CW00348398

CLASSES, CULTURES, AND POLITICS

Classes, Cultures, and Politics

Essays on British History for Ross McKibbin

Edited by
CLARE V. J. GRIFFITHS
JAMES J. NOTT
WILLIAM WHYTE

OXFORD
UNIVERSITY PRESS

Great Clarendon Street, Oxford OX2 6DP

Oxford University Press is a department of the University of Oxford.
It furthers the University's objective of excellence in research, scholarship,
and education by publishing worldwide in

Oxford New York

Auckland Cape Town Dar es Salaam Hong Kong Karachi
Kuala Lumpur Madrid Melbourne Mexico City Nairobi
New Delhi Shanghai Taipei Toronto

With offices in

Argentina Austria Brazil Chile Czech Republic France Greece
Guatemala Hungary Italy Japan Poland Portugal Singapore
South Korea Switzerland Thailand Turkey Ukraine Vietnam

Oxford is a registered trade mark of Oxford University Press
in the UK and in certain other countries

Published in the United States
by Oxford University Press Inc., New York

First published 2011

British Library Cataloguing in Publication Data
Data available

Library of Congress Cataloging in Publication Data
Data available

Typeset by SPI Publisher Services, Pondicherry, India
Printed in Great Britain
on acid-free paper by
MPG Books Group, Bodmin and King's Lynn

ISBN 978–0–19–957988–4

1 3 5 7 9 10 8 6 4 2

Preface

Through his writing and teaching, Ross McKibbin has had a significant impact on the historiography of modern Britain. He has made important contributions to the scholarly literature, notably through his books *The Evolution of the Labour Party* and *Classes and Cultures*, and his stimulating collection of essays: *The Ideologies of Class*. As college tutor, graduate supervisor, author, and commentator, he has also influenced and inspired many other books and articles. Over the past three decades, his postgraduate students have produced studies that are testimony to the breadth of his interests and the productive ways in which his ideas have been able to stimulate others. He never cultivated a 'school' of McKibbinites, but his influence is there to see in books as diverse as Paul Johnson's *Saving and Spending* (1987), Nicholas Fishwick's *English Football and Society 1910–1950* (1989), and Joseph McAleer's *Popular Reading and Publishing in Britain 1914–1950* (1992).[1] Two of the editors of this present volume were also his doctoral students, and produced their first monographs under his supervision—Clare Griffiths' *Labour and the Countryside* (2007) and James Nott's *Music for the People* (2002).[2]

Ross McKibbin's impact on other branches of literature may be less familiar. He is memorialised by his former student Vikram Seth in *A Suitable Boy*, where we encounter 'Jock McKay, a cheerful bachelor in his mid-forties who was one of the directors of the managing agency of McKibbin and Ross.'[3] He was also the inspiration for Anna Ramsay's Mills and Boon classic of 1988, *Heartbeat*, where he is re-imagined as Dr Ross McDonnell—a brilliant but irascible eye surgeon whose broken heart has led him to practise in the wilds of East Africa. Firm of jaw and firm of thigh, self-confident, formidable, and with the sort of eyes that made the 'recollection of their power . . . like an icy finger tracing the channel of [the] spine', 'Dr Ross' is an unforgettable hero. 'Yes, Ross could be rude and impossible and casual; but these in themselves were attractively provoking qualities and set the adrenalin flowing in a most exciting manner.' The slight 'twang of an Australian accent' only makes him more appealing. 'Life with the ferocious Dr Ross is never boring!' reflects the heroine, just before she kisses him; and, it is admitted that in a tie he looks 'quite frighteningly handsome'. The conclusion is thus entirely unsurprising. Reader, she marries him.[4]

[1] Paul Johnson, *Saving and Spending: The Working-Class Economy in Britain c.1870–1939* (Oxford, 1987); Nicholas Fishwick, *English Football and Society 1910–1950* (Manchester, 1989); Joseph McAleer, *Popular Reading and Publishing in Britain 1914–1950* (Oxford, 1992).

[2] Clare V. J. Griffiths, *Labour and the Countryside: The Politics of Rural Britain, 1918–1939* (Oxford, 2007); James J. Nott, *Music for the People: Popular Music and Dance in Interwar Britain* (Oxford, 2002).

[3] Vikram Seth, *A Suitable Boy* (London, 1993), p. 389.

[4] Anna Ramsay, *Heartbeat* (Richmond, 1988), pp. 15, 23, 30, 53, 55, 71, 84, 111, 125, 187.

This book, then, is one of many volumes that have been inspired by Ross McKibbin. It represents the bringing together of one particular group of people who have in some way been shaped by his work. Some—like Clare Griffiths, Paul Johnson, Joseph McAleer, Gregg McClymont, and James Nott—were taught by him. Others—like Martin Caedel, Peter Ghosh, Janet Howarth, Ben Jackson, Andrzej Olechnovicz, and William Whyte—have worked with him. Still others—like Robert Colls, Peter Mandler, and Tony Mason—have more indirect connections. Yet all these contributors acknowledge Ross McKibbin's influence and seek to celebrate his importance as an historian. Using three key terms that he himself has deployed to analyse twentieth-century Britain—the idea of classes, cultures, and politics—this book is a tribute to a man who suggested new ways of analysing and explaining the recent past. From very different perspectives, and addressing a wide variety of themes, each of the contributors engages with aspects of Ross McKibbin's work and points to ways in which his interpretations have opened up fresh topics for historical analysis.

Ross McKibbin is, without question, one of the most influential writers on modern British history—the author of seminal works on the history of politics, on cultural history, and the history of class. A gifted stylist and talented essayist, his concise interventions in the field have often distilled to a few thousand words what others might have laboured over in the length of a monograph. His articles and essays—including, notably, 'Why was there no Marxism in Great Britain?' (1984) and 'Class and conventional wisdom' (1988)—are standard points of reference in the historiography of class and politics in modern Britain. 'The franchise factor' (1976), written jointly with Colin Matthew and John Kay, ignited a long-lasting debate in the scholarly literature. Fans and critics alike have been provoked by his ideas, and this book can only explore a few themes from his work. But by combining chapters on subjects as diverse as international football and Liberal internationalism with Boyd Hilton's biographical sketch and Peter Ghosh's historiographical survey, we hope that this volume can pay tribute to Ross McKibbin's work, assess its importance, and situate his contribution within a wider context. McKibbin is acknowledged as 'one of the leading historians of twentieth century Britain', but also as 'a somewhat enigmatic figure'.[5] This book is intended to highlight the first statement and explore the second. We seek in this way to aid those who are coming to McKibbin's books for the first time or who are trying to tease out the subtle meanings and implications within his arguments.

Beyond this, the essays that follow serve two further purposes. In the first place, they seek not only to praise, but also to critique, Ross McKibbin's work, bringing new insights to bear on his conclusions and providing a critical assessment of his achievements. In some cases—as with Peter Mandler's chapter on the

[5] Steven Fielding reviewing *Classes and Cultures* in *Contemporary British History*, 13 (1999), p. 170.

sociologist Geoffrey Gorer—this means challenging the sources that McKibbin used in his work. In other cases—as with Andrezj Olechnowicz's chapter on the monarchy—this means revising some of McKibbin's conclusions. All of the chapters critically engage with his writing and each is intended to shed new light on particular aspects of his analysis.

Secondly, this book is intended to follow McKibbin's example by using innovative sources and approaches to illuminate the history of modern Britain. Sometimes this means exploring the use of literary material as a means of exposing contemporary attitudes to politics and society—as in Joseph McAleer's and William Whyte's chapters. Sometimes it means listening to witnesses who have been marginalized by previous writers—as in John Davis's investigation of London taxi drivers, or Janet Howarth's discussion of working-class women. Sometimes, it means addressing areas that have been disregarded by many academic historians—as with Paul Johnson's account of working-class finance, or the nightclubs that feature in James Nott's chapter. Sometimes it means approaching more traditionally mainstream topics from an original and even oblique angle. Hence, the essays that follow include studies of the neo-liberal take on trades unions; on the role of history within the Labour Party; and on the hard-drinking, freewheeling socialists of the Edwardian period. Our contributors thus highlight the continuing value of McKibbin's insights whilst also contributing original arguments in their own right.

Classes, Cultures, and Politics had its origins in a series of seminars held at St John's College, Oxford, in 2006. The editors subsequently invited the contributors to a two-day workshop, at the St John's College Research Centre in April 2009. We are immensely grateful to all who attended. In addition to those whose work is included in this book, we must thank Matthew Grimley, Brian Harrison, Mary Hilton, Sue Matthew, Margaret Pelling, Robert Saunders, Keith Thomas, Philip Waller, and—of course—Ross McKibbin, for making it such an enjoyable and profitable occasion. We are also extremely grateful to Professor Linda McDowell, Director of the Research Centre, and to St John's College, for their material support for this project.

Neither the workshop nor the book itself would have been possible without the help of numerous other friends. The editors particularly thank Stephanie Ireland at OUP, Jeremy Crang, David Salter, Philip Williamson, Zoë Waxman, and Nahum Whyte. Above all, we are indebted to Eve Colpus for her magnificent efforts in organising the workshop, co-ordinating the contributors, and keeping the editors in line. The *Festschrift* would not only have been unthinkable without her work, it would also have been far less fun to produce.

Ross McKibbin has been a major voice in modern British history for over forty years—ever since he published his first article on the subject in the 1970 volume of the *Journal of Modern History*. His commentaries and reflections on modern politics in the pages of the *London Review of Books* have brought—and continue to bring - his ideas and unique perspectives to an audience outside academia. With the publication of *Parties and People: England 1918–1951*, he has shown that his importance and his originality are undiminished. Although *Classes, Cultures, and Politics* marks his retirement, it should in no sense be seen as signalling the end of his career. Rather, it is intended to acknowledge his immense contribution to the discipline—and to the work of all those who have written for this volume.

Clare Griffiths, James Nott, William Whyte

Sheffield—St. Andrews—Oxford,
1 June 2010.

Contents

List of Contributors

Martin Ceadel is fellow, tutor, and professor of politics at New College, Oxford.

Robert Colls is professor of English History at the University of Leicester.

Eve Colpus is a graduate student at New College, Oxford.

John Davis is fellow, praelector, and university lecturer in history at Queen's College, Oxford.

Emma Eadie is head of history at Loughborough High School.

Peter Ghosh is fellow, tutor, and university lecturer in history at St Anne's College, Oxford.

Clare V. J. Griffiths is senior lecturer in history at the University of Sheffield.

Boyd Hilton is professor of history and fellow of Trinity College, Cambridge.

Janet Howarth is an emeritus fellow of St Hilda's College, Oxford.

Ben Jackson is fellow, praelector, and university lecturer in history at University College, Oxford.

Paul Johnson is vice chancellor of La Trobe University.

Joseph McAleer an independent scholar and author living in Connecticut.

Gregg McClymont is MP for Cumbernauld, Kilsyth, and Kirkintilloch East.

Peter Mandler is professor of history and fellow of Gonville and Caius College, Cambridge.

Tony Mason is emeritus professor of history at De Montfort University, Leicester.

James J. Nott is lecturer in history at the University of St Andrews.

Andrezj Olechnowicz is lecturer in history at the University of Durham.

Rosemary Sweet is professor of urban history at the University of Leicester.

William Whyte is fellow, tutor, and university lecturer in history at St John's College, Oxford.

Mary-Kay Wilmers is editor of *The London Review of Books.*

Abbreviations

Bod	Bodleian Library
DLB	*Dictionary of Labour Biography*
DNB	Dictionary of National Biography
EHR	*English Historical Review*
FA	Football Association
FIFA	Fédération Internationale de Football Association
GLC	Greater London Council
HIA	Hoover Institution Archives
H-M&B	Harlequin and Mills & Boon Archive
IEA	Institute of Economic Affairs
ILP	Independent Labour Party
IRSH	*International Review of Social History*
LPL	Lambeth Palace Library
LMA	London Metropolitan Archives
LRB	*London Review of Books*
LNU	League of Nations Union
NVA	National Vigilance Association
ODNB	*Oxford Dictionary of National Biography*
PMC	Pubic Morality Council
PP	*Past and Present*
RUL	Roehampton University Library
SDF	Social Democratic Federation
SW	*Steering Wheel*
TGWU	Transport and General Workers Union
TLS	*Times Literary Supplement*
TNA	The National Archives
TRHS	*Transactions of the Royal Historical Society*
TSSA	Transport and Salaried Staffs Association
TT	*Taxi Trader*
UDC	Union of Democratic Control
WL	Women's Library

INTRODUCING ROSS MCKIBBIN

1

Ross McKibbin: A Biographical Introduction

Boyd Hilton

Ever since my wife Mary and I moved from Oxford to Cambridge in 1974, Ross has visited us regularly several times a year. While our children were young he was 'Uncle Ross', effortlessly one of the family, fooling about, riding on swings, or 'having a chuck' of a ball. Nowadays the three of us often spend the afternoon visiting local sites of interest including, about ten years ago, the display of historic aircraft at the Imperial War Museum in Duxford. I was interested only in the magnificent hangar designed by Norman Foster, but Ross was in his element as he moved between exhibits with continual exclamations of recognition. First the goodies: Hurricane! Spitfire! Lancaster! Avro Anson! B17 Flying Fortress! Then the enemy: Fokker DR1! Messerschmitt Bf109! *Schwalbe* Swallow! He was equally familiar with parts: liquid cooled engines, overhead camshafts, a ventral tail gunner turret, and a Heinkel 111 tail fin. I had never heard him speak of these things before and wondered why he was so knowledgeable. Was it because his father had been in the Royal Australian Air Force? No, his father had never spoken about the war. Apparently it went back to his schooldays in New South Wales, when there had been a craze for reading flight magazines, cutting out cardboard models, and swapping cigarette cards dedicated to Second World War aviation. He had forgotten that he knew so much, but it came flooding back that afternoon in Duxford.

The above anecdote illustrates the extraordinary range and often arcane nature of Ross's knowledge, his powers of recall, and his still vivid memories of childhood. It also touches on a central ambiguity facing his biographer. The battles that so fascinated him as a boy mainly took place over western Europe, 12,000 miles away, yet in the later stages of the war Australians mainly fought in the Pacific to defend their own homeland, not the mother country. If Ross remains hard to pin down culturally, it is partly because he grew up in a colonial society still dominated by ties to Britain and Europe, yet was part of the first generation consciously to reject those old loyalties.

Ross was born in Sydney in January 1942, the product of four or five generations of New South Wales stock on both sides. His grandfather's forebears had come from Northern Ireland as free immigrants in the 1860s, unlike some earlier members of the family who had been relocated at Her Majesty's pleasure.

Ross's branch of the family was fiercely Protestant. One uncle was a Methodist Moderator, another was a big shot in the Salvation Army, while his paternal grandfather, legal clerk and secretary to the vice-chancellor of Sydney University, was a member of the Loyal Orange Order and highly suspicious of Catholics, a hostility that was not unusual in the Australia of his time. Ross's father Arnold, usually known as 'Mac', had the ambition and aptitude to become a lawyer, but since this was not affordable he had to be satisfied with a qualification in teaching. It was during 'Mac's' third appointment in the little coastal town of Bega that he met Nance Spence whom, after several years of persistent wooing, he finally persuaded to marry him. Why she allowed herself to be persuaded was a question Ross would often ask his mother in later years. Part of the answer must have been that 'Mac' offered her a way out of Bega, and also a means of escape from her father, Clarence Spence, whose alcoholism was having a destructive effect on family life. A bank manager by profession, Clarence was a member of the quasi-Fascist New Guard and kept a gun under his bed. 'Mac' by contrast was a gut Labour man and a committed anti-Fascist, who in 1940—the year before he and Nance married—had anticipated conscription by volunteering for the RAAF. He became a commissioned Flight Lieutenant (Signals) and had risen to Acting Squadron Leader by the time he was demobilized in 1946. Meanwhile his wife and their baby son were forced to live peripatetically, staying with various relatives in turn. It is not absolutely certain that Ross even met his father until he was about four, though he retains an impression of 'a man in blue uniform', which suggests that he probably did.

After two fulfilling years as an instructor on the Commonwealth Reconstruction Training Scheme for ex-servicemen, 'Mac' McKibbin went to teach English and History at the North Sydney Boys' High. He was regarded fondly by pupils and chalked up impressive exam results, but for reasons that remain obscure he moved, in 1951, to be subject master at an intermediate high school in the tiny wheat growing and sheep rearing township of Forbes (population: 6000) in western New South Wales. The nine-year-old Ross found the flat surrounding countryside an enjoyable place to explore, especially by bicycle, while Forbes had occasional excitements, such as the floods of 1953 (from which he had to be rescued by helicopter) and the occasional unexpected landing of an aeroplane on one of its two main streets. In 1956 'Mac' was promoted to school inspector and the family moved to Orange, a fruit growing town in the foothills of the Great Dividing Range. About three times as large as Forbes, Orange contained a somewhat self-conscious professional elite to which the McKibbins clung. Discriminating social observation is a defining feature of Ross's historical writing, and it may well be that his antennae were made all the sharper by his having exercised them first in a country which pretends so aggressively to be classless. Although class was never overtly mentioned in rural New South Wales, everyone knew everyone else's religion, not least because their children attended different schools. Ross remembers feeling genuinely puzzled when he spotted some slightly older members of the different tribes talking animatedly together at a social function.

Though by no means literally so, Forbes and Orange are often colloquially described as being 'back of Bourke', as in 'back of beyond' or 'woop woop'. The young McKibbin was unequivocally a country boy, yet it might not have been so. Here we encounter a small mystery, a moment of amnesia. At the age of twelve he was interviewed for and accepted by his father's own old school, Sydney Boys' High, *the* crack establishment in a state where, unlike in Victoria, most of the crack establishments were in the public rather than the private sector. Both parents seemed keen, the uniform was bought, and arrangements made for Ross to board with a family friend. But at the eleventh hour it was decided that he should not go after all. Why were his prospects in the Sydney fast stream aborted? Ross has no recollection. Being a slightly anxious only child he might have baulked at the prospect of competing with the Jewish high fliers of the Eastern Suburbs, yet there is no evidence to suggest that the decision to withdraw from Sydney High was Ross's own. Whatever the truth, the upshot was that he remained metaphorically 'back of Bourke' where, in most respects, he received a decent education. He worked hard, was top of the class for most of his primary years, and remembers without much bitterness being mocked when a temporary lapse forced him to move (literally) down a place. At home he read avidly—*Biggles*, the *William* books, some Blyton, later the English classics, but almost no Australian literature. At Orange High he excelled in the Humanities but had to be privately coached to get him through the final examination in Mathematics. Since qualification in that subject was a requisite of going on to University, this sparked off a minor crisis. Meanwhile sport was a passion, especially swimming, at which he was exceptionally proficient, and tennis (tellingly his boyhood hero was the great Ken Rosewall, not the great Lew Hoad).[1] There was no school cricket team, nor did he have a cricketing hero to set alongside Rosewall, but that may be because England held the Ashes while Ross was aged eleven to sixteen. Australians are always inclined to pretend that cricket is unimportant whenever England win the Ashes.

At that time all Orange's school leavers were expected to write an essay on the subject of 'What ANZAC Day means to me', the entries to be judged by the Returned Soldiers' League, and prizes awarded. 'ANZAC' was the name given to the annual day of wartime remembrance throughout the Antipodes, while the RSL was a highly conservative organisation, loyal to Crown and empire, and as such hardly to 'Mac' McKibbin's taste. In 1958, Ross's final year, one of his classmates flatly refused to write an essay, others followed her lead, and a rumpus ensued, which placed Ross in an awkward situation. Though he and his father sympathised with the rebels, it would hardly do for the son of a local inspector to join them, so he decided to write a spoof. He would write what the judges wanted to read, but in such an obviously exaggerated way as to send up the whole exercise. His entry ended with the following risible stanza by Mary Gilmore:

[1] Telling because, according to Robin Briggs and Philip Waller, his long-time antagonists in squash and tennis respectively, Ross plays the percentages, exploits all angles, eschews flamboyant shots, displays no temperament, and wins more often than not.

We are the sons of Australia,
of the men who fashioned the land;
We are the sons of the women
Who walked with them hand in hand;
And we swear by the dead who bore us,
By the heroes who blazed the trail,
No foe shall gather our harvest,
Or sit on our stockyard rail.

Unfortunately his ruse rebounded on him. Either the RSL judges deliberately called his bluff, or else they failed to recognise the satire. They awarded him third prize, and if it was excruciatingly embarrassing for Ross to read about his own success in the *Central Western Daily*, it was no less so for his father, who had agreed to announce the winners in front of the town memorial.

Might this episode explain why, in his current political commentaries, Ross refrains from using irony or sarcasm? It is this self-restraint that helps to explain why his attacks on government seem so angry, despite their generally restrained tone. At any rate his bungled act of rebellion was mildly portentous. In the following year the Sydney University student magazine *Honi Soit* also mocked ANZAC Day, which it saw as little more than an excuse for a binge, while in 1960 Alan Seymour used the annual celebrations to explore a developing generational divide in his brilliant play *The One Day of the Year*. These gestures of subversion led to the founding of *Oz* magazine by Richard Neville and Richie Walsh in 1963, conventionally seen as the point at which the deeply conservative 'Liberal' political regime began to crack; and it reminds us that, translated into British or American terms, Ross was a child of the 'sixties'. Not the mainly American 'sixties' of Woodstock, flower power, and student revolution, which came later, but the satirical and mainly British early 'sixties' of *TW3*, *Beyond the Fringe*, and *Private Eye*. However, whereas its corrosive effect on authority and conventional morality was almost immediate in Britain, in Australia it would take another decade and the Vietnam war for the carapace to crack.

In 1959 Ross went up to Sydney University. At about the same time his father was appointed to high-level managerial posts in the education department of that city, so the family stayed together. This was perhaps a pity for Ross's relations with his father were becoming increasingly strained. They had much in common, including a love of reading, especially in History, a commitment to Labour politics, and a visceral hatred of Toryism in all its forms. Earlier as a teacher and now as a bureaucrat, 'Mac' McKibbin won universal praise for his competence, vision, and graceful charm, and Ross was deeply appreciative at one level. Yet 'Mac's' explosive and unpredictable behaviour at home made his marriage to Nance little short of a disaster.[2] At this time he was almost certainly being groomed for the post of Chief Education Officer, and it may be that the stresses of his job, exacerbated by incipient coronary disease, led him to take his anxieties

[2] After some years of widowhood Nance was to achieve happiness in her relationship with Bob Wood, whom she had known for some time. She died after a long illness in 2008.

out on his wife and son. He was not physically violent, but his psychological bullying and temper tantrums—he once swept the entire contents of a table laid for dinner on to the floor—kept Nance and Ross on permanent tenterhooks.

Ross's student days seem to have been fulfilling in a slightly low-key way. Clive James, who left as Ross arrived, has provided a joyously indelible impression of the ethos in his *Unreliable Memoirs*, and though Ross had little to do with the literary set, now dominated by Germaine Greer and Richard Neville, he enjoyed the company of a lively and supportive peer group. He was active in the Labor Club, then passing through a 'Stalinist' phase, and shortly afterwards helped to form a break-away group, the ALP [Australian Labor Party] Club. His historical training was fairly broad, for though he did nothing ancient or medieval he took in the Reformation, nineteenth- and twentieth-century Europe including Britain, America, India, and Australia (including its Aboriginal origins). He wrote a dissertation on the social origins of early Australian nationalism and was thrilled by his introduction to the archives.

He loved his fourth-year Honours, did extremely well in Finals, and won a university prize medal. Through most of this his mentor, guiding light, and later close friend was the man to whom he would subsequently dedicate his volume on *The Ideologies of Class*: Ernest Bramsted, an Augsburg Jew who had written his doctorate under Meinecke, had been expelled from Frankfurt in 1933, and had published widely on Nazi propaganda and on the interwar German aristocracy and middle classes. It should be borne in mind that Sydney was a more provincial city than Melbourne, then the artistic, cultural, social, and business 'capital' of Australia, and Sydney University had far fewer Jewish intellectuals than its Victorian counterpart. Bramsted stood out because he represented a great German intellectual tradition, and made the other teachers, almost all of whom were Sydney products, seem (perhaps unfairly) introverted and provincial. Hearing him lecture for the first time in a wretched English accent, Ross found himself thinking, 'This is history!' Bramsted was almost certainly instrumental in setting Ross to work on the subject of his first (and still frequently cited) periodical publication on the social groups that voted for the Nazis in the German general elections of 1932–3. All this being so, the question then arises as to why Ross decided to become a historian of the *British* Labour Party. No doubt it was partly because, at a time when the Australian Labor Party seemed all but washed up, he found the idealism of Crosland and the chutzpah of Wilson refreshing. It may also be that he did not wish to continue a line of research that could 'only end in Auschwitz'.[3]

In 1964 Ross went to Oxford to research for a D.Phil. That is a fact, though to what extent he has ever 'left' Australia in emotional terms remains unclear. During that decade many enterprising graduates left for Europe or America to escape the stultifying atmosphere of the later Menzies years and their aftermath.

[3] This phrase occurs in Ross McKibbin, 'Timothy Wright Mason (1940–1990)', in Colin Matthew and Brian Harrison (eds.), *Oxford Dictionary of National Biography* [*ODNB*] (Oxford, 2004).

For some, like Barry Humphries, Clive James, and Germaine Greer, the big wide world exerted an almost gravitational pull, as conveyed by the title of James's second volume of memoirs, *Falling Towards England*. Some, like the cultural critic Peter Conrad, closed the door firmly behind them, not in disparagement or rejection, but to preserve an idyll. Others left intending to return after a year or two but then, like my wife, became personally or professionally entangled overseas. Some went back only after the cultural renaissance of the Whitlam years removed the irony from the phrase 'Lucky Country'. None of these scenarios quite fits Ross. He had been happy at Sydney, and stardom has never been much of a concern. The prosaic fact was that he wished to be a historian of Britain, and Britain was where the archives were. After three satisfying years in Oxford, of which more below, he would return to Sydney as a Lecturer in his old Department (1968–9), and once again he would have a 'terrific time', but as before he would not be able to do without the archives, which is why, in 1970, he returned to Oxford to complete the doctorate and effectively dedicate his life to British history. Only then did he make a clear-eyed decision to become part of Australia's 'lost generation', a decision re-affirmed in the 1980s when, after some internal deliberation, he rejected the tempting offer of a Chair of History at Sydney University. But to set against the fact that he has been an Oxford fixture for more than forty years is the increasing amount of time he has spent in Australia. A factor of course was his closeness to his mother, coupled perhaps with guilt at not being permanently on hand during her eight last stricken years, but all the indications are that in retirement he will continue to spend not much less than half the year down under. His extended family and that of his stepfather remain emotionally important to him. As for taking out British citizenship, I doubt that the idea has ever entered his head.

Max Hartwell, a much more 'professional' Australian than Ross, used to remark that whenever he was in Oxford he wished he were in 'Oz', and vice versa. Ross by contrast seems content to enjoy each in turn. And why not? Many will envy a man who can divide his life between the most beautiful city in England and the second most handsome city in Australia. And indeed Ross does seem to be a contented person. Not inanely so—one can tell when he is pissed off—but if he broods, he broods alone. Yet his hovering between two homes may also reflect a slight vicariousness and an unwillingness to commit fully to either. Philip Waller points to the curious fact that in pre-email days Ross never used to date the notes and letters that he sent, an idiosyncrasy that seems especially strange in a historian. Was it, perhaps unconsciously, another way of remaining elusive, of leaving no trail and not being pinned down?

On going to Oxford in 1964, Ross had the wit or good fortune to choose a graduate college, St Antony's, which he loved. An antidote to the 'Brideshead' side of Oxford life, it was full of lively and clever students working mainly on European history and politics, while its many international networks guaranteed a constant stream of visiting academics. He formed close and lasting friendships with scholars such as Sheila Fitzpatrick and James Joll, but the biggest influence on his intellectual development was that of the 'liberal-Marxist' historian Tim

Mason (described by Ross as 'a powerful and impressive presence', 'a remarkable historical intelligence'),[4] who was preoccupied by the experience of the working classes under Nazism. The seminar on social history that Mason ran with Gareth Stedman Jones and Joaquin Romero Maura offered Ross a theoretical counterpoint to the (likewise fascinating but relentlessly empirical) anthropology of Raphael Samuel's Ruskin History Workshop. Important in a different way was Ross's research supervisor, Pat Thompson. Their interaction was informal, as was often the manner in those days, when students were largely left to get on with it. (Thompson's contribution was to come later, after Ross returned to Oxford in order to write his thesis up in 1970. Though he published little of his own research, he was a brilliant midwife, critical, meticulous, and conscientious. He and his late wife Mary remained close counsellors and friends.) Aside from work, Ross became a Labour Party activist and helped in the campaign to win the Oxford seat for his St Antony's colleague Evan Luard in the 1966 general election. He found Swinging London 'terrific', and sometimes inhaled, but he was even more excited by the Underground. What he did not fall for were Oxford's 'dreaming spires'. He left for home in 1967 having hardly met an undergraduate or entered an undergraduate college.

This changed in 1970 when he became a Research Lecturer at Christ Church where, incidentally, he stumbled across Colin Matthew and me. The white-tied hearties of Peckwater Quadrangle were not to his taste, and there was the occasional 'Oz in Oxford' moment on High Table, as when he made semi-insulting remarks about Hugh Trevor-Roper and the first Earl Haig in consecutive sentences without realising that the colleague he was talking to was the stepson of one and the grandson of the other. (Fortunately James Howard-Johnston has a good sense of humour.) There was at this time a very slight prickliness, not helped by the fact that the stereotypical Australian of those days was the beer-swilling cartoon 'Okker' of Earls Court, Barrie Mackenzie. In Philip Waller's words, Ross was then 'inclined to perceive slights, especially from those with braying voices and apparently little between the ears, and whose forebears had considered Gallipoli something of a breeze'. However, any such tensions were eased in 1972 when he was elected to a tenured Tutorial Fellowship at an even richer and more congenial college, St John's.

I shall skip briefly over the biographical details of Ross's subsequent career, since what mainly matters can best be gleaned from Peter Ghosh's commentary on his work. Because status means little to him, he never applied for one of Oxford's recently introduced titular professorships, but he received the accolade of an FBA in 1999, and reached what many regard as the pinnacle of his profession when he became the Ford Lecturer in 2008. For thirty-five years or more he had been an extremely conscientious undergraduate tutor and research supervisor, in both of which roles he was much in demand. He had maintained a wise if largely back-room presence in the History Faculty, ably advising in the cause of syllabus

[4] Ibid.

reform or whatever, but rarely bestriding the parapet or playing a dominant part on committees. Likewise in College, where he served his turn as Senior Tutor, his had been a wise and amiable albeit mainly unassertive presence.[5] The partnership that he formed for many years with his tutorial colleagues Keith Thomas and Howard Colvin had made St John's one of the most exciting colleges in which to read History. Ross acknowledges that he was 'intellectually challenged' by Keith—'made to think about things in ways I had not thought of before'—while Keith acknowledges that Ross helped him to put himself in touch with his gossipy side. Quite simply, they hit it off. Ross's friendship with Howard and Christina Colvin, both much older than him, was also remarkable. Howard's artistic and architectural expertise enormously expanded his cultural horizons on the scores of visits that they made to Continental cities and English stately homes. In the appreciation of music, on the other hand, and especially opera, Ross had no need of assistance. Wagner remains a profound inspiration.

There is not room to list his many important friendships, and I could not do it anyway for he tends to compartmentalise; but mention must be made of Peter Parsons—a wise and jovial companion since the Christ Church days—and his late wife Barbara. Also of Colin and Sue Matthew, into whose family life he became thoroughly insinuated, and with whom he chewed much cud, both historical and political.[6] Colin's sudden death in 1999 devastated him, as did his mother's stroke and descent into serious illness a few months later. This 'worst time of my life', as he called it, followed a long period of frustration and uncertainty that had ended with his decision to abandon his volume for the New Oxford History of England series, and to use the material he had amassed in his magnum opus, *Classes and Cultures* (1998). In retrospect the acclaim accorded to the latter must have more than compensated for his withdrawal from the Oxford series, but at the time the change of tack was a somewhat dispiriting one. Finally in 2005 Ross took early retirement from his formal teaching posts. Like many of his contemporaries he was alienated by the bureaucratic demands increasingly made on university teachers, the nonsensical targets and time-wasting exercises in accountability, and the attempts to shift the balance of power within the higher reaches of Oxford's governance from academics to 'failed businessmen'.

Meanwhile, beginning in 1989, Ross had found a new voice as a regular political commentator for the *London Review of Books*, a surprising move insofar as he had never previously sought the limelight. His contributions are highly regarded and have brought him a good deal of fame, but here I must restrict myself to just two points, the first of which concerns their distinctive tone. Other historians who have pronounced on current politics in the media—A. J. P. Taylor and John

[5] He is particularly proud of his service on the St John's College Building Committee. Indeed, he and I both take pride in our central roles in turning our respective colleges into Richard MacCormac designed Valhallas.

[6] Ross has discussed his collaboration with Colin Matthew in Peter Ghosh and Lawrence Goldman (eds.), *Politics and Culture in Victorian Britain: Essays in Memory of Colin Matthew* (Oxford, 2006), pp. 28–34. See also Ross McKibbin, 'Henry Colin Gray Matthew (1941–1999)', *ODNB.*

Vincent for example—have invariably adopted the stylistic traits of the journalist, at least to some extent, but there are no such histrionics in Ross's essays. Exceptionally forthright judgments are delivered in a didactic but resolutely conversational, almost matter-of-fact prose. There is condemnation aplenty, indeed there is frequently very little else, but sentence is delivered dispassionately like a judgment in the Court of Appeal or a chartered accountant's audit report. The tonal restraint partly masks the very remarkable self-assurance with which Ross pronounces his various anathema. Very few historians these days suppose that their expertise qualifies them to act as public seers, but Ross apparently does think this, though he never makes the claim explicitly. And yet, it might be asked, how can he be so confident about what the Chancellor of the Exchequer, say, or the Home Secretary, ought to do next, given that he is not an economist and has hardly ever engaged in politics himself, even at the humdrum level of the university committee? And especially, how can he be so confident given that many of his judgments are unique to himself and original, so utterly unaffected by the conventional wisdoms of the 'Today' programme and blogosphere? The answer, according to his café regular Martin Ceadel, is that Ross (one of whose listed hobbies is gardening) allows himself to be guided by his own 'green fingers', a phrase used by A. J. P. Taylor to express his much less justified belief that he knew instinctively what was historically true. Self-evidently in his *LRB* pieces, more subtly in his historical writings, Ross draws heavily on his instincts, something that only someone with his capacious and detailed knowledge of facts could possibly do.

In terms of content Ross's *LRB* pieces are full of passion, but it is easier to tell what he is against than what he is for. He has a deep-seated contempt for what he sees as the 'born-to-rule' pretensions of many traditional Tories; he especially hates social-market Thatcherites; he despises New Labour for its Thatcherite tendencies and betrayal of the Left, yet he is certainly no Old Labourite, albeit sympathetic to some of its ethos. In general terms he supports the aims of the German Social Democratic Party, and perhaps, if things had fallen out differently, he might have followed Luard into the UK's SDP. (He has voted for the Lib. Dems. in recent elections for the West Oxford and Abingdon constituency, but only for tactical reasons.) There is also a suggestion, put to me by Philip Waller, that whereas Ross can contemplate the ruination of the UK with a certain detachment—hence the coolness of tone referred to above—what made him increasingly incandescent was the fear that Prime Minister Howard was turning Australia into a nightmarish replica of Thatcher's Britain. In letters written to Philip from Australia in 2003–4 he denounced the Liberal Government for its hostility to asylum seekers, its increasingly punitive penal policies, and its sequence of repellent budgets, evidently designed to 'complete the destruction of the universities', emasculate the unions, wreck the health service, and more generally undermine the country's fundamental egalitarianism. 'Australian govt. obsessed with terrorism, crucial nature of Aust. presence in Irak [sic] (all 450 of them); no time to abandon US alliance, etc. Wholly politically driven for this year's election. A truly odious gang', he scribbled in March 2004.

People who know Ross McKibbin only from the *LRB* sometimes comment on his anger, earnestness, and lack of humour. This must astound those who know him personally, especially the last, but attempts to describe what he is 'really like' are hampered by my sense that his is a multifaceted personality. Indeed, his demonstrated ability to form close, loyal, and long-lasting relationships owes a lot to the fact that he can be solemn, confidential, cerebral, flippant, giggly, raucous, risqué, or whatever other characteristic is required by the company he happens to be keeping. This ability may have something to do with his historical powers of empathy, but it also marks him down as something of a chameleon.

In his moving essay on Tim Mason for the *Oxford Dictionary of National Biography*, Ross ponders the question of why Mason chose to wear a Hamburg docker's cap, and speculates that it 'was, in a way, the badge of a carefully nurtured loyalty'. I have never asked Ross why he wears a northern working man's flat felt cap. Rather than ask him now, I prefer to speculate that, by mimicking sartorially a group to which he so obviously does not belong, Ross is once again affirming his determination not to be categorized or pinned down.[7]

[7] I am especially grateful to Keith Thomas and Philip Waller, with whom I have held extensive and very fruitful discussions. Other friends of Ross whom I have consulted include Robin Briggs, Martin Ceadel, Mary Hilton, Sue Matthew, Peter Parsons, Margaret Pelling, Valerie Thomas, and William Thomas.

2

The Guv'nor: The Place of Ross McKibbin in the Writing of British History*

Peter Ghosh

When Ross McKibbin's *magnum opus Classes and Cultures* appeared in 1998,[1] it was affectionately greeted as showing 'once again that, in his chosen field of political-cum-social history, the author of *The Evolution of the Labour Party* [1974] and *The Ideologies of Class* [1990] is still the Guv'nor'.[2] Yet though historians of twentieth-century Britain do not need to be told of his eminence and presence, there remains plenty of room for historiographical scrutiny of his work. Agreement that it has to be reckoned with does not imply agreement on what it signifies. Across a series of critical engagements within the disputatious world of labour and social history, we find that in 1985 he was accused of 'cultural determinism'; in 1990 he was seen as a political reactionary who had betrayed the classical Marxist agenda; in 1994 he was a methodological reactionary who reaffirmed 'the old labour history'; while in 2003 his type of originality was merely one 'in which familiar elements are given novel interpretation and arrangement'. '*Socialism*... is a word that McKibbin rarely has any use for.'[3] Now such verdicts reflect primarily on those who utter them; otherwise they are mistaken. Nonetheless, they illustrate that while his intellectual course has in fact possessed a powerful inner consistency, this has not been obvious to outsiders. Hence the response of another reader who described him simultaneously as 'one

* This essay draws on both personal sympathy and critical detachment. It has been my privilege to know Ross McKibbin personally since 1979 and to admire his work for still longer. Nonetheless such affinities have had no influence on my own practice in the writing of history, which is evidently very different to his. Warm thanks to Philip Waller for documentary assistance (see n. 54 below) and to Philip Williamson and Philip Waller for reading this essay in draft.

[1] *Classes and Cultures: England 1918–51* (hereafter *CC*) (Oxford, *1988*).

[2] Ben Pimlott, 'Tell me the old, old story', *New Statesman* 27.3.98, p. 47.

[3] Jay Winter, 'Trade unions and the Labour Party in Britain', in W. J. Mommsen and H. G. Husung (eds.), *The Development of Trade Unionism in Great Britain and Germany 1880–1914* (London, 1985), pp. 364, 367; an unidentified reviewer cited by Harold Perkin, 'Just holding together', *TLS* 15.6.90, p. 637a; Terry Irving, 'Introduction: labour history, crisis and the public sphere', in *Challenges to Labour History* (Sydney, 1994), p. 3; John Callaghan, 'Ross McKibbin: Class cultures, the trade unions and the Labour Party', in John Callaghan et al. (eds.), *Interpreting the Labour Party* (Manchester, 2003), pp. 116, 131.

of the leading historians of twentieth-century Britain' but also as 'a somewhat enigmatic figure'.[4] Such critical verdicts further remind us of the elementary genre distinction between two quite different kinds of historiographical analysis: that which serves the purposes of current practitioners in a particular field of study—British history *c.*1880–1950; and that which seeks to construe the historian as a historical subject in his or her own right—in this case as a part of the history of ideas in Britain after *c.*1970. Here we shall pursue historiography in the second sense: as history, not as the contested preamble to the writing of history.

I

The starting point for any inquiry into the 'real' McKibbin does not lie in his doctoral thesis of 1970, or in *The Evolution of the Labour Party*, the heavily revised monograph which derives from it, even if enthusiasm for 'the history of gee-gees', and the Bobby Bear annuals culled from the children's page of the *Daily Herald*, give us an early glimpse of his instinctive preferences.[5] This may seem a very brusque dismissal of a pioneering body of work, which is still uncontested in its scholarship. Yet in doing so we follow a path that McKibbin himself has marked out. As he stated in 1990, the thesis project was undoubtedly part of an overall inquiry into 'the social character of the British working class in the period we conventionally think it to be most "mature" . . . from the early 1880s to the early 1950s', yet 'it excluded much that we would need to know about the working class and it omitted almost everything to do with the working class' relations with the rest of society'.[6] In other words, it was too narrowly 'institutional': too close to party and trade union structures. It reflected an early (and understandable) deference on the part of a young graduate to the influence of an Oxford 'school' of labour history, in particular Hugh Clegg, Alan Fox, and A. F. (Pat) Thompson. They had recently commenced a multi-volume *History of British Trade Unions since 1889* (1964), and Thompson would be his doctoral supervisor. The lynchpin of McKibbin's institutional analysis was Arthur Henderson, at once the 'chief architect of the Labour Party' and 'almost a perfect representative of the manner in which the [trade] unions had moulded the Party'.[7] In 1974 he even went so far as to announce a future biography of Henderson, and *The Evolution of the Labour Party* would be followed by a number of essays developing and expanding the institutional perspective, including 'Arthur Henderson as Labour Leader' (1978).[8] Even so by this date his 'final' and 'most important' conclusion regarding

[4] Stephen Fielding reviewing *Classes and Cultures* in *Contemporary British History*, 13 (1999), p. 170.

[5] 'The evolution of a national party: Labour's political organization, 1910–1924' (1970), p. 112 (citing James Sexton), p. 395 n. 3.

[6] 'Preface', *The Ideologies of Class* [hereafter *IC*] (Oxford, 1990), p. vii.

[7] 'The evolution of a national party', p. 433.

[8] See *The Evolution of the Labour Party 1910-1924* (hereafter *EL*) (Oxford, 1974), p. 91 n. 11 on the Henderson biography. The essays loyal to its political and institutionalist framework are: 'The economic policy of the second Labour government, 1929–1931', *PP* 68 (1975); 'The franchise

Henderson was that 'In almost every way the *labour movement* developed against his wishes'[9]—and in this way the institutional creator of the *party* was transcended by a broader perspective. Blessed with the today unimaginable freedom supplied by the simple fact of academic tenure, McKibbin was able to stand back from the history of the party and unions in order to confront working-class life in its entirety. The result was a set of four essays on the themes of 'Social class and social observation' (1978), 'Working-class Gambling' (1979), 'Work and hobbies' (1983) and 'Why was there no Marxism in Great Britain?' (1984).[10] These essays are only a fraction of his mature output, and yet they are a complete statement of a historian's perspective and of a historical world.

As readers quickly realised, these essays constitute a quantum leap. They took 'the vitally important step from labour to working-class history',[11] taking as their premise the study of the working class as a social body in its own right, independent of any institutional context. It is a step with which Ross McKibbin's name will always be associated. Previously we can find historians such as Eric Hobsbawm (whom McKibbin has always admired) and Henry Pelling (who was his initial choice as a doctoral supervisor on arrival at Oxford in 1967) calling for, and indeed pioneering, the 'social' history of the working class before 1914. Nonetheless, their efforts were limited: in Hobsbawm's case by parameters laid down by Marx and Engels, above all economism and the idea of a labour aristocracy, and in Pelling's by a continued reliance on institutional, political, and legal sources, so that the firm footing supplied by these well-defined fields is always clearly in view. Equally revealing in this light is the work of a Marxist of McKibbin's own generation, Gareth Stedman Jones's essay on 'Working-Class Culture and Working-Class Politics in London, 1870–1900' (1974). This was the most important study 'pre-McKibbin' which sought to tackle the nature of working-class culture head-on, but still it started from an extraneous and Marxist premise: the 'failure' of radical and socialist politics in late nineteenth-century London, which was in turn a symptom of the economic decay of the artisan trades. The efflorescence of working-class culture was a compensation for political and economic failure, and was marked by it—it was a culture of passivity, lack of vitality, apathy, escapism and fatalism.[12] This was a view that would evoke vigorous criticism from McKibbin, who denied both Stedman Jones's premise—that working-class culture was a mere dependency of working-class politics—and also his pessimistic conclusion. In reality (he held) cultural and political life should be seen as complementary and even competing activities,

factor in the rise of the Labour Party', *EHR* 91 (1976), written with Colin Matthew; 'Arthur Henderson as Labour leader', *IRSH* 23 (1978).

[9] *IRSH* 23 (1978), p. 99 my emphasis.

[10] Respectively in (1) *TRHS* 5th Ser., 28 (1978), pp. 175–99, read 14 October 1977; (2) *PP* 82 (1979), pp. 147–78; (3) Jay Winter (ed.), *The Working Class in Modern British History: Essays in Honour of Henry Pelling* (Cambridge, 1983), pp. 127–46; (4) *EHR* 99 (1984), pp. 297–331.

[11] Harold Perkin, 'Just holding together', *TLS* 15.6.90, p. 637b.

[12] *Languages of Class* (Cambridge, 1983), e.g. pp. 181–2, 225, 234–5.

while working-class culture itself was to be seen in a strongly positive light: 'this was not an inert or apolitical culture.'[13]

McKibbin's quest was not unlike that of feminist historians at roughly the same date. Where they asked about the missing female half population who had been 'hidden from history', he wished to understand the lives of the vast working-class majority, who hitherto had hardly been treated as a subject in their own right. The point is best brought out in 'Social class and social observation in Edwardian England', the first of this group of four essays to be published and in a real sense a foundation for all his subsequent work. Overtly this is an examination of working-class life through three Edwardian social investigators, Helen Bosanquet, Margaret Loane, and Lady Bell. But the subtext is an implied parallelism between their investigations and that of the historian: hence the prominence of 'Social Observation' in the title, a methodological category. The mode of investigation of these women was 'essentially psychological and cultural', an obvious pointer to McKibbin's subsequent interest on 'cultures',[14] while the fundamental question posed in this essay is practically the starting point for all his later inquiries: 'how could the members of one social class ever understand another (a methodological question)?' If the social investigators could answer this question in anything like an adequate manner, then so could he, and their reflections on method became echoes of his. 'At every point', he states, 'their writings suggest that this was a difficult, if not actually impossible, task'. However, 'it was possible, [Margaret Loane] suggested, to penetrate the working-class, not by accepting or understanding its codes—that *was* impossible—but by counterfeiting them; and much of the fascination of her writings for the historian lies in her accounts of how this was done. The first quality a district nurse had to learn was self-effacement.' Hence the need for 'what she curiously called "interclassic sincerity"'.[15]

The inherent difficulty of the task is in one sense simply evidential: the fact that 'Historians for their part necessarily observe the working class very largely through the eyes of . . . other classes'—a frequently repeated trope.[16] But the stakes are a good deal higher than this, for what is ultimately at stake is the personal relationship which necessarily exists between the historian and his or her subjects, just as it does for the Edwardian investigator. Seen in this personal light there is a further equivalence between Ross McKibbin the historian and the early social observers: he is middle class, just as they are. Hence enthusiastic support for the observers as being 'entirely without condescension and sentiment . . . Precisely because they had a "total" view of classes, their work is not marked by the single-minded and single-issue moralizing that disfigures the work of other observers of the period:

[13] 'Why was there no Marxism in Great Britain?', *EHR* 99 (1984), pp. 307–10, here p. 309; reiterated *IC* pp. 295–6.

[14] 'Social class and social observation in Edwardian England', *TRHS* 28 (1978), p. 176 cf. pp 182, 184 on 'mental culture' and *IC* p. 169.

[15] Ibid., pp. 178, 185, 186–7 resp.

[16] *IC*, 'Preface' (1990), p. vii.

Booth... Masterman... Rowntree... Sherwell'.[17] However, the same honesty that excludes sentiment and moralizing also requires a frank admission of distance. There should always be 'interclassic sincerity', but there could be none of that assumed and frankly spurious identification with the working class which was common amongst Marxist intellectuals in the 1960s and 70s. In later life, McKibbin would lay great stress on the political and committed nature of historical writing. However, the foundation of all his writing lies in an intellectual rigour which is rooted in social detachment; and it is precisely the yoking of rigour and commitment that gives his work its steel and its distinction.

'Social class and social observation' was not simply a tract on method. It also laid bare the elementary foundations of working-class life. For example, 'the primary difference' between the classes, 'the one that (so to speak) generated all others, was in attitudes to time'.[18] Unlike its 'betters' the working class in its work, pay, health, expenditure and culture lived from week to week, and not with the kind of long time horizon whereby one might (for example) write for 'posterity' or accumulate property for the next generation. This was an immense advance in understanding when compared to Marxist theory. The most explicit confrontation of this kind comes in the essay on 'Work and hobbies'. Here McKibbin tackled head-on Marx's proposition that 'the worker feels himself at home outside his work and feels absent from himself in his work', subjecting it to a merciless empirical critique (though one which would have fascinated the author of *Capital*, had he been alive today).[19] He did not deny that work could be boring and alienating, especially in certain sectors of the economy such as the clerical, distributive, and packing trades, but this was far from the whole or even the principal truth. In a fundamental sense workers liked and lived through their work and the workplace, because the industrial economy had left plenty of room for intense craft 'pride of work', while the evidence suggested that British workers were fascinated by machinery—a portrait that climaxes in Alfred Williams's glorious anecdote of the 'frame-shed foreman, "an inventor himself," who could not keep his hands off other people's machinery'.[20] 'Furthermore, for men, more than for women, the workplace was an important social institution. Men did not just *work* there, it was in the factory more than anywhere else that they had their social being.'[21] *Contra* Marx, not only did the worker feel himself at home in his work, he felt himself more at home in his work than he did at home.[22]

Here was a major reversal of Marxist thought. When it is set alongside an equally stringent critique of romantic ideas about the necessary unity of the working class—in reality workplaces (British firms) were notoriously small

17 'Social class and social observation', p. 198.

18 Ibid., p. 184.

19 'Work and hobbies in Britain, 1880–1950', in Jay Winter (ed.), *The Working Class in Modern British History: Essays in Honour of Henry Pelling* (Cambridge, 1983), p. 127.

20 Ibid., pp. 137–8.

21 Ibid., p. 140.

22 'Why was there no Marxism?', pp. 304–5.

and multifarious; working-class communities might have displayed mutuality but 'they were also marked by backbiting, gossip and a jockeying for social superiority'[23]—it is easy to see why the move 'to' working-class history was for some a false move 'away' from traditional labour (and Labour) history. Now at first sight McKibbin's procedures may look like simple empiricism. Yet he is no simple empiricist. Ultimately he appeals to a set of qualities which he perceives in all human nature, and this universalism leads to original and sometimes surprising conclusions. For example, boredom is a universal quality which can be avoided in a variety of ways. 'Pride of work' is one, but so too are the breaking of factory routine by workplace talk, 'the creation of tension via strikes, unofficial stoppages', and the claims of *St Monday.* Working and striking are psychologically *analogous.*[24] More generally, he assumes that his principal historical subject, the British working class, had an inevitable interest in creating its own psychological satisfactions, which can be described in universal categories recognisable to all people and in all times and places. A list of these satisfactions supplies the kernel of his definition of a working-class 'hobby':[25]

> First, it was an activity freely chosen . . . Second, it was neither random nor disorganized, but required regularity and physical and/or intellectual discipline. Third, it demanded knowledge and sustained interest. Finally, it was usually accompanied by the creation and discharge of some kind of mental or physical tension.

This kind of psychological modelling highlights McKibbin's sense of affinity not only with social observers in the past, but also with contemporary sociology and *its* constructions of human conduct. He has freely acknowledged his indebtedness to figures such as Eric Dunning and Roger Caillois,[26] and such a cast of mind is readily understandable in the composition of essays which, at the time of writing, admitted no frontier between the historical periods under discussion and the present day, and which explored territory practically devoid of literature by historians. In his own work the psychological categories he associates with hobbies embrace all areas of working-class life. Not only does the 'hobby' cover all disciplined, energetic and intellectual activities outside the workplace, but in most cases 'hobbies had all the characteristics of work: indeed that is their fundamental quality'.[27] Now in itself this is a plausible, empirical thesis—the view that the hobbies of skilled workmen will most likely entail a higher degree of skill than those of the unskilled. It also attaches a whole new conceptual or theoretical dimension to the category of 'work'. But what underlies it all is a view of human nature. For McKibbin it is unthinkable that, providing external conditions permit, *any* large group of people should not wish to engage in

[23] Ibid., p. 305 cf. pp. 302–6 *passim.*

[24] 'Work and hobbies', p. 140 cf. p. 138.

[25] Ibid., p. 129.

[26] 'Working-class gambling in Britain 1880–1939', *PP* 82 (1979), p. 147 n.1; 'Class, politics, money: British sport since the First World War', *Twentieth Century British History* [hereafter *TCBH*] 13 (2002), p. 192.

[27] 'Work and hobbies', p. 142.

activities which are active, mentally stimulating, and disciplined; which take up and release their energies to the fullest degree. He is neither a class theorist nor a simple empiricist, but the creator of a historical universe in which men and women live. In this most fundamental respect he is *like* Marx. He certainly shares Marx's elementary premises, if not his conclusions: 'real individuals, their activity and their material conditions of life.'[28]

Universal assumptions produce a striking balance between human commonality and class specificity. The working class might be excluded from the particular forms of middle-class activity, yet both classes were active, intellectual, and energetic to an identical degree. Now this identity might facilitate the diffusion of ideas and practices from one class to another, and in his early writings he is happy to draw attention to this 'interclassic' aspect. But what was more intriguing and more common was a qualitative identity of behaviour within separate class spheres. So in another striking inversion of previous stereotypes McKibbin finds that, within specific contexts, the working class could be 'intensely competitive' and possessed of 'a jaunty and attractive individualism' where individualism and the competitive spirit are integral parts of the model of an active, energetic humanity.[29] In this case it is not merely the romantic stereotype of the working class as a simple undifferentiated community which is overridden; so too is the equally unthinking identification of individualism, energy and competition with capitalist entrepreneurs and private ownership. On this occasion the implied target is not Marx but modern neo-liberal thinking. Accordingly Thatcherism would later appear not as individualism per se but as a form of 'reductionist individualism'.

McKibbin's celebration of human activity and working-class intellectuality reaches a high point in the essay on 'Working-class gambling'. Even the most acclaimed of social observers (Rowntree) and outstanding social theorists (Veblen, Hobson) had seen nothing in a mass culture of betting and gambling besides economic profligacy and 'an abandonment of reason'.[30] Accordingly there had been no historical treatment of the subject. But for McKibbin the abandonment of reason lay with those who, overwhelmingly because of their class situation, were unable to enter sympathetically into the everyday practice of millions. In fact working-class gambling (which was quite different from that of rich) was eminently 'rational',[31] because (first) it placed a premium on having as much information as possible about sporting form so as to reduce the element of chance in the bet to a minimum. Betting was a 'quasi-intellectual activity' in another sense because it had a high mathematical quotient.[32] One of the outstanding characteristics of working-class betting was the placing of extremely complex bets, of combinations and permutations—one might say it was a facet of Richard Hoggart's working-class

[28] *Die deutsche Ideologie I. Feuerbach,* MEGA I/5 (Moscow and Leningrad, 1933) p. 10.

[29] 'Work and hobbies', p. 144; 'Why was there no Marxism in Great Britain?', p. 299, cf. pp. 299–301, 327.

[30] 'Working-class gambling', p. 165 citing Hobson.

[31] Ibid., pp. 168, 178.

[32] Ibid., p. 169.

'baroque'[33]—and this was indeed its primary satisfaction. Making money in this way was an incentive for some, but such a material outcome was indeed luck: by definition no betting industry can survive if the mass of punters make money. What was certain was the mental stimulus and excitement to be gained from making calculations of extreme complexity backed by the placing of very small bets, so that the money supply for thrills might be extended as far as possible within the limit allowed by the working-class budget, say '6d. up to 2s. a week'.[34] Now this was a triumph of historical explanation based on the close empirical scrutiny of a particular class situation; but it could not have taken place at all without a universal human sympathy, and McKibbin has always been careful to describe class satisfactions in universal terms. For the unemployed in the 1930s betting was 'a way of spending one's time in . . . discussion, analysis and decision with a seeming sense of purpose and ultimate achievement'[35]—a description of conduct which could as well apply to the most heroic capitalist entrepreneur. Though the working class might be 'excluded from the particular forms of middle-class intellectual and economic activity', the commonality of cross-class behaviour was not to be denied: what, after all, was middle-class insurance but the hedging of bets based on actuarial calculation, albeit in accordance with a quite different timescale? [36] *Prima facie* there is an intellectualist bias in McKibbin's assumptions about human nature, as there is in his use of the term 'culture' to describe the life activity of ordinary people. Yet no one could be less vulnerable than he to the kind of objections that J. S. Mill exposed himself to, when he exalted the cultivation of the 'higher faculties' and the reading of poetry over the child's game of pushpin, since for McKibbin the essential quality of any really good game (setting aside mindless and mechanical pursuits such as bingo or lotteries) is that it is an exercise of the higher faculties.[37] There have been few essays of which one could say in absolutely unqualified terms, 'this was pioneering', but it was so in this case. His sympathetic exploration of the mass culture of betting and gaming has since given rise to an ample and fruitful literature, but inevitably none of it possesses the air of first discovery which accompanied the original.

The fourth and last of this group of early essays, 'Why was there no Marxism in Great Britain?', is very different in character. Not only was its political subject matter not new, but at its core there lay one of the oldest—if not the oldest—'ideas' in modern English and British history: the unique structure of the political institutions which since 1688 had differentiated and safeguarded Britain from a series of Continental ills: despotism, dictatorship and revolution. Yet it was vitally important for a historian mapping out the range and extent of working-class society to confront this alternative political universe. Without in any way yielding his 'social' starting point or confining himself to the institutional premises of his earliest work, it was essential for McKibbin to measure just

33 *The Uses of Literacy: Aspects of Working-Class Life* (London, 1957), V.b. Cf. *CC*, p. 514.
34 'Working-class gambling', p. 156 citing the *Royal Commission on Lotteries and Betting, 1932–3.*
35 Ibid., pp. 169–70 citing the Pilgrim Trust.
36 Ibid., p. 178 (quotation), p. 162.
37 Ibid., p. 166 (on bingo) cf. Mill, *Utilitarianism* [1861], ch. 2.

how far the 'social' world extended, and what were the boundaries between the realms of society and politics. In this sense, the inquiry was new. Hitherto it had hardly seemed necessary to ask why the British working class was reformist rather than an analogue of the Continental Marxist parties of the Second International, because the answer had been presumed to be self-evident. Given the nature of Britain's institutions, there never had been and could not be a credible revolutionary threat. It might perhaps be necessary to defend this position in the years of Chartism and Continental revolution *c.*1789–1848, but it was surely not the case for the late nineteenth and early twentieth centuries, when political stability was axiomatic. Now however the politics of the later period became a subject for systematic inquiry, and in making this move he commenced a seam of inquiry that has preoccupied him down to the present day.

The result was 'something old, something new'. McKibbin was well persuaded of the power of British institutions, and he accepted that the potential for a rejectionist socialist political movement had been snuffed out by long recognised forces: the theatrical show put on by the Bagehotian monarchy; the 'open self-satisfaction' displayed by the working classes as much as any others 'at being British and not foreign'; and the role of parliament which worked according to a set of strictly formalized procedures and so secured 'strict fairness' in adjudicating between the interests of the various classes of society.[38] But if the matter of this was conventional, its treatment and placement were not. McKibbin, like all historians of his generation, was oppressed by the tedium of an appeal to the all-sufficient goodness of the unique British Constitution, an appeal which by the mid-1980s was palpably obsolescent and decadent, as the unique political good fortune Britain had experienced comparable to her European neighbours became just a memory. He did not deny its relevance in an earlier period, but there is a strong sense that he, like Marx, felt that 'the past "weighs like a nightmare on the brain of the living"', and given his voluntaristic and activist conception of human nature, he has always been sceptical and critical of the inertial power of tradition and the *longue durée*.[39] His modern social history may deal in 'mentalities and structures', but it has nothing to do with French structuralism or the *Annales*: 'emphasising the unchanging character of mentalities and the comparative insignificance of historical "events" ... has a very conservative political implication'.[40] This view might be taken as a symptom of the difference between the historical depth of the English and Australian political traditions; but in any case it helps explain why he was happy to add an entirely new component to the traditionary culture of constitutional continuity and reformist hegemony. Thus British institutions were also powerful because of their links to 'the great British sporting tradition', since voting, elections and parliament 'gained even more

[38] 'Why was there no Marxism?', pp. 316, 313, cf. p. 310.

[39] Ibid., p. 310.

[40] Resp. *CC*, p. v; 'Is it still possible to write labour history ?', in T. Irving (ed.), *Challenges to Labour History* (Sydney, 1994), p. 38. Cf. Stefan Collini, 'Labour's lost chance', *TLS* 17.4.98, pp. 3a, 4b–c.

ideological acceptability when . . . they became assimilated to the rules of the game', a sporting code which was crucial to their equitable character.[41] Even so there were strict limits to the power of the Constitution, since it could not override the central reality of modern social life: it might succeed 'in defining and narrowing the conventions of the class struggle', but it could never abolish it. Classes had adversarial interests whether one liked it or not. So the outer limit of the achievement of the British state was 'the exclusion of the market from the "politics"'. Hence the creation of 'a "politics" that permitted a viable class-neutral state'.[42] The final outcome was 'a highly cohesive but poorly integrated nation', a conception consonant with another feature of English or British exceptionalism which had already appeared in the essay on 'Work and hobbies'.[43] Because of the practical withdrawal of the state from the economy, the working class enjoyed a degree of autonomy in its industrial relations to which there was no parallel on the Continent. Granted there might be socialist and formally revolutionary parties across the Channel, but at least in Britain there was 'no "kow-towing" to management': 'within certain broadly defined [limits] the British workman went his own way.'[44]

'Why was there no Marxism?' tells us a good deal about its author. First and foremost, it shows that McKibbin's desire to get away from narrowly institutional analysis should never be confused with a lack of interest in politics and political history. The idea that he might have oscillated between an early political phase when writing *The Evolution of Labour* (1974), followed by a middle 'social' and 'cultural' phase which climaxed with *Classes and Cultures* (1998), before a later return to politics in his Ford Lectures of 2008 on 'Parties, People and the State *c.*1914–1951' is quite mistaken. He has always adhered to the common-sense view that society and politics, though they might appear distinct at times, are two spheres which go together and must always be conceived together. This 1984 essay is also notable as supplying the 'other face' of his intellectual relationship with Marx. In his purely 'social' essays McKibbin appeared as a radical subverter of Marx. Even his fundamental reliance on 'a central organizing theme—social class—that gives unity to material that would otherwise appear antiquarian and discrete' is traced there not to Marx but to a native English discourse.[45] Yet when he turns to politics and political culture, the picture changes. He finds that 'ideology' in what he holds to be its classical Marxist sense, and 'class struggle' are clearly present within the depths of the peaceful British society *c.*1914. Accordingly 'Why was there no Marxism?' wrestles with the political implications of 'class struggle' and offers a reading of Engels' famous Introduction (1895) to Marx on *The Class Struggles in France*, though to be sure this is in the revisionist or 'social-democratic' sense made famous by Eduard

[41] 'Why was there no Marxism?', p. 314.

[42] Ibid., p. 320.

[43] 'Work and hobbies', p. 146; cf. 'Why was there no Marxism?', p. 329; 'Foreword' to Lawrence Black et al., *Consensus or Coercion? The State, the People and Social Cohesion in Post-war Britain* (Cheltenham, 2001), p. vii.

[44] Resp. 'Why was there no Marxism?', pp. 329, 319; 'Work and hobbies', p. 146, cf. p. 143.

[45] 'Social class and social observation', p. 199.

Bernstein: that class conflict was consistent with the procedures of parliamentary democracy.[46] So for all that he disagrees with Marx, we can readily see why he holds that 'Marx is undoubtedly the most formidable thinker that any historian has to confront',[47] even if this is a Marxism which must be 'confronted', and which is consistent with classic British constitutionalism.

There is however no mystery here and McKibbin's occasional remarks on the subject are entirely consistent. An obvious starting point lies in the distinction between 'Marxism . . . as a political goal and as a method of historical explanation'.[48] His own avowedly social-democratic political preferences have nothing to do with political Marxism, or with the Marxist belief that historical explanation and analysis is ultimately tied to a particular political outcome. Yet he has a firm belief in Marx as an immensely powerful critical analyst of politics. His most sustained reflections on this subject have been triggered by engagements with Eric Hobsbawm (though his friend and contemporary Tim Mason is another case in point). He dismisses Hobsbawm's Marxist political premises while displaying warm admiration for his Marxist history, and in doing so tells us something about himself. Like Hobsbawm, he absorbed Marx's ideas through a reading of 'the classics', those texts which were widely available outside university libraries, such as *The Eighteenth Brumaire* or *Class Struggles in France*—and it is no accident that it is precisely these texts which are cited in 'Why was there no Marxism?'.[49] Such Marxist influences as he has absorbed are 'largely atheoretical . . . strongly historical . . . and thus popular'. Again: 'it is the strength of this kind of Marxist history that it provides a way of seeing the world that actually coheres with individual experience: even for people who themselves are anything but Marxist, or not even political.'[50] It is a view of Marx which has absolutely nothing to do with the Cold War, or the fall of the Berlin Wall in 1989, and everything to do with Marx himself, and the early generation of 'bourgeois' theorists who both admired him and reacted against him—Weber, Sombart, Durkheim, Labriola, Croce . . . Understandably, then, this is a view of 'Marxist theory' which has 'much in common with liberal tradition'.[51] In particular it looks to 'Marx the historian',[52] for historical and critical weapons to use in analysing of the role of 'ideology' in sustaining and maintaining class structures. However, we should not fall into the error of supposing that Marx is in any way an exclusive idol, even in this restricted sense. I have already noted McKibbin's instinctive openness to a range of critical thinkers and sociologists or even (more speculatively) Byzantinists and historians of medieval religion[53]—figures whom he utilises conceptually in just the same way

46 'Why was there no Marxism?', p. 319.

47 'Did my question ever change?', Seminar presentation in Oxford 25.6.06.

48 'Hobsbawm today', *LRB* 22.6.89, pp. 1a cf. 2c.

49 Review of Eric Hobsbawm, *Interesting Times*, *EHR* 119 (2004), p. 156. For citation of *The Eighteenth Brumaire* see 'Why was there no Marxism?', p. 310, quoted in the text above at n.38.

50 Ibid., pp. 156–7.

51 'Is it still possible to write Labour history?', in T. Irving (ed.), *Challenges to Labour History* (Sydney, 1994), p. 35.

52 'Mason, Timothy Wright', *ODNB* (2004).

53 Cf. 'Mass-Observation in the Mall', *LRB* 2.10.97, p. 3a.

he uses Marx; and if Marx is nonetheless extremely prominent, still he is not the only figure of this magnitude in the intellectual pantheon, where J. M. Keynes must certainly be set alongside him. In McKibbin's view both were outstanding critical analysts of modern industrial society, who 'had much in common: both believed that capitalism was dynamically unstable; both believed that a capitalist society was inhabited by classes whose interests were irreconcilable; both believed that the ordinary precepts of political economy were "false" when universalised.'[54]

'Why was there no Marxism?' may legitimately be seen as the completion of a circle of inquiry. Having first established the terms on which one could know the working class as a social body, McKibbin had examined the culture of its work; its leisure; and then its political culture. Whether he himself would see this group of early texts in such sharply defined terms, I don't know. The analytical divisions erected by the outsider inevitably do violence to the continuous experience of real life. It may also be suggested that 'Why was there no Marxism?' points forward to the more overtly political and ideological concerns informing his later writings, while the claim for an overall continuity is unarguable: the historical universe created in these early writings is undoubtedly the same universe which lies at the heart of all his subsequent work. Nonetheless, seen through the eyes of a 'outsider' or 'observer' (to borrow a McKibbinite category), we may fairly mark a caesura at this point.

II

Two major changes affected his work from the beginning of the 1980s. They were purely external impacts, but no less powerful for that. The first was his acceptance *c.*1980 of a major publishing commission—to write a volume for the *New Oxford History of England* covering the period 1918–1951. As early as April 1981 we find him sketching out a draft plan of contents for this volume,[55] and after the completion of 'Why was there no Marxism?' *c.*1982 he abandoned the late Victorian (or Second International) starting point that had been uniform in the essays that we have been considering hitherto and moving forward to 1918. The two central statements of his later career, *Classes and Cultures* (1998) and the 2008 Ford lectures on 'Parties, People and the State', both stem from this root. Once we understand this shift in perspective, it will be clear that the essay collection *The Ideologies of Class* (1990) was a composite, which gathered material from three distinct phases of work: McKibbin's earliest political and institutional phase, including such famous conceptual provocations as the 1976 essay on the impact of 'The Franchise Factor' in 1918 (written with Colin Matthew); the four 'social' essays we have just examined; and then two later essays written in preparation for the *New Oxford History*.

54 'Extravagance', *LRB* 2.2.89, p. 5d.
55 Untitled facsimile, dated 8 April 1981. This was drawn to my attention by Philip Waller.

One on 'The "Social Psychology" of Unemployment in Interwar Britain' (1987) was an extension of the socio-cultural perspectives of his 'second' period—seeking a sympathetic understanding not merely of work and leisure but of worklessness—and would be taken over without difficulty into *Classes and Cultures.*[56] As such it highlights the element of continuity in McKibbin's career. The second on 'Class and Conventional Wisdom: The Conservative Party and the "Public" in Interwar Britain' was more unusual and more ambitious. Driven by the requirement of the *New Oxford History* to write a comprehensive history, this essay is practically a sketch of the entire volume: elections, the three political parties, fiscal and economic policy, the material bases and ideological stereotypes of class—all are there. Yet what may sound like an *omnium gatherum* is pervaded by a profound unity, since the starting point of the essay is a single problem: the need 'to explain the most visible of [working-class] defeats—the remarkable electoral success of the Conservative Party in the inter-war years'.[57] This for McKibbin was surely the single most pressing historical problem confronting him in the *New Oxford History*, and working-class defeat and Conservative hegemony remain the premise of *Classes and Cultures.* Note too that the essay also embraces the purely political deviation in English social history marked out by war in 1939–40—a crucial conundrum which would preoccupy McKibbin first in *Classes and Cultures*, and would then provide an obvious catalyst for the writing of the Ford lectures.[58] 'Class and Conventional Wisdom' is now outmoded in one important respect: its snapshot of the interwar middle class as an essentially unchanging, anti-socialist and class-sensitive body has been superseded by the 'political life-cycle' outlined in *Classes and Cultures*, such that the confrontational class of the 1920s (and of the original essay) is replaced by the modern, scientific and even democratic body of the 1930s before reverting to anti-socialist type in the 1950s.[59] Nonetheless, this remarkable essay, like the cluster of earlier 'social' essays, exceeds the scope of his later writings in important respects (above all in what it says about Keynes), even if the latter are more massive and developed in others. Viewed in a literary perspective, it shows McKibbin at the peak of his mastery of the essay form.

Yet if *The Ideologies of Class* was composite in origin, it was also a readily identifiable position statement of just where McKibbin stood at the end of the 1980s. Most of the essays in the volume were substantially revised, or else a different significance was attached to them. The tenor of these revisions and rethinkings was uniform: a heightened, and sometimes quite new, emphasis on class confrontation in British history and its ineradicably political character, especially for the period after the Great War.[60] This is particularly evident in 'Class and Conventional Wisdom', but it pervades the rest of the volume as well. Some of his early essays on political history, a vein he might appear to have left behind *c.*1978, now took on new meaning. When first published in 1975 'The

[56] Originally published in *Politics and Social Change in Modern Britain* (Sussex, 1987), ch. 7. Cf. *CC*, pp. 151–63.

[57] *IC*, p. viii cf. p. 258.

[58] *IC*, pp. 286–92; *CC*, pp. 531–6.

[59] Compare *IC*, pp. 270–4 with *CC*, pp. 50–69.

[60] Cf. *IC*, p. vii.

Economic Policy of the Second Labour Government' was an invaluable, historicist riposte to the view that there was a readily available Keynesian solution to the economic crisis of 1929–31. It was a classical exercise in the avoidance of anachronism—one should not translate the economic thinking of the 1960s back to the 1930s—but otherwise it appeared to have little wider significance. In *The Ideologies of Class* the text is only lightly revised, but it has acquired a quite new force. It now 'suggests . . . that the structure of power and ideological interest within Britain did not permit the adoption of alternative policies' by Labour.[61] In other words, a Keynesian policy friendly to working-class interest was not merely an anachronism, but was impossible on class grounds and because of an ideological accompaniment to class embodied in the conventional economic wisdom ('the Treasury view', the Labour-cost doctrine). By contrast, 'there are many reasons for thinking that the Conservatives could have ridden out the [economic] storm in a way impossible to Labour'[62]—not indeed because they would have been allowed to adopt a Keynesian and inflationary policy (on this point the essay was unchanged), but because the politics of deflation suited them and their class interests so well. 'The "Social Psychology" of Unemployment' presents a different case, but it was revised in much the same direction. This was a very recent text which was (as we saw) in most respects a continuation of established perspectives. In 1987 McKibbin had already devoted substantial attention to the politics of the unemployed, and yet it was precisely this point in the text that he chose to buttress still further when it was republished in 1990.[63] It was at this point too that in 1987 he had delivered the dictum that '*everyone* has a politics'.[64] Now in context this remark applied to the unemployed—those who were least capable of having politics, still had them in fact—but the force of that minatory '*everyone*' was not to be overlooked. If the unemployed were capable of having politics, so too were educated and socially privileged historians, and the remark is (I suggest) the immediate precursor to a series of reminders appearing from 1990 onwards that 'the writing of history is the most political of all creative actions'.[65] Of course this was not a new view—his milieu both before and after his first arrival in England in 1966 was intensely political. What was new was the need to say it out loud; and if there was no intellectual discontinuity, still it can be said that the tone of his work from the later 1980s has carried a more sombre and embattled note.

Here is the second change which affected McKibbin in the 1980s: the 'desolating' experience of public life; the growing sense (as he put it in 1991) that 'no one can contemplate except with dismay the wasted hopes and opportunities of the last 20 years.'[66] One reflection of the incursion of this changed world came in 1989 when he took up the role of an occasional political

[61] Ibid., p. viii. [62] Ibid., p. 293 cf. pp. 26, 302. [63] *IC*, pp. 250–3.

[64] 'The "social psychology" of unemployment', *Politics and Social Change in Modern Britain* (Sussex, 1987), p. 176; cf. *IC*, p. 246. Original emphasis.

[65] [Ross McKibbin and John Rowett], 'Editorial', *Twentieth Century British History* 1 (1990), p. 8; cf. *CC*, p. vi, 'Did my question ever change?'.

[66] 'With or Without the Workers', *LRB* 25.4.91, p. 6b.

commentator in the *London Review of Books*, and he has contributed something like sixty articles over the twenty years since. One would never think of him as a journalist, and this was not an intended career movement; yet it has suited him well. It has led to the production of a unique public record, which should certainly be collected and reprinted. But it is also, of course, a personal testimony. So what relation does it bear to his historical writing? In one sense it evidently stands apart. He is writing an engaged polemic addressed to the citizen of today, and any historical audience is placed at some fairly remote point in the future—the day 'when historians come to account for the *dégringolade* of modern British politics'.[67] Nonetheless, it is equally clear that this present-day commentary is written by a historian. He believes that the citizens' and politicians' forgetfulness of the past is frequently damaging—above all New Labour's abandonment of its past in response to the onslaught of 'Thatcherism'[68]—and if we wish to understand our present, then historical and genetic explanation will be found as powerful a tool as ever it was in more confidently historicist eras. So there is a wealth of historical reference. The 1994 Borrie Report on Social Justice is compared at length to Beveridge in 1942; the currency politics of sterling and the ERM to those of 1925–31; the 1990 Poll tax to the 1902 Education Act; Tony Blair to Ramsay MacDonald;[69] and Mrs Thatcher's government to that of Neville Chamberlain—though also to late Tsarist Russia and decadent eighteenth-century Spain.[70] One motto which runs throughout is that 'Before they'—the politicians—'appropriate history, history should appropriate them.'[71]

However, the links between political journalism and academic history can be drawn more tightly than this. The *LRB* articles cite identical material to that used in *Classes and Cultures*: for example, the widespread belief by workers that trade unions and employers colluded at their expense—'they piss in the same pot'—or the sharp rebuke of Attlee for failing to attack and reform such thoroughly undemocratic institutions as the MCC.[72] Indeed they sometimes deploy material that was evidently considered for inclusion in *Classes and Cultures* or *The Ideologies of Class* but was omitted.[73] More substantially, arguments and categories central to the academic writings are continually employed, and sometimes reworked, in the political commentary. For example, the 'public' is a central category in the essay

[67] 'Radical democrats', *LRB* 7.3.91, p. 10a.

[68] e.g. 'Homage to Wilson and Callaghan', *LRB* 24.10.91, pp. 3–5; 'Why they did it', 25.5.95, pp. 3–4; 'Very Old Labour', 3.4.97, pp. 3–6.

[69] Resp. 'On the defensive', *LRB* 26.1.95, pp. 6a–7d; 'What Is Labour to Do?', 27.2.92, p. 7d (cf. 'When Labour last ruled', 9.4.92, pp. 6b–c); 'Mrs Thatcher's Ecstasy', 24.5.90, p. 3a; 'If/when Labour gets in', 22.2.96, p. 3d; 'Very Old Labour', 3.4.97, pp. 3b–c; 'Make enemies and influence people', 20.7.00, p. 3c; 'Defeatism, defeatism, defeatism', 22.3.07, p. 26c.

[70] Resp. 'Hobsbawm today', *LRB* 22.6.89, pp. 10a–b; 'Mrs Thatcher's Ecstasy', 24.5.90, p. 5d; 'What a progressive government will have to do', 30.8.90, p. 8a.

[71] 'Diary', *LRB* 6.12.90, p. 25a.

[72] Resp. *CC*, p. 148 cf. 'Customers of the state', *LRB* 9.9.93, p. 7c; *CC*, p. 339 cf. 'When Labour gets in', 25.5.95, p. 3d.

[73] 'The summer of discontent', *LRB* 17.8.89, p. 6c cf. 'Class and conventional wisdom', *IC*, p. 268 (on the *Daily Mail*), *CC*, p. 71.

on 'Class and Conventional Wisdom' (1990), but the idea of the 'public', the agglomeration of the middle classes that promoted 'conventional wisdoms' of a 'universalized and apparently class-neutral' kind at the expense of organized (unionised) labour,[74] is also a lynch-pin of *LRB* argument. This is for a very good and obvious reason: in both the academic and the journalistic contexts McKibbin wishes to explain the cross-class appeal and electoral hegemony of Conservatism. In one case this means Stanley Baldwin and Neville Chamberlain, in the other Margaret Thatcher, but the conceptual instrument is the same. The identification at the time of the 1992 election of 'a large passive electorate which has no material interest in a Conservative government [in fact], but also has no confidence in its own political capacities' or the still blunter statement that 'the electorate, or its largest part, chooses to live in a dream', derive from this root.[75] Such too is the foundation for the parallel drawn between Mrs Thatcher and Neville Chamberlain (but not Baldwin).[76]

In fact a whole series of distinctively McKibbinite conceptual fingerprints appear in the *LRB*, going far beyond practically inescapable categories such as the state and social class. Note, for example, the appeal to Marx's *Eighteenth Brumaire* as a central text for decoding not merely the class hegemony of Edwardian England (as it was in 'Why was there no Marxism?') but the ideological spell woven by Thatcherism.[77] There is also parallel historical and contemporary usage of McKibbin's original, populist construction of 'ideology' in the form of 'conventional wisdom' or 'folklore' (as distinct from the 'ideology' created by ideologues and theorists), something which was first expounded in 'Class and Conventional Wisdom',[78] as of his veiled but insistent appeal to the force of 'elites' as an alternative conservative social grouping to that of class.[79] Of course, the employment of these tools is not always identical in the earlier and late twentieth-century contexts. For example, the separation between the market and the state which (as we saw) was of major importance to the argument of 'Why was there no Marxism?' is significantly reworked in a present-day context. Nigel Lawson might have a genuine interest in markets, but Mrs Thatcher did not: 'insofar as her Thatcherism has a clear focus, it is the establishment of a reactionary moral and political order in which the free market performs a disciplinary and not an allocationary function.'[80] And this line of thought would lead on to a pungent scepticism regarding New Labour doctrines about pseudo-consumer and market

[74] *IC*, pp. 284–5.

[75] 'What is Labour to do?', *LRB* 27.2.92, p. 7b; 'The sense of an ending', 28.5.92, p. 3b; see also *LRB* 17.8.89, p. 6a; 24.5.90, p. 3a; 25.4.91, p. 6d etc.

[76] See *CC*, p. 96; 'The tax-and-spend vote', *LRB* 5.7.01, p. 14a, the latter perhaps assisted by Philip Williamson's *Stanley Baldwin* (Cambridge, 1999).

[77] e.g. *LRB* 22.6.89, p. 8d; 11.1.90, p. 5d.

[78] Compare *IC*, pp. 259, 271, 274, 281 ('primitive convictions') with *LRB* 23.11.89, p. 25d; 24.5.90, p. 4a; 24.10.91, pp. 3a, 4d; 22.9.94, p. 10a ('folk-memory'), 8.2.2001, p. 13c etc.

[79] *LRB* 11.1.90, p. 5d; 5.11.92, p. 6d; 9.9.93, p/6d; 24.2.94, p/18d; 26.1.95, p/6a; 25.5.95, p. 3b etc.

[80] 'Diary', *LRB* 23.11.89, p. 25a cf. 'Skimming along', 20.10.94, pp. 7c–d.

'choice' in areas where in fact no real market existed.[81] More generally the immense research foundation of McKibbin's historical work cannot be matched by his present-day reading, extensive though it is. Nonetheless, the later arguments run in close parallel to the 'academic' ones, and the intellectual world of political commentary is seamlessly connected with that of more formal history. To appreciate and understand Ross McKibbin, even as a purely academic author, the two must be taken together.[82]

III

We come lastly to Ross McKibbin's most 'mature' and even classical works: to *Classes and Cultures* (1998) and its political complement, the 2008 Ford Lectures, now published as *Parties and People: England, 1914–51* (2010). I suggest that *Classes and Cultures* is the most important statement about modern British social and political history since E. P. Thompson's *Making of the English Working Class* (1963). At first sight this may seem an unlikely remark. There is no intellectual tradition linking Thompson and McKibbin—as we have seen, he finds Eric Hobsbawm a far more sympathetic Marxist historian—and the two books appear radically unalike when we look at their structures, their authors' views, or the tone and literary styles which accompany them.[83] Unlike Thompson, McKibbin is not tied to an obviously vulnerable historical thesis, such as that the English working class was somehow 'made' in the years before 1832. Nonetheless, some large similarities remain: both embrace political and social history as a unity; and both combine tangible political and ethical commitment with radical academic innovation. The reader who traverses these books knows that there is one response which is inadequate and unacceptable: indifference. We know it, first, because the historical statement that is being made also claims a universal human status; and next because of the author's personal presence—a *persona* which embodies political-ethical and intellectual-historical commitment in indissoluble unity. McKibbin's political commitment is no more (and no less) than an ideal, an ideal which knows itself to be historically conditioned: hence mutable and uncertain. As such it sits easily with the writing of empirically flexible and intellectually open history. Here, for example, is one of the best short statements of the values he upholds. It is a statement of undeniable grandeur, yet there is also an implicit pathos, since it is couched not in his own name but as a proposition about a world that he supposes has largely passed away:[84]

[81] e.g. 'Nothing More Divisive', *LRB* 28.11.2002, p. 5a.

[82] Here the full text version of this essay goes on to discuss the negotiation between past and present in McKibbin's work; the way his conception of twentieth-century British history changed and was unchanged; and his view of socialism.

[83] See e.g. 'Against it', *LRB* 24.2.94, p. 18b on 'Edward Thompson . . . a born member of nature's awkward squad'; also 'Making Things Happen', *LRB* 26.7.90, p. 6d.

[84] 'Very Old Labour', *LRB* 3.4.97, p. 3a.

Old Labour had all the familiar aims of traditional social democracy: an emphasis on the collective, on equality, on a rational political discourse, on the redistribution of power and wealth, on social and economic modernisation, and a sense that the nation exists only to the extent that its poorest and most deprived feel part of it.

Even a statement as restrained as this does not appear in his academic writings, but it is an excellent guide to what he understands by the 'democracy'—the creed of the 'ordinary man', which is his alternative to an unattainable 'socialism'. In turn it offers a guide to the emotional charge behind *Classes and Cultures*, which was originally intended to carry the sub-title *A Study of a Democratic Society*, though this was regrettably deleted.[85] 'Democracy', and more particularly 'the social-democratic definition of democracy',[86] is the underlying standard of judgement which informs the book, just as it does Parties and People. The prominence of 'democracy' is indeed a central distinguishing feature of the later works when compared to the position he occupied *c.*1990 in *The Ideologies of Class*, where his stance too easily appears as simply critical and without this wider vision. In reality the instinctive equation of Labour with social democracy and (however loosely) 'the classic social-democratic parties' of Western Europe has always been with him, in the later 1980s as much as at any other time.[87] However, from this root, reference to 'democracy' and 'social democracy' as explicit criteria by which to judge both Labour and British politics emerged gradually in the early 1990s as the prospects of a Labour government revived.[88] So it was that in McKibbin's academic work the treatment of democracy in *Classes and Cultures* marks a real discontinuity and, we may say, final maturity.

In its construction the radicalism of the book far outstrips any competitor, since it offers an English history where politics is covered only by the study of its 'social and ideological foundations'.[89] Any conventional account of formal or high politics is omitted. To some extent this was an accident of publishing. As we saw, *Classes and Cultures* began life as a part of the *New Oxford History of England*, an eminently conventional project which continued to pay lip service to the largely obsolete prescription of its early twentieth-century precursor, the *Oxford History*, in calling for 'a comprehensive account [of each period], in which politics is always likely to be prominent'.[90] Having completed his account of the 'foundations', McKibbin did not demur at fulfilling the rest of his comprehensive brief in a second volume: there was plenty here to interest him, and he had done a large amount of work for it—Keynes and interwar economic policy are outstanding examples.[91] However, the publisher's desire for a series of uniform, single-volume treatments prevailed, and *Classes and Cultures* was published in splendid isolation,

85 'Postscript' [2002], p. 154 n.4. 86 *CC*, p. 533.
87 e.g. 'Hobsbawm today', *LRB* 22.6.89, p. 8d.
88 e.g. 'What is Labour to do?', *LRB* 27.2.92, pp. 7–8.
89 *CC*, p. vi.
90 [J.M. Roberts] 'General Editor's Preface' [1989], p. viii.
91 For evidence of this: 'Extravagance', *LRB* 2.2.89, p. 5b; 'Class and conventional wisdom', *IC*, p. 266 n.17, 274 nn.34–6, pp. 282–4 nn.49, 54.

as a free-standing volume without the political or other forms of accompaniment which were originally intended. So there was always ample scope for a completion or supplement—and the political history later delivered in the Ford Lectures is only the most prominent example of this process. Already in late 1997, before *Classes and Cultures* was even published, McKibbin was sketching out 'The Structure of Politics in Britain 1918–51: An Interpretation',[92] while his conception of the Second World War as the central example of a purely autonomous, political intervention in recent British history—and the ultimate justification for writing the Fords—had been established in his mind at least a decade previously, when planning the original *New Oxford History* volume.[93]

Nonetheless, the underlying radicalism of the original design is not to be gainsaid. For McKibbin society and ideology, classes and cultures, were the foundations of any history, and of political history above all. As such they had to be prioritised. And this same social priority informs the Ford Lectures. They are an essay in 'the political sociology of parties',[94] an account of the working out (or ideological obstruction) of social class within high politics, and by no means a reversion to self-sufficient political history. It would be wrong to say that *Classes and Cultures* was not shaped in some degree by the original *New Oxford History* requirement to be comprehensive. The account given of classes and cultures aims to be comprehensive, and one may at least wonder whether McKibbin would otherwise have offered treatments of classes (such as the upper class, ch. I) or cultures (religion, ch. VII) which are either problematic as subjects or of less intrinsic interest to him. Again, the extraordinary care with which a plurality of variables apart from class is kept in view throughout—gender above all, but also religion—is either indebted to, or at least confirmed by, the need to be systematic. But still what stands out is the author's determination to pursue his own unitary agenda. The peril confronting any volume in the *New Oxford History* is that comprehensiveness of coverage will in fact render it a giant compendium which is otherwise intellectually inert. By contrast the power of *Classes and Cultures* derives from the extraordinary unity of its concerns across a broad canvas; the omission of even a stripped down treatment of high politics enhances this unity, and with it the sense of a truly radical break with past historiography. In this fundamental sense liberation from the constraints of the *New Oxford History* was a blessing.

If the book's major themes and approach were first sketched out in the quartet of early essays, still these outlines were now filled out in massive fashion, and there was a great deal that was visibly new. Perhaps the outstanding novelty is the prominence of the 'cultures' signalled in the book's title. Now this is instantly recognisable as a theme of much broader relevance given the picture of the evolution of recent historical writing which is conventionally accepted today. According to this the immediate precursor of present-day historiographical

92 The title of a seminar presentation given in Oxford in late November 1997.

93 'Class and conventional wisdom', *IC*, pp. 290–2; 'Hobsbawm Today', *LRB* 22.6.89, p. 8d.

94 Lecture I 'The First World War and the party system': delivered 18.1.2008.

practice lies in the domination of ideas about class and materialism in the 1960s, which in turn represented the ultimate triumph of a loosely Marxist frame of reference that had been gathering force since *c.*1890. However, by the 1980s this matrix had been dissolved in favour of 'cultural' themes such as gender and ethnicity. Hence the commonplace appeal to a 'linguistic' or 'cultural' turn in historiography.

McKibbin is evidently a central exemplar of a real individual at work to set alongside this simple sketch. The trader in stereotypes could easily seize hold of the institutional and trade union framework of *The Evolution of Labour* in 1974 and contrast this with the agenda of *Classes and Cultures* in 1998 and proclaim that the stereotype was vindicated. But of course this is nonsense, as the retained presence of *Classes* indicates. Conversely, McKibbin's concern with the 'mental culture' of class behaviour (as of all social groups) was established from the moment he undertook to investigate social class rather than the parties and institutions.[95] In this sense his work has always been about both classes and cultures. However, this statement cuts both ways: if he has always thought culturally, his thinking has been equally consistent in upholding the material and quantitative premises which attach to class. So it would be a mistake to suppose that culture was his exclusive concern in the construction of class, though it was surely the most innovative one. For example, his identification of that elusive body the middle classes derives in the first instance from census and occupational statistics, and the 'cultural' history which follows is entirely consistent with, and formally determined by, this statistical foundation.[96] The working class is no doubt easier to identify, but even so its hegemony in English history—and hence its prominence in the account he chooses to give—is in the first instance a statistical fact, as is its decay since 1950.[97] Statistics of employment remind us that McKibbin's conception of class *starts* from the idea of material interest, so that in principle, and subject to political contingency, the working-class constituted 'a large mass of voters whose "objective class position" was probably better served by Labour than by the Conservatives'.[98] This was 'the *a priori* presumption for the rise of the Labour Party' at the expense of the Liberal Party—a presumption which he still endorses 'to a considerable extent', after scrutinising the revisionist historiography on this much contested subject. Yet use of the term *a priori* is exact and not dogmatic: class and material interest are the ideal-typical assumptions one begins with, but the historical end-product may be very different. The active, expressive and intellectual qualities of human nature stand entirely outside class and lead (even within a class context) to a spectrum of interest where 'some men emphasised wages, some job-interest'.[99] And then there is class delusion or deviancy: the case (noted before) of 'a large passive electorate which has no material interest in a Conservative government, but also has no confidence . . . in [the capacities] of people, like the Labour Party, who

[95] 'Social class and social observation' 183, 'Working-class gambling', *PP* 82 (1979), p. 162.
[96] *CC*, pp. 44–9. [97] *IC*, p. vii; *CC*, pp. 106–11.
[98] 'Postscript' [2002], p. 162. [99] *CC*, p. 133.

claim to speak for it'.[100] In such a case, 'if we look simply at "objective" self-interest we get more or less nowhere'.[101] Now on the face of it, this is virtually a complete reversal of the materialist starting point. Yet the qualifications entered here ('simply', 'more or less') are not to be overlooked: the perceived historical outcome—working-class Toryism, a culturally inflected end-point—only makes sense or assumes significance when measured against the material starting point. In this respect McKibbin is a neo-Weberian who rejects any 'one-sided' interpretation of history. So for all his pronounced interest in 'cultures', he also makes authorial interventions which the cultural determinist will not relish, and what happens 'in fact' does not necessarily correspond with what 'contemporaries thought'.[102] Consider what is for him the central example of middle-class hostility to the working-class in the first half of the twentieth century. Its principal defining characteristic was that it was 'ideological', and yet 'this fear was usually expressed in non-ideological, matter of fact terms: loss of income, an inability to maintain a "middle-class" existence'.[103] In other words, cultural evidence of overt class hostility is largely wanting; the basis of the analysis goes back to material class interest, and the only cultural symptoms are oblique at best.

Having said this, McKibbin is unquestionably a historian of ideas or, in an older terminology, an exponent of *Kulturgeschichte.* In its elementary taxonomy the history of ideas falls into two parts: the study of canonical authors, who reflect at a very high level of sophistication and abstraction; and the observation of wider currents of thought which cannot be captured within the microcosm of privileged texts. Yet whether we pursue the high road or the low, the macrocosm or the microcosm, the ultimate premise and rationale of study must be the same: that is, the history of the mental world of societies in their totality, and not the fetishism of individuals in isolation. McKibbin is an advocate of the macrocosm—albeit explicit advocacy is all done and dusted in ten lines—and he applies its principle with typically stringent consistency. Neither in *Classes and Cultures* nor, still more revealingly, in the 'comprehensive' 1981 Plan of Contents for the *New Oxford History*, is there any room for 'high culture', hence canonical texts, for the simple reason that 'the great mass of the English people' was unmoved by them.[104] This does not exclude authors, filmmakers, sociologists and sexologists who spoke to, and about, the wider culture; nor does it dispense with the idea of a set of 'elites', which includes a cultural elite; but it is a radical omission all the same. It is not at all a new position and yet within the recent history of ideas, which has fetishised high theory even in England,[105] it appears so.

[100] 'What is Labour to do?', *LRB* 27.2.92, p. 7b.
[101] 'Class and conventional wisdom', *IC*, p. 270.
[102] *CC*, p. 529.
[103] Ibid., pp. 104–5, cf. p. 50.
[104] *CC*, p. vi, cf. 'Why was there no Marxism?', *EHR* 99 (1984), p. 324 n.1.
[105] Stefan Collini's *Absent Minds* (Oxford, 2006) offers an oblique but authentic expression of this priority.

What then is the idea of culture present in *Classes and Cultures*? Evidently the book title establishes the use of 'cultures' as an umbrella term of equal status to 'classes'. Such sweeping usage cannot be found previously in McKibbin's *oeuvre*, so what does this linguistic innovation signify? In the quartet of essays from 1978–84 a range of words are used alongside 'culture' to describe the acts which later fall under this heading: 'intellectual world', 'mental' and 'intellectual environment', 'intellectual horizon', 'intellectual' and 'quasi-intellectual activities', 'exertion of mind', as well as 'social values', or even 'the rules of the game'.[106] The prominence of the epithet 'intellectual' here reminds us that these labels attach to what McKibbin conceives as culture in its purest or least distorted form: the unconstrained, creative, and active expression of mind. However, this positive idea of culture has a roughly equal and opposite negative face. This is the realm of ideology—that is, culture employed in a distorting and constraining sense, most obviously in the political sphere as an instrument of class conflict. When we read about 'the institutions of civil society which had *ideological* value to their members',[107] we know that there is a struggle going on, polite and peaceable though its form may be. Now the early essays have relatively little to say about 'ideology'—a reflection of a content that in three out of four cases is non-political, as also of their distance from the developing conflicts of British politics in the 1980s. 'Ideology' is first elevated to a position of prominence in the title of *The Ideologies of Class* (1989), just as this idea is central to 'Class and Conventional Wisdom'—conventional wisdom *is* ideology—the one essay written specially for this collection and its undoubted keynote. 'Culture' too has a more elevated formal status by this date, but still it appears primarily as 'the internal culture of the working classes',[108] a counterpart to ideology: so it is only one half of the story. Seen in this light the elevation of 'cultures' in *Classes and Cultures* appears as a kind of balanced synthesis: finally both the negative and positive faces of 'culture' are embraced under this umbrella term. But though I believe that this narrative has force, it goes without saying that the core components of this view, both positive and negative, cultural and ideological, were always present in McKibbin's mind. Even the *Evolution of Labour*, the high point of his 'institutionalist' deviation from culture, begins with the granite-like pronouncement that 'Political action is the result of social and cultural attitudes which are not primarily political' (a fairly extraordinary opening to a book which *was* primarily political).[109] 'Ideology' too is already present in the early essays, albeit only occasionally. Thus when they turn to the competing claims of the classes, this inevitably evokes a reference to 'the British ideology'; and though these claims were settled within that most consensual of political cultures, British constitutionalism, still the latter is by definition 'an ideological environment'.[110]

[106] 'Working-class gambling', pp. 147, 162, 165, 169, 171, 178; 'Work and hobbies', p. 145; 'Why was there no Marxism?', pp. 310, 314.

[107] *CC*, p. 535, original emphasis.

[108] *IC*, p. 101.

[109] *EL*, p. xiii.

[110] Resp. 'Work and hobbies', p. 146; 'Why was there no Marxism?', p. 310.

McKibbin's critical conception of ideology deserves notice, since his thinking here is far from obvious, and is fully as innovative as its obverse—the sympathetic conception of culture as creative, expressive and rational. The crucial step forward occurs in 'Class and Conventional Wisdom', where ideology appears variously as conventional wisdom, 'common-sense', 'a . . . universe of sentiments and primitive convictions', and 'folklore'.[111] As usual, one can find early anticipations of this idea in the form of 'codes, conventions, habits', or 'traditions, superstitions, habits, folkways',[112] the first of which looks forward to the use of 'social codes' in *Classes and Cultures.* But at this early stage they are more symptoms of backwardness, a want of that intellectuality and rationality which McKibbin prizes in any culture; they do not yet constitute ideology, an agency of political and class-competitive constraint. In the lexicon deployed in 1989–90 (whether academic or journalistic)[113] much the most common term is 'folklore'. The term is slightly curious—unintended overtones of rusticity and preciousness may blind the reader to its significance—but once we have got over this hurdle, the force of the idea is evident: the cultural distortion which underlies profound political distortion is not an affair of great texts and formal argument but of the 'received ideas' of ordinary people.[114] And, as is abundantly clear from the portrayal of the working class in *Classes and Cultures,* cultural and ideological distortion is not simply the result of influences from outside, however important the latter may be. The greatest weakness of the interwar working class was not (in the first instance) its liability to succumb to the blandishments of Stanley Baldwin but its own internal social disintegration: it 'was almost certainly more riven than any other class'.[115] This process began quite literally at home, with gender segregation and the failure of husbands and wives to communicate at a culturally significant level. The result was an entrenched 'matrilocality' which in turn 'tended to freeze social values, perpetuate folk wisdom, and subvert the sense of social reality'.[116] In this way the working class generated its own ideological constraints.

Now this is an original nexus of ideas, and though McKibbin's own commendations might imply that student reading of Karl Marx was his inspiration, this can hardly be true except in a most general sense. The *Eighteenth Brumaire* undoubtedly offers a brilliant critique of a political regime, and this was surely a strong encouragement not to take either Baldwin or Mrs Thatcher at face value. But the *Eighteenth Brumaire* is not an exposé of the workings of ideology nor, in any strict sense, of the instruments of class persuasion. Those who support Louis Napoleon in 1851 do so not because of ideological delusion but out of class interest, albeit of a most curious and unexpected kind. Marx's equally famous critique of *The German Ideology* is a condemnation of fatuity at the level of high theory; it does not engage with the demotic and diffused beliefs that concern

[111] *IC,* pp. 274, 281, 271 resp. [112] 'Social class and social observation', pp. 176, 198.
[113] See *CC,* e.g. pp. 57, 58 n. 41, 88 n. 38, 139, 175, 190, 291, 293, 305; *LRB* e.g. 23.11.89, p. 25d; 24.5.90, p. 4a; 24.10.91, p. 3a, 4d; 22.9.94,p. 10a.
[114] *CC,* p. 499 cf. pp. 312, 523 for variants. [115] Ibid., p. 198. [116] Ibid., p. 175.

McKibbin. Besides Marx we should also consider the modern sociologists who had identified working-class Tory voting as a major problem, because it was at variance with 'objective' class interest. Frank Parkin writing in 1967 is an important example, and one whom McKibbin has always held in high esteem. Parkin took the important step of trying to explain political behaviour by reference not only to class but also to 'a set of... core values' generated by 'the dominant institutional orders' of a society—a miscellany which included recognisably McKibbinite items such as 'the public schools and ancient universities, the élites of the military establishment, the press and the mass media, the monarchy and the aristocracy'.[117] As such he went to the brink of the socio-cultural explanation pioneered by McKibbin, but he did not undertake it in fact. He assumed that there was a set of dominant values 'in close accord' with Conservatism, but as a self-confessed exponent of 'armchair theorizing' he did not examine what they were or how they were generated.[118] Furthermore, his premise supposed that voting for a Labour or socialist party was 'a symbolic act of deviance' in any capitalist society. Parkin had no political agenda in saying so, but still in his analysis it was Labour voting which was 'deviant'. Thus any occasional references to 'the ideology of Conservatism' entirely lack the critical note that McKibbin injected into the term.[119] In short, the sophisticated and original construction of ideology which emerged in the 1980s was surely McKibbin's own. It was in fact a mirror of his equally innovative analysis of the legitimate or undistorted face of culture.

So whatever the broader course of historical thought in the late twentieth century may have been, the picture in McKibbin's case is not one of simple evolution 'from classes to cultures', but of a single primary moment of innovation embracing ideas about both class and culture. Any subsequent development was at most a working out of the implications of the initial conception. Again, the political component in his thinking—the idea that historical writing is a political act, without which his ideas of class and culture have little meaning—is much more obviously a constant, not a developing, feature. All the same, there remains some life in the model of simple evolution. First, because the point at which he was free to pursue his innovatory agenda was delayed until the late 1970s by the presence of a powerful institutionalist—and so anti-cultural—context; and although in principle his mind did not change, the *scale* of his engagement with both classes and cultures was immensely expanded in the twenty years between the publication of 'Social class and social observation' in 1978 and *Classes and Cultures*.

This expansion of focus can be viewed in various lights. One is simply quantitative. 'Classes' and 'cultures' were never separate entities: the evocation of class is founded on the evocation of cultures and sub-cultures such as 'the

[117] 'Working-class Conservatives: A theory of political deviance', *British Journal of Sociology* 18 (1967), p. 280.
[118] Ibid., pp. 280, 289.
[119] Loci cit. Cf. the criticism of Parkin in 'Class and Conventional Wisdom', *IC*, p. 293.

culture of work',[120] just as an interest in specific cultural fora such as sport, literature, and cinema is primarily directed to the ways in which the various classes participated within them. Nonetheless there is a formal separation in *Classes and Cultures* between these two categories—a series of chapters on classes (chs. I–V) is followed (after an institutionalist interim on education) by another series on cultures (chs. VII–XIII)—and this is a mark of just how much more there was to say. Another measurement of change over time is supplied by the draft plan of contents for the *New Oxford History* drawn up in 1981. There were to be eight primary subject areas or sections (A-H), of which the first would be a section of three chapters on the '*Social Classes*': 'The Old Elite (incl. monarchy)', the middle and working classes.[121] Now this looks very like the treatment of 'Classes' in 1998. However, the putative section (E) which is in effect the precursor to 'Cultures' is rather different:

Social Conditions

[ch.]16 Living standards (statistics here): poverty and wealth, conditions of unemployed, distribution of wealth etc. Techniques of calculating poverty, social surveys.

17 Family, structure of—role of women here.

18 Work and Leisure—attitudes to work, mechanization—mass sport, hobbies, holidays.

19 Reading and cinema—how 'literate' England, what did people read? What sort of 'images' did they get from cinema.

Of course, it would be unfair to place too much weight on a draft outline of future work—self-evidently a piece of ephemera. Still, it is striking that the section as a whole is not conceived in terms of 'cultures', but as a movement from external and material conditions to more internal and cultural ones. In itself this is not so surprising: as we saw, this is a sequence which can still be found in 1998. But what is noticeable is the modesty of the space allotted to 'cultures'. There is indeed room for the ideas about 'culture' mapped out in the early essays—the linkage between 'Work and Leisure' in ch. 18 clearly derives from the scheme of the essay on 'Work and hobbies' which had been written at just this time—but still they are allowed just two chapters within the section, which means two out of thirty chapters in the book as a whole. In such a small space it is hard to see how the elaboration of class analysis and differentiation *within* specific 'cultures' which is so essential to the final account, could have been adequately realised. Seen in terms of subject headings, the most striking changes between 1981 and 1998 lie in the creation of new chapters on Religion and Sexuality. At the same time items which had always been on McKibbin's agenda took on much more weight and scale. Sport (and by inference gambling) is an obvious example from the 1981 listing; but the category of the 'obvious' surely includes all those aspects of popular culture which were 'perfectly recognizable to anyone acquainted with English cultural traditions'—where 'anyone' included

[120] *CC*, p. 106 cf. pp. 129, 151, 161–3. [121] See n. 54 above.

'Australian middle-class schoolboys of the 1950s'.[122] Thus the inclusion of literature and film in the 1981 outline must surely be entered as 'obvious' and of long standing, given the existence of a famous work such as Richard Hoggart's *The Uses of Literacy* (1957), to which the outline refers when it asks 'how "literate" [was] England?'[123] or the listing of cinema as a hobby in 'Work and hobbies'.[124]

One of the most dramatic expansions of focus is more an underlying theme than a particular subject: that of the Americanization of popular culture and thus of English life as a whole—a theme which becomes so prominent in the later chapters of *Classes and Cultures* that for a time 'America' becomes a variable to consider alongside 'class, sex, age, geography'.[125] Seen in purely empirical terms, this was an immense advance. It may seem practically a truism to explore the outlines of 'a familiar, common Anglo-American culture' in a systematic survey of English life,[126] when that culture has had a continuous life since the first English settlement of the New World; and yet this theme was untouched to a degree that now seems extraordinary. McKibbin's interest here, as in so much of his English history, is in part autobiographically driven: he cannot see why what is self-evidently a part of everyday life should be excluded from history; and he, growing up in Australia, as much as any Englander, was aware of 'the Aladdin's cave of America's (unearned) wealth' in the decade after 1945.[127] The one obvious difference between himself and the English was (I suggest) that his sense of dependency on cultural importation was so much stronger. As always he sees culture as standing in a relation to politics, but (as always) he proceeds from socio-cultural 'foundations' to politics rather than *vice versa.* In particular he is on the look out for the historical origins of 'the predominant Anglo-American political tradition' of 'asocial liberalism', 'reductionist individualism' and 'social decay',[128] which he sees as instrumental in the remaking of the civic culture throughout the period from Mrs Thatcher down to the present. But though such origins certainly can be found, still there is a considerable distance between the 1940s and the late twentieth century: 'It was . . . difficult, even in the late 1940s and early 1950s, for the élites to co-opt "America"—as they did a generation later—in an "anti-socialist" crusade', since both the elites (an elusive body) and the 'classes' (middle and working) continued to harbour considerable reservations about America and 'the possibility of an Americanised individualist democracy'.[129] This corresponds to a period division around *c.*1950 that became important to McKibbin after 1980, as he began to recognise the Thatcherite present as the embodiment of discontinuity.

[122] *CC*, p. 472 and n. 43. [123] Cf. ibid., p. 477.
[124] 'Work and hobbies', p. 129. [125] *CC*, p. 477. See esp. chs. XI–XII.
[126] Ibid., p. 526. [127] Ibid., p. 65 citing David Lodge, *Out of the Shelter.*
[128] Resp. 'With or without the workers', *LRB* 25.4.91, p. 6a; 'The sense of an ending', 28.5.92, p. 3b.
[129] Resp. *CC*, p. 524; 'Postscript' [2002], p. 159.

It is particularly important to view this theme according to McKibbin's own perspective, in order to place the omissions that go with it in due proportion. When Americanisation is brought so thoroughly under the microscope, consistency demands that we examine Britain's relation to European culture with equal rigour. Once we have started down this path, the picture will only be completed by an equally close calibration of British insularity; and this then leads into the question of national identity, which is surely one of the most discussed subjects in both public and academic life in the years since 1980. But though McKibbin is much interested in the frontier marking off England from America—this is what underlies the chapter heading 'The Cinema and the English' (ch. XI)—his treatment of these other themes is occasional at best; and an ambitious assertion such as that 'whole areas of English life . . . came under strong continental influences, particularly via Jewish emigration, and in many cases were subject to a long-overdue Germanization' only serves to remind us of the fact.[130] It may be true but it is hardly supported here. This is certainly not because of cultural disqualification or disinclination—he reads fluently in French and German, and has always taught French and German texts. But although comparison between England and Europe (Germany in particular) is a frequent presence in his work, this has only been for illustrative purposes;[131] it does not serve a major conceptual agenda. 'Why was there no Marxism?' is very much the exception that proves the rule. It starts from an essentially European premise—the Marxism of the title means the Marxism of the Second International before 1914, 'political Marxism's classical moment'[132]—but concludes by accepting the classical view of British singularity. Europe occupies a similarly subdued position in the *LRB* articles between 1989–97, a position quite at variance with the feverish coverage in the news media at that time, or with the view of an academic contemporary (Peter Clarke) who, in trying to sum up twentieth-century British history in 1996, roundly asserted that 'the most obvious missed opportunity' of the entire period lay in Britain's failure to join the EEC in 1957.[133] Implicitly the Anglo-American focus in *Classes and Cultures* appears as an acknowledgement of Britain's cultural distance from Europe. But if this is so, no personal preference is being expressed. McKibbin's scepticism about America is far too deeply rooted. He would like to think 'that Britain is primarily a European society'; and that 'if we must have a special relationship, it should be with Germany'.[134] Nonetheless, his historical sense of an indissolubly fused Anglo-American cultural tradition is so strong, that he neither advocates nor rigorously investigates the alternatives. When he says that the British 'are as European as anyone else', this turns out to be a confession of agnosticism: 'they are ambivalent: Europeans in some contexts; not Europeans

[130] *CC*, p. 526. [131] See eg. *EL*, Index s.v. Germany.

[132] 'Why was there no Marxism?', *EHR* 99 (1984), p. 297.

[133] Peter Clarke, *Hope and Glory. Britain 1900–1990* (London, 1996), p. 403.

[134] 'Pure New Labour', *LRB* 4.10.07, p. 17a.

in others.'[135] So the simplest and safest conclusion must be a declaration of 'unfinished business' at this point.

The expansion of focus in *Classes and Cultures* embraced classes as much as cultures. McKibbin had always recognised that the social history of one class, the working class, could properly be understood only in relation to others: a class on its own, like a party, is not a self-sufficient category.[136] However, it appears to have been the *New Oxford History* commission that confronted him with the need to supply a social and cultural history of the middle classes—though it is revealing that he continues to describe the latter as 'the not-working class',[137] and to conceptualise it primarily as 'anti-working class',[138] so betraying his point of origin. Now here there is an obvious problem, of which he is well aware. As the word 'middle' indicates, the middle class (or ranks or classes) is a residual construct, embracing all those persons 'in the middle' between two positively defined social groups: the working class and the traditional landed class. *Prima facie* its class identity is a purely negative one, if indeed it is an identity at all, and it bears no resemblance to a Continental *bourgeoisie*, a group positively defined as urban and anti-feudal. This is why (as McKibbin tells us) 'Agatha Christie's middle class, while it does include colonels and vicars' wives, also includes secretaries, commercial salesmen, shopkeepers, receptionists, shopgirls, nurses, solicitors, housewives, doctors and dentists'.[139] He calls it 'the "broad" middle class'.[140] Of course, given his reliance on the dualism between middle or not-working class and working class, he seeks to combat the problem posed by middle-class breadth or diffuseness, and the unity (or implied unity) of the middle class is both derived from and sustained by the idea of class conflict. Another, less obvious but equally fundamental problem posed by Agatha Christie's catalogue is that of historical method. Regardless of any final verdict on the nature of the middle class—as either a unitary agent or a diffuse residuum—a much simpler question remained: how was it possible to know or construe such a miscellany in the first place? In particular there was an absence of social survey materials—as we saw, one of McKibbin's most valued sources—when one definition of the class was that it was not a social problem, not entitled to state assistance, and so not commonly subject to investigation.[141] In short, the methodological leap he had performed in getting to know the working class and its culture was of little help, and the feat would have to be performed all over again.

There was of course no panacea; no single magic source. Nonetheless, there was one element in his solution to this conundrum which stood out by its ingenuity and novelty. It also opened up a whole new vein of source material, which he has continued to mine to this day. This was popular fiction. In 'Class

135 'The tax-and-spend vote', *LRB* 5.7.01, p. 13d.
136 e.g. 'Social class and social observation', *TRHS* 28 (1978), p. 197.
137 *IC*, pp. vii–viii, 101, 270, 289–99 *passim.*
138 *CC*, pp. 50, 57, 68.
139 Ibid., p. 483.
140 *CC*, p. 485; cf. 'Politics and the medical hero: A. J. Cronin's *The Citadel*', *EHR* 123 (2008), p. 656.
141 *CC*, p. 44; cf. S. Glynn and J. Oxborrow, *Interwar Britain* (London, 1976), p. 47.

and Conventional Wisdom' (1990) he proposed Warwick Deeping's best-selling 'middlebrow' novel *Sorrell and Son* (1925) as something like 'a "representative text"' for middle-class social attitudes in the interwar period.[142] Although the historical usage of literary sources was generally emergent at the time and has become much more frequent since, still McKibbin's idea was very much his own, and preceded other pioneering literary-historical studies for this period.[143] If there was a precursor, the obvious one was Ernst Bramstedt, the émigré German-Jewish scholar who taught McKibbin as an undergraduate at the University of Sydney, and is the dedicatee of *The Ideologies of Class*. Bramstedt is plainly of great significance as a route by which high European and German culture came down to McKibbin (and may well lie at the root of his faith in the power of Jewish émigrés on English culture). However, he also exerted a more specific influence through his doctoral thesis submitted to the LSE, published as *Aristocracy and the Middle-Classes in Germany. Social Types in German Literature 1830–1900* (1937, 1964^2). Here the importance of class analysis, and specifically middle-class analysis; of a contested political context; and the appeal to 'single, apparently accidental, works of literature [which] acquire a symbolic function in connection with the society of their age' are all clear anticipations of McKibbin's later approach.[144] The one significant difference lies in McKibbin's carefully calculated interest in best-selling 'middlebrow' authors—a category which was only invented in Britain in the mid-1920s to cater for the rupture caused by 'highbrow' literary modernism—as compared to Bramstedt's looser reliance on a group of social novelists who sold 'widely' but without any precise measurement of that width. Even so some of his principal figures, such as Gustav Freytag, were indubitably the 'middlebrows' of their day, while others, such as Fontane, had no difficulty in spanning the pre-modernist spectrum that embraced middle- and highbrow readers alike—just like Orwell, Waugh, and Graham Greene.

A decade later this form of literary analysis had been greatly expanded in *Classes and Cultures*, where it formed the bulk of an entire chapter (ch. XIII) on the reading habits of all classes, genders, and age groups. The displacement of this material away from the history of class per se to that of literary culture also signified an enhanced allowance for purely literary categories. However, any such displacement is purely formal. As noted above, the history of classes in *Classes and Cultures* is in no way separate from that of cultures; and class, together with a restrained but firm identification of 'middlebrow' with middle-class, remains central.[145] In the interim McKibbin had also discovered a new 'representative text', Vincent Cronin's *The Citadel* (1938)—again a prodigious best-seller.[146] We saw above that his narrative history of the interwar middle classes could have

[142] *IC*, p. 272.

[143] See esp. D. L. LeMahieu, *A Culture for Democracy: Mass Communication and the Cultivated Mind in Britain Between the Wars* (Oxford, 1988); Alison Light, *Forever England: femininity, literature and conservatism between the wars* (London, 1991). 'Chess and Conventional Wisdom' was first presented as a Seminar paper in Oxford on 25 February 1988.

[144] Ernst Kohn-Bramstedt [Ernest K. Bramsted] *Aristocracy and Middle-Classes in Germany* (London, 1937), pp. 6–7.

[145] *CC*, p. 488.

[146] Ibid., p. 485; cf. 'Politics and the medical hero', pp. 651–78.

been derived from census and occupational statistics, so it is a mark of his virtuosity that approximately the same story can be told in the transition from the ex-officer Sorrell—a very traditional social starting point—to the Scottish doctor Manson (the hero of *The Citadel*), where the latter is representative of the developing technical and scientific profile of the 1930s middle class. However, the novel outstrips the statistics in that it is also, through Cronin's association with Victor Gollancz, a component in the culture of the Left Book Club and Penguin Specials, as well as an important light on the pre-history of the NHS. Indeed his interest in the historical uses of literature accompanied by the discovery of valuable archival materials would lead McKibbin to write a more extended study of Cronin—and this was in fact the first of the 'supplementary studies' that followed in the wake of *Classes and Cultures.*

It was then followed by his 2004 edition of Marie Stopes, *Married Love,* yet another representative literary text for the interwar middle classes. However, in this case the histories of sexuality and gender relations overshadow those of class. It is a salutary reminder that for McKibbin class may be a uniquely powerful organizing category for a particular period of English and European history, but it is no more than that. The be-all and end-all of history is not class but the happiness, knowledge, activity, and free expression of 'the ordinary man' and woman. His interest in Stopes, and *Married Love* (1918) in particular, is an elegy to the liberation and happiness which can be brought about through knowledge: 'Only knowledge could dispel misery because it alone dispelled ignorance.'[147] In upholding these themes, he was in some sense returning to the world of his early essays—to a world governed by a broadly Weberian social evolution towards greater knowledge and rational understanding; a world which appears to the outsider as less constrained and more free than that of *Classes and Cultures, a fortiori* the *LRB* articles.

IV

After classes and cultures come politics. In any description of McKibbin's *oeuvre* this is the inevitable third term. His premise that ordinarily the understanding of politics should begin with social class, will be clear by now. However, he is neither a doctrinaire, nor a historian of society and ideology alone. Nor are all political circumstances 'ordinary' and the impact of war in 1939–45 offers an outstanding example: this was the time of 'The Party System Thrown Off Course'.[148] Furthermore, he has always had a consciously Australian belief in the power of the state to intervene to rectify social imbalance and difficulty, a belief well in advance of ordinary British practice. This leads to verdicts of the kind that 'Historically the "problem" of the British economy has not been the strength of the state but its weakness'; or persistent complaints about the

[147] 'Introduction', *Married Love,* xliv cf. pp. xlvi–li; *CC,* pp. 319–20.
[148] *Parties and People,* c. 4.

'excessive voluntarism' of English sport, where want of state intervention went hand-in-hand with social conservatism and amateurism, so leading to a rapid decline in its international standing.[149] The question of the relation between the two tiers of social and political history raises an obvious problem of method, but it is one of which he is well aware. Hence frank acknowledgement of 'the methodological difficulties of establishing connections between "formal" or "high" politics, and their necessarily contingent nature, with the complex and slow-moving relationships within which politics operates.... Not everything "fits"'.[150] The Ford lectures offer an ample and dispassionate account of how social relationships might 'fit' with high politics in the years 1914–51. They are often original—most obviously in the claim that politics in the 1920s represented a perpetuation of Edwardian assumptions out of kilter with a social and cultural foundation that had shifted markedly—yet they are also soberly compatible with the work of historians whose starting point is different, who take politics as (in the first instance) a self-sufficient world rather than as an epiphenomenon of society. Philip Williamson's portrait of *Stanley Baldwin* (1999)—a work as central to political historiography as *Classes and Cultures* is to the alternative 'social' tradition—is an obvious case in point, since both he and McKibbin highlight the theme of 'democracy' and Baldwin's capacity to adapt to it.[151] Here McKibbin's 'culture' and Williamson's post-Cowlingite 'doctrine'[152] converge on what is in effect the common ground between society and politics (although the shade of Maurice Cowling may lament the mellowing of a once very animated divide).[153]

When measured against McKibbin's early writings, the coverage of cultures in *Classes and Cultures* reveals an obvious omission: there is no treatment of political culture to match that offered in 'Why was there no Marxism in Britain?' To be sure, this statement must be qualified. *Classes and Cultures* has a good deal to say about the depoliticisation of English culture and social behaviour as an instrument of class and Conservative hegemony between the wars. There may be no account of political culture, but there is a vivid, if scattered, picture of an apolitical culture. For example, we are told that the middle-class premium on sociability

> led to a host of bans and taboos—particularly sexual and religious—which constantly surprised and bemused visitors to England. It also promoted a lack of seriousness in personal relations: never to talk about politics or religion is, after all, never to talk about two of the most interesting subjects in human history. By encouraging the belief that all relationships, however intrinsically political, could be depoliticised, this social style

[149] 'What a progressive government will have to do', *LRB* 30.8.90, p. 7d; *CC*, p. 380.

[150] 'Postscript' [2002], p. 153 cf. 160.

[151] Besides 'Postscript' [2002], p. 159, n.16, compare *Parties and people*, pp. 88–105 with Philip Williamson, *Stanley Baldwin* (Cambridge, 1999), esp. ch. 7.

[152] Cf. Williamson, 'The doctrinal politics of Stanley Baldwin', in Michael Bentley (ed.), *Public and Private Doctrine: Essays... presented to Maurice Cowling* (Cambridge, 1992), ch. 9.

[153] See *EL*, p. 112 n.1: a legendary footnote.

became crucial to the development of an 'apolitical' anti-socialist vocabulary: it was the Labour Party which dragged 'politics' into everything, which took everything so 'seriously', which politicised human relationships by emphasising conflict instead of good humour.[154]

Now this passage is important because its theme is so important. If one aspires to a conceptual understanding of modern English and British history as a whole, it is really *the* most important theme—and yet it is so little studied. Simply to open the agendum is a major step. Nonetheless, I suggest that the treatment here is incomplete, and that this was one of the costs of breaking away from the framework of the *New Oxford History*.

It should be said (first) that the evidence for English 'depoliticisation' long precedes 1918 and any class configuration that might have appeared then. For example, the object of university education in later Victorian and Edwardian Oxbridge was not, as it was in Germany, to study law, *Staatswissenschaft* or theology in a vocational sense, where the discussion and definition of political and religious positions was a necessary accompaniment of education; on the contrary the aim was a consensual 'liberal education', a general training of the mind which all could share. Political argument was bad form and religious still more so. Hence the classical answer to an equally classical question from the seventeenth century: what was 'the religion of all sensible men'? 'Sensible men never tell.'[155] These were indeed subjects not to be talked about—and there is no novelty about an English social code which persists even today, and which McKibbin finds so impoverishing.[156] Again, the psychological characteristics he associates with English depoliticisation between the wars—Puritanism, emotional restraint, withdrawal and inhibition[157]—were cultural stereotypes that had been part of the English identity since the 17th century at least. A considerable number of them were assembled in what is perhaps the most famous foreign portrait of pre-1914 Englishness, Max Weber's 'Protestant Ethic' (1904–5). In fact what these stereotypes signify is not interwar depoliticisation, but an entrenched ideological uniformity and consensus unique in Western Europe. An equally telling reflection of this ideological uniformity lies in the shallowness of the identities of the English (hence British) political parties. In the words of Disraeli (when Prime Minister), 'gentlemen must all be of the same opinion if not on the same side'.[158] In the Western European states there was a plurality of world-views or 'ideologies': to be Liberal or Catholic or Socialist was to occupy a position which could not be exchanged except at a cost comparable to that of religious denial. In England by contrast there was only one ideology. As McKibbin himself stated in 1982 this was 'the British ideology' (singular),[159] where the fundament of all parties lay in their common loyalty to the unique constitution,

[154] *CC*, p. 98.
[155] See e.g. Leslie Stephen, *An Agnostic's Apology* (London, 1893), ch. VII; *Notes and Queries* 9th Ser. X (4 Oct. 1902), p. 271.
[156] *CC*, p. 97. [157] e.g. *CC*, pp. 204–5, 327, 382, 433, 445, 522.
[158] B. Disraeli, *Endymion* (1880), ch. LXXI. [159] 'Work and hobbies', p. 146.

an entity which, because it was the product of an historical accumulation going back to the Anglo-Saxons, could not be theorised or repeated elsewhere. Empirically the difference between English and European institutions was epitomised by the contrast between English liberty, order, and prosperity since 1688 and Continental despotism in the eighteenth century, revolution in the nineteenth, and dictatorship in the twentieth centuries. This was hardly a neutral perspective, but on any reading it lent extraordinary power to perceptions of a shared, national identity.

Such was the classical 'constitutionalist' perspective which found its mid-century academic deposit in the famous works of T. H. Marshall, of Shils and Young, works which McKibbin invoked in 'Why was there no Marxism?' albeit, as we saw, with a significant degree of inner detachment. However, six years later 'Class and Conventional Wisdom' posited a drastic change in 'the British constitutional and political system' as a result of the Great War: now it appeared that this system and its class strategy 'had not simply faltered, it had failed'.[160] The 'constitutional classes' became the class coalition which enforced interwar Conservative electoral hegemony, so that constitutionalism was narrowed down to 'constitutional Conservatism'.[161] The same assumption underlies *Classes and Cultures*, where—insofar as the subject is mentioned at all—'constitutional principles' are either obsolete, 'an essentially Edwardian political rhetoric', or else a form of self-deception, a device 'to conceal from people what they were actually doing'.[162] It followed then that the perceived national unity of the 1940s, which to contemporaries was simply a renewal of the traditional constitutional consensus was, quite explicitly, 'not the product of the long evolution suggested by Shils and Young'.[163] Here again it will be clear that McKibbin is far from being a cultural determinist, since the overt cultural evidence stands so strongly against him.[164] Indeed his sense of class-cultural denial here is not too far removed from his outrage at Thatcherite Britain where 'delusion has become almost a way of life'.[165] All the same, this line of argument is an obvious and consistent correlative to the idea of depoliticisation and as such, whether we agree or not, one might suppose that there was an end of the matter.

However, the subject will not lie down so easily even within McKibbin's own *oeuvre*. The constitutionalist paradigm is tenacious because, as he notes, it was constitutional principles and the 'fair play' that it upheld, which secured the unique political stability of interwar Britain in sharp contrast to the political turmoils of Western (let alone Eastern) Europe.[166] Nor was this simply to be measured in terms of the differences between home and abroad; it necessarily carried over into the conduct of domestic class relations. The 'ritualized

160 *IC*, p. 259.

161 Ibid., pp. 284, 280 resp. Cf. *Parties and People*, p. 62.

162 *CC*, pp. 385, 59 resp.

163 Ibid., p. 535.

164 Cf. Richard Hoggart, *The Uses of Literacy* (1957), 87; George Orwell, *The Lion and the Unicorn* (1941)—a text passed over in silence in *CC*.

165 'Making things happen', *LRB* 26.7.90, p. 7d.

166 *CC*, pp. 98, 385, 530.

parliamentarism' which lay at the heart of the constitutional idea 'continued to restrain labour's opponents [after 1918]: while the labour movement was decisively defeated in the inter-war years, it is not clear that the non-working classes decisively won'[167]—a remark from 1990 which stands in contrast to the flatter, bleaker pronouncement in *Classes and Cultures* that 'the middle class, as a whole, had won', though here too the idea of class restraint remains in evidence.[168] We should also consider the extensive treatment this subject receives in his *LRB* articles. By the 1990s the deficiencies of a now dated 'traditional civic culture' were clear. Hence the need to get beyond 'Crown-and- Parliament ideologies' so as to create a properly 'democratic civic culture' in the future. And yet, Labour's enthusiastic endorsement of constitutionalism in the era of Attlee was 'not an absurd calculation', even if it now turned out to be 'the wrong one'.[169] Whatever the deficiencies of a now obsolescent constitutionalism, the modern alternative was far worse: 'Lady Thatcher as prime minister was entirely open in her determination to destroy those quasi-constitutional conventions of British political life which underlay the hated "consensus".'[170] Having 'denuded the public mind, and thus England's political culture, of almost any sense of the "collective" or "social"', traditional class restraint was at an end: 'The aim of the Conservative party' had always been 'to preserve inequalities' but now it wished 'actually to increase them'.[171] Of course, Conservative 'disfranchisement of the public sphere' was by no means new; but whatever the forms of depoliticisation and disfranchisement enacted between the wars, their more recent development evoked a 'nostalgic recollection of a particular culture . . . which, for all its imperfections, was decidedly superior to the one that has been put in its place'.[172] 'The old restraint' which accompanied 'a more civilised and consensual politics' was not a trivial matter.[173]

So constitutionalism remained a considerable reality long after 1918, and as such it calls out for historical examination. But this is not the full extent of the lacuna left by *Classes and Cultures* in regard to political culture, and the same is true of *Parties and People.*[174] As we have seen, working on the *New Oxford History* forced McKibbin to isolate '*The Role of the State*'[175] and to consider its interaction with social evolution. Since then the nature of this political-social interaction has been a primary concern, but it has left undecided a crucial preliminary question: what exactly was the state? There can be no doubt that so scrupulous a conceptual thinker has an answer to this question (if not necessarily a simple one); but it is hard to read it off from the texts we have, where the implied answers he gives are intriguingly

[167] 'Conclusion', *IC*, p. 297. [168] *CC*, p. 483 cf. 98.
[169] 'With or without the workers', *LRB* 25.4.91, pp. 6c–d.
[170] 'After Smith', *LRB* 9.6.94, pp. 10b–c.
[171] Resp. 'Labour blues', *LRB* 11.2.92, p. 13c; 'Stormy and prolonged Applause', 5.11.92, p. 6d.
[172] Resp. 'It all gets worse', *LRB* 22.9.94, p. 11d; 'Skimming along', 20.10.94, p. 8a.
[173] 'After Smith', *LRB* 9.6.94, pp. 10b–c.
[174] Although it states that it is 'a study of England's political culture' (p. vi), in reality it offers only occasional remarks on the attitude of the political parties to 'the state and its institutions' (p. 198).
[175] 'Conclusion', *IC*, p. 300.

diffuse. One typically capacious definition links 'the institutions of the state and of civil society'. Another, in the same spirit, targets 'those of the country's institutions where power lies', which are then itemized as follows: 'the judiciary or legal system, the Civil Service, Parliament, the peerage, the monarchy . . . the MCC or the Football Association'.[176] But of course this list is by no means complete. The rubric surely includes the Church and the armed forces,[177] while the category of the 'Civil Service' might mean medical officers of health, the staff at labour exchanges, or the higher civil service in Whitehall.[178] The 'legal system' takes in not just the judiciary but the police—the subject of a set of fragmentary and tantalising notices in *Classes and Cultures*;[179] while 'Parliament' is not only a source of bipartisan law but of political manoeuvre. Thus the great intervention of 'the state' in British politics in 1940 meant in reality 'the entry of Labour into government', where it acquired a 'legitimacy bestowed by the *Conservative Party*'.[180] No wonder then that the original, 1981 plan for the *New Oxford History* provided for an entire chapter in this sense (ch. 8): 'Structure of the state—here civil service . . . ', nor that 'the absence of an adequate theory of the state' is deemed to be a major failing of Keynesian economics.[181]

McKibbin's reliance on the idea of an 'elite' or 'elites' also provokes inquiry. They are a constant presence in both his academic and political writings. As with the state, this is not simply a political category—besides political and bureaucratic elites there are social and military elites, as well as cultural elites such as the BBC and F. R. Leavis;[182] but nor is it a class category. This sort of conceptual ambivalence is captured in the remark that 'Highbrow [literary] culture was the culture of an élite, which was, in class terms, probably upper-middle-class; but many of its members were not upper-middle-class in their social origins.'[183] It reminds us in turn of the difficulties attaching to the definition of 'the upper class' in the opening chapter of *Classes and Cultures*. McKibbin does not shy away from the problem of definition here but in effect comes to no conclusion: 'there was undoubtedly an upper class, if only because there were people who could be categorized in no other way'.[184] However, the reality of the social argument that permeates the rest of the book is that there is no upper class. It plays no role in class relations, because there is only the dualism of the working class and the middle or 'non-working' classes. As a result the upper class is seen to be perpetually on the brink of collapsing into the 'upper middle class', though in fact this only happens after 1945 when it dissolves 'into a number of overlapping coteries which had only a limited notion of themselves as constituting a single class'. For the same reason the bulk of the chapter entitled 'The Upper Class' is not about class at all but about a culture, about 'Society, which was the popular

176 Resp. *CC*, p. 535; 'Why did they do it?' *LRB* 25.5.95, pp. 3c–d.
177 Cf. *CC*, p. 35.
178 Cf. *CC*, pp. 157, 313, 430, 510.
179 Ibid., pp. 328–30, 372–3, 451–2, 501, 522.
180 'Postscript' [2002], p. 162. Original emphasis.
181 Resp. n.54 above; '"They mean us no harm"', *LRB* 8.2.01, p. 13d.
182 *CC*, pp. 475, 477. 183 Ibid., p. 477. 184 Ibid., p. 2.

idea of the upper class'.[185] I find this quite brilliant: a quintessential example of McKibbin's capacity to show how prominent and yet (gloriously or horribly) 'vulgar' components of present-day life have a significant history—*Glamour* was once an idea and today it is a magazine; but still it is not class analysis. In this respect the 1981 Contents plan for the *New Oxford History* is more accurately drawn, when it begins with 'The Old Elite (incl. monarchy)' before moving onto class dualism. And this is indeed the scheme of the rest of *Classes and Cultures*, most obviously the long chapter on Education, where those educated at public school and Oxbridge appear as 'élites' (ch. VI §§ 2–3). All the same whatever the difficulty attaching to elites as a social construct, it is clear that they must have a political and ideological component. Thus the political writings commonly refer to 'the old élites' who epitomise the decadent consensus of the 1960s and '70s: 'a senescent political system based on a popular monarchy, a defeatist former ruling élite' and much else, including 'a timid social-democratic party'.[186] The elites are therefore closely tied to the old constitutionalist culture, as in the case of Tony Blair who 'like so many of the country's elite . . . cannot actively contemplate a reform of something ["our constitutional arrangements"] which is associated with Britain's past grandeur'.[187] A further unanswered question lies in the fact that the idea of an elite cuts across and comprehends all the political parties; yet one of the distinctive features of McKibbin's class analysis is how tightly it is linked to the competing fortunes of Labour and the Conservatives. Here then are three interlocking ideas, constitutionalism, the state and the elites, all of which are major components of political culture; they are all ideas about which McKibbin has thought considerably, and these subjects must have featured in the *New Oxford History*, had he been allowed to complete it. But as of today his thinking in this area is unclear to us. Might I then propose a treatment of political culture and the structures that accompany it as one of the possible 'supplements' to *Classes and Cultures*?—alongside one on J. M. Keynes and the Macmillan Committee.

V

It will now be clear why I believe that Ross McKibbin's work will long continue to be read. It embraces an unprecedented range of the life and activities of the 'ordinary man'; it combines the most generous human sympathies with a stringent intellectual discipline; and it embodies a radical and novel conceptualization of the recent past, so that we retain a rich sense of the present as part of an ongoing history, in defiance of the attempted repudiation of that past by our political 'masters' today. Still there is one final trait to notice. McKibbin is a wonderful prose stylist in the spare, terse manner of the twentieth-century

185 Ibid., pp. 37, 43, 31 resp.
186 'Against It', *LRB* 24.2.94, p. 18d.
187 'What Blair threw away', ibid., 19.5.05, p. 7d.

English tradition epitomised by Waugh and Orwell. The common sense of the matter was well caught by the reviewer of *Classes and Cultures* who said that 'this is a people's history that many people might actually enjoy reading'.[188] No doubt much of the praise here is directed towards McKibbin's subject matter: his ability to render the connections between the recent past and the present so transparent and accessible, and to do so at a level of high significance. Even so, the statement surely includes a tribute to his literary and formal mastery. It is no accident that a major chapter in *Classes and Cultures* is entitled not 'The Community of Letters' or 'Literature' (though these are the principal subjects) but of 'Language', and contains a good deal of reflection on that theme. When McKibbin comments on George Orwell in this regard, he tells us much about himself: 'Much of Orwell's power . . . is, in fact, linguistic—a high austerity of style seductively modified by surprising demotic touches.'[189] McKibbin combines the clarity, sobriety, and economy which make up 'high austerity' to such an extraordinary degree, that to find even one loose word in a quarter of a million is something of a shock.[190] Pellucid prose without an ounce of fat is another, even a principal, reason why a large audience may actually enjoy reading him both today and in generations to come. Here again he takes the part of the democracy.

188 Stefan Collini, 'Labour's lost chance', *TLS* 17.4.98, p. 3d.
189 'Making things happen', *LRB* 26.7.90, p. 6b.
190 I find 'stratospheric' just a little low: *CC*, p. 503.

3

Ross McKibbin: A Bibliography*

Peter Ghosh

1967

'The reaction of British public opinion to the rise of Nazism', MA thesis, University of Sydney, listed in 'New Research', *Australian Historical Studies* 13, October 1967, p. 137.

1969

'The myth of the unemployed: who did vote for the Nazis?' *Australian Journal of Politics and History* 15, 1969, pp. 25–40.

1970

'James Ramsay Macdonald and the problem of the independence of the Labour Party, 1910–1914', *Journal of Modern History* 42, 1970 pp. 216–35.
'The evolution of a national party: Labour's political organization, 1910–1924' (Oxford D. Phil. Thesis), 1970.

1974

The Evolution of the Labour Party, 1910–1924 (Oxford University Press), 1974.

1975

'The economic policy of the second Labour Government, 1929–1931', *Past and Present* 68, 1975, pp. 95–123.
(Revised text in *The Ideologies of Class*, 1990.)

1976

'The franchise factor in the rise of the Labour Party', *English Historical Review* 91, 1976, pp. 297–331.
(Revised text in *The Ideologies of Class*, 1990.)

* The listing of book reviews in academic journals is selective only. It has been limited to those which are of particular weight or else make a significant comment about the writer himself.

1978

'Social class and social observation in Edwardian England', *Transactions of the Royal Historical Society*, 5th Ser., vol. 28, 1978, pp. 175–99.
(Revised as 'Class and poverty in Edwardian England', in *The Ideologies of Class*, 1990)
'Arthur Henderson as Labour leader', *International Review of Social History* 23, 1978, pp. 79–101.
(Revised text in *The Ideologies of Class*, 1990.)

1979

'Working-class gambling in Britain 1880–1939', *Past and Present* 82, 1979, pp. 147–78.
Shortened version translated as 'Le "Temps" des bookmakers' in *L'Histoire* 57, 1983, pp. 26–33.
(Revised text in *The Ideologies of Class*, 1990.)

1981

'Big acts', review of Kenneth and Jane Morgan, *Portrait of a Progressive*, *London Review of Books*, 19 February 1981, p. 16.
Review of Bruce Murray, *The People's Budget*, *Times Literary Supplement*, 29 May 1981, p. 610.

1983

'Work and hobbies in Britain, 1880–1950', in Jay M. Winter (ed.), *The Working Class in Modern British History* (Cambridge: Cambridge University Press), 1983, pp. 127–46.
(Revised text in *The Ideologies of Class*, 1990.)

1984

'Why was there no Marxism in Great Britain?', *English Historical Review* 99, 1984, pp. 297–331.
(Revised text in *The Ideologies of Class*, 1990.)
Review of R.A. Soloway, *Birth Control and the Population Question*, *Journal of Modern History* 56, 1984, pp. 150–1.

1985

Review of H. A. Clegg, *A History of British Trade Unions*, vol. 2, *TLS* 18 October 1985, p. 1164.

1986

'History and the Universities', *Oxford Magazine* no. 8 (6th week, Hilary Term), 1986, pp. 3–6.

'Losers' [review of books on Upper Clyde Shipbuilders, the miners' strike of 1984–5 etc.], *London Review of Books* [*LRB*] 23 October 1986, pp. 10–11.

1987

'The "social psychology" of unemployment in inter-war Britain' in Philip J. Waller (ed.), *Politics and Social Change in Modern Britain* (Sussex: Harvester Press), pp. 161–91.

(Revised text in *The Ideologies of Class*, 1990)

'Progressive causes', *Oxford Magazine* no. 21 (10th week, Trinity Term), pp. 2–3.

1989

Articles in the *LRB*: 'Extravagance' [review of Peter Clarke, *The Keynesian Revolution*] 2 February 1990, pp. 5–6; 'Hobsbawm today', 22 June, pp. 8–10; 'Ross McKibbin on the summer of discontent', 17 August, pp. 6–8; 'Diary', 23 November, p. 25.

1990

The Ideologies of Class. Social Relations in Britain 1880–1950 (Oxford: Clarendon Press), 1990.

New texts: 'Preface'; 'Class and conventional wisdom: the Conservative Party and the "public" in inter-war Britain'; 'Conclusion'. Chapters 1–8 revise and reprint essays listed above, 1990. (with John Rowett) 'Editorial', *Twentieth Century British History*, 1, pp. 1–8.

Articles in the *LRB*: 'The way we live now' [review of Stuart Hall and Martin Jacques, *New Times*], 11 January 1990, pp. 3–5; 'Mrs Thatcher's ecstasy' 24 May, pp. 3–5; 'Making things happen' [review of R.W. Johnson, *Heroes and Villains*], 26 July, pp. 6–7; 'What a progressive government will have to do' [review of Ben Pimlott et al., *The Alternative*], 30 August, pp. 7–8; 'Diary' 6 December, p. 25.

1991

'Foreword to the 1991 impression', *The Evolution of the Labour Party, 1910–1924* (Oxford: Oxford University Press), 1991.

Articles in the *LRB*: 'Radical democrats' [review of books by Tony Benn and Paul Foot], 7 March 1991, pp. 10–11; 'With or without the workers' [review of David Marquand, *The Progressive Dilemma*] 25 April, pp. 6–7; 'Homage to Wilson and Callaghan', 24 October, pp. 3–5.

1992

Articles in the *LRB*: 'What is Labour to do ?', 27 February 1992, pp. 7–8; 'When Labour last ruled' [review of Burk and Cairncross, *Goodbye, Great Britain*], 9 April, 1992 pp. 6–7; 'The sense of an ending', 28 May, pp. 3–4; 'Stormy and prolonged applause . . . ' [review of Ian Gilmour, *Dancing with Dogma*], 5 November, pp. 5–6.

1993

'Oxford and the General Strike, 1926', *Oxford Magazine* no. 98 (2nd week, Michaelmas Term), 1993, pp. 5–6.

Review of Peter Baldwin, *The Politics of Social Solidarity*, *Journal of Modern History* 65, 1993, pp. 827–30.

Articles in the *LRB*: 'Labour blues' [review of R. Heffernan and M. Marqusee, *Defeat from the Jaws of Victory*], 11 February 1993, p. 13; 'Customers of the State', 9 September, pp. 6–7.

1994

'Is it still possible to write labour history?' in Terry Irving (ed.), *Challenges to Labour History* (Sydney: UNSW Press), 1994, pp. 34–41.

Articles in the *LRB*: 'Against it' [review of Christopher Hitchens, *For the Sake of Argument*], 24 February 1994, p. 18; 'After Smith', 9 June, p. 10; 'It all gets worse' [review of Neil Milward, *The New Industrial Relations?*] 22 September, pp. 10–11; 'Skimming along', [review of A. Seldon and D. Kavanagh (eds.), *The Major Effect*], 20 October, pp. 7–8.

1995

Articles in the *LRB*: 'On the defensive . . . who's afraid of the Borrie Report [?]', 26 January 1995, pp. 6–7; 'Why they did it . . . ?' [Tony Blair and Clause IV], 25 May, pp. 3–4.

1996

Article in the *LRB*: 'If/when Labour gets in . . . ' 22 February 1996, pp. 3–5.

1997

'World Wide Webb', review of R. Dahrendorf, *LSE: a History . . . 1895–1995*, *Oxford Review of Education* 23 (1997), pp. 235–40.

Articles in the *LRB*: 'Very Old Labour', 3 April, 1997 pp. 3–6; 'Why the Tories lost', 3 July, pp. 3–7; 'Mass-Observation in the Mall' [the death of Princess Diana], 2 October, pp. 3–6.

'Mass-Observation in the Mall' was reprinted in M. Merck (ed.), *After Diana. Irreverent Elegies* (London: Verso), 1998.

1998

Classes and Cultures. England 1918–1951 (Oxford: Oxford University Press), 1998.

Articles in the *LRB*: 'Why One-Nation Tories can no longer make an impression . . .', 16 April, 1998 pp. 8–9; 'Third Way, Old hat', 3 September, pp. 3–5.

1999

Foreword to Michael Apted, *7 Up: 'Give me the child until he is seven, and I will show you the man',* [ed. Bennett Singer] (London: Heinemann), 1999, pp. xiii–xix.

The cover of this paperback is (as Granada TV admitted at the time) 'not very professional' in that it suggests that the foreword is by 'Ross McKibben' (*sic*). The text inside is however clean.

'New Labour's timid hearts and minds' [review of Dick Leonard (ed.), *Crosland and New Labour*], *New Statesman* 26 March 1999, pp. 53–4.

Article in the *LRB*: 'Mondeo man in the driving seat', 30 September 1999, pp. 8–10.

2000

'Treading water?' in *New Left Review* 4, July-August 2000, pp. 69–74.

Articles in the *LRB*: 'The Iceman Cometh', 6 January 2000 [review of Tony Adams and Ian Ridley, *Addicted*], pp. 31–2; 'Make enemies and influence people', 20 July, pp. 3–5.

2001

'Foreword' to *Consensus or Coercion? The State, the People and Social Cohesion in Post-war Britain* (Cheltenham: New Clarion Press), 2001, pp. vii–x.

Articles in the *LRB*: 'They mean us no harm' [review of Robert Skidelsky, *John Maynard Keynes*, vol. 3], 8 February 2001, pp. 12–13; 'The tax-and-spend vote', 5 July, pp. 13–15.

2002

'*Classes and Cultures*: A Postscript', in Stefan Berger, (ed.), *Labour and Social History in Great Britain: Historiographical Reviews and Agenda, Mitteilungsblatt des Instituts für soziale Bewegungen* 27, 2002, pp. 153–65.

'Class, politics, money: British sport since the First World War', *Twentieth Century British History* 13, 2002, pp. 191–200.

Review of Jonathan Rose, *The Intellectual Life of the British Working Classes, Albion* 34, 2002, pp. 685–8.

Articles in the *LRB*: 'The luck of the Tories' [review of Martin Westlake, *Neil Kinnock*], 7 March 2002, pp. 8–9; 'Non-party man' [review of Peter Clarke,

The Cripps Version], 19 September, pp. 8–9; 'Nothing more divisive', 28 November, pp. 3–6.

2003

Articles in the *LRB*: 'Why did he risk it? . . . on Blair and the War', 3 April, 2003 pp. 7–8; 'How to put the politics back into Labour', 7 August, pp. 3–5.

2004

Marie Stopes, *Married Love*, edited with an Introduction and Notes (Oxford: Oxford University Press), 2004.

Oxford Dictionary of National Biography, 2004 'Joll, James Bysse', 'Mason, Timothy Wright', 'Matthew, Henry Colin Gray'.

Review of Eric Hobsbawm, *Interesting Times*, *English Historical Review* 119, 2004, pp. 155–7.

Articles in the *LRB*: 'Why did it end so badly?' [review of John Campbell, *Margaret Thatcher*, vol. 2], 2004, pp. 11–12; 'How to dislodge a leader who doesn't want to go', 8 July, pp. 18–19.

2005

Articles in the *LRB*: 'Perhaps a Merlot' [review of David Miers, *Regulating Commercial Gambling*], 3 March 2005, pp. 16–17; 'What Blair threw away', 19 May, pp. 7–8.

2006

'Colin Matthew: A Memoir', in Peter Ghosh and Lawrence Goldman (eds.), *Politics and Culture in Victorian Britain. Essays in Memory of Colin Matthew* (Oxford: Oxford University Press), 2006, pp. 28–34.

Review of Steve Nicolson, *The Censorship of British Drama*, vol. 1, *English Historical Review* 121, 2006, pp. 340–2.

Articles in the *LRB*: 'The destruction of the public sphere', 5 January, 2006 pp. 3–6; 'The reshuffle and after', 25 May, pp. 11–12; 'Sleazy, humiliated, despised', 7 September, pp. 3–6.

2007

'Great Britain', in R. Gerwarth, (ed.), *Twisted Paths: Europe 1914–45* (New York: Oxford University Press), 2007, pp. 33–59.

Review of Callum Brown, *Religion and Society in Twentieth-Century Britain*, *English Historical Review* 122, 2007, pp. 1464–8.

Articles in the *LRB*: 'Defeatism, defeatism, defeatism', 22 March 2007, pp. 23–26; 'Pure New Labour', 4 October, pp. 17–18; 'Who's on the Ropes Now?', 1 November, p. 3.

2008

'Politics and the medical hero: A.J. Cronin's *The Citadel*', *English Historical Review* 123, 2008, pp. 651–78.

'Parties, people and the state: Politics in England *c.*1914–1951', *Oxford Historian* Issue 6, October 2008, pp. 38–41.

A brief 'account' of the Ford Lectures, presented under this title in early 2008.

Articles in the *LRB*: 'Not pleasing the tidy-minded' [review of David Kynaston, *Austerity Britain*], 24 April 2008, pp. 30–1; 'An element of unfairness', 3 July, pp. 7–10; 'What works doesn't work', 11 September, pp. 20–2; 'What can Cameron do ?', 23 October, pp. 7–8.

2009

Review of John Baxendale, *Priestley's England*, *English Historical Review* 124, 2009 pp. 486–7.

'Pat Thompson', *The Guardian*, 30 October 2009, p. 39.

Articles in the *LRB*: 'Will we care when Labour loses?', 26 March 2009, pp. 7–8; 'Will we notice when the Tories have won?', 24 September, pp. 9–10; 'At the Tory Conference', 22 October, p. 20.

London Review Blog, 2009 [www.lrb.co.uk/blog]: 'Good cop, bad cop', 22 May; 'The candidate of the United States' [Blair], 27 July; 'Deathbed conversions', 30 September; 'Half the argument', 24 October.

2010

Parties and People: England 1914–1951 (Oxford: Oxford University Press), 2010.

Articles in the *LRB*: 'Good for Business', 25 February 2010, pp. 9–10; 'Time to Repent', 10 June, pp. 11–14; 'Nothing to do with the economy', 18 November, pp. 12–13.

London Review Blog, 2010: 'Sub-tabloid', 4 January 2010; 'Coercive solutions', 26 February; 'Half proposals', 8 April; 'Contradictory aims', 15 June; '[Australian] Labor's warring factions', 7 September; 'Not so Red Ed', 30 September.

CLASSES

4

In Pursuit of Prudence: Speculation, Risk, and Class in Victorian Britain

Paul Johnson

Prudence was the most quintessentially Victorian of the bourgeois virtues.[1] It embraced calculation, forethought and self-restraint—or thrift, self-help, and character, to use three of Samuel Smiles's favourite terms.[2] To the bourgeoisie, prudence was the modest, measured, and mature way to cope with the challenges of an unpredictable world, particularly the financial challenges that affected almost all people in the monetised economy of nineteenth-century Britain. To socialists it was a mere smokescreen for aggressive self-interest. Prudence, like beauty, was in the eye of the beholder. It could not be collapsed into a set of approved and mechanistic behaviours, nor was it a constant in place or time. This essay examines ways in which economic response to financial risk either was, or was not, deemed to be prudent in Victorian Britain. It reveals the importance of social convention and class position in assigning prudential motive to economic behaviour.

The starting point for the discussion, however, is what may seem to be the least prudent of economic activities—gambling. Few educated Victorians could see any virtue in gambling, whether lowly sixpenny each-way bets or princely stakes on the classic races. The churches were unwavering in their hostility: to trust to luck was to deny the righteous order of the Lord. Economists proposed more worldly reasons for eschewing the thrill of the odds. Alfred Marshall concisely noted that 'gambling involves an economic loss, even when conducted on perfectly fair and even terms'.[3] Parliament had its say, and was unequivocal. In 1808 it had already itemised the alleged effects of gambling on society in the following alarmist fashion: 'idleness, dissipation, and poverty are increased, the most sacred and confidential trusts are betrayed, domestic comfort is destroyed, madness often created, crimes, subjecting the perpetrators of them to the punishment of death[,] are inflicted and even suicide itself is

[1] For a discussion of bourgeois virtues, see D. N. McCloskey, *The Bourgeois Virtues: Ethics for an Age of Commerce* (Chicago, 2006).

[2] These terms being the titles of three of Smiles's books.

[3] Alfred Marshall, *Principles of Economics* (London, 1890), bk. 3, ch. 6, para 95.

produced.'[4] Action eventually followed the words. The Gaming Act of 1845 declared wagering contracts to be unenforceable at law and made it a criminal offence to keep a gaming house.[5]

This Victorian consensus about the economic and moral folly of gambling has been challenged by Ross McKibbin. His pioneering study of working-class gambling in late nineteenth and early twentieth-century Britain was one of the first attempts to analyse the economic and cultural significance of risk in the lives of manual workers.[6] Far from viewing gambling as that 'abandonment of reason'[7] which so preoccupied middle-class anti-gambling campaigners, McKibbin revealed an internal financial and cultural purpose to mass betting which made it 'the most successful example of working-class self-help in the modern era'.[8] Betting on horses did not cast the fortune of working-class families to the winds of chance, but instead required careful study of past performance and evaluation of odds. It represented a specifically working-class form of intellectual activity 'where the whole point was to *eliminate* chance from the bet'.[9] McKibbin inverted the arguments of the late Victorian and Edwardian anti-gambling movement. Rather than working-class gambling being indulgent, wasteful, degrading, and pauperising, he instead presented it as rational, controlled, and socially integrative—a specifically working-class representation of the bourgeois virtue of prudence.

Gambling was far from being the only stratagem to deal with financial risk that was adopted by people from all classes in nineteenth-century Britain. This essay focuses on two other responses that lay at opposite ends of the spectrum of popularity. The first—the purchase of life insurance—was ubiquitous, with all sections of society participating in this form of risk-sharing. The second—the purchase of shares—was a minority activity, even among prosperous middle-class households, throughout Victoria's reign. It was, however, not an activity confined to the prosperous middle class, as became clear at various moments of stock-market turbulence. Both these financial strategies encountered a degree of moral censure from the Church and from other quarters, but whereas the anti-gambling movement was resolute in its oppositional stance, regardless of the context and social standing of the individuals concerned, the critique of life insurance and stock purchase evolved in a distinctly class-conscious manner. These activities, which were initially considered to be morally tainted, became legitimised and institutionalised over the course of the nineteenth century. This was, however, a process of legitimation in which virtue came to depend heavily

[4] House of Commons Select Committee on the Evils Attending to Lotteries, 1808, Appendix 8, 157.

[5] Public Acts, 8 and 9 Vict. c. 109.

[6] Ross McKibbin, 'Working-class gambling in Britain, 1880–1939', *Past and Present* 82 (1979), pp. 147–78.

[7] J. A. Hobson, 'The ethics of gambling', in B.S. Rowntree (ed.), *Betting and Gambling: A National Evil* (London, 1905), p. 5.

[8] McKibbin, 'Working-class gambling', p. 172.

[9] Ibid., p. 165.

on the status of the actor rather than the form of the act. Prudence, it seemed, could only ever be a middle-class girl.

I

By the end of the nineteenth century life insurance was big business in Britain. The major life insurance offices were large-scale employers and, increasingly, large-scale investors.[10] Their products were sold through an extensive network of agents—mainly solicitors and accountants—to a largely middle-class clientele both within the UK and, through subsidiaries, to overseas clients, particularly in the empire. Life insurance was mainstream, part of the establishment. A remarkable sociological analysis of membership of the House of Commons published in 1868 identified the insurance industry as coming behind only the railways and banks in its claim on the allegiance of parliamentarians: 'the railways, which have hardly any voters at the polling booth . . . have 179 railway directors in the House of Commons, who represent only shareholders, not railway travellers. The banks have 78 bankers and bank directors in the House, the insurance offices 53.'[11] This legislative influence was complemented by the physical presence of insurance company head offices in Holborn and the City, designed to exude a sense of grandeur and permanence. There was no clearer sign of the standing of life insurance in the nation than the conferment of a knighthood in 1897 on Henry Harben, the driving force since 1851 behind the growth of the nation's largest and most successful life insurance company, the eponymous Prudential.

It had not always been so. Life insurance had a tainted history. Geoffrey Clark has explored the origins of life insurance in Britain from its essentially speculative early eighteenth-century origins through to its 'scientific' reformulation by the Equitable Assurance Society in 1762 and the development of actuarially-weighted premiums.[12] Throughout this period there was a tension in public discourse between those who viewed life insurance as immoral betting on life, and those who saw it as prudential action to underwrite personal and family security. Life insurance gambling for pure financial gain was widespread, and according to Clark, widely tolerated in the first half of the eighteenth century. The wagers could be made in the betting books of gentlemen's clubs, by the underwriters at Lloyd's, or through the issuing of policies by the established life assurance offices. Formal life insurance policies had an advantage over personal wagers because they could be assigned to

[10] The assets of British life insurance companies rose from £109m in 1870 to £530m in 1913. Over this period the proportion invested in securities (including government bonds) rose from 24.4 to 50.6 per cent: R. C. Michie, *The London Stock Exchange* (Oxford, 1999), p. 73. For the development of the life insurance industry see B. S. Supple, *The Royal Exchange Assurance: A history of British insurance 1720–1970* (Cambridge, 1970).

[11] Bernard Cracroft, *Essays, Political and Miscellaneous* (London, 1868), p. 118. The essay 'Analysis of the House of Commons in 1867' (pp. 95–113) was originally published in the *Saturday Review.*

[12] Geoffrey Clark, *Betting on Lives* (Manchester, 1999).

third parties, and thus had a clear resale value. Viscount Bolingbroke, Robert Walpole, and the Duchess of Marlborough were just a few of the many prominent public figures who had their lives insured—without their knowledge—by the Amicable Assurance Society, purely as a gamble.[13] The callousness of some of the bets on life, together with the possibility that a gambling policy-holder with substantial sums to win on someone's death might hasten nature's path, produced a shift in moral sentiment which was reflected by the passage of the Gambling Act of 1774. This introduced a requirement that the purchaser of a life insurance policy should have to demonstrate a legitimate financial interest in the life of the insured. The Gambling Act was an important step in shifting the discourse around life insurance from one which focused on chance and speculation to one that emphasized the prudent manner in which commercial families could secure their financial futures in the face of mortal disaster. Despite the initial disquiet about the morals and motives surrounding the insurance of life, by the early nineteenth century the practical utility offered by life insurance to the upper and middling classes had trumped all serious concerns about legitimacy.

Not so, however, in the case of working-class insurers, who played in a different market space—the penny-a-week industrial life assurance market. Far from this section of the market being lauded with honours, it was loaded with restrictions (restrictions which existed quite independently of the general middle-class lament that it was a ridiculously expensive way to purchase a form of insurance which was not needed and usually squandered). In 1846 parliament forbade any penny-a-week insurance on the life of a child less than six years of age through a restrictive clause inserted into the Friendly Societies Act of that year. In 1850 and 1855 this limit was altered and extended to cover all children aged under ten. This insistent parliamentary attention was driven by a concern that working-class parents as a group were indeed prepared to gamble on the lives of their children, and sacrifice these lives to the lure of lucre—the very same discourse that had previously been developed with respect to the middle-class insurance market, and roundly dismissed by the beginning of Victoria's reign.

This was not just a mid-century aberration. In the early 1870s it was claimed—in evidence to the Royal Commission on Friendly Societies—that the high infant mortality rate and extensive infant life insurance in Lancashire was proof that children were being killed for cash.[14] A decade later, a further parliamentary inquiry into friendly societies produced the claim that infant insurance in some cases led to murder and frequently led to negligence. The Society for the Prevention of Cruelty to Children was, from its inception as a London society in 1884, and a national society four years later, adamant that working-class infant insurance was evil. The Director of the Society, Revd Benjamin Waugh, was quite certain, in his parliamentary evidence, that 'infant

[13] Clark, *Betting*, pp. 49–53.

[14] Fourth Report of the Royal Commission on Friendly and Benefit Building Societies, PP 1874 xxiii, pt 1, pp. cxxxiii–cxli.

life insurance is a direct incentive to the destruction of infant life.'[15] Not content with stating the case, the Society worked with the Bishop of Peterborough to bring to the House of Lords in 1890 a bill proposing that any sums payable on the death of young children should be handed direct to the undertaker and not to the parents or guardians who had paid the premiums. Doctors, coroners, and judges were called to give evidence that infant life insurance put temptation in the path of the poor: it was 'an incentive to cruel neglect, and what is, morally speaking, murder'.[16]

This middle-class fear of the effect of working-class life insurance, as with middle-class censure of working-class gambling, derived from a prejudicial view of the psychology of the masses. It was not the act, but rather the actors, that justified the concern. Workers were less restrained, less able to plan for the future, to defer gratification, or to control their base animal instincts. They were, in a fundamental sense, different people; they lacked the bourgeois virtue of prudence, and they required different treatment. It was left to Will Crooks, the lone working-class voice invited into their Lordships' house, to present the contrary view:

> I find always mothers willing and very ready to make every sacrifice to keep their children alive, and it seems to me to be the case that the most thrifty of the very poor always insure. I do not find in my experience anyone who has not that maternal affection for their children which it seems to be the general opinion that we lack as poor people.[17]

Although the Bishop of Peterborough's Bill lapsed, the financial limits on penny-a-week life insurance for children remained in force until after the First World War. By the late-Victorian period, middle-class life insurance was seen as the epitome of prudence, whereas the working-class equivalent was seen as generally profligate, and, in the case of insurance of children, a moral threat.

II

If life insurance tested Victorian notions of propriety and prudence, then the stock market did the same in spades. From the very establishment of the London Stock Exchange in 1801 there existed a concern that the structures of financial markets, and particularly of the Stock Exchange, led, and even forced, decent men to behave dishonourably. As early as 1816 an anonymous pamphleteer had remarked that, although individual traders on the Stock Exchange 'generally speaking are respectable members of society', nevertheless the collective body of the Stock Exchange 'exists by manoeuvres and deceptions'.[18] The particular focus of this and many other complaints was that the majority of Stock Exchange trades were driven not by 'real' transactions, but by the trade in options, or 'time

15 Select Committee on the Friendly Societies Act 1875, PP 1889 x, q. 3746.

16 Select Committee of the House of Lords on Children's Life Insurance Bill PP. 1890 xi, qq.10, 50, 1876, 1201.

17 Ibid., q. 2274.

18 Practical Jobber, *The System of Stock Jobbing Explained* (London, 1816), p. 12.

bargains'. Time bargains, it was claimed, created price movements that were unnatural, and which thereby could disadvantage honest investors. More importantly, time bargains were immoral, because they were nothing more than a gamble: 'This practice, which is really nothing else than a wager concerning the price of Stock, is contrary to law; yet it is allowed to be carried on to such an alarming extent, that almost the whole city of London, and many at distant parts, have become gamblers.'[19]

The law in question was Barnard's Act, which, from enactment in 1734 to repeal in 1860, made illegal 'the frequent and mischievous practice' of dealing in time bargains—future contracts in which settlement was determined not by exchange of stock or commodities, but by exchange of money between the contracting parties, depending on whether the price had risen or fallen in the intervening period. From the outset this law was a dead letter; dealers in stocks and shares habitually settled accounts with each other periodically (fortnightly once the Stock Exchange was established in 1801) rather than daily, and so necessarily carried 'short' or 'long' positions for some days. Furthermore, many dealers deliberately entered into 'put' (sell) or 'call' (buy) options covering longer periods in order to speculate on price movements, though in 1821 the Stock Exchange limited the length of options to 14 days, in order to limit systemic risk in the market (an interesting case of a private institution publicly regulating an activity that was formally illegal).[20]

The critique of time bargains arose in part from the general evangelical assault on gambling which held that it undermined morals and weakened the habits of industry. This pressure contributed to the abolition of public lotteries in 1826.[21] Time bargains were also held to create incentives for corrupt behaviour, because the lapse in time between initiation and execution of the contract provided an opportunity to distort the 'true' market price. By the 1840s the financial commentator David Morier Evans felt able to write, with some equanimity, that the majority of stock market trades were 'purely of a gambling nature'.[22] Evans was writing in the middle of the 'railway mania' which had drawn many thousands of novice investors into dealing in shares. When the bottom dropped out of the stock market in October 1845, a huge number of investors were left holding almost worthless paper in the thousand or so railway companies that had been provisionally registered over the preceding nine months. The railway mania confirmed the views of stock-market sceptics that dealing in shares had little in common with legitimate trade or investment: a distinction—in the words of Thomas Chalmers—between 'solid commerce' and 'excrescent trade'.[23]

[19] Ibid., p. 15.

[20] Charles Duguid, *The Story of the Stock Exchange* (London, 1901), pp. 48–50; Michie, *London Stock Exchange*, pp. 47–50.

[21] G. R. Searle, *Morality and the Market in Victorian Britain* (Oxford, 1998), pp. 230–3.

[22] D. M. Evans, *The City; or, the physiology of London business* (London, 1845), p. 37.

[23] T. Chalmers, *On Political Economy*, 229–32, cited in Boyd Hilton, *The Age of Atonement: The Influences of Evangelicalism on Social and Economic Thought, 1785–1865* (Oxford, 1988), p. 122.

There were two discrete objections. First, speculation was immoral, because whereas legitimate trade added to the nation's wealth, speculation was a form of plunder in which one person's gain was another's loss (an argument that was difficult to square with one of the key tenets of classical political economy, which held that exchange only takes place when the parties to the trade each obtain benefit). Second, speculation was unmanly, because it permitted men to gain wealth by 'dexterity and trick' rather than by 'patient industry'.[24]

Regardless of moral criticism and practical setbacks at times of financial and commercial crisis, stock-market speculation continued to develop. By mid-century there existed a ready supply of advice to readers of a new genre of investment manuals. One such guidebook, purportedly penned by 'a late MP', was addressed to:

> The active, the intelligent, the far-seeing men of the world, of quick eye and energetic grasp of mind; to these we say, the field of enterprise is open to you in the FUNDS, wherein millions of pounds are lost and won *almost daily*, in the RAILWAY SHARE MARKET, a source of gain which has enriched thousands, BANKING SHARES, MINING SHARES, LAND SPECULATION, etc., all these various modes of making money we mean to discuss *seriatim*.[25]

In 1852 Walter Bagehot was of the view that gambling, in the guise of stock-market speculation, was becoming part of the national character as an increasing number of people misguidedly sought easy winnings through trading shares: 'John Bull can stand a great deal, but he cannot stand Two per cent . . . Instead of that dreadful event, they invest their careful savings in something impossible.'[26] Five years later the *Economist* castigated the naivety of investors: 'The public, always unreasoning and generally unreasonable, want the security of Consols without submitting to the low interest—they want the high profits of speculating business without incurring the risk attending them, and without taking the labour and trouble of looking after them.'[27]

The scope and appetite for stock-market speculation was undeniable; the issue of contention was whether, and for whom, this speculative activity produced harmful results. In 1878 the Royal Commission established to investigate the practices of the Stock Exchange after many investors lost considerable sums they had committed to foreign loans floated on the exchange, drew a distinction between appropriate and excessive levels of stock-exchange trading:

> It is an undoubted fact that the great facilities afforded by the Stock Exchange for the unlimited purchase or sale of all sorts of securities, coupled with the system of making bargains for the "account", that is, for a future day, open a wide door to mere gambling as

[24] *Cobbett's Weekly Register*, 12 February 1825, cited in James Taylor, *Creating Capitalism: Joint-stock enterprise in British politics and culture, 1800–1870* (Woodbridge, 2006), p. 59.

[25] Anon [A Late M. P.], *How to make money; or hints to speculators* (Birmingham, 1857), p. 5.

[26] Walter Bagehot, 'Investments', *Inquirer*, 31 July 1852, quoted in Taylor, *Creating Capitalism*, p. 60.

[27] *Economist*, 17 January 1857, quoted in J. Taylor, 'Company fraud in Victorian Britain: The Royal British Bank scandal of 1856', *EHR* 122 (2007), p. 713.

well as to legitimate speculation. And where this has been carried to excess or undertaken by people of limited means, frequently with ruinous results to creditors, the blame by many persons is thrown upon the Stock Exchange.[28]

Just as Victorian novelists tended to account for financial scandals and defalcations by reference to the character flaws of individuals, this Royal Commission whitewashed the Stock Exchange as an institution, explaining away perceived problems by reference to the excessive desire or limited means of investors (no surprise given that membership of the Commission included both the chairman of the Exchange, S. R. Scott, and Nathaniel de Rothschild). This was despite the fact that bargains for 'mere differences' were wagers within the meaning of the 1845 Gaming Act. The Stock Exchange had openly ignored the provisions of Barnard's Act, and it also ignored the legal prohibition on enforceable wagers.

The key characteristic of a wager was the intention to settle a forward contract by payment of the difference in price, rather than through exchange of goods. This characteristic existed regardless of the means of the parties involved, or the place in which the wager was struck. Yet it was clear by the 1880s that Parliament and the courts were content with a practical distinction between wagers on the stock market and wagers in any other environment. There was a fine line between Victorian perceptions of gambling (immoral, sinful, and, depending on the context, illegal) and speculation (robust, reliable, and required for the good functioning of any market). Where the dividing line was drawn depended on the circumstances of the observer, and the circumstances of the observed; as the author of an anti-gambling tract published by the Society for the Promotion of Christian Knowledge conceded in 1897, 'it will always be difficult to say where it is exactly that legitimate speculation ends and gambling begins'.[29]

Attempts by religious moralists to define and delineate illegitimate speculation foundered in a sea of inconsistent or illogical definitions. According to the Archdeacon of Westmoreland, 'legitimate speculation submits to no uncertainty except such as is inevitable; it courts no risk', whereas illegitimate speculation or gambling 'traffics in uncertainties. Risk and chance are its chief commodities'.[30] But in practice there never was a risk-free transaction, except in the stylised market of classical economics where buyers and sellers transacted instantly and effortlessly, without the messy encumbrance of contracts that needed to be enforced. All trade was, to some extent, speculative: a gamble on whether market prices would rise or fall, on whether the counter-party would honour the contract. The benefit to speculators of the use of 'put' and 'call' options on the stock market was that they could massively leverage their capital, since the cost of the option was only ever a small fraction of the face value of the stock. However, the speculative principle was the same, whether or not the deal was leveraged.

28 Report of the Royal Commission on the Stock Exchange, PP 1878 xix, p. 20.
29 A. T. Barnett, *Why are Betting and Gambling Wrong?* (London, 1897), p. 20.
30 Archdeacon Diggle, *Speculation and Gambling* (London, 1899), pp. 6–7.

By the 1890s the operation of the Stock Exchange and all the speculative opportunities offered by company flotation were fully accepted in Victorian society, and were so much a part of the establishment that in 1893 they were satirised by Gilbert and Sullivan in their operetta *Utopia*. The absurdist plot had the king of the imaginary Pacific island of Utopia adopt the very latest English fashion by converting each of his citizens into a limited liability company. The king's daughter proudly announced that 'there is not a christened baby in Utopia who has not already issued his little Prospectus!' to which her lover added: 'Marvellous is the power of a Civilization which can transmute, by a word, a Limited Income into an Income (*Limited*).'[31]

In 1870 only a small minority of the 250,000 stock exchange investors held company shares (most held fixed-interest government bonds), but by 1900 roughly half the one million investors held shares.[32] By this date almost half of MPs were directors of listed companies.[33] It is no surprise, then, that when Francis Hirst, editor of the *Economist*, wrote a guide to the Stock Exchange in 1911, he recognised speculative behaviour as being ubiquitous: 'even in an old and conservative country like England the average investor is a speculator in the sense that he not only wishes his investment to yield him interest but also hopes and expects that he will some day be able to sell out at a profit. Such an aspiration is perfectly natural and legitimate.'[34]

Stock Exchange activity in Victorian Britain underwent a process of moral laundering as language and attitudes changed. The change is clearly articulated in a statement attributed to Sir Ernest Cassell, banker to the rich and famous, including Edward VII:

> When I was young, people called me a gambler. As the scale of my operations increased I became known as a speculator. Now I am called a banker. But I have been doing the same thing all the time.[35]

Yet this moral laundering had a class dimension. Most purchasers of shares were middle class, but not all of them were, as became clear whenever financial crisis struck. When the Royal British Bank collapsed in 1856 it was found that among the bank's 280 individual shareholders were twenty-eight spinsters and ten widows, together with butlers, household servants, clerks, shopkeepers, artists, and publicans—a group described by the *Times* as 'a class of small people . . . who live entirely outside of the great commercial world, are wholly unacquainted with

[31] See libretto at Gilbert and Sullivan archive: http://math.boisestate.edu/gas/utopia/html/index.html.

[32] Michie, *London Stock Exchange*, pp. 71–2; E.V. Morgan and W.A. Thomas, *The Stock Exchange* (London, 1962), table V.

[33] *Directory of Directors for 1898* (London, 1898).

[34] F. W. Hirst, *The Stock Exchange* (London, 1911), p. 164.

[35] Quoted in Edward Chancellor, *Devil take the hindmost: a history of financial speculation* (London, 1999), p. ix.

trade on a large scale, and to whom, therefore, all the machinery of this great world of business and all its proceedings are as simple mysteries as if they were matters of another world.'[36] The Royal Commission on the Stock Exchange had identified 'people of limited means' as being key to the accusation of gambling, because for this group any significant loss involved financial ruin, and it was the outcome, rather than the cause, that generated public criticism. The mingling of lords and labourers in the shareholder lists of joint-stock companies was a form of 'social promiscuity' that risked undermining the new legitimacy of the investment market.[37]

Further access to the stock market for people of limited means emerged in the 1880s when companies began to issue fully paid-up low denomination shares valued at £1 or less.[38] By the end of the century the entry price to the shareholders' club was well within the reach of lower income households with money to save. But such activity was deemed to be imprudent. This was no longer because the sale and purchase of shares was generally held to be morally dubious, but rather because small-scale speculators were uninformed. The respectable investor was conceptualised as a wealthy man of business who moved in the same social and business circles as the directors he elected: who gained his information through informal links that allowed him to minimise risk. The imprudent investor followed the financial press with naïve credulity, became swept up in bubbles and manias: was essentially nothing more than a gambler.

IV

In his summary of attitudes to working-class gambling, Ross McKibbin wrote: 'While the upper and middle classes were being taught that gambling was on the whole no longer acceptable behaviour, and were abandoning it, the working class, excluded from the particular forms of middle-class intellectual activity, practised an intellectualised betting as one way of expressing the more rational and controlled culture of the late nineteenth century.'[39] The carefully controlled and well-informed thought-patterns, expectations, and behaviours of working-class betters were remarkably similar to those of the well-connected, large-scale stock-market traders and speculators of the late nineteenth century. Yet working-class gambling was seen to be the antithesis of prudence, while stock-market investment was the epitome. Although the definition of prudential activity changed markedly over the course of the nineteenth century, it remained resolutely middle-class in attribution—an embedded bourgeois virtue.

[36] *Times*, 18 September 1856, p. 8.

[37] Searle, *Morality*, 84; Taylor, *Creating Capitalism*, pp. 80–9.

[38] J. B. Jefferys, 'The denomination and character of shares, 1855–1885', *EHR* 16 (1946), pp. 45–55.

[39] McKibbin, 'Gambling', p. 178.

Postscript

The collapse of Lehmann Brothers in September 2008, and the subsequent contagion that spread across global financial markets, revealed that the guardians of Prudence had let their ward run riot. Bankers, brokers, financial regulators, and even national governments appeared to have crossed that invisible but crucial line between legitimate speculation and gambling. Investments that had been repeatedly verified as solid and secure became worthless overnight, and contagion spread from North American financial markets to businesses and households around the world. After two centuries, the description provided by the House of Commons in 1808 of the evils attending lotteries seemed to have renewed relevance: 'idleness, dissipation, and poverty are increased, the most sacred and confidential trusts are betrayed, domestic comfort is destroyed, madness often created.'[40]

Financial institutions that had been established to minimise and contain risk undertook actions that massively multiplied it, all in pursuit of additional profit. Whether the cause was greed masquerading as market efficiency, or naivety masquerading as professionalism, it is clear that the Victorian middle-class commitment to calculation, forethought and self-restraint had been abandoned, and this abandonment had come in a rush. Prudence had remained a good middle-class girl throughout most of the twentieth century. Manual workers continued to bet on horses and, from the 1920s, on the football pools, while upper-middle class households continued to pursue what was deemed to be prudent investment on the stock market. In 1986 Prudence had a dalliance with working-class Sid, when Margaret Thatcher used the privatisation of British Gas to attempt to create a nation of shareholders—though most of the new shareholders recognised they had done nothing more than place a bet and took their profit when the time came.[41] What really did for Prudence was globalisation. She was lured from London to New York in the late 1990s by the prospect of sharing in the ever-increasing returns being manufactured by supposedly invincible financial engineers on Wall Street. She lost her inhibitions, cast self-restraint to the winds, but in the end lost her soul. The denouement came in a Gladstonian moment in 2008 when Prudence, the fallen woman, was rescued from the dark streets of the City of London by a British Prime Minister wielding a stimulus package.[42]

[40] See above, note 4.

[41] The privatisation of British Gas in 1986 was heavily advertised to the non-shareholding members of the British public with the slogan 'Tell Sid'.

[42] For Gordon Brown's association of his economic policy with prudential values see William Keegan, *The Prudence of Mr Gordon Brown* (London, 2003). For Gladstone's 'rescue work' with fallen women see H. C. G. Matthew, *Gladstone* (Oxford, 1997), pp. 90–5.

5

Britain's 'Quasi-Magical' Monarchy in the Mid-Twentieth Century?

Andrezj Olechnowicz

For one reviewer *Classes and Cultures* 'provides as good a snapshot of the Windsors, warts and all, as one could hope to find'. The conundrum at the heart of the book is, he noted, why '[in] the high period of class consciousness . . . in the most working-class country in the world' the working class was 'roundly trounced, both politically and economically'. To this Ross McKibbin 'does not offer a single, direct solution . . . although in a sense his book offers a thousand solutions'.[1] The same multi-causal outlook characterises McKibbin's approach to the British monarchy in the mid-twentieth century: why did the monarchy not only survive but strengthen its 'hold on the popular imagination' to the point that 'after 1918 it had a cultural centrality to British life possessed by hardly any other British political institution'?[2] There was, he accepts, an element of contingency to this survival and popularity: the Second World War offered the monarchy 'a lucky escape, given George VI's commitment to Chamberlainite Conservatism'.[3] However, consistent working-class attachment is 'surprising but not inexplicable';[4] and the explanation consists of five distinct but related practices and beliefs.

First, by the late nineteenth century the monarchy had acquired a 'politically uncontentious' character, enabling it to function as 'the even-handed guarantor of the class-neutrality of Parliament'—a role 'acceptable to all classes'. Publicly and also privately the monarchy embraced 'the stylised vocabulary of "fairness"'.[5] Second, McKibbin endorses Ernest Jones's Freudian analysis of 'the psychology of constitutional monarchy': once a ruler is decomposed into two persons, the 'murderous potentialities in the son-father (i.e. governed-governing) relation' are satisfied by the ordered opportunities for the 'destruction' of the prime minister, leaving the monarch 'guarded from adverse criticism' and able to present (in the case of England) 'a magnified and idealized picture of the most homely and familiar attributes' which release ordinary people 'for a moment . . . from the

1 R. W. Johnson, 'Mr Shepperd to you', *London Review of Books*, 21 May 1998.
2 Ross McKibbin, *Classes and Cultures: England, 1918–1951* (Oxford, 1998), p. 7.
3 Ibid., p. 534.
4 Ross McKibbin, *The Ideologies of Class* (Oxford, 1990), p. 17.
5 Ibid., p. 19.

inevitable sordidness and harassing exigencies of mundane existence'.[6] Third, McKibbin is sceptical of a crude Durkheimian analysis exemplified by Edward Shils and Michael Young that the monarchy 'came to represent certain commonly held values': though they did not claim that agreement in any society 'even the most consensual, is anywhere near complete', McKibbin argues that the monarchy could only represent common values of 'the most trite kind' since it divorced itself 'from most of those areas of British life where moral unity was not possible'.[7] Fourth, the press, radio and cinema played an important role in projecting a public, ceremonial, glamorous but also domestic monarchy, though only Edward VIII embraced 'glamour' unreservedly.[8]

Fifth, McKibbin argues that the monarchy possessed a 'quasi-magical character' and this 'partly magical' monarchy, made more powerful by being at the same time 'ordinary' and domestic, was 'largely, though not entirely, a product of the interwar years'.[9] This was evidently far more than the pleasure of Bagehotian 'dazzle' and 'mystery'.[10] It was reinforced by 'the age-old notion that royalty is magical'; and it accorded with 'people's mentality' in the mid-twentieth century, which subscribed to 'various kinds of religious and quasi-religious belief... the belief in semi-religions, vaguely transcendental doctrines, spiritualism and various superstitions'.[11] McKibbin has cautioned that people do not express their opinions 'in ways that please the tidy-minded; they are usually partial, fragmented, often scattered by the daily struggle of life'—the products of lives that are also fragmented.[12] Nonetheless, he finds the evidence for such a popular mentality in three quarters. There were 'archaisms' promoted by George V: 'most self-consciously archaic of all, [he] reinstituted the giving of Maundy Money in 1921.' In Geoffrey Gorer's *Exploring English Character* (1955) is the evidence of 'the widespread belief in astrology, spiritualism, an afterlife, in the power

[6] Ernest Jones, 'The psychology of constitutional monarchy' [1936], in *Essays in Applied Psycho-Analysis*, vol. 1 (London, 1951), pp. 229–30, 232; McKibbin, *Classes*, pp. 13–14. McKibbin also endorses Jones's analysis in explaining why the 'hold on our emotions' of Princess Diana was 'in direct relation to her political powerlessness': Ross McKibbin, 'Mass-Observation in the Mall', in Mandy Merck (ed.), *After Diana: Irreverent Elegies* (London, 1998), p. 20.

[7] McKibbin, *Classes*, p. 13; McKibbin, *Ideologies*, p. 19; see Edward Shils and Michael Young, 'The meaning of the Coronation', *Sociological Review* 1 (1953), 65. Certainly, a participant-observer study of contemporary royalists concludes that the identification of the monarchy with the nation—'it's about being British'—is at the core of their beliefs: Anne Rowbottom, '"The real royalists": folk performance and civil religion at royal visits', *Folklore* 109 (1998), p. 85.

[8] McKibbin, *Classes*, pp. 7–9.

[9] Ibid., pp. 14, 3. In 'Why was there no Marxism in Britain?', however, McKibbin described the authority of the monarchy as 'quasi-hieratic': McKibbin, *Ideologies*, p. 20.

[10] Ibid., p. 17; Walter Bagehot, *The English Constitution* [ed. Miles Taylor] (Oxford, 2001), p. 41.

[11] McKibbin, *Classes*, pp. 15, 522. McKibbin makes a similar case for very many people having a 'quasi-religious view' of Princess Diana and investing her with 'semi-magical qualities': McKibbin, 'Mass-Observation', pp. 19–20.

[12] Ross McKibbin, 'Not Pleasing the Tidy-Minded', *London Review of Books*, 24 April 2008, 31; idem., '*Class and Cultures*: A Postscript', in Stefan Berger (ed.), *Labour and Social History in Great Britain: Historiographical Reviews and Agendas* (Mitteilungsblatt des Instituts Für Sociale Bewegungen series, Essen, 2002), p. 153; idem., *Classes*, p. 289.

of prayer, charms and good luck'; and McKibbin endorses Gorer's attribution of this belief to 'the feeling of helplessness which . . . so many people had about their own lives', with the implication that 'as life became increasingly dominated at all levels by "rational" procedures, arguably the magic became yet more acceptable to the public'. Most decisively, Kingsley Martin's *The Magic of Monarchy* (1937) cites 'a number of widely noticed atavisms' in the latter part of George V's reign, which constitute *direct* evidence of a 'recrudescence of sheer superstition':

> much publicity was given to a crippled Scottish boy who learnt to walk 'after' having met George V; in 1935 there was endless talk of the providential nature of the 'royal weather'; as late as 1939 villagers near Southwold (Suffolk) pressed around George VI to 'touch' him in order to ward off disease.

McKibbin notes that such examples represented 'a revival as well as an atavism' and that 'the crown itself encouraged such archaisms'.[13]

This is a challenging and heterodox argument, largely by virtue of McKibbin's fifth point: very few 'royal' writers, let alone academic historians, have been willing to make the argument for a '(quasi-) magical' monarchy as strongly as this.[14] The object of this chapter is to offer a friendly critique of this view. First, it will point to the need to distinguish 'magic' and 'religion', because it will be argued that there was a deliberate intensification of the sacred and Christian character of the monarchy by royal servants and the leaders of the Church of England, but not its magical character.[15] Second, it will suggest that neither the 'evidence' of Gorer nor of Martin is as compelling as it appears; and that there is a dearth of other evidence, notably for the coronations of 1937 and 1953 from Mass-Observation, a body keen to highlight atavisms. Third, it will argue that in the 1930s Martin's perspectives were affected by his preoccupation with the threat of fascism, which he understood—as did many across the political spectrum—as an irrational doctrine akin to monarchy. Martin was too ready to condemn Britain's 'magical' monarchy because he was too ready to believe that the British people were vulnerable to the 'irrational' appeal of fascism. Finally, the chapter will emphasise the *purely* conventional sense in which the word 'magic' has been and is associated with the term 'monarchy'; and it will argue that a tone of 'knowingness' marked—and continues to mark—working-class engagement with the monarchy, which 'punctured official knowledges and preserved an independent popular voice'.[16]

[13] Ibid., p. 14.

[14] Though Pimlott did argue that 'the persistence of the belief in the special access of Monarchs and by extension other royals to divine grace, alluded to by Bagehot, may indeed point in the direction in which we should be looking': Ben Pimlott, *The Queen* (London, 2001), pp. 646–7.

[15] For a study of the religious dimension, see Ian Bradley, *God Save the Queen* (London, 2002).

[16] Peter Bailey, 'Conspiracies of meaning: Music-hall and the knowingness of popular culture', *Past and Present* 144 (1994), 168.

I

What should we understand by 'magic'; and should it be distinguished from 'religion'? McKibbin seems to treat the two as identical ways of thinking—a view in accord with much anthropological and historical literature.[17] He endorses Gorer's view of a 'magical' universe as entailing 'a passive cosmology where there was no perceived connection between effort and outcome', and where 'Fate ruled all and the most fortunate were the most lucky'. According to McKibbin, popular attachment to this cosmology was the product of 'a real social powerlessness'. This, he argues, offers an acute insight into popular mentalities at a time when most of the English also 'believed themselves (one way or another) to be Christian';[18] and 'magic' is certainly often used in a weak sense to describe 'an inexplicable and remarkable influence producing surprising results'.[19] However, there is a strong sense of 'magic' which is at odds with Gorer's view, and is incompatible with Christian religion and resisted by ecclesiastical authorities. Here magic is a 'form of activity in which different elements and forces, physical, supernatural and verbal, are manipulated in order to bring about certain results. The symbolic or ritual component of magic sets it apart from merely technical activity'.[20] A magical universe would therefore not be one in which 'Fate ruled all'; rather charms and spells would be believed to work mechanically and impersonally to bring about change, provided that the correct ritual had been observed. Religion, on the other hand, entails 'recognition on the part of man of some higher unseen power as having control of his destiny, and as being entitled to obedience, reverence, and worship', with prayer, a supplication to God which carries 'no certainty of success'.[21] Durkheim suggested sociological reasons why religion and magic, 'though related', must be distinguished. Religion comprised both beliefs and rites; the former presupposed the division of the world into sacred and profane domains; and the latter had a 'sacred character as well . . . There are words, speeches, and formulas that can be spoken only by consecrated persons; there are gestures and movements that cannot be executed by everyone'. Religious beliefs and rites are always held and observed by a group which is thereby united 'in a single moral community called a church'. Although magic

[17] Dorothy Hammond, 'Magic: A Problem in Semantics', *American Anthropologist* 72 (1970), pp. 1349–56; Adam Kuper, *Anthropologists and Anthropology: The British School 1922–72* (Harmondsworth, 1975), pp. 38–41; John Wolffe, 'The religions of the silent majority', in Gerald Parsons (ed.), *The Growth of Religious Diversity*, vol. 1 (London, 1993), p. 310. Wolffe terms 'activities and beliefs relating to the supernatural, however people perceive it' as 'common religion', and those without an 'explicit supernatural reference' but relating to 'people's perception of their place in the cosmos' as 'invisible religion'. A further consequence of such a view is to rule out *ex hypothesi* any possibility of a 'secular' society.

[18] McKibbin, *Classes*, pp. 291–2, 272.

[19] 'Magic', in *Oxford English Dictionary Online*, http://dictionary.oed.com, accessed on 1/12/2009.

[20] Alan Bullock and Stephen Trombley (eds.), *The New Fontana Dictionary of Modern Thought* (London, 1999), p. 496.

[21] 'Religion', in *Oxford English Dictionary Online*, http://dictionary.oed.com, accessed on 1/12/2009; Keith Thomas, *Religion and the Decline of Magic* (London, 1971), p. 41.

too consists of beliefs and rites and the magician invokes forces 'not only similar in nature to the forces and beings addressed by religion but often identical', it does not create a church. Moreover, there is 'hostility' towards religion among believers in magic, and a 'marked repugnance' for magic is a general characteristic of the Judaeo-Christian religious tradition.[22] It is especially important to take care to distinguish between a 'magical' monarchy and a 'sacred' one in the case of England where the monarch is 'Supreme Governor of the Church of England'.[23]

Though newspapers sometimes presented the monarchy as 'magical' in a weak sense, royal ritual in this period *always* projected the monarchy as 'sacred' and Christian; and it is improbable that this had little or no effect in developing an exclusively religious understanding of the institution.[24] The example of Maundy Money is a case in point. Royal Maundy had a continuous history from the thirteenth or fourteenth century as a religious ceremony.[25] As *The Times* declared in 1932, Royal Maundy was 'a symbol and a religious ceremony, at once the declaration and the sanctification of the monarch's service of the people'.[26] What George V was persuaded to do by his advisers was not to reinstitute the ceremony, but to perform it in person for the first time in over two centuries in 1932;[27] and this in no way changed its long-established meaning. Other 'new-old' interwar royal ceremonies also had a clear Christian meaning:[28] for example, George V's broadcast to his peoples during his Silver Jubilee in 1935 expressed 'thankfulness to God' for the past and sought 'God's help' for the future.[29] Moreover, as Philip Williamson has observed, the first half of the twentieth century saw the emergence of 'a new type of special worship' termed 'national days of prayer' which proved to be 'even more numerous than the fast and thanksgiving days' in the mid-nineteenth century and were characterised by the monarch's support 'now expressed as personal approval or

[22] Emile Durkheim, *The Elementary Forms of Religious Life* (Oxford, 2008), pp. 36–46.

[23] Though not of Scotland, where Jesus Christ is seen as the 'Divine Head' of the Church of Scotland and the monarch is merely an ordinary worshipper.

[24] Sennett regards ritual as 'an emotional unity achieved through drama', and therefore its impact 'disappears the moment the ritual ends': Richard Sennett, *Authority* (London, 1993), pp. 3–4. Lukes, however, suggests that ritual has 'a cognitive role . . . serving to organise people's knowledge of the past and present and their capacity to imagine the future': Steven Lukes, *Essays in Social Theory* (Basingstoke, 1977), p. 68.

[25] The washing of feet by the monarch, recalling Jesus washing the feet of his disciples before the last supper, ended in 1698 and the practice ceased altogether after 1736. The custom of relating the number of recipients to the age of the monarch dates back to at least 1363. Between 1822 and 1954 specially minted Maundy coins carried the inscription 'by the Grace of God King of All the Britons, Defender of the Faith' (from 1954 'by the grace of God Queen, Defender of the Faith'). The practice of giving Maundy money started in 1662. See 'The Royal Maundy. A Long Historical Tradition', *The Times*, 23 Mar. 1932, which claimed that the ceremony had a continuous history from 400.

[26] *The Times*, 24 Mar. 1932.

[27] Ibid., 22 Mar.; 24 Mar. 1932.

[28] On the supposed interwar 'invention' of 'new-old royal ceremonials', e.g. Queen Alexandra's funeral and George V's Silver Jubilee, see David Cannadine, *Class in Britain* (New Haven, 1998), p. 141.

[29] *His Majesty's Speeches: The Record of the Silver Jubilee of His Most Gracious Majesty King George the Fifth, 1935*, pp. 21–2. The formal observance of a Jubilee in the Christian tradition started in 1300 as a special year of forgiveness of sins and of pardon (cf. Isaiah 61: 1–2).

request, not by exercise of the royal supremacy'.[30] The most archaic ceremony of all was the coronation. In 1937 essentially 'the same service was used for King George VI as had been used for the Saxon kings before the Normans came here'. Nor was it a simple blessing of the monarch; rather it was 'the consecration of the sovereign to a definitely ecclesiastical position', with the Archbishop of Canterbury during the Anointing calling on God, who 'by anointing with oil didst of old make and consecrate kings, priests, and prophets' of Israel, to 'bless and sanctify thy chosen servant GEORGE, who by our office and ministry is now to be anointed with this Oil, and consecrated King'.[31] All media reinforced this meaning, and the celebrations were 'unescapable': 'people who tried to avoid them found themselves going back to the radio on one ground or another'.[32] Although there was no commentary throughout the service on the radio, the order of service with an explanation of its religious meaning was available in the *Radio Times*, newspapers, and coronation guides and souvenirs. The BBC Director of Religion and a Chaplain to the King, Frederic Iremonger, offered 'guidance for the thoughts and prayers of listeners' during the most sacred part of the Communion, its special significance marked by the Abbey microphones being shut off for its duration. Moreover, the Archbishop of Canterbury had a 'free hand' to cut from the newsreel films of the coronation anything 'unsuitable for the public at large to see'.[33] By order of the two archbishops, Coronation Day and the Sunday before were days of special Church of England services, and other churches had their own services.

The coronations of 1937 and 1953 were subjects of investigation by Mass-Observation. What is striking is the absence of evidence of people adopting a 'magical' or 'mystical' interpretation of the two events, even though Mass-Observation labelled the 1937 Coronation 'macabre and atavistic' and in 1953 explicitly requested reports of '"folk" ceremony'.[34] Malinowski took the organisation to task for not observing and analysing 'the most important religious aspect, the fact, namely, that the monarchy is still to the people "by the Grace of God"' in 1937.[35] His criticism was unfair, however, for what is equally striking is

[30] Philip Williamson, 'State prayers, fasts and thanksgivings: public worship in Britain 1830–1897', *PP* 200 (2008), 167.

[31] F. C. Eeles, *The Coronation Service: its Meaning and History* (London, 1952), pp. 10, 13, 35. Like other writers, Eeles points to the similarity between services for the consecration of a monarch and of a bishop in the medieval period. See also B. Malinowski, 'A Nation-Wide Intelligence Service', in Charles Madge and Tom Harrisson, *First Year's Work 1937–38* (London, 1938), p. 112. Elizabeth II too was 'consecrated' to the service of God: e.g. J. A. C. Roberts, *Coronation: published for the Girl Guides Association* (London, 1953), p. 6; *Guardian*, 3 Jun. 1953.

[32] Humphrey Jennings and Charles Madge (eds.), *May the Twelfth: Mass-Observation Day-Surveys, 1937* (1937; London, 1987), pp. 91, 267.

[33] Ibid., pp. 15, 16–17.

[34] Ibid., p. 325; Special Jobs, May 1953, TC 69/1/B, Mass-Observation Archive, University of Sussex. References to 'the beautiful Fairy Coach' and to Princess Margaret Rose looking 'very much a little princess from a story book' were the few instances of an 'enchanted' view of the monarchy; but these were wholly 'conventional' descriptions and suggested no supernatural dimension: *May the Twelfth*, pp. 116, 137; cf. p. 335.

[35] Malinowski, 'Nation-Wide Intelligence Service', p. 114 fn. 2. Mass-Observation's 1964 survey reported that 30 per cent agreed that the Queen was specially chosen by God, and that 34 per cent had done so in 1956, causing Ziegler to speculate that in 1937 it would have been

that Mass-Observation found little evidence of a religious interpretation. Rather there was 'no extreme interest in what the function of a King may be or the significance of his Coronation . . . And so far as the King himself becomes an object of emotion he is conceived in family or "Freudian" relations, not as a person who might do anything'. The fact of the King's speech impediment 'seems to have aroused general sympathy, even among anti-monarchists . . . though this sympathy was closely connected with the feeling of embarrassment'.[36] Celebrations reflected local loyalties, and people treated Coronation Day as 'a public holiday and festival like any other, to be enjoyed in the usual ways':[37] when coal-owners in Treharris refused to give a day's holiday with pay, the miners decided to go to work as usual on Coronation Day.[38]

The unpublished Mass-Observation files on the 1953 Coronation lead to a similar conclusion, with a more 'instrumental' set of attitudes perhaps more evident.[39] There is no reference to the 'magical',[40] and barely any reference to the religious character of the monarchy or of the event. One schoolgirl wrote that 'on Coronation morning as soon as I awake I will say a prayer for our beloved queen'; while the 72-year-old wife of a labourer said that 'it's a thing that has to be. It's a very sacred thing'. The very few other mentions of a religious dimension were much more vague: a view that 'from the spiritual & religious side it's wonderful'; and a Sunday school teacher opining that 'it will bring God's love from heaven to people on earth'.[41] Though many of the school children answered a question about the meaning of the Coronation along the lines that it enabled the monarch to 'pledge him or herself to God and the people' or her subjects to 'give the Queen her sacred rights', these were conventional, expected and sometimes confused replies, and most children were more heartfelt in condemning a degree of commercialization which put 'portraits of the Queen on such things as shoeshines'.[42] For the rest, there was a miscellany of 'secular' emotive and instrumental reactions: it was right because the Queen and all the Royal Family were 'lovely people'; it would be 'the thrill of a lifetime', and 'it's only once in a lifetime you

surprising if less than half the population had seen some special link between God and the King: Leonard Harris, *Long to Reign Over Us* (London, 1966), p. 43; Philip Ziegler, *Crown and People* (Newton Abbot, 1979), p. 36. Setting aside the vagueness of the claim, it then becomes inexplicable why there was not a greater trace of this link in *May the Twelfth*, even allowing for any 'bias' in the observers and the imprecision of 'attitudes'.

36 *May the Twelfth*, pp. 270, 279, 294, 301.

37 Ibid., pp. 169, 92, 91, 35, 53.

38 Ibid., p. 35.

39 This paragraph relies on 'Coronation Questions put to National Samples. February 1953. May 1953. October 1953', TC 69/2/A; and a large collection of essays written by thirteen- and fourteen-year-old school children on how they spent Coronation Day and how they felt about the Coronation, TC 69/3/A-D, M-O Archive.

40 Only one schoolgirl intimated an 'enchanted' view, declaring that 'the Duke of Edinburgh . . . looked very proud of the fairytale Queen at his side': TC 69/3/B4, M-O Archive.

41 TC 69/3/C25, and see also C11, C26; 'Coronation Questions', pp. 4, 8, 'Rectory . . . 3 September 1953'.

42 e.g. TC 69/3/B1, B4, B10, B11, B12, B14, B16, B20, B23, B26, C1, C5, C8, C18, C21, C22, C31, D1.

see anything like it'; pomp and tradition were matters of national pride, and 'the Yanks would die to have a little bit of English pageantry to boast about'; it was 'important and necessary for international reasons', and would 'raise our prestige abroad—and it needs it'; it would 'help the trades people no end', and was 'an excellent way of bringing money & tourists into the country'; and several women were 'very much interested in Coronation Fashions'.[43]

Turning to the 'magic' documented by Gorer and Martin, what is striking is how unsatisfactory their 'evidence' is Gorer's work is 'little acknowledged today', in part because of 'his readiness to produce generalizations for the whole of a complex society'.[44] Yet we need to be clear about *precisely* what he was claiming. He argued that 'about a quarter of the population' held a view of the universe which could 'most properly be designated as magical', in the sense that the future is 'pre-determined and knowable by various techniques which are not connected with either science or religion'. He found that half the men and a third of the women who responded read horoscopes 'without taking them seriously', and 4 per cent of the women and 2 per cent of the men said that they regularly followed the advice in horoscopes, with a further 29 per cent of the women and 16 per cent of the men doing so 'occasionally'. Gorer regarded these figures as 'quite astounding';[45] but it is not obvious that they are. Similarly, between three-quarters and four-fifths of the population did *not* believe that luck was 'controlled mechanically', according to his own findings.[46] Martin's book is impressionistic and tendentious. Of the three instances cited by McKibbin, there is no indication of the extent of the publicity for the healed crippled boy; there is hardly 'endless talk' about 'royal weather' in, say, newspapers, commemorative publications or the Mass-Observation surveys;[47] and the villagers of Southwold appear to have been uniquely—not typically—gullible. Martin acknowledged that these might be regarded as 'extreme examples', but stated that he 'could cite many other illustrations of the existence of a magical theory of Monarchy'. He was especially critical of Archbishop Temple's remark that the King was the 'incarnation' of his people, which he regarded as either 'meaningless' or endorsing 'an even more primitive conception than that of divine right'.[48] Temple wrote to Martin that he could not understand why Martin had been 'so perplexed at that very innocent remark of mine':

[43] 'Coronation questions', pp. 20, 1, 9, 4, 14, 12, 24. Such instrumental reactions were also common in 1937: *May the Twelfth*, pp. 298–301.

[44] Jeremy MacClancy, 'Geoffrey Gorer', *ODNB.*

[45] Geoffrey Gorer, *Exploring English Character* (London, 1955), p. 269.

[46] Ibid., p. 265. This does not mean that there were not particular occupational communities where the belief in 'luck', 'fate' and 'misfortune' was more pervasive, and explained by the extraordinary danger of the work: e.g. Zweig, *Men in the Pits*, pp. 114–15, 171, where miners held that 'mining is really gambling'.

[47] This is hardly surprising since e.g. Coronation eve in 1937 was marked by 'almost continuous rain in the morning and afternoon', leaving some decorations badly damaged; and many people were 'greeted by a dull wet morning' on Coronation Day in 1953: *May the Twelfth*, pp. 81, 82; 'Coronation Day feelings. 3.6.53', TC 69/6/D.

[48] Kingsley Martin, *The Magic of Monarchy* (London, 1937), p. 9.

It is so evident that the function of the Crown is primarily symbolic that it never occurred to me that anyone could suppose that my use of this phrase referred back to the outlook of primitive tribes or the rest. On the other hand most English people's conception of a symbol, when that word is used, is so meagre that it seemed more advisable to leave it out.

Martin remained unconvinced.[49] Martin's very few other illustrations are similarly unpersuasive: a society paper suggesting that 'the very pheasants . . . are fortunate enough to fall to the Royal gun'; or a letter to a newspaper extolling 'the extraordinary miracle of a royal birth'. What was extraordinary was Martin's contention that the 'most convincing proof' of a magical theory was 'the complete absence of serious discussion of Monarchy'.[50] But there was, in fact, serious discussion,[51] which also highlighted the fundamental weakness of Martin's analysis. Martin took it for granted that what was said about the monarchy in newspapers or by figures in authority was popularly believed, and made no distinction between magical, religious and Freudian interpretations of the monarchy but interchanged them indiscriminately.[52] This lack of rigour was not a consequence of Martin being an 'idiot journalist';[53] rather it reflected the book's origin as a response not only to the Abdication, but also to the success of fascism in the 1930s.

II

Remembering that decade, the Fabian Martin wrote that 'the confusion and perplexity of that time are now hard to communicate'. He had thought that the future of the bankrupt capitalist system lay in fascism or war, unless a Popular Front succeeded.[54] Moreover, as Tony Wright notes, Martin was 'evidently obsessed by the possibility of a British fascism'.[55] Already in 1927 he feared that Communist propaganda would 'disintegrate the Labour Party and lead to revolutions and strikes and a Fascist government in Great Britain'.[56] In the wake of the British Union of Fascists' Olympia meeting, he wrote in his diary in

[49] Id., *Editor: A Second Volume of Autobiography 1931–45* (London, 1968), pp. 183–4. Martin had sent a copy of his book to Temple.

[50] Id., *Magic*, pp. 104, 7, 9.

[51] Though it was true that when discussed, it was 'not as a constitutional device but rather as a trait in the national character, as an old and ingrained social habit': Maurice Amos, *The English Constitution* (London, 1934), p. 1.

[52] Thus Martin also endorsed Jones's Freudian explanation of why a king was 'above criticism' (and why George V was very frequently spoken of as 'a father to us all'); and argued that the 'taboo' surrounding the monarchy was a consequence of 'its sacred character': Martin, *Magic*, pp. 18, 15–16, 10.

[53] Isaiah Berlin, *Enlightening: Letters 1946–1960* [ed. Henry Hardy and Jennifer Holmes] (London, 2009), p. 469 (12 Jan. 1955).

[54] Kingsley Martin, *Father Figures: A First Volume of Autobiography 1897–1931* (London, 1966), pp. 203–4.

[55] A. W. Wright, *G. D. H. Cole and Socialist Democracy* (Oxford, 1979), p. 221n.

[56] Beatrice Webb, *The Diary of Beatrice Webb*, vol. 4 [ed. N. and J. MacKenzie] (London, 1985), p. 115 (7 Feb. 1927); and see also p. 337 (13 July 1934), p. 347 (22 Feb. 1935).

September 1934: 'I see no way of stopping Fascism in this country now.'[57] During the Abdication he was alarmed by Mosley's support for Edward VIII, and believed that the growth of a 'King's Party' was a 'real danger' over the weekend of 5–6 December 1936.[58] He wrote of Mrs Simpson in his diary that 'it is true that she is pro-Nazi and likely to lead the King in a Fascist direction'.[59] In *The Magic of Monarchy* he drew attention to 'the stories of the pro-Nazi sympathies of the King's friends and even of the King himself', but drew back and stated that there was no evidence—'as far as I know'—that Edward VIII held other than 'common British views' that Versailles had been unfair and friendship was necessary for peace.[60] Together with part of the British left, he feared that the National Government had fascist tendencies, evidence for which he found in the press becoming 'a good deal more pro-Fascist and subject to Government influence'.[61]

Not only Martin, but *most* interwar writers and politicians across the British political spectrum would have agreed with a definition of fascism as 'the sum total of all the *irrational* reactions of the average human character'.[62] Martin believed that in countries where the struggle of the powerful to preserve their wealth had reached its 'most acute form', propaganda was 'the chief weapon of reaction'; and this fascist 'reaction against reason and common sense' had already gone to 'extravagant lengths' on the Continent.[63] Martin's mentor at the LSE, Laski, considered that the Nazis had endeavoured to make Hitler 'in a real sense a god to the people'.[64] Cole regarded fascism as an 'atavistic doctrine' which reverted 'to the savage tribe celebrating its ritual propitiation of the unmastered forces of nature'.[65] Huxley noted how in 'modern dictator-worship' the name and title of the dictator were invoked 'as though they had the force of magic spells'.[66] Malinowski wrote that reason and free thought had been 'so far impotent to withstand the new mysticisms and the new mythologies'.[67] For Collingwood, the beliefs of fascism and Nazism were 'silly', founded on

[57] Quoted in Wright, *Cole*, p. 221n. [58] Martin, *Magic*, pp. 76–7.

[59] Quoted in id., *Editor*, p. 181 (24 Nov. 1936).

[60] Id., *Magic*, p. 97. He drew attention to dinner parties where 'the King or his immediate entourage' and 'prominent Nazi spokesmen' had been present. Edward VIII later claimed that he had regarded Hitler as 'a somewhat ridiculous figure', but had admired the German people, and 'sympathized with many of their aspirations': *A King's Story: The Memoirs of H.R.H. the Duke of Windsor K.G.* (London, 1951), p. 277. The Nazis appear to have had 'genuine respect' for Edward VIII's *Volksnahe* (proximity to the people): Gerwin Strobl, *The Germanic Isle: Nazi Perceptions of Britain* (Cambridge, 2000), pp. 108–12.

[61] Kingsley Martin, 'The freedom of the press', *Political Quarterly* 9 (1938), 387; see also id., *Fascism, Democracy and the Press* (London, 1938).

[62] Wilhelm Reich, *The Mass Psychology of Fascism* (Harmondsworth, 1983), p. 16 (Preface to 3rd edn, 1942).

[63] Martin, *Magic*, pp. 103, 112.

[64] H. J. Laski, 'The meaning of Fascism', in *Reflections on the Revolution of Our Time* (London, 1943), p. 118.

[65] G. D. H. and M. I. Cole, *The Condition of Britain* (London, 1937), p. 427.

[66] Aldous Huxley, 'Emperor-worship up to date' [1935], in D. Bradshaw (ed.), *The Hidden Huxley* (London, 1994), p. 193.

[67] Malinowski, 'Nation-wide intelligence service', pp. 120–1.

'conjuring up a social order based on the superstitious adoration of individual leaders'.[68] Barker and A. D. Lindsay thought that fascism substituted mass enthusiasm for 'the reasoning and reasonable process of discussion', and found the 'obvious irrationality' of its doctrines troubling.[69]

Martin's object in *The Magic of Monarchy* was to establish that before the Abdication 'we were abandoning reason and common sense for hysteria and magic' in 'deifying' George V; that the Abdication had broken the royal 'taboo', making an 'honest analysis' possible, as it had been possible in the nineteenth century; but that 'today the Press, the platform, and the pulpit are again hard at work to try to build up the new King into a god'. He accepted that a constitutional monarch acting as 'a symbol and a figurehead' was 'not incompatible with an increasingly rational attitude towards public affairs'; but what he feared was that 'an intense propaganda by public men, in the Press, and in the cinema' was deliberately fostering 'an irrational feeling about the whole Royal Family' in the interests of 'the powers that be'.[70] In short, the revival of monarchy 'worship' was, for Martin, a further step along the British road to fascism.[71]

Though not as alarmist as Martin, several prominent figures on the left observed that the interests sheltering behind the monarch could manipulate him towards anti-democratic ends. Laski, for example, relished recounting the sycophancy surrounding the monarch;[72] but was concerned that 'the democratic contacts of the Throne' were 'superficial', and that in an emergency the King could ignore the advice of his ministers if, 'in his judgement', it violated the 'essentials of the Constitution'.[73] Probably a more common opinion on the left was that the monarchy served, as one reviewer of Martin's book put it, 'a useful negative purpose in drawing-off from our heads the lighting of a Fascist dictatorship'.[74] Beatrice Webb, a close friend of Martin's, shared his distaste for the Coronation in 1937, and the 'revolting role' of the bishops within it; she also felt that the popular reaction to the King and Queen demonstrated that the

[68] R. G. Collingwood, 'Fascism and Nazism', *Philosophy* 15 (1940), pp. 172–3, 176n.

[69] Ernest Barker, 'The conflict of ideologies', *International Affairs* 16 (1937), 352, 355.

[70] Martin, *Magic*, pp. 10–13, 94, 103, 112. One means to this end this was to put pressure on English publishers to withdraw unsuitable books: M. M. Knappen, 'Review article: The abdication of Edward VIII', *Journal of Modern History* 10 (1938), 249.

[71] The British 'constitutional monarchy' is so insistently projected as the product of uniquely indigenous conditions that it is easy to miss that, in fact, there have been several periods when it has been seen, at least by some public figures, as influenced by authoritarian, Continental models: e.g. Dilke's attack on the monarchy in 1871 and criticism the Royal Titles Act in 1876 both arose out of the anxiety that the monarchy was attempting to move towards the sort of 'Caesarism' which had been established by Napoleon III in France: Miles Taylor, 'Republics versus empires: Charles Dilke's republicanism reconsidered', in David Nash and Antony Taylor (eds.), *Republicanism in Victorian Society* (Stroud, 2000), pp. 25–34; Richard Williams, *The Contentious Crown: Public Discussion of the British Monarchy in the Reign of Queen Victoria* (Aldershot, 1997), p. 116.

[72] M. D. Howe (ed.), *Holmes-Laski Letters 1916–1935*, (London, 1953), p. 1289 (11 Oct. 1930); see also H. J. Laski, 'The danger of being a gentleman: reflections on the ruling class in England [1932]', in *The Danger of Being A Gentleman and Other Essays* (London, 1939), pp. 26–7.

[73] H. J. Laski, 'The monarchy', in *Parliamentary Government in England: A commentary* (London, 1938), pp. 394, 424.

[74] F. Hardie, 'Review: *The Magic of Monarchy* by K. Martin', *Political Quarterly* 8 (1937), 461.

'idolization of persons on account of their assumed and exceptional goodness and infallible wisdom' was not confined to the 'so-called totalitarian states'; but she argued that, unlike Hitler and Mussolini, the objects of the British people's adulation had no power, and constituted a safe channelling of 'a dangerous human instinct'.[75] Opinion on the left was not even uniformly troubled by the emotion unleashed by royal ceremonies: the celebration of George V's Silver Jubilee aroused in Winifred Holtby's staunchly Labour Sarah Burton not 'mass hysteria and empty shouting', as a socialist predicted, but a 'democratic' awareness that 'we are members one of another . . . this is what it means, to be a people'.[76]

Martin was too fixated on the idea of the imminence of fascism in Britain to reflect on flaws in his analysis or alternatives to it. His fixation required that the monarchy should be 'magical', and that ordinary people should be susceptible to its 'magic'. He was therefore willing to clutch at straws in 1937.[77]

III

It is unnecessary to invoke a 'partly magical' monarchy in order to account for its popularity. The four other components of McKibbin's explanation are sufficient without this fifth. In particular the notion of a 'politically uncontentious' institution might be developed. Once the monarchy could no longer credibly be criticised as partisan, it was bound to remain popular as long as the political system commanded popular legitimacy—and this was not in doubt in this period.[78] Moreover, as Williamson has argued, royal public language in this period articulated 'values which most public and voluntary bodies considered essential for the general interest'—'constitutionalism, social cohesion, the empire, Christian witness, and public morality'. The 'most ubiquitous' royal trope was that of 'service'.[79] Words were very publicly matched by deeds as the whole

[75] Webb, *Diary*, vol. 4, pp. 388 (14 May 1937), 435 (24 Jun. 1939).

[76] Winifred Holtby, *South Riding: An English Landscape* (London, 1936), pp. 576, 585–7. The socialist's anxieties in the novel were, however, evident among the opinions Mass-Observation collected in 1937: a typist in London reflected that 'reviewing it all calmly afterwards, one sees how very dangerous all this is – the beliefs and convictions of a lifetime can be set aside so easily': *May the Twelfth*, pp. 303–5.

[77] Martin published a second book on the monarchy in 1962, and its argument is in some respects markedly different from that in his 1937 work. George VI is credited with restoring 'the ideal conception of the domestically correct and conventional monarch'; the emphasis is on the 'glorified, religious view of royalty' rather than the 'magical' view; the monarchy is now the subject of 'fairy tales which help the imagination'; and the main criticism is that the monarchy is 'still the head of the Establishment rather than the nation': Kingsley Martin, *The Crown and the Establishment* (Harmondsworth, 1963), pp. 117, 12, 120, 178, 179.

[78] McKibbin argues that after the early nineteenth century the working class imagined no alternative to Parliament, and concurs with Lukes' view that participation in elections is a 'symbolic affirmation of the voters' acceptance of the political system and their role within it': McKibbin, *Ideologies*, pp. 20–1. Turnout in the seven interwar elections was 57% (in the disrupted circumstances of 1918), 73%, 71.1%, 77%, 76.3%, 76.4%, and 71.1%.

[79] Philip Williamson, 'The monarchy and public values 1900–1953', in Andrezj Olechnowicz (ed.), *The Monarchy and the British Nation, 1780 to the Present* (Cambridge, 2007), pp. 231–2, 252.

Royal Family patronised a wide, socially diverse range of charities, which even allowed it to claim a 'hybrid form of republican virtue'.[80] So entrenched was the idea of charity as the 'job' of the monarchy that as Mrs Dalloway sees Queen Mary's car, she can only think: 'The Queen going to some hospital; the Queen opening some bazaar'.[81] Not only did the monarchy attend to the welfare of its people, it shared their prejudices and pastimes. As Colin Matthew observed, George V's 'middle-brow remarks became something of a hallmark of his peacetime reign', and he enjoyed and attended spectator sports.[82] A great deal was made of George VI's sportsmanship as he sought to establish himself after the Abdication.[83] The Monarch's words and actions meant that it became common between the Wars to celebrate Britain's 'democratic monarchy', and to contrast it with the 'totalitarian' regimes. 'The monarchy has become so truly democratic nowadays', declared *The Times* leader on Coronation Day in 1937.[84] Moreover, and contrary to Martin's insinuation, the Church fostered the Christian idea of a democratic national community held together by faith, distinguishing it from the fascist notion of a *Volk* decided by blood.[85]

Williamson is careful to establish that 'this is not to argue that the monarchy reflected some "natural" moral consensus in British society'. See e.g. G. M. Trevelyan, 'Twenty-five momentous years', in *King and People, 1910–1935. Reprinted from the Silver Jubilee Number of The Times, May 3, 1935* (London, 1935), p. 13: 'The popularity of King George and of his Queen and Family, due to their personal qualities and to the long, faithful, and affectionate service that they have for twenty-five years rendered to their subjects, gives soul and reality to this form of government.'

[80] Frank Prochaska, *The Republic of Britain, 1760–2000* (London, 2000), p. xviii; id., *Royal Bounty* (New Haven, 1995), chs. 6–8. The Palace ensured that the monarchy's contributions were publicised: e.g. 'You are at liberty to publish the fact that the King has given £100 and the Queen £50 to this work', Privy Purse Office to L. F. Ellis, National Council of Social Service, 7 Nov. 1933, Unemployed Box 3, File Grants-in-Aid, National Council of Voluntary Organisations Archive, Bedford Square, London.

[81] Virginia Woolf, *Mrs Dalloway* (1925; London, 2000), p. 17.

[82] H. C. G. Matthew, 'George V', *ODNB*.

[83] e.g. J. T. Gorman, *George VI: King and Emperor* (London, 1937). Queen Elizabeth created a sensation by playing darts at Slough: Mass-Observation, *The Pub and the People: A Worktown Study* (1943; Welwyn, 1970), p. 300 'women flock to follow the Queen's lead at darts'. Edward VII and Edward VIII too had been commended as 'sportsmen': e.g. for James Joyce's Henchy the King was 'just an ordinary knockabout like you and me', and 'a good sportsman': James Joyce, *Dubliners* (1914; London, 2000), p. 129; *Edward VIII Souvenir Book. Our Sportsman King* (n.d). It is unfortunate that there is as yet no comprehensive study of the monarchy and sport. As Zweig remarked (and McKibbin explored in *Classes and Cultures*), sport contributed to 'the ethical code of society', meaning in the worker's mind 'first of all fairness and keeping the rules and customs which are a solid frame for fairness, and secondly the avoidance of arbitrariness and dictation': Ferdynand Zweig, *The British Worker* (Harmondsworth, 1952), pp. 124, 126.

[84] Quoted in *May the Twelfth*, p. 84. See also e.g. Amos, *English Constitution*, p. 1; Louis Wulff, *Silver Wedding: The Record of Twenty-Five Royal Years* (London, 1948), pp. 12–13; G. M. Gathorne-Hardy, 'The democratic monarchy', *International Affairs* 29 (1953), 273–6; John Wheeler-Bennett, *King George VI: His Life and Reign* (London, 1958), pp. 165–72.

[85] Matthew Grimley, *Citizenship, Community, and the Church of England: Liberal Anglican Theories of the State between the Wars* (Oxford, 2004), pp. 200–1. This was evident in Temple's correspondence with Martin concerning his use of 'incarnation' in which Temple was at pains to draw a distinction between the state and the community, and insist that 'what the King embodies symbolically is not the State but the Community' – a point Martin ignored: Martin, *Editor*, p. 184.

Does 'magical' monarchy play therefore no role? Not quite. First, as McKibbin noted, monarchy had for many centuries been associated with 'magic', and the term continues to be used in an entirely habitual and unreflective way. It is the term which for centuries has been at hand, and still continues to be, when many people mention the monarchy.[86] We might even speculate that acknowledging the magic of the monarchy was simply another of the 'techniques designed to avoid embarrassment or the giving of offence', which McKibbin has identified as critical in British life.[87] Nonetheless, people are perfectly aware of the 'powerlessness' of royalty in the sense that despite great privilege they are not free to do as they will.[88] Second, to take the vulnerability of people to a 'magical' monarchy too seriously is to take people's 'knowingness' not seriously enough. There is much evidence of ordinary people not directly refuting official languages, but always engaging in a 'countervailing dialogue that sets experience against prescription, and lays claim to an independent competence in the business and enjoyment of living'.[89] Mass-Observation recorded in 1937:

Lancashire. (CO.36) *Self.* Last night ____ and I had a walk round, when we came to a house with a picture of Albert Edward and Elizabeth tacked up, and underneath to bathe it in an aura of light was an electric lamp. ____ said, 'Oh, look at this holy image,' then out it popped. She said, 'Now look what our derision's done'.

And:

Belfast. (CO.30. A sanitary inspector.) I went into the general office in order to await any cases of infectious diseases or nuisances which may arise during the day (inspector on duty) and chatted with the clerk on duty. He had a Coronation souvenir paper and read aloud the heading 'Smiles that charm all subjects' and added in a disappointed tone 'they have failed to charm me'.... A workman remarked that the King and Queen would be a longer time without a meal to-day and the clerk said, amid laughter, that they would take

[86] e.g. Woolf, *Mrs Dalloway*, p. 18; Anne Ring, *The Story of Princess Elizabeth, Told with the Sanction of Her Parents* (London, 1930), p. 124; Harold Nicolson, *King George the Fifth: His Life and Reign* (London, 1952), p. 525, there was 'magic' in the first Christmas broadcast in 1932; Robert Lacey, *Princess* (London, 1982), Diana's 'youth, beauty, and glamour' had brought new meaning to 'the old magic of monarchy'; Arthur Edwards, *Magic Moments: The Greatest Royal Photographs of All Time* (London, 2008).

[87] McKibbin, '*Classes and Cultures*: A Postscript', p. 164.

[88] Indeed, it might be argued that this is in part a reason for their popularity: in the fact that even royalty cannot do as they will, ordinary people have found a compensation for their own restricted lives, an illusory reminder that money does not buy freedom: Andrzej Olechnowicz, '"A jealous hatred": royal popularity and social inequality', in Olechnowicz, *Monarchy*, pp. 280–314.

[89] Bailey, 'Conspiracies', 155, 168–9. Harrison noted 'a knowingly sarcastic tone' in recent writing on the monarchy; but this was the tone of many ordinary people long before academics gave up reverence: Brian Harrison, *The Transformation of British Politics, 1860–1995* (Oxford, 1996), p. 347. Perhaps knowingness is one of the causes of that 'lack of consistent commitment to general values of any sort' which undermines Shils and Young's argument, and supports Mann's: Michael Mann, 'The social cohesion of liberal democracy', *American Sociological Review* 35 (1970), 423–39.

a snack in their pockets. From this evolved facetious and imaginative remarks on the crowning ceremony. [90]

Knowingness, however facetious or grim, usually remained subordinated to official languages;[91] but it could coexist with anti-monarchism; and it can pardon a working life spent toasting 'Queen and Country'.

[90] *May the Twelfth*, pp. 278, 245. See also e.g. Michael Billig, *Talking of the Royal Family* (London, 1992), pp. 57–8; *The Sun*, 3 Apr. 2000: 'The mum-to-be, June Jones, 65, was honoured when the Queen Mother visited her garden in Bow, East London, in 1965. . . . "At the time I had two sons and I was hoping for a daughter, so as she left the Queen Mum said: 'I do hope you get your girl.' I told my husband, 'We're bound to have a girl now. We've got the Royal seal of approval.' But we didn't".'

[91] e.g. 'Towards the end of the war, we were so fed up we wouldn't even sing "God Save the King" on church parade. Never mind the bloody King we used to say, he was safe enough; it should have been God save us': Martin Middlebrook, *The First Day of the Somme: 1 July 1916* (London, 1971), p. 300.

6

Classes and Cultures in England after 1951: The Case of Working-Class Women

Janet Howarth

Classes and Cultures is one of the few histories of modern English society to treat gender systematically. It draws on a rich contemporary literature of social observation which took gender as one major focus of interest. An equally rewarding and if anything more varied range of sources is available for the later twentieth century, with input from cultural studies, oral history, and feminist ethnography as well as mainstream social scientists, social commentators, and journalists. These sources have yet to be fully exploited by historians. Class analysis, challenged by postmodernists, became for a while unfashionable and some recently published surveys on British social history have avoided using class as a framework.[1] Even before that, questions were being asked about the survival of class identities in the affluent post-war era. 'It is often said that there are no working classes in England now', wrote Richard Hoggart in 1957; and though that view is resisted in *The Uses of Literacy*, he did see influences making for a 'culturally classless society'.[2] If that had come about, there would be little point in attempting to pursue the story of 'classes and cultures' much beyond the 1960s. The aim of this essay is to suggest that we can in fact fruitfully continue to ask questions about the history of gendered class experience in the second half of the twentieth century. My focus will be on change and continuity in the lives of working-class women, which are actually much better documented in those decades than ever before.

Current developments in sociology do nothing to discourage the writing of class history. The notion that affluence would in itself erode class differences by an inexorable process of *embourgeoisement* was shown to be wrong in the classic study of high-paid workers in Luton published more than forty years ago by John Goldthorpe and his collaborators.[3] The divisive impact of immigration within the working classes, much in evidence in the 1960s and after, is now seen as

[1] For example F.M.L. Thompson, *The Cambridge Social History of Britain, 1750–1950* (Cambridge, 1990); Ina Zweiniger-Bargielowska (ed.), *Women in Twentieth-Century Britain* (Harlow, 2001).

[2] Richard Hoggart, *The Uses of Literacy* (London, 1957), p. 15.

[3] J. H. Goldthorpe et al., *The Affluent Worker in the Class Structure* (Cambridge, 1969).

having receded.[4] Since the late twentieth century there has been renewed interest in the study of working-class identities and in understanding the ways in which class consciousness manifests itself.[5] A persuasive case is made by Mike Savage and others for the central importance of class analysis in contemporary society, and for aiming to produce a 'class focused account of social change'.[6] In theoretical terms the approach now favoured draws less on Marx and Weber than would have been the case in earlier generations. Instead the emphasis is on a cultural mode of understanding social class, largely inspired by the work of Pierre Bourdieu, which has—allowing for differences in academic style—a good deal in common with Ross McKibbin's approach to writing social history.

The continuing significance of class in contemporary Britain is borne out by empirical evidence. Social survey data confirm that a large majority of people, when asked, do still place themselves in a social class. The British Election Studies for the period 1964 to 2005 show remarkable continuity in this respect. The proportion of respondents in these surveys who identified as working class fell, as one would expect in an era of deindustrialisation—from 64 per cent in 1964 to 57 per cent in 2005—with a corresponding increase in the numbers placing themselves in the middle class; but the proportion refusing to identify with any class was as low as 6 per cent in both years.[7] Class, as defined in the traditional way according to occupation, does moreover still correlate (although more weakly than in the past) with voting behaviour—and with life expectancy, access to higher education, diet and much else too. 'Affluence' has not eroded economic inequality between social classes in the way that was once anticipated. An apparently well established trend towards greater equality in incomes was sharply reversed in the 1980s. The rate of unemployment between 1980 and 1995 approached inter-war levels. Poverty, far from decreasing, became more widespread. In 1991 the proportion of the population with incomes below half the average income was twice as large as it had been in 1961.[8] Inequality in pay at the turn of the century—measured by comparing wage levels at the top, bottom and middle of the wage distribution (the 90th, 10th, and 50th percentiles)—was at a level 'higher than at any time since the 1920s'.[9] At the same time the demand for domestic servants—at one stage regarded by modernisation theorists as destined to vanish in the developed world—grew rapidly. A Mintel survey found that between 1987 and 1996 the amount spent on waged domestic workers in the UK rose from £1.1 billion to £4.3 billion. Except in some areas of London, where domestic service is dominated by migrant workers, most English families recruit

[4] See e.g. Paul Gilroy, *There Ain't No Black in the Union Jack* (London, 1987; 2002 edn.), pp. xiii–xvii; and his *Black Britain. A Photographic History* (London, 2007), pp. 219–23.

[5] Michael Savage, 'Working-class identities in the 1960s; revisiting the *Affluent Worker* Study', *Sociology* 39 (2005).

[6] Michael Savage, *Class Analysis and Social Transformation* (Buckingham, 2000), p. 151; Fiona Devine et al., *Rethinking Class: Culture, Identities and Lifestyles* (Basingstoke, 2004).

[7] Anthony Heath, Jean Martin, and Gabriella Elgenius, 'Who do we think we are? The decline of traditional social identities', *British Social Attitudes* 23 (2007), p. 4.

[8] Joseph Rowntree Foundation, *Inquiry into Income and Wealth* (York, 1995), vol. 2, p. 34, fig. 18.

[9] Florence Kondylis and Jonathan Wadsworth, 'Wages and Wage Inequality, 1970–2000', in Nicholas Crafts et al. (eds.), *Work and Pay in Twentieth-Century Britain*, (Oxford, 2007), p.80.

cleaners, nannies and the like largely from the native working and lower-middle classes.[10] A hierarchy of social classes was in some respects more entrenched at the turn of the century than in the England of the 1950s, a country still affected by 'wartime policy and rhetoric . . . [of] equality of sacrifice and provision'.[11]

Admittedly, there are questions—to some extent new ones—about the nature of the class system. Why do so many people still claim to be working-class? Who counts as working-class? A mere 38 per cent of the workforce were manual workers by 2001, compared with over 72 per cent in 1951: and even if low-grade clerical workers and the unemployed are counted as working-class, only about 50 per cent of the workforce would qualify by occupation. Yet responses to social surveys do not necessarily reflect the current occupational structure. Upwardly mobile working-class men and women often continue to regard themselves as working class.[12] Deindustrialised areas may retain their working-class ambience and culture.[13] Responses to surveys differ, moreover, according to how the question is put, at different points in time—the numbers identifying without any prompting as working class shot up in the 1983 election survey—and in different parts of the country.[14] Gendered patterns of class identification vary too. A study in north-east England in the early 1990s found women more likely to identify as working class than men, in contrast to the findings of other surveys.[15] One group of working-class women enrolled in 'caring' courses at a north-western Further Education college, also in the early 90s, are described by Beverley Skeggs as positively 'disidentifying' themselves as working class—not with any thought of upward mobility but rather as a way of asserting their respectability.[16] On the other hand Fiona Devine found upwardly-mobile teachers and doctors in Manchester quite happy to speak spontaneously of their origins in respectable working-class families.[17] Circumstances clearly alter perceptions of class and the way people talk about it, and may always have done so. In the later twentieth century there is perhaps a stronger tendency than in the past to fall back on the argument (not itself a new one) that the most important distinction is not between the middle and working classes but between what Bernice Martin terms 'respectable middle England' and a feckless proletariat or

[10] Bridget Anderson, *Doing the Dirty Work. The Global Politics of Domestic Labour* (London, 2000), pp. 86–7; Nicky Gregson and Michelle Lowe, *Servicing the Middle Classes. Class, gender and waged domestic labour in contemporary Britain* (London, 1994), pp. 122–51.

[11] Ross McKibbin, *Classes and Cultures. England, 1918–51* (Oxford, 1998), p. 531.

[12] See e.g. Brian Jackson and Dennis Marsden, *Education and the Working Class* (London 1962), p. 171.

[13] On Cheadle in Greater Manchester, see Michael Savage et al., 'Local habitus and working-class culture', in Devine, *Rethinking Class*, pp. 95–122.

[14] Compare e.g. Harriet Bradley, *Gender and Power in the Workplace* (Basingstoke 1999) and Michael Savage et al., 'Ordinary, ambivalent and defensive: class identities in the Northwest of England', *Sociology* 35 (2001), pp. 875–92.

[15] Bradley, *Gender and Power*, p.146; cf. Pamela Abbott and Roger Sapsford, *Women and Social Class* (London, 1987), pp. 94–5.

[16] Beverly Skeggs, *Formations of Class and Gender: Becoming Respectable* (London, 1997), pp. 75–97.

[17] Fiona Devine, 'Talking about class in Britain', in Fiona Devine and M. C. Waters (eds.), *Social Inequalities in Comparative Perspective* (Oxford, 2004), pp. 201–7.

'underclass'.[18] And yet this should not tempt us to change the categories of class analysis. 'Underclass' is not on the whole an identity that people choose to adopt; and when it is defined by objective criteria such as poverty or unemployment, or quantified as the 'bottom 20 per cent', it becomes clear that this is an unstable category—individuals and families move into it from, and out of it into, the ordinary working class.[19]

So the argument for carrying on writing about working-class history does seem fairly persuasive. As far as women are concerned, however, there are some further issues. Their place in the class has never been the same as that of men. McKibbin noted the '"politically" fractured' character of the working-class family, reflecting the traditional segregation of gender roles within the male-breadwinner household.[20] The housewife might identify as a consumer rather than a manual worker—one explanation for the gender gap in voting that was revealed when opinion poll data became available in the 1940s and 50s, and which may also have been present in the 1930s, reinforcing the Baldwinian Conservative ascendancy.[21] Insofar as they were waged workers, moreover, girls and women were less likely to have manual jobs; and the proportion of the female workforce that was in manual—and especially skilled manual—work declined steadily from 1931 onwards.[22] This meant that working women were much less likely to be unionized than men: before the expansion of white-collar and public-sector unions in the 1960s and 70s, organized labour was an overwhelmingly masculine world. How far women really belonged at all in a working class defined by male occupational status became a live issue among Marxist-feminist social scientists in the 1970s.

For sociologists there was also a practical issue that became increasingly fraught as the numbers of married women in paid employment grew after the Second World War. How should the class identity of such women be decided? Up to that point the accepted convention was that a woman's social class was determined by that of the head of the household she belonged to, normally her father or husband. Becoming an office worker or shop assistant, nurse or elementary schoolteacher, would not necessarily raise questions about the class identity of a working-class girl, given that she was unlikely to remain in employment after marriage (or at least after the birth of her first child). That system of classification had the advantage of simplicity, as it categorised the population by household. It also incidentally highlighted a gender gap in working-class social

[18] Bernice Martin, *A Sociology of Contemporary Cultural Change* (London, 1981), p. 57.

[19] See John Welshman, *Underclass: A History of the Excluded* (London, 2006), pp. 157–81; K. P. Sveinsson (ed.), *Who Cares about the White Working Class?* (London, 2009).

[20] *Classes and Cultures,* pp. 204, 518.

[21] Ina Zweiniger-Bargielowska, 'Explaining the gender gap: the Conservative Party and the women's vote, 1945–1964', in Martin Francis and Ina Zweiniger-Bargielowska (eds.), *The Conservatives and British Society, 1880–1990* (Cardiff, 1996), pp. 197–8.

[22] A. H. Halsey and Josephine Webb, *Twentieth-Century British Social Trends* (London, 2000), p. 295, Table 8.10.

mobility. Daughters were more likely to improve their class position by marriage than sons were to experience upward occupational mobility. When Ferdynand Zweig found girls in the 1950s less willing to accept the label 'working-class' than boys, he believed that was partly because they cherished hopes of making a good marriage.[23] But by the 1970s and 80s not only had it become normal for married women to return to the workforce after childbirth, the wives of manual workers were also increasingly likely to be employed in clerical or lower professional jobs. This prompted the question, why should a dual income, mixed-class household automatically be classified according to the occupational status of its male 'head'? To this there could be no wholly satisfactory answer.[24]

Much more rewarding for the study of working-class women than the traditional British, occupation-based definition of class is the cultural approach associated with Bourdieu.[25] For Bourdieu, social classes were 'the basis of the systems of classification which structure perception of the social world'; and gender was central to the way he conceptualized class. In a much quoted passage he wrote, 'Sexual properties are inseparable from class properties as the yellowness of a lemon is from its acidity: a class is defined in an essential respect by the place and value it gives to the two sexes and to their socially constituted dispositions'.[26] Moving away from the assumption that the resources at the disposal of families could be assessed in terms simply of income and material wealth, Bourdieu introduced the concepts of cultural and social capital—resources that are often provided by, or embodied in, women. He also elaborated on the role of taste and style in preserving the social order through hierarchies of class authority reinforced by symbolic violence.[27] For feminist academics who are 'scholarship girls' from working-class backgrounds this approach has been especially appealing, offering theoretical perspectives on their own experience of the class system—the pain of being made to feel inferior, of seeing parents humiliated, of feeling disloyalty to one's roots on moving up the social ladder, never quite belonging or getting it right. The historian Carolyn Steedman was one of the first to explore these themes in a book about her mother's life and her own South London childhood, *Landscape for a Good Woman* (London, 1986).[28] In sociology and cultural studies they are developed by scholars such as Valerie Walkerdine, Beverley Skeggs and Diane Reay. The continuing power of class cultures expressed through taste and style is a common

[23] Ferdynand Zweig, *Women's Life and Labour* (London, 1952), p. 122.

[24] Helen Roberts, 'The women and class debate', in David Morgan and Liz Stanley (eds.), *Debates in Sociology* (Manchester, 1993), pp. 52–68.

[25] See e.g. 'Representing the working classes', in Beverly Skeggs, *Class, Self, Culture* (London, 2004), pp. 96–118.

[26] Pierre Bourdieu, *Distinction. A Social Critique of the Judgment of Taste* (Abingdon, 1986), pp. xiiiiv, 107.

[27] Ibid., pp. 244–56, 511.

[28] For a more positive view of the upwardly mobile working-class girl, see her 'Writing the self: the end of the Scholarship Girl', in Jim McGuigan (ed.), *Cultural Methodologies* (London, 1997).

refrain. 'From house to dress, from accent to appearance, Eliza Doolittle is as present in the early twenty-first century as she was in the 1900s.'[29]

Recent work by feminist writers on popular discourses about working-class women invites comparison with the pioneering (if impressionistic) study of Ferdynand Zweig on 'women in industry' half a century ago. Zweig saw the working-class girl's class consciousness as quite different from that of a man, but very deeply felt. She 'suffers a great deal from the snobbishness of other classes', he wrote: so within the working-class community 'snobbishness is regarded as the worst of sins'. The girl who 'speaks posh' or gives herself airs will be ostracised. She aims to dress like a middle-class girl—to 'pass'—but can't quite bring it off because the clothes she can afford are too brightly coloured and made of cheap materials. This contributes to the profound sense of inferiority of working-class women, which Zweig considered 'in itself the distinguishing mark of the class'.[30] In the same way Skeggs's Further Education students worry obsessively about looking 'tarty' or 'dead common', while resenting the middle-class health visitors who compel them to prove their respectability.[31] The language of class is not used so overtly today as in the 1950s, and yet it is implicit in terms like 'chav' or 'Essex girl' and their regional equivalents.[32] These are class stereotypes which clearly can become a vehicle or pretext for symbolic violence. The 'Essex girl', unlike the 'Essex man', is apolitical—she is vulgar, brassy and oversexed, and may well be that familiar bogy in modern discourse of the 'underclass', the young working-class single mother or 'teenage pram-pusher'. She may be portrayed with some affection, as in the 1990s BBC sitcom 'Birds of a Feather'.[33] But abuse aimed at real-life Essex girl and TV celebrity Jade Goody—'the most hated woman in Britain', 'a slapper with a face like a pig'[34]—tells another story. Angela McRobbie has argued that we should see the early twenty-first century BBC television makeover show 'What Not To Wear' as an exercise in class-based 'symbolic violence'.[35] The audience watched with amusement as a 'victim', typically lower-middle or working-class, was subjected to humiliating inspection by two well-educated upper-middle class 'experts' and given tips about how to bring her appearance up to scratch.

The message is that the class consciousness of the working-class woman is—and has been historically—scarred by the abuse and condescension heaped upon

[29] Valerie Walkerdine, Helen Lucey and June Melody, *Growing Up Girl. Psychosocial Explorations of Gender and Class* (Basingstoke, 2001), p. 53. See also Pat Mahony and Christine Zmroczek (eds.), *Class Matters. Working-Class Women's Perspectives on Social Class* (Abingdon, 1997).

[30] Zweig, *Women's Life and Labour*, pp. 121–5. The book is based on interviews in Lancashire, Cheshire, Staffordshire, Yorkshire, and London.

[31] Skeggs, *Formations of Class and Gender*, p. 3.

[32] Imogen Tyler, 'Chav mum, chav scum. Class disgust in contemporary Britain', *Feminist Media Studies* 8 (2008), pp. 17–24. For regional synonyms for 'chav' see pp. 20–1.

[33] See also Germaine Greer, 'Long live the Essex girl', *Guardian*, 5 March 2001.

[34] Press comments cited by Michael Parkinson, *Radio Times*, 8 April 2009.

[35] Angela McRobbie, 'Notes on "What Not To Wear" and post-feminist symbolic violence', in Lisa Adkins and Beverly Skeggs (eds.), *Feminism after Bourdieu* (Oxford, 2004), pp. 99–109.

her by social superiors. Lacking the positive, workplace-based collective consciousness of the male manual worker, a woman tends to regard 'working-class' as a 'spoiled identity'.[36] The point can be overstated—there are positive values associated with working-class women's nurturing, family roles, and also with the identification with 'ordinary' people against the pretensions of the 'snobs'. But it is nevertheless worth keeping in mind as we ask how things have changed for working-class women in the past half-century.

The focus in this essay will be on published sources on women's roles in family and community, and the experiences of workplace and education. But one must first sketch in a context. A woman who lived through these decades would have experienced four very different trend-periods: the affluent post-war era—real incomes rose by 42.7 per cent between 1950 and 1965—which featured the mid-century marriage boom and baby booms; the strike-prone, inflationary 1970s, when accelerating divorce and illegitimacy rates were accompanied by feminist criticism of the traditional family; the 1980s, with accelerated deindustrialisation, labour market deregulation, privatization, and unemployment—bringing for some working-class families significant long-term economic deterioration, in relative terms at least; and the more prosperous 1990s. The impact of economic change varied a great deal regionally and locally, moreover, as did the impact of immigration. One early assessment of the effects of deindustrialisation on women's work contrasted the north-eastern coalfields, where new production-line factory jobs became available for women as mining contracted, with Lancashire, where there was little new industrial development as the cotton industry declined, creating significant female unemployment in an area with a long tradition of women's industrial work. The effects of globalisation in East London differed again. In the clothing trade there, women—many of them home workers—kept their jobs but experienced wage cuts and intensification of work pressures.[37] London did of course offer opportunities to qualified women in the service sector. But for the poorest, carers especially, in inner-city areas there was a moment of acute crisis as benefit and welfare service cuts coincided with the recession of the early 1980s.[38]

Studies of the working-class family and community in the 1950s and 60s still reflected traditional assumptions about married life; and they showed an expectation that the modern middle-class 'companionate' relationship between husband and wife would become the norm, replacing the traditional working-class partnership in which there tended to be a rigid division of gender roles.[39] But the most important finding of these studies—first spelled out fully in Young and Willmott's work on Bethnal Green—was the importance of extended family

[36] Skeggs, *Formations of Class and Gender*, p. 95; Savage, *Class Analysis*, pp. 109–13, 116.

[37] Linda McDowell and Doreen Massey, 'A woman's place?', in Doreen Massey and John Allen (eds.), *Geography Matters! A Reader* (Cambridge, 1984), pp. 137–46.

[38] Paul Harrison, *Inside the Inner City* (London, 1985), pp. 171–9, 246–52.

[39] On the optimistic tone of this literature see Angela Davis, 'A critical perspective on British social surveys and community studies and their accounts of married life', *Cultural and Social History* 6 (2009).

networks in the traditional working-class community.[40] Dominated by women and with a particularly strong mother-daughter bond, these networks were the most important element in neighbourhood mutual support systems and added greatly to the resources (in Bourdieu's terms, the social capital) of the nuclear families that made them up. Although the community study came in for criticism as a genre for its lack of theoretical rigour, both sociologists and historians have broadly accepted this emphasis on the extended family and 'neighbouring' as hallmarks of working-class community life.

There was also a good deal of interest in the sexual politics of working-class families, and an attempt to associate extreme patriarchal or matriarchal variants of the family with communities of different sorts. This was rather more controversial. Madeline Kerr's study of an inner-city Liverpool slum district led Josephine Klein to suggest that the Lancashire Irish might be inclined towards matriarchy.[41] The community Kerr called 'Ship Street' did seem to fit that model, with married daughters actually living with their mothers whenever this was feasible and husbands in a very peripheral role. But this district, where families with over ten children were still common, was highly atypical of mid-century England, and it was chosen for study for precisely that reason. Kerr was a social psychologist who had done fieldwork in Jamaica and wanted to replicate her research in an equally deprived English community. She chose 'Ship Street' because the results of psychometric tests carried out at a local play centre resembled those of Jamaican peasant children rather than English children of the same age. On the other hand, the patriarchal ethos of the traditional, role-segregated northern working-class family may have been exaggerated in *Coal is Our Life*, a classic study of a mining community near Leeds.[42] The authors (three male academics) saw the married women of 'Ashton' as downtrodden and under their husbands' thumbs, not apparently aware that some Yorkshire miners' wives took a different view. In the words of one wife, quoted in the *New Left Review*, 'In reality [the woman is] the pivot of the whole community. She bolsters him, he hands over his money to her, she runs the home without any interference from him. She herself brings up the children. She also bolsters up his self-esteem and makes it possible for him to go on thinking of himself as a fine fellow'.[43] A woman might display confidence and autonomy even within the archetypal male-breadwinner family. In practice, as Elizabeth Roberts's oral history evidence suggested, whether the husband or the wife had the upper hand in a marriage was likely to depend on personality as much as anything else.[44]

[40] Michael Young and Peter Willmott, *Family and Kinship in East London* (London, 1957).

[41] Madeline Kerr, *The People of Ship Street* (London, 1958); Josephine Klein, *Samples from English Cultures* (London, 1965), vol. 1, p.176.

[42] Norman Dennis et al., *Coal is Our Life* (London, 1956).

[43] John Rex, 'Weekend in Dinlock: a discussion', *New Left Review*, May-June 1960, p. 3. On the background to this feature on a film by Clancy Sigal, which also depicted the miner's wife as a victim of male oppression, see Stuart Laing, *Representations of Working-Class Life, 1957–1964* (Basingstoke, 1986), pp. 47–57.

[44] Elizabeth Roberts, *A Woman's Place* (Oxford, 1984), pp.110–24.

More convincing as representative of post-war experience was the series of community studies, contemporary with or following the Bethnal Green research, which set out to investigate the effects of socio-economic change on working-class families. What happened when they were rehoused on a council estate, or moved to a mixed-class suburb, or lived in an expanding industrial town, or became significantly better off?[45] Similar questions were asked in the *Affluent Worker* study in Luton, which used the social survey method. To summarise the findings very broadly, it turned out that such families might develop some features of the middle-class family but not others. Extended family contacts became more limited when people moved out of traditional working-class communities, lifestyles became more domestic and centred on the nuclear family, the roles of husbands and wives more 'symmetrical'. But patterns of sociability remained distinctive, even among affluent workers—more focused on family and neighbours, with less participation in local associational groups and less entertainment in the home than was typical of the middle-class lifestyle. The working-class wife now went out to work and shared more leisure activities with her husband, but she was less likely to develop new roles as hostess or committee woman.

One development noted in various genres of writing was the decline in the status and authority of 'Mum'. Based above all on her role as manager of the household budget for families on the edge of poverty, and possibly—as McKibbin notes—stronger than ever in wartime and the depression of the 1930s, her authority contracted in the post-war decades as poverty receded.[46] There are interestingly gendered perspectives on this phenomenon. It was working-class men who had chiefly dwelt on, and sometimes sentimentalised, her image and it was men who chiefly lamented the disappearance of the powerful maternal figure.[47] For women, whether family members or social observers, she often represented a problem—manipulative, conservative, apt to take self-sacrifice too far for her own good or that of the family, but sometimes also very hard on her daughters, not to speak of daughters-in-law.[48] One might expect, too, that mothers and grandmothers themselves would have welcomed the transition to a regime in which children could be indulged rather than dominated. Yet Elizabeth Roberts did find some signs in her north Lancashire interviews in the late 1980s of unhappiness at the perception that 'a mother's work was not so

[45] J. M. Mogey, *Family and Neighbourhood. Two Studies in Oxford* (London, 1956); Peter Willmott and Michael Young, *Family and Class in a London Suburb* (London, 1960), and *The Symmetrical Family* (1973); Margaret Stacey, *Tradition and Change* (Oxford, 1960).

[46] McKibbin, *Classes and Cultures*, pp. 169–79, 519.

[47] Young and Willmott, *Family and Kinship*, pp. 44–61, 187–92; Richard Hoggart, *The Uses of Literacy* (London, 1957), pp. 38–47; Jeremy Seabrook, *What Went Wrong?* (London, 1978), pp. 122–5. For a defence of Hoggart against the charge of sentimentality, see 'Hoggart and women', in Sulan Owen (ed.), *Richard Hoggart and Cultural Studies* (Basingstoke, 2008).

[48] See e.g. Carolyn Steedman, *Landscape for a Good Woman*; Margery Spring Rice, *Working-Class Wives* (London, 1939); Annette Kuhn, *Family Secrets* (London, 1995). Madeline Kerr made no bones about her distaste for the domineering matriarchs of 'Ship Street'.

important as it had once been'.[49] Cultures associated with motherhood were by no means classless at the end of the century: for example, women from manual working-class families were two and a half times as likely to have a birth outside marriage as women from non-manual backgrounds.[50]

At the turn of the century two snapshots of change are provided by research projects which have replicated the mid-century Bethnal Green study and a study of Swansea that was modelled upon it.[51] The contrast in the way change is reported in these 'restudies' could hardly be more stark. This is partly due to social differences between the communities they describe, and above all the effects of immigration in East London. Swansea's population was now more stable than it had been in 1960, whereas Bethnal Green is described as 'changed so profoundly that it was hardly any longer the same place'. Back in the 1950s, 83 per cent of its population had been born in London: in 2001 35 per cent of the population of Tower Hamlets was born outside the UK.[52] Conflict between the white working class and the mainly Bangladeshi immigrant community over access to welfare support, education, and housing are issues that dominate *The New East End.* It was above all amongst the older *women*—'the local granny—the archetypal East End "Mum" . . . with a busy extended family revolving around her'—that hostility to Bangladeshis was strongest.[53] But the authors dwell too on destructive effects on the family of the 'new individualism', and of a welfare system focused on individual rights that weakens marriage and men's family roles. Women lose out in this account, as the 'social capital' created by the extended family is eroded by the state. They may become single mothers for strategic reasons, as a way of securing benefits and preferential access to social housing. But most single mothers would prefer to be married and have the support of female in-laws. Many older women have no contact with their sons' children. In the Swansea study, on the other hand, the emphasis is on important elements of continuity in parenting and partnering, and the adaptation of the extended family to high rates of divorce and remarriage. Women, as the authors comment, are 'still at the heart of kinship networks'.[54]

A common feature of social change in Swansea and East London is the increase in women's employment—indeed the authors of *The New East End* were struck by the feminisation of the Bethnal Green labour market, with the decline in industry and expansion of paid work in caring and '*human relations* activities', much of it under the auspices of the welfare state. 'Working for the National Family' is their description of women's employment in occupations of that

[49] Elizabeth Roberts, *Women and Families. An Oral History, 1940–70* (Oxford, 1995), pp. 150–4.

[50] 'Trends in births outside marriage', *Population Trends*, 81 (1995), p. 17.

[51] Geoff Dench et al., *The New East End; Kinship, Race and Conflict* (London, 2006). Colin Rosser and C. C. Harris, *The Family and Social Change: A Study of Family and Kinship in a South Wales Town* (London, 1965) is rerun as Nickie Charles et al., *Families in Transition. Social Change, Family Formation and Kin Relationships* (Bristol, 2008).

[52] Dench et al., *New East End*, pp. 14, 23.

[53] Ibid., p.187. [54] Charles et al., *Families in Transition*, pp. 224–5.

kind.[55] For some it offered a decent living and an escape from dependence on uncongenial husbands and relatives, as well as status within the community. How far labour market changes for working-class women can in general be seen in such a favourable light is however open to question.

The increase in all social classes of women's paid work is a major feature of the later twentieth century. In 1950 40 per cent of women between the ages of 16 and 59 were in employment; in 2001 the proportion was 70 per cent. Working-class single women had of course always had paid jobs: the new development was the rise in workforce participation of married women, with older women returning to work as the children grew up, and by the 1980s and 90s mothers continuing to work through the child-bearing years in their 20s and 30s.[56] What made this possible was the increased availability of part-time employment—in 1951 only about 11 per cent of women's jobs were part-time; in 2001, 46 per cent.[57] Oral history testimony and contemporary social surveys make it clear that there was little desire on the part of working-class housewives to reject the traditional male-breadwinner/female homemaker family arrangement.[58] As real wages rose in the middle decades of the century that became a feasible basis for the family economy for more and more working people. Wives worked for extras for the home, to improve the family lifestyle, but their identity remained primarily that of housewife. They remained at a disadvantage in the labour market partly for that reason.[59] Part-time work was particularly badly paid and this has continued to be the case despite equal pay legislation in the 1970s and after.[60] Women, carers especially, accept low pay because of the convenience of part-time work. And yet—as always—many women were not supported by a breadwinner's wage; and as men's jobs in industry were lost in the last quarter of the century the numbers of women doing low-paid part-time jobs to provide a basic subsistence for their families increased. Nor did this necessarily improve their status within the workforce. The classic process of de-skilling, in which cheap female labour is used to reduce the number of skilled men's jobs, was a general feature of the British clothing industry in the 1970s. In the 1980s women trapped by a desperate need to earn—including older women, ethnic minorities, and carers—were used to pave the way for systematic wage cuts when NHS cleaning services were privatised.[61] Trade Unionists understandably lamented

[55] Dench, *New East End*, pp 124–7.

[56] Sara Connolly and Mary Gregory, 'Women and work since 1970', in Crafts, *Work and Pay*, p. 169.

[57] Halsey and Webb, *Twentieth-Century British Social Trends*, p. 276.

[58] See e.g. Roberts, *Women and Families*, pp. 131–3, 234–5; Margaret Stacey et al., *Power, Persistence and Change. A Second Study of Banbury* (London, 1975).

[59] Marilyn Porter, 'Standing on the edge; working-class housewives and the world of work', in Jacline West (ed.), *Work, Women and the Labour Market* (London, 1982).

[60] Connolly and Gregory, 'Women and work', pp. 161–2.

[61] Angela Coyle, 'Sex and skill in the regulation of the clothing industry', in West, *Work, Women and the Labour Market;* and her 'Going private', in Feminist Review (ed.), *Waged Work: A Reader* (London, 1986).

the substitution of part-time women's jobs for 'real', full-time jobs. The assumption that women worked for pin-money lingered on.[62]

Sallie Westwood's ethnographic study of workers at a Leicester hosiery firm is one of several grim accounts of women's factory work in the 1970s and '80s. Often segregated in one way or another as 'women's work', most of it was unskilled or semi-skilled, hard and monotonous—and it did not pay a living wage. All of the women Westwood worked with as a participant observer in this project wanted to keep their children out of the factory.[63] Of a West Midlands car components factory she had worked in Ruth Cavendish wrote, 'If you were a woman, you could walk into the factory on your sixteenth birthday, get a job on the assembly line, and stay there till you retired at sixty. There was no promotion off the line'.[64] At Churchman's tobacco factory in Bristol, as described by Anna Pollert, unskilled women's work was regarded as inferior to unskilled men's work by both women and men. Girls dreamed of escaping from the factory on marriage but often found they had to continue because they could not manage without the money. But even the married women who worked full-time regarded themselves as housewives and felt guilt at neglecting the housework. 'Work' was the province of men.[65] If we compare these Marxist-feminist accounts with Dennis Marsden's description of 'mill girls' and factory culture in mid-century Huddersfield, there is agreement that the factory could remain a very male domain and a hard place for a woman to keep her respectability and self-respect.[66]

Yet there is also much evidence to support McKibbin's observation that men and women workers would often react in similar ways in the workplace when in similar circumstances.[67] Male semi-skilled and unskilled workers as well as women disliked the tyranny of the production line. Complaints of 'speeding up', work intensification, and authoritarian management are common to both sexes, as they had been intermittently for the previous century. New office technology and management systems in the 1980s meant that stress of this kind was now experienced by white-collar as well as manual workers.[68] But management styles varied. Kate Purcell, working in 1980 in a north-western electrical engineering factory that was run on more relaxed and friendly lines, found that women enjoyed workplace sociability as much as men.[69] Trade

[62] R. A. Hammond, 'The Trade Unions and the conflict between work and home', in T. S. Epstein et al., *Women, Work and Family in Britain and Germany* (London, 1986); Sallie Westwood, *All Day, Every Day* (Leicester, 1984), p. 73.

[63] Ibid., pp. 222–3.

[64] Ruth Cavendish, *Women on the Line* (London, 1982), p. 76.

[65] Anna Pollert, *Girls, Wives, Factory Lives* (Manchester 1981), pp. 73–125.

[66] Dennis Marsden, 'In the mill', in Brian Jackson, *Working-Class Community* (London, 1968), pp. 80–4.

[67] McKibbin, *Classes and Cultures*, pp. 136–7, 143–4.

[68] Bradley, *Gender and Power in the Workplace*, p.121, reports widespread complaints that working conditions for office workers had deteriorated, particularly in the public sector.

[69] Kate Purcell, 'Female manual workers, fatalism and the reinforcement of inequalities', in David Robbins et al. (eds.) *Rethinking Social Inequality* (Aldershot, 1982); cf. McKibbin, *Cultures and Classes*, pp. 136–7.

Union associational culture remained largely a male preserve because out-of-hours functions and meetings were hard to reconcile with women's domestic commitments. But women workers were increasingly likely to belong to a trade union, and as with male workers circumstances affected their perceptions of it. It was not only women who suspected the unions at times of colluding with management against the interests of the workers—or felt, towards the end of the century, that trade unions were simply too weak to be much use.[70] Purcell argues persuasively against the stereotype of women as 'passive and fundamentally exploitable workers'. There were elements of fatalism in the outlook of the women workers she got to know, but the same was true of unskilled and semi-skilled male workers, and in both cases it reflected an accurate perception of their powerlessness.

So has there been any movement in the past half-century towards a sense of the woman's identity as a worker and the rebalancing of commitments to work and the home? Survey responses show a significant difference between the attitudes of parents in the routine manual and professional classes towards women's roles: manual workers are less likely to agree that mothers should work full-time when their youngest child starts school, and more likely to think that 'being a housewife is just as fulfilling as working for pay'.[71] A recently reported study of low-earning young adults in Bristol found that traditional attitudes to gender roles still prevailed.[72] On the other hand Harriet Bradley's 1990s study of five workplaces in the Tyne and Wear area found signs that 'a new gender order' was emerging there, in which 'women were almost as ambitious as men for promotion' and 'were as likely as men to make statements indicating strong commitment to employment'. 'In the North East at least', she writes, 'dual-earning is becoming the *social norm*, replacing the expectation of breadwinner male and dependant wife'.[73] Interestingly, this new commitment to work was displayed more strongly by factory workers in a pharmaceutical plant than by women workers in the four service sector organisations in her study—a bank, a supermarket chain, a group of hospitals and a branch office of a civil service agency.[74] But a turn-of-the-century survey of call centres—often thought of as a particularly proletarianised form of white-collar work, 'human battery farms'—showed that 50 per cent or more of the managers were women in most of the firms included in the study. Many female employees were not looking for promotion, but for those who did there were opportunities, and it seemed that promotion went by merit.[75]

70 Ibid., p. 148; Bradley, *Gender and Power in the Workplace*, pp. 196–9.

71 Geoff Dench, 'Exploring parents' views', *British Social Attitudes* 25, 2009, Table 5.5, p. 119.

72 Harriet Bradley, 'Catching up? Changing inequalities of gender at work and in the family in the UK', in Devine and Waters, *Social Inequalities.*, pp. 271–5.

73 Bradley, *Gender and Power in the Workplace*, pp. 103–4.

74 Ibid., p. 108.

75 V. Beit, 'A female ghetto?' and D. Holman, 'Employee well-being in call centres', in Stephen Deery and Nick Kinnie, *Call Centres and Human Resource Management. A Cross-National Perspective* (Basingstoke, 2004).

In Bradley's study it was, unsurprisingly, the younger women who were most ambitious. What can we say about the education of working-class girls in this half-century? Here again there is evidence of some change in attitudes towards employment and family roles, and this fits with the pattern of modestly improving achievement by working-class girls in the past three decades. A study of Ealing secondary schoolgirls in the 1970s which was repeated in the 1990s found the later generation much more assertive about plans for a job or career. For the white girls in these surveys this went with a more cautious view of marriage—in 1972 82 per cent said they wanted to marry compared with 45 per cent in 1991, when 46 per cent were unsure and nearly one in ten were clear that they did not. It also went with a more positive view of the advantages of being a girl—in 1972 25 per cent would have preferred to be a boy, in 1991 only 16 per cent.[76] Already in the 1970s girls were achieving better results than boys in 16-plus school examinations and between 1979 and 1991 the rate of improvement in results was faster for girls than boys in all social classes. By 1993–4 more girls than boys were getting three A Levels.[77] But this did not lead to a significant increase in the chances for a working-class girl of going to university. Participation rates in higher education remained grossly unequal across the social classes: in 1998–9 these stood at 72 per cent for the professional class, 29 per cent for skilled non-manual, 17–18 per cent for skilled and semi-skilled manual, and a mere 13 per cent for children from the unskilled manual working class.[78] Within the working classes, it was not until the twenty-first century that more girls than boys went on to higher education. Even then they tended to avoid the more traditional universities, preferring post-1992 universities where they could study vocational courses while living at home.[79] And girls from the poorest families, those entitled to free school meals, were more than three times less likely to go on to higher education (9 per cent as against 30 per cent) if they were from a white working-class as distinct from an ethnic minority background.[80] Distinctive class patterns of behaviour clearly remain entrenched despite change over time. What lay behind them?

A problem of persistent working-class underachievement in education was diagnosed half a century ago, although it was not until the 1970s and '80s that questions began to be asked specifically about the underachievement of girls. Studies in the 1960s and after found evidence of very different styles of pre-school child rearing in middle and working-class families. Working-class

[76] Sue Sharpe, '*Just Like a Girl*'. *How Girls Learn to be Women: From the Seventies to the Nineties* (London, 1994), pp. 239–92. West Indian and Asian girls had a more negative view of both marriage and the advantages of being a girl, although responses from Asian girls also suggested that things had improved between the '70s and the '90s.

[77] Andy Furlong, 'Education and the reproduction of class-based inequalities', in Helen Jones (ed.), *Towards a Classless Society?* (London, 1997).

[78] Office for National Statistics, *Social Trends*, 30 (2000), p. 56 table 3.13.

[79] Sarah Evans, 'In a different place. Working-class girls and higher education', *Sociology*, 43 (2009).

[80] Stijn Broecke and Jospeh Haned, *Gender Gaps in Higher Education Participation* (DIUS Research Report OG-14, 2008).

mothers spoke to and played with their children less and were more authoritarian. The outcome was that they began school with a less-developed command of language.[81] Valerie Walkerdine and others argue persuasively that the effect of such research has been to pathologise working-class family life, and mothers especially.[82] Class differences in parenting are the result of poverty and inequality: working-class women spend more time on housework and have to train children to do without what cannot be afforded. But there is general agreement that a mismatch between the culture of home and the norms of the schools can affect the prospects of working-class children from the time they start school. As they go on to secondary school this disadvantage may be compounded not only by material factors but by their parents' lack of understanding of the system, perhaps too by a preference not to send their children to a 'posh' local school which will be the school of choice for middle-class families (insofar as these use the state system rather than educating their children privately).

A further dimension of disadvantage is identified in peer-group cultures that may develop amongst working-class schoolchildren. For girls this may not take on the aggressively anti-school tone found among working-class boys.[83] But it does entail resistance to school work, investing time in friendships, appearance, 'grooming' for marriage.[84] Girls who work hard run the risk of rejection by the peer group as 'snobs'. This is a culture that imposes its own limits on achievement and employment prospects. Yet a study of six Birmingham schools in 1979 found that in practice jobs open to female school-leavers were for the most part far from attractive. Factory work was seen as 'boring, insecure and unpleasant'. Office work offered less prospect of promotion than was sometimes imagined and required girls to 'pass' as middle class by 'talking posh and acting snobby'. Sexual harassment was common in both and girls who objected were liable to be dismissed. In the recession of 1979–84, things got worse, as the local unemployment rate rose to 15 per cent.[85] Incentives to do well at school, insofar as these are influenced by job prospects, were evidently not strong. Incentives to look for fulfilment in family roles were as strong as ever and doubtless do much to explain the continuing high rate of teenage pregnancy amongst working-class girls in the later twentieth century at a time when, in the middle classes, the mean age at first childbirth was rising sharply.[86]

In the 1980s and after labour market changes did create more opportunities for girls with some qualifications, while openings for those without became

[81] National Children's Bureau, *From Birth to Seven* (London, 1972).

[82] Valerie Walkerdine and Helen Lucey, *Democracy in the Kitchen. Regulating Mothers and Socialising Daughters* (London, 1989); Gillian Plummer, *Failing Working-Class Girls* (Stoke-on-Trent, 2000).

[83] P. E. Willis, *Learning to Labour: How Working-Class Kids Get Working-Class Jobs* (Farnborough, 1977).

[84] Angela McRobbie, 'Working-class girls and the culture of femininity', in Women's Studies Group, Centre for Contemporary Cultural Studies, *Women Take Issue* (London, 1978); Valerie Hey, *The Company She Keeps. An Ethnography of Girls' Friendships* (Buckingham, 1997).

[85] Christine Griffin, *Typical Girls?* (London, 1985).

[86] Although McRobbie's research on Birmingham schoolgirls (above, n. 84) suggests that it also had something to do with a taboo on contraception for girls who were not 'going steady': the risk of pregnancy was less threatening than the risk of losing one's reputation.

increasingly scarce. As divorce rates rose and marriage rates fell there was less reason to count on a secure future as a wife and mother. Schools came under pressure to improve success rates at GCSE and A Level, and with the coming of mass higher education universities became less forbidding places for the working-class girl. In the 1980s feminists celebrated and the media even glamourised the opening of higher education to mature working-class women students.[87] Willy Russell's play *Educating Rita,* first performed in London in 1980, became an awarding-winning film (1983) starring Julie Walters and Michael Caine. By the early twenty-first century more working-class families were expecting their children to go on to higher education.[88] Yet it still remained less straightforward for such girls to go on to university than for their middle-class peers.[89] The latter were bound, with family support, on a path that was intended to secure their future as professionals, within the same social class. There was no sense of betraying one's class, treating one's parents' culture as inferior, imposing an excessive financial burden on family resources. The pervasiveness of class cultures in education is well captured by feminist researchers who pay attention to subjectivities and to class as a component in young women's identities.

Interestingly—perhaps surprisingly—it is in politics that change in gender roles appears to be most clearly marked. The 14–17 per cent gender gap in voting found in the 1940s and '50s, with women favouring the Conservatives, had all but vanished by the 1980s. Women born in the 1940s and '50s proved to be more likely to vote Labour than their male contemporaries.[90] Nor does this half-century look altogether like one in which—to quote McKibbin's verdict on 1918–51—'state and economy were dominated by men, and this changed little over the period'.[91] White and ethnic minority women staged some high profile strikes in the 1960s and '70s—the Ford sewing machinists (1968), Imperial Typewriters (1974), Grunwick (1976–8)—and, more importantly, were active in the public service strikes of the 1978–9 'Winter of Discontent', in the 1985–6 'Battle for Fleet Street' and in support groups for the miners' strike of 1984–5. Much has been written about entrenched opposition within the labour movement to women's activism, and not only from trade union or party officials. 'The first hurdle you have to get over is your husband', a Midlands woman told Bea Campbell, describing her experience as a shop-steward in the hospital workers' dispute.[92] Oral history based studies are however beginning to appear suggesting that a 'reconfigured' pattern of working-class politics was emerging in the 1980s

[87] Taking Liberties Collective, *Learning the Hard Way. Women's Oppression in Men's Education* (Basingstoke, 1989).

[88] Ted Wragg and Mark Johnson, 'Higher Education: a class act', *British Social Attitudes*, 16 (2000).

[89] Diane Reay et al., *Degrees of Choice. Class, Race, Gender and Higher Education* (Stoke on Trent, 2005), pp. 83–107.

[90] Pippa Norris, 'Gender: a gender-generation gap', in G. Evans and P. Norris (eds.), *Critical Elections. British Parties and Voters in Long-Term Perspective* (London, 1999), pp. 151–61.

[91] *Classes and Cultures*, p. 518.

[92] Beatrix Campbell, *Wigan Pier Revisited. Poverty and Politics in the Eighties* (London, 1984), p. 193.

in which more leadership roles were taken by women within some trade unions and in non-traditional forms of community politics.[93]

A survey on this scale can do no more than sketch the contours of the subject and sample the available sources, but I hope it has shown that working-class women in England still do have some sort of collective history, and that it has in the process lent support to the case for a 'class-focused' study of social change in the contemporary world. The aim, to echo McKibbin, is not to treat class categories as rigid, but to use social class as a framework that 'allows us to generalize while accepting that there are exceptions to every rule'.[94] Without such a framework social historians will find it difficult to make effective use of the sources available to them, or to understand the complex pattern of shifts and continuities in gender regimes in England since the mid-twentieth century.

[93] Tara Martin, 'The beginning of Labor's end? Britain's "Winter of Discontent" and working-class women's activism', and Jean Spence and Carol Stephenson, '"Side by side with our men?" Women's activism, community, and gender in the 1984–1985 British Miners' Strike', in *International Labor and Working-Class History* 75 (2009).

[94] *Classes and Cultures*, p. v.

7

The London Cabbie and the Rise of Essex Man

John Davis

In order to understand why Labour never did become the 'natural party of government' in the post-war years, we need to look at those working-class groups whose support for the Labour Party proved to be conditional—in particular at the working class outside blue-collar industry and outside the Labour heartlands. They are epitomised by the 'Essex man' of the 1980s, culturally working-class but politically beyond Labour's reach during the Thatcher years. London's taxi drivers belonged to this group, their reflectiveness and articulacy making them fruitful research subjects.

I

London's taxi drivers formed a kind of medieval guild in the 'swinging city'. Cabbies were free spirits, protective of their status and their rights, both sheltered and inhibited by elaborate trade regulation. Their trade originated in the seventeenth century, but it had assumed its modern form in the mid-Victorian period, the principal subsequent change being motorisation in the 1900s. Many of its regulatory provisions were, though, remnants of the horse age: the notorious, if unenforced, requirement to carry a bale of hay, for example, or the rule preventing drivers from leaving their cab unattended for fear that it might bolt. The regulatory framework enforced by the Home Office and the Metropolitan Police was reminiscent in its elaborate nature of the rules governing early railways. The dimensions of cabs were prescribed along with, after motorisation, their tight turning circle. Similarly, vehicles were subjected to stringent annual tests and decommissioned after ten years, but these quality controls were augmented by provisions suggesting—at least to those touched by them—that the cabbie was still regarded as a coachman without a master, potentially unruly unless firmly controlled. Cabmen had to satisfy a character test to gain their badge, which they had to wear at all times when on duty and during court appearances. They were obliged not merely to demonstrate familiarity with the metropolis and an ability to read a map, but to recite by rote, during a notoriously demeaning inquisition, arbitrarily constructed routes across the capital.

Drivers resented much of this regulation, and its application by what they considered an over-zealous police force, but regulation defined the London taxi fraternity more sharply than was the case in any other city, giving the licensed drivers an *esprit de corps* lacking amongst their minicab rivals. And, as with most guilds, regulation conferred privileges as well as drawbacks. The purpose-built 'black cab' cost roughly as much as a Jaguar, but it offered brand recognition, being as much of a London icon as the Routemaster bus. The right to 'ply for hire' which the badge conferred—the exclusive right to pick up a customer hailing him in the street—was the licensed taxi-driver's greatest commercial asset. It *was* a right rather than a duty: a licensed driver was not required to stop when hailed, even if his cab was empty and advertising itself as for hire.[1] Having stopped, however, a driver could not refuse a trip within a six-mile radius of the point of hire.[2] These regulations provided the taxi-driver with an element of serendipity in his working day, as he tried to gauge whether a potential customer would request a 'roader'—the lucrative outing to Southampton or Norwich—or demand an irksome trek to a suburb on the other side of London from his garage or home, with little prospect of a return fare.

The pros and cons of the regulatory regime were demonstrated most strikingly by 'The Knowledge'. Only by passing the Knowledge of London test, applied with sadistic rigour by the Public Carriage Office examiners since 1843, could a driver gain the green badge allowing him to ply for hire across London (suburban drivers working only in their home area gained a yellow badge from a less exacting test). To pass 'the Knowledge' a driver had to master 400 theoretical trips devised by the PCO and recite those chosen by the examiner. The Knowledge was essentially an extremely demanding memory test, compared by drivers to learning the works of Shakespeare by heart.[3] 'Knowledge Boys' learned their routes 'on the ground', covering them by moped, and the majority also had to learn their routes while doing a day job to sustain them. Many found the burden intolerable: the drop-out rate in 1969 was 57 per cent.[4] Almost all who stayed the course eventually passed, however, but in the 1960s the ordeal took about two years. Drivers nonetheless liked the Knowledge once they had passed it. It was a selling point, reassuring customers that cab drivers—unlike those driving most minicabs—knew their way around an intricate city. Moreover, as the authorities had no power to limit the number of badges issued, the Knowledge provided protection against a driver surplus. It was an apprenticeship, and valued as such.[5]

[1] *Report of the Departmental Committee on the London Taxicab Trade* [Maxwell Stamp Committee], Cmnd. 4483, London, HMSO, (1970), 11.

[2] Beyond six miles driver and passenger could negotiate a fare, at least until 1969, when longer trips became chargeable at double the metered rate, largely to end the exploitation of tourists arriving at Heathrow Airport.

[3] Maurice Levinson, *Taxi* (London, 1963), p. 24.

[4] Maxwell Stamp Committee, *Report* 24.

[5] Transport and General Workers Union, Cab Section, 'Evidence to the Committee on the London Cab Trade', 20 November 1968, TGWU Archive, Modern Records Centre, University of Warwick, MSS.126/TG/RES/P/16/2, 2.

It inevitably influenced recruitment, ensuring that London's licensed taxi service was never exactly an 'entry trade' like taxi services elsewhere—a first step on the ladder for new immigrants. The Knowledge disadvantaged those unfamiliar with London and with the English language. It favoured those from cabbing backgrounds, like Reuben Cohen, whose family produced thirteen drivers from 1889 and who passed the Knowledge in four weeks in 1971.[6] Sixty per cent of 'Knowledge Boys' surveyed in 1969 had relatives in the trade.[7] It also favoured those with the capital to allow them to study full-time: Alf Townsend, learning the Knowledge in the early 1960s, noted that the Jewish boys 'were subsidised by their dads, many of them already cabmen'.[8]

The strong Jewish presence in the business suggests that cabbing *had* been an entry trade in the late nineteenth century. It explained the location of so much of the industry, before the decline of the major garages after 1960, in London's East End, where 'from the cobbled back streets of Hackney, Bethnal Green and Shoreditch, diesels clattered day and night'.[9] The *Jewish Chronicle* estimated in 1971 that 5,000 of London's 13,000 drivers were Jewish; 32 per cent of Hackney's Jewish population in that year's census worked in transport, most of them as cabbies.[10] The entrepreneurially-minded sought to become owner-drivers or garage proprietors, but cabbing was itself seen as a 'good' job for a working-class Jew: a 'fond Jewish grandmother in St John's Wood' would want her grandson to become a doctor or an accountant, but 'if you ask the same question in Ilford or Stamford Hill, the answer is likely to be a taxi-driver'.[11]

Later immigrant groups were less conspicuous. A group of Cossack refugees from the Bolshevik revolution drove London cabs for the best part of fifty years, dreaming of returning to Russia and their estates,[12] but few of London's post-war immigrants adopted cabbing as an entry trade or established cab dynasties on the Jewish model (even today only five per cent of cab drivers come from the black, Asian, or 'other' ethnic minorities comprising a third of the London population).[13]

Cabbies were normally white and male; beyond that, generalisation was dangerous. A survey of 150 'Knowledge Boys' in the trade journal *Steering Wheel* in 1969 found that almost half the 'Boys' were over the age of thirty and that aspirant cabbies came to driving from a variety of other jobs. Many came from the transport industry, driving buses or lorries, but no single occupation accounted for more than 5 per cent of respondents.[14] Drivers' life stories

[6] *Steering Wheel [SW]*, 29 May 1971.

[7] 'On the "Knowledge"', *SW*, 9 August 1979.

[8] Alf Townsend, *Cabbie* (Stroud, 2003), p. 19.

[9] A. Fresco, 'Where have all the garages gone?', *SW*, 7 September 1979.

[10] C. Field, 'Taxi! The Jews behind the wheel', *Jewish Chronicle Colour Magazine*, 30 April 1971; Barry A. Kosmin and Nigel Grizzard, *Jews in an Inner London Borough. A Study of the Jewish Population of the London Borough of Hackney Based on the 1971 Census* (London, 1975), p.27.

[11] Field, 'Taxi!'.

[12] 'Should the lid go on the melting pot?', Taxi Trader [*TT*], February 1969.

[13] 'Black cabbies for black cabs', *TSSA Journal*, December 2007/January 2008, www.tssa.org.uk/article-259.php3?id_article=3841 (consulted 20 March 2009).

[14] 'On the "Knowledge"!', *SW*, 9 August 1969.

confirm this occupational eclecticism. The 'Cabbies of London' interviewed by the *Evening News* in 1961 included a former seller of secondhand tablecloths, a Bevin Boy, a trainee doctor unable to stand the sight of blood, a tailor ruined in the depression, a failed barrister's clerk, three boxers, a film stuntman and wrestler and a violinist who had once performed on stage with a tap-dancer but 'found taxi-driving a more secure profession'.[15] Interwar unemployment had driven many to cabbing, but with jobs plentiful in post-war London, it was more likely to be an aversion to industrial routine which drove men onto the Knowledge. A cabman, wrote the Chairman of the Owner Drivers Association in 1965, was often a man who 'has sampled industry and cannot fit in'.[16] 'Clocking on and off would get on my nerves', explained William Hull of Roehampton in 1961.[17]

Drivers regularly described themselves as individualists. They were *necessarily* economic individualists. An informal chivalry governed conduct on the road—never overtake an empty cab to reach a fare first, etc.[18]—but cabbing was inescapably competitive. '*Every* other taxi on the road is my competitor', wrote driver Roger Annoute in 1970, 'It doesn't do me one iota of good when people ride in other taxis, it doesn't put a brass farthing in my pocket'.[19] Technically, all drivers were freelance. Those working for garages were not the employees of the proprietors, but bailees, hiring cabs daily or weekly. None, consequently, had much claim upon the welfare state or access to occupational perks: taxi-driving was 'a job where there is no promotion, no pension, no workmen's compensation, no overtime pay at weekends'.[20] 'Journeymen' engaged by garages were employed persons for National Insurance purposes[21] and might receive sick pay, but owner-drivers were self-employed and denied such benefits. There was no occupational pension; in fact many drivers appreciated the chance to work beyond retirement age: 'there is not another like the Taxi Trade where an old age pensioner can work for an odd day or two a week', argued 'Jack from Mons' Cohen, a First World War veteran who continued driving into the 1970s.[22] Driver Joe Polski died at the wheel at the age of seventy-five.[23]

Like J. S. Mill, cabbies used the term 'individuality' in preference to 'individualism', suggesting that they were free spirits rather than mere economic men.[24] There was truth in the popular view that cabbies' favourite freedom was the freedom of speech. Robert Buckland spoke of '"the full-flowing river of speech" that only a London taxi-driver can command',[25] and the Maxwell Stamp

[15] 'Cabbies of London', *Evening News*, 16, 24, and 25 October, 3, 9, 10, 13, 14, and 15 November 1961.

[16] A. Sheehan, 'If', *TT*, April 1965.

[17] 'Cabbies of London, 17', *Evening News*, 31 October 1961; *SW*, 9 April 1966.

[18] Townsend, *Cabbie*, p. 45.

[19] R. Annoute, 'Why DO taxi drivers . . . ??', II, *SW*, 5 September 1970.

[20] Levinson, *Taxi*, p. 190.

[21] J. Pilkington, Department of Health and Social Security, letter in *SW*, 28 June 1969.

[22] J. Cohen, letter to *SW*, 23 March 1968.

[23] *SW*, 24 June 1972.

[24] e.g. Levinson for drivers' 'strong streak of individuality', *SW*, 9 April 1966.

[25] Robert Buckland, *Share My Taxi* (London, 1968), p. 82.

Committee on the taxicab trade noted laconically in 1970 that 'there was no dearth of views for the Committee to consider'.[26] Cabbie aphorisms of the *Private Eye* type can be found in the printed record—'pay policemen well above the average and maybe London will again have a force that will make the toughs think twice';[27] 'I say we should come out, we are throwing good money after bad. I think this Common Market is a bad thing';[28] 'very straight-faced was Mr Ribbentrop . . . Didn't surprise me a bit when we went to war with that lot'[29]—but it would be misleading to depict cabbies merely as purveyors of unpolished street wisdom. The trade, after all, always sustained at least three journals, written almost entirely by working drivers.

Most cabmen came from working-class backgrounds and had received only limited formal education,[30] but the Knowledge required at least precision and a retentive memory. Many developed an antiquarian interest in London history. Trade journals routinely carried London quizzes, with questions such as 'why is Piccadilly so called?' or 'where is London's costliest drinking fountain?'.[31] Garage proprietor Harry Baylis established a London Guide School for cabmen in 1973, while in July 1974 London Taxi Guides offered guided tours.[32] The future *Mastermind* winner Fred Housego was named top guide by the London Tourist Board in 1977.[33]

The restless employment history of many drivers perhaps indicated intellectual frustration. Philip Mintz had left grammar school at fifteen because his friends considered it 'sissy' to stay. He drove through London 'knowing full well that had the dice been on his side, he might have been a graduate . . . It's a fact that sticks hard in the throat'.[34] Buckland suggested that taxi-driving attracted 'men whose talents and aspirations range far beyond the job they are doing'.[35] For example, Gary Sherrick, captivated at school by the Romantics, recited his own verses to passengers, 'to make them feel as if they had escaped from the mad rush of London into my world of poetry'.[36] Joe Polski loved languages and chemistry, Fred Whiten mathematics and meteorology, while Michael Freedman conducted Bartok's *Concerto for Orchestra* at Wembley Town Hall.[37] Several drivers—Herbert Hodge before the war, Maurice Levinson, Buckland, Ron Barnes, Townsend, and Walter Geake—

[26] Maxwell Stamp Committee, *Report*, 2.

[27] E. Sussman, 'Is Britain soft?', *TT*, January 1960.

[28] F. Braverman, 'What Cabmen think of the Common Market', *Cab Trade News*, 29 March 1975, TGWU Archive.

[29] Joe 'Rubberface' Wiltshire, 'Cabbies of London' 11, *Evening News*, 23 October 1961. Wiltshire had driven von Ribbentrop, German Ambassador 1936–8, during the refurbishment of the German embassy.

[30] Buckland, *Share My Taxi*, p. 185.

[31] *Cab Trade News*, 9 August 1973, *TT*, January, February 1968.

[32] *SW* 7 July 1973, 18 August 1973, 20 September 1974.

[33] *SW* 22 April 1977.

[34] P. Moger, '"Carnaby Street" Cabbie', *Acton Gazette*, 6 April 1967.

[35] Buckland, *Share My Taxi*, pp. 185–6.

[36] 'Gerry Sherrick—poet—taxidriver', *Cab Trade News*, 25 January 1975, TGWU Archive.

[37] *SW* 16 November 1968, 16 December 1967; Maurice Levinson, *The Taxi Game* (London, 1973), p. 141; M. Schiman, *SW*, 9 March 1979.

wrote cabbing reminiscences.[38] Barnes and Levinson wrote autobiographies and Levinson was a published novelist.[39] Sam Raingold compiled an idiosyncratic London tourist guide and Charles Poulsen wrote London local history.[40]

Cabbies' intellectual independence made them, in Hodge's words, 'philosophical anarchists with a contempt for all law and order imposed from above'.[41] Buckland considered cabbies 'difficult people to fit into a socialistic or totalitarian state'.[42] They encountered authoritarianism only in the dilute form of the Metropolitan Police, but that relationship was antagonistic enough. In 1939, 11,000 licensed drivers incurred around 3,000 summonses a year, coming 'to look on the police-court dock as a normal trade risk'.[43] Things had improved by the 1960s, but drivers felt that the Met still saw the cab trade as a branch of the East End criminal class. Entrapment was frequently alleged, often by 'blue trees'—policemen who hid behind trees to catch taxis jumping lights.[44] Verbatim accounts of police-cabbie exchanges enlivened the London magistrates' courts—' "bugger off. You're power crazy. Don't think you can tell me what to do because you're in uniform . . . That's why you bastards get shot at" ', ' "You can't treat me like an animal" . . . "I treat all b—— cabmen as animals" ', and similar.[45]

Sympathy for society's outcasts accompanied this contempt for authority. A driver had to be of good character to gain his badge, but, for Levinson, crooks and cabbies were 'on the same spiritual level, even if one is honest and the other isn't'. Criminals habitually used cabs, tipping well and never inviting police attention by fare-dodging.[46] Levinson also considered homosexuals 'usually good passengers'.[47] With many drivers, he felt an affinity with prostitutes, who likewise plied for hire, suffered police harassment and lived off fleeting encounters with anonymous members of the public.[48]

Prostitutes, moreover, never looked down on taxi-drivers.[49] A fear that the trade retained a servile image made cabbies more sensitive to condescension than

[38] Herbert Hodge, *Cab, Sir?* (London, 1939); Levinson, *Taxi* and *Taxi Game*; Buckland, *Share My Taxi*; Centerprise Trust, *Working Lives. II* for Barnes; Walter Geake, *What's Next? Incidents Recorded whilst Driving a London Licensed Taxicab* (London, 1999); Townsend, *Cabbie*.

[39] Ron Barnes, *A Licence to Live: Scenes from a Post-war Working Life in Hackney* (London, 1975); Maurice Levinson, *The Trouble with Yesterday* (London, 1946); *The Woman from Bessarabia* (London, 1964); *The Desperate Passion of Henry Knopp* (London, 1962); *Greek Street Tragedy* (London, 1964).

[40] S. Raingold, *A Taxi Driver's Guide to London* (London, 1973); Charles Poulsen, *Victoria Park. A Study in the History of East London* (London, 1976).

[41] Hodge, *Cab, Sir?*, p. 238.

[42] Buckland, *Share My Taxi*, p. 86.

[43] Hodge, *Cab, Sir?*, p. 238.

[44] Barnes in Centerprise, *Working Lives*, p. 156.

[45] Hugo Clarke, tried at West London Magistrates Court, *Owner Driver*, March 1963; V.Gale and an unidentified police constable, Marlborough Street Magistrates Court, *TT*, May 1965. Gale was acquitted of driving without due care and attention, but Clarke was imprisoned for driving his cab at PC Sidney Lear.

[46] Levinson, *Taxi Game*, p. 100.

[47] Ibid., p. 98.

[48] Levinson, *Taxi*, p. 106; Buckland, *Share My Taxi*, p. 55.

[49] Levinson, *Taxi Game*, p. 73.

most groups. Many 1960s cabbies had entered the trade in the 1930s, when the upper classes had provided almost the only custom in a thin market. Buckland remembered living off 'the Clubmen, those denizens of St James's and Pall Mall whose lives seemed to be devoted to driving by taxi from their town houses to their clubs, and back again to their houses'. He 'hated [the clubman] in proportion as I needed his patronage'.[50] Jack Cohen remembered being 'looked upon as dirt' by 'the wealthier section of the community' before the War.[51] In the buyers' market of the 1930s, cabmen had bitten their tongues, but in the permissive 1960s they could speak their minds:

> You f—— people make me sick. You give me, the bloke who does the work, a 6d. piece, and you give the bloody doorman a 2s. piece. I used to get 6d. before the war. What can I spend with 6d. now, you ——?[52]

General affluence and a decline in the real level of fares meant that 'we can find work . . . in Brixton as well as Kensington'.[53] Taxi slang remained redolent of class warfare—'Rowton House' for the Ritz, 'Den of Thieves' for the Stock Exchange, 'The Cow Shed' for the Ladies' Carlton Club[54]—but with the broadening of his customer base, Levinson suggested, the 1970s cabbie 'on his social rounds . . . might even go to the same places as his passengers'.[55] Dealing with the whole of society rather than just its upper levels, he developed the contempt for his fares that service providers habitually display towards their clients—what one driver described as 'the need-hate relationship that exists between the taxi and its customer'.[56] 'I love my trade', driver Albert Levy told the *Evening Standard* in 1979, 'It's the people I don't like.'[57]

Three-quarters of 'Knowledge Boys' in 1969 thought they had 'good' relations with the public, but Levinson expected the 'butterboy'—taxi slang for a newly qualified driver—eventually to 'wake up to the fact that politeness doesn't pay'.[58] Street hiring implied 'terse instructions barked at the driver in hurried conditions' and the knowledge that driver and passenger were unlikely to meet again produced a 'mutual couldn't-care-less attitude'.[59] So did taxi design. The partition between the driver's cab and the body of the vehicle, along with the noise of the diesel engine, hindered conversation with passengers: 'we carry around 30,000,000 people a year and have very little means of communication with

[50] Buckland, *Share My Taxi*, pp. 21–2.

[51] 'Personality Page, No.1. Jack (from Mons) Cohen', *SW*, 13 January 1968.

[52] Myer Franks, summoned at Bow Street court for using insulting language to a Belgravia company secretary, *SW*, 1 July 1967.

[53] P. Roma, letter to *SW*, 12 May 1962.

[54] H. Pearman, 'Glossary of cockney cabology', *TT*, January 1971; Buckland, *Share My Taxi*, p. 25.

[55] Levinson, *Taxi Game*, p. 141.

[56] G. Bocca, 'Taxi drivers of the world, I', *SW* 30 December 1967, referring to London, Paris, and Rome.

[57] 'Why London's cabbies are so miserable', *Evening Standard*, 9 November 1979.

[58] 'On the "Knowledge"', *SW*, 9 August 1969; Levinson, *Taxi*, p.69.

[59] Editorial, 'Pride or prejudice?', *SW*, 7 August 1971.

them', argued the Owner Drivers Society in 1970.[60] Cabbing became an oddly solitary business.

Cabbies' dealings with their customers became starkly commercial, and drivers judged passengers according to their generosity. Fare evasion was rare: a driver could expect to be 'bilked' only once every four years.[61] The real point of conflict was the tip. As Hodge put it, 'a "good" rider is one who tips lavishly, though he may have the manners of a pig'. The worst riders were therefore the 'legals', who paid only the metered fare—most prominently Church of England clergymen.[62] Winston Churchill was a hero to the nation but not to the trade, being 'a bit tight when it came to tipping'.[63] Royalty was 'not thought of by cabmen as being conspicuously generous', apart from the Duke of Windsor, a good tipper whose populist repertoire as Prince of Wales had extended to buying drivers breakfast in their shelters.[64] Cab lore held that the poorest fares gave the largest tips—'Bermondsey nearly always tips better than Belgravia'.[65] London's expanding tourist trade allowed drivers to extend the comparison to most of the planet, producing league tables of visitors ranked by generosity, with Australians invariably at the bottom and Japanese and Chinese at the top.[66] Levinson noted that London's Chinese, many of them restaurateurs, understood the importance of the tip.[67] Other New Commonwealth immigrants were, though, considered bad tippers—'the black person (on average) tips badly, if at all'[68]—explaining drivers' tendency to ignore them and their consequent reputation for racism.

Moreover, the act of tipping was inherently condescending, threatening, Levinson believed, 'to push the London taxi-driver lower down the social scale'.[69] Socialist drivers like Ron Barnes loathed the tip, advocating instead 'a basic wage and a bonus'.[70] The TGWU Cab Section campaigned sporadically for a basic wage,[71] which would have made tips less frequent, but gained limited support from drivers. One consideration was that the tip was hard to tax. A driver declaring only his metered fare income would invite 'searching enquiries from his local Inspector of Taxes',[72] but with even the Prices and Incomes Board admitting that 'nothing . . . is known of the true earnings' of most London cabbies, the

60 K. E. Drummond, in 'The Maxwell Stamp Committee Report', *SW*, 14 November 1970.
61 Editorial, 'Bilking', *Owner Driver*, February 1962.
62 Hodge, *Cab, Sir?*, pp. 78, 89.
63 H. Pearman, 'Call me cabby', II, *TT*, July 1971.
64 Ibid.; G. Stedman, letter to *SW*, 20 September 1974.
65 Hodge, *Cab, Sir?*, p. 95; Buckland, *Share My Taxi*, p. 84.
66 Buckland, *Share My Taxi*, p. 84; R. Annoute, 'Why DO taxi drivers . . . ??', IV, *SW*, 19 September 1970; W. J. D'Arcy in D. Orgill, 'Hail and Fare Well', *Daily Express*, 15 November 1973.
67 Levinson, *Taxi Game*, p. 107.
68 'The taxi driver and race relations', *SW*, 6 February 1971.
69 Levinson, *Taxi Game*, p. 91.
70 Centerprise Trust, *Working Lives. II*, p. 141.
71 e.g. *SW*, 11 March 1967.
72 Buckland, *Share My Taxi*, p. 88.

tax authorities were at a disadvantage.[73] But cabbies also feared that a basic wage 'would mean the loss of the freedom which we now have', in favour of the work discipline that drivers had joined the trade to avoid.[74] It was also unclear how a basic wage could be applied to owner-drivers, whom the TGWU considered regrettable anomalies, but who were becoming increasingly numerous. Contained in the issue of the tip were wider questions concerning the trade's organisation and self-image.

II

'You cannot organise individualists', wrote the chairman of the Owner Drivers Association in 1971. 'Logically, if you could you would cease to have individualists.'[75] A union of London taxi-drivers had nonetheless been created in 1894 and absorbed by the Transport and General Workers Union on its formation in 1922. The TGWU's Cab Section had organised a major strike in 1932 and had offered the only defence against appalling trade conditions in the 1930s.[76] That decade cast a long shadow over cabmen. Those who had cruised the streets for £2.10s per week[77]—perhaps as little as 7/6d per week in slack periods [78]—never forgot the experience. The TGWU's response, from 1935 onwards, was to call for limitation of entry to the trade, and for fifteen years or so after the war it made limitation—later called 'stabilisation'—its major objective. It had made no headway, however, either by industrial action or by lobbying government, before the advent of the minicabs made talk of limitation otiose.

In June 1961 Welbeck Motors, run by the private hire operator Michael Gotla, released 200 yellow Renault Dauphines onto London's streets, starting the 'minicab war'.[79] Private car hire had previously been a luxury; Gotla aimed to make it an everyday facility by claiming the licensed trade's greatest advantage: the right to ply for hire. Although his vehicles were radio-controlled, would-be passengers were encouraged to hail one, whose driver would hand the customer a telephone enabling him to book a cab—in practice the same cab—through Welbeck's control room.[80] The Home Office thought this trick illegal,[81] but showed no eagerness to bring a test case, reinforcing trade suspicion that they favoured Gotla's initiative.[82]

[73] National Board for Prices and Incomes, Report no 87, *Proposed Increase in London Taxicab Fares*, October 1968 (Cmnd. 3797, 1968), p. 12.

[74] 'Jack from Mons' Cohen, *SW*, 7 February 1970. Cohen had been a TGWU member since 1926; *SW*, 23 March 1968.

[75] A. Sheehan, 'On unity', *SW*, 6 February 1971.

[76] W. Fox, *Taximen and Taxi-Owners. A Study of Organisation, Ownership, Finances and Working Conditions in the London Taxi Trade* (London, 1935), p. 5.

[77] Figures for a journeyman driver in 1938: 'Proposals of the Transport and General Workers Union for the Limitation of the Number of London Taxicabs and Drivers', TNA, HO 45/25256.

[78] 'Cabbies of London, 4', Alec Weldon, *Evening News*, 12 October 1961.

[79] 'Pioneer of minicabs exudes innocence and ambition', *Times*, 19 June 1961.

[80] B. Cardew, 'Minicabs will start taxi war', *Daily Express*, 6 February 1961.

[81] Memorandum by A. Hewins, 28 March 1961, TNA HO 385/7.

[82] A. Sheehan, 'The last word', *Owner Driver*, June 1961.

The authorities' failure to make difficulties for Welbeck angered licensed drivers. Minicab drivers escaped the Knowledge, the character test, and the advanced driving test faced by cabbies. The ferocious trade reaction reflected both resentment of a competitor, and frustration at the authorities' refusal to liberalise regulations from which that competitor was exempt. Much direct action followed Welbeck's arrival, ranging from hoax booking calls to assaults on minicab drivers. Reports of minicabs being boxed in or having their radios torn out—even assaults on minicab passengers—surfaced during Welbeck's first week.[83] This open warfare led to thirty-seven taxi-drivers being prosecuted in the autumn of 1961.[84] In November two cabmen were imprisoned for dangerous driving—hemming in a minicab driver who had picked up a passenger—and another for forcing a minicab into the kerb.[85] A six-month sentence in January 1962 for assault on a Welbeck driver underlined the magistracy's impatience with 'jungle law and mob rule'.[86]

The cab war subsided after the High Court decision in *Rose v. Welbeck* in May 1962 reaffirmed the licensed trade's exclusive right to ply for hire. Though rogue minicab drivers continued to ply, minicab firms no longer openly attempted to circumvent the law. Private hire tacitly acknowledged that the two operations were complementary—the licensed trade concentrating on the centre, the minicabs on the suburbs. Casual plying for hire was most profitable in the centre, and, as Sid Pearce, a Richmond cabbie with an LSE Economics degree, pointed out, the mandatory initial hiring charge made the return per mile highest for journeys below two miles. Longer journeys within the six-mile limit were appreciably less lucrative, and although the return rose above six miles, the prospect of finding a return fare diminished.[87] In 1974 the GLC established that the average journey by licensed cab covered a mile and three-quarters and lasted twelve minutes. Three-quarters of trips were made in the City and West End, Kensington, or Paddington.[88] As one yellow-badge driver put it, 'Inner London's paved with gold day and night—the suburbs are but a cart track.'[89]

Black cabs consequently neglected the suburbs. It was estimated in 1969 that only seventy licensed cabs worked south London,[90] and minicabs captured the area. Licensed drivers exploited the lucrative City and West End business, while minicabs focused upon individual suburbs, where the street map was simpler and lack of the Knowledge mattered less. Welbeck collapsed in 1965, largely because operating a dedicated vehicle fleet at loss-leader rates was uncommercial, but subsequent hire firms succeeded by simply equipping drivers' private cars with

83 *SW*, 8 July 1961.

84 P. Warren, 'Welbeck Minicabs—the Tip of the Iceberg. Part 3', *Cab Trade News*, 17 October 1974, TGWU Archive.

85 Marlborough Street magistrate Leo Gradwell, quoted in *TT*, December 1961; Warren, 'Welbeck Minicabs'; *Daily Mirror*, 21 November 1961.

86 *TT*, January 1962.

87 S. Pearce, 'Fares. Time for a change?', *SW*, 4 July 1975, etc.

88 M. F. Talbot, *Greater London Transportation Survey. A Study of Taxi Trips*. GLC Research Memorandum 307 (1974), pp. 17, 43.

89 Arthur Goldwater's Column, *SW*, 13 December 1969.

90 'South London businessman and minicab user', letter to *TT*, March 1969.

radios. By the late 1970s the private hire sector operated 27,000 vehicles, but between 1961 and 1977 the number of licensed cabs had also nearly doubled, from 6 500 to 12,452,[91] sustained by the businessmen, shoppers, theatre-goers, and tourists in the central area.

The minicab issue remained, though, an open wound for licensed drivers. The taxi press obsessed over the 'pirates' threatening drivers' livelihood, issuing lugubrious predictions of the death of the black cab.[92] Driver resentment focused on the TGWU. The Union had necessarily urged restraint during the violence of 1961–2, but lacked purchase on a Home Office uninterested in limitation. It struggled to retain driver support, and a succession of splinter groups challenged its authority.

In April 1967 the '12,000 Group' staged a protest in which 1,000 cabs and 4,000 drivers blockaded the House of Commons.[93] In May a meeting at the Festival Hall attended by 2,500 drivers transformed this group into the Licensed Taxi Drivers Association, 'dedicated to end the operation of minicabs'.[94] Some 4,500 members were soon recruited. Rivalry with the TGWU was immediately evident, reflecting fundamental divisions over the role of a trade body. The LTDA believed that little was gained by being a small part of a large general union.[95] It worked 'for Licensed cab men alone, without the need to consider dockers, busmen, kitchen porters, road sweepers and dustmen'.[96] Unencumbered by TGWU caution, it mounted guerilla actions like the 1967 boycott of the Park Lane Hilton, which forced the hotel to renounce minicabs. The TGWU, conversely, projected itself as an estate of the realm, with the ear of government and a troop of sponsored MPs. Militancy was beneath it: 'cab-drivers must learn the difference between getting publicity in the House of Commons and getting legislation through the House of Commons.'[97]

Behind these tactical divisions lay deeper questions of status. The TGWU Cab Section considered itself an industrial union, representing the trade's proletariat—the 'journeymen' drivers hiring cabs from proprietors. The LTDA saw itself as a genuine trade association. It included proprietors on its executive, contrary to the Union's belief that 'the struggle for improvement in pay and conditions is one against the proprietor'.[98] By 1967 this was a somewhat sectarian view: proprietors and drivers had campaigned together for stabilization and against the minicabs in the early 1960s. What *was* true was that journeymen and owner-drivers—'mushes' in taxi slang—had different interests. Where the journeyman looked to his union to gain from garages a higher percentage of

[91] Metropolitan Police figures in Michael E. Beesley, 'Competition and supply in London taxis', in his *Privatization, Regulation and Deregulation* (2nd edn., 1997), Table 8.1, pp. 112–13.

[92] e.g. letter by J. Lovegrove, *TT*, September 1970, predicting that the licensed trade would last no longer than five years.

[93] *SW*, 22 April 1967.

[94] 'London taxi drivers "Close their Ranks"', *Times*, 17 May 1967.

[95] Levinson, *Taxi Game*, p. 42.

[96] J. Toff, *SW*, 16 December 1967.

[97] R. Fletcher, 'Taxicabs and Parliament', *SW*, 3 June 1967. Fletcher was the TGWU-sponsored MP who spoke for the taxi trade.

[98] TGWU Cab Section Bulletin, 23 May 1967, quoted in *SW*, 3 June 1967.

takings, the owner-driver essentially sought protection against the risks involved in running his own business. The LTDA accordingly enhanced its appeal by offering accident, sickness, and disablement benefit to its members from the start,[99] courting the charge of being 'a predominantly "mushes" union'.[100]

This rivalry soon acquired a political edge, making reconciliation unlikely. The TGWU accused its competitor of gulling members into believing 'that they don't have anything in common with a working man, but are destined to become tycoons'.[101] The LTDA's Public Relations Officer indeed suggested that 'we have a choice to be classed as workers . . . or in our *own* true perspective of Professional men with our own Professional Association'.[102] The LTDA was apparently advised by Michael Ivens, later Director of the free-market lobby group Aims of Industry, and its secretary, Bill D'Arcy, was accused of welcoming the Tory victory in 1970.[103] The TGWU's critics, conversely, alleged that the Cab Section was run by Communists.[104]

The LTDA benefited from these turf wars because conventional industrial politics was losing relevance. In the 1950s most drivers had been journeymen, working fixed shifts which allowed their garage to use cabs continuously. They were paid 'on the clock', keeping around 40 per cent of metered fares from each shift. This percentage commission system offered a means of regulating the workforce *and* a basis for collective bargaining, and was therefore acceptable to proprietors and Union alike.[105] The alternative—for those who could not afford their own cabs—was the flat hire system, by which drivers paid a fixed rate to hire a cab for a week, keeping the fares gained. In the 1930s, drivers had disliked 'the flat', as slack trade made it difficult to pay the rental.[106] In the more buoyant 1970s, though, drivers saw 'the clock', with 60 per cent of fare income going to the proprietor, as 'the swiftest way to the bun-house ever devised'; it was rejected by 'drivers who wish to earn good money'.[107]

The popularity of 'the flat' also reflected the migration of many taxi-drivers, along with much of the East End population, to outer London—one Redbridge street was christened 'Green Badge Alley'.[108] These suburbanites resented commuting to a garage to do a shift. Garages began to offer drivers transport to and

[99] See Schedule II of the LTDA Rule Book, 1969, in 'Licensed Taxi Drivers Association', TNA NF 2/708.

[100] Letter from Mrs M. Kupler, 'A taxi driver's wife', *SW*, 13 July 1968.

[101] Editorial, 'Disagreement', *Cab Trade News*, 10 September 1975, TGWU Archive.

[102] Joe Toff, letter to *SW*, 15 July 1967.

[103] Letter from H. Bennett, *SW*, 31 March 1973; *Cab Trade News*, 19 October 1977, TGWU Archive. Both claims refer to articles in taxi journals which have not survived. Both were made by hostile witnesses, but the second cites an article by Ivens himself.

[104] 'Taxidermy', *SW*, 2 December 1977.

[105] Michael E. Beesley, 'Regulation of taxis', *Economic Journal* 83/1 (1973), p. 171.

[106] Hodge, *Cab, Sir?*, pp. 273–4.

[107] Barnes, in *Working Lives*, II, p. 138; S. Pearce, 'On putting up or shutting up', *SW*, 17 December 1976.

[108] Maxwell Stamp Committee, *Report*, 38; Dick Hobbs, *Doing the Business. Entrepreneurship, the Working Class, and Detectives in the East End of London* (Oxford, 1988), p. 178.

from home, hoping to retain their labour force,[109] but they were swimming against a tide carrying drivers away from dependence upon garages altogether. Most drivers saw driving on 'the flat' as a step towards owner-driving. In 1961 27 per cent of drivers had been mushes. Twenty years later this figure stood at 44 per cent.[110] Most of the Knowledge boys surveyed in 1969 aspired to owner-driving—'to be my own guvnor'.[111] Facing fixed prices, rising costs, and a driver shortage, many garages went under. Their demise hurt the TGWU, which paid the price for remaining a journeymen's union. In 1967 the TGWU Cab Section had claimed 3,500 members, representing 90 per cent of garage drivers.[112] Ten years later its membership was estimated at 800.[113]

As the Union had feared, owner-driving appealed to cabbies' entrepreneurialism: 'where else will an investment of £1500 buy you your own independent business?'[114] It was a concomitant of suburbanisation, owner-occupation and the escape from proletarian status. Crucially, it offered a means of paying for this improved lifestyle. It was not clear that owner-driving was any more lucrative *per hour* than working as a journeyman. What mattered was that the owner-driver, like the 'flat' driver in the garages, was not restricted by garage shifts. Owner-driver witnesses before Maxwell Stamp described working twelve-hour days.[115] Levinson spoke of 55 to 60 hour weeks: he himself had taken only one day off a month when raising his family and paying off his mortgage.[116]

Inflation raised the stakes: Levinson considered it 'the most disturbing feature about the taxi trade'.[117] Maxwell Stamp had noted Whitehall's tendency 'to consider taxi fare increases in the light of the Government's general economic policy',[118] and for several years in the mid-1970s the tariff was frozen, like nationalized industry prices in the same period, in the hope of containing inflation. The real cost of taxi trips fell sharply; Pearce believed that 'the growth in cab utilisation owes more to declining real prices than to any fundamental change in the structure of the market'.[119]

Forty years earlier the cab trade had suffered real poverty, to which trade unionism had been a realistic, if inadequate, response. By the 1970s things were different. The cab trade had shared in the affluence of the post-war years: 'today cabmen do not, as they had ample reason to do in the past, complain over much

[109] Beesley, 'Regulation of taxis', p. 170.

[110] Figures from the Annual Reports of the Commissioner of Police of the Metropolis, taking the number of drivers owning one cab as a proxy, although many with two, three or four cabs would also have thought of themselves as owner-drivers rather than proprietors. By 1986 the figure stood at almost 60 per cent.

[111] 'On the "Knowledge"!', *SW*, 9 August 1969.

[112] 'Note of a Meeting Held on 23 September [1968]', Working Party on Taxi-Cab and Private Car Hire Trades in London', London Metropolitan Archives (LMA), GLC/DG/GP/1/103.

[113] Editorial, *SW*, 28 January 1977.

[114] Field, 'Taxi!', p. 15.

[115] Maxwell Stamp Committee, *Report*, p. 36.

[116] Levinson, *Taxi Game*, p. 20.

[117] Ibid., p. 19.

[118] Maxwell Stamp Committee, *Report*, p. 29.

[119] S. Pearce, 'Fares. Time for a Change?, *SW*, 29 August 1975.

about the job's financial rewards', as *Taxi Trader* noted in 1972.[120] Many drivers owned their homes and their cabs and paid some income tax at 35 per cent,[121] but they considered their relative comfort precarious in an inflationary age, when the price of their services was fixed. They responded in two ways: by pushing themselves harder but also by seeking to maximise their returns. Circumstances allowed this. In the 1930s demand for their services had been inadequate; by the 1970s demand was strong. No 1930s cabbie would have turned away a fare as not worth his while; by the late 1970s drivers were routinely (and illegally) rejecting unrewarding jobs—'"Get one going the other way, will you dear?', they say wearily"'[122]—to maximise engaged mileage on lucrative work. This also discouraged collective action: more time spent on the road meant less time on the rank, where Union proselytizing had been easiest and 'a bond [had been] formed throughout the trade—which today seems to be disappearing'.[123] 'Only the sick, lame and lazy rank up these days', Pearce noted in 1978.[124] The TGWU's decline has been described, but the LTDA, having failed to kill the minicab, also lost ground after its enthusiastic start. By 1976 it was estimated that only 20 per cent of drivers belonged to either organisation.[125] In 1978 driver Peter Schendel urged *Steering Wheel*'s readers to join the National Federation of Self-Employed, at a cost of £12 p.a., and the journal printed the Federation's application form.[126]

This doubtless supported the charge of class betrayal made by TGWU militants against those beyond their ranks, but the self-image of the owner-driver as a successful but hard-pressed entrepreneur was widely accepted. 'As an owner-driver I am doing very well thank you', wrote 'A. Musher' in *Steering Wheel* in 1979:

> I'm not afraid to work in order to pay my mortgage and have two cars plus a good holiday. Yes my wife does go to work so does my neighbours', who is a police superintendant, as does my bank managers wife. If we want the good things in life we must work for them, without trampling on our fellow citizens.[127]

It is unsurprising that taxi drivers proved receptive to the new Toryism of the 1970s. Previously drivers had largely been bred in the East End socialist tradition; Hodge wrote in 1939 that the number of cabmen on London Borough Councils fluctuated with the strength of the Labour vote.[128] In the mid-1970s, though, the leader of the Conservative minority on the GLC, Horace Cutler, courted the taxi vote, opposing Labour proposals for GLC control of the

[120] Editorial, 'Image', *TT*, January 1972.
[121] Editorial, *SW*, 1 July 1977.
[122] K. Whitehorn, 'Spiels on Wheels', *Observer*, 29 April 1979.
[123] P. Philips, 'As I see it', *SW*, 6 April 1979.
[124] S. Pearce, 'Minimum hirings and maximum profits', *SW*, 7 April 1978.
[125] Editorial, *SW*, 24 September 1976.
[126] P. L. Schendel, 'True representation', *SW*, 5 May 1978.
[127] 'A. Musher', 'I'm doing very well', *SW*, 9 February 1979 (original spelling and punctuation).
[128] Hodge, *Cab, Sir?*, p. 262.

service,[129] and later calling for drivers to be allowed to set their own fares.[130] In the 1977 GLC elections, the Tories ran taxi-driver Arnold Kinzley in Ilford South, a constituency containing 1,000 cabbie voters.[131] He turned a 1,100 Labour majority into a 5,600 Conservative one, while the 1,600 drivers in neighbouring Ilford North presumably contributed to another Tory gain, with a massive 10,000 increase in their poll.[132] In 1978 a parliamentary by-election occurred in Ilford North. The Labour candidate, Tessa Jowell, advocated financial support for would-be owner-drivers, but the Tories' Vivian Bendall impressed *Steering Wheel* with 'his grasp of trade matters'.[133] The Conservatives captured a Labour seat, on a swing less spectacular than in recent by-elections, but anticipating their national performance in 1979.

III

'Madam', wrote driver J. M. Marcelle in an open letter to Margaret Thatcher before the 1979 election, 'as self-employed persons, it seems to me that we should believe in enterprise, expansion, and business.'[134] Perhaps it is unsurprizing that these self-professed individualists, with their suspicion of officialdom and their arm's length relationship with the taxman, should have been recruits to Thatcherism, but it remains striking that an outcome which would have appeared unlikely in 1960 appeared natural by 1979. For generations, cabbies' apparently Conservative instincts had been offset by other influences: by their embedding in an east London community—often an east London Jewish community—that was tribally socialist, and by their proletarianization in the larger garages. From the early 1960s, though, they had sought to break out of the garages and flee the East End while becoming increasingly disenchanted with industrial trade unionism and with collective action generally. In these years cabbies' shift from a pointed hatred of the rich to a generalized low-level misanthropy is paralleled by a shift from class-war socialism towards an economic liberalism consistent with the new Conservatism of the 1970s. They became almost stereotypical Thatcherite material, enjoying a prosperity which they could plausibly attribute to their own hard work, but, working as they did or they had on a fixed tariff, feeling sensitive to the danger of inflation. Doubtless the cultural elements of Thatcherism—English nationalism, or the no-nonsense approach to crime and punishment[135]—also resonated with this white working-class group, but the roots of their political evolution ran deeper than that,

[129] H. Cutler, letter to *Taxinews*, March 1977, in 'Taxi and car hire', LMA GLC/DG/AD/5/23.
[130] *SW*, 6 April 1979.
[131] 'Ilford South votes!', *SW*, 22 April 1977.
[132] *Ilford Recorder*, 12 May 1977.
[133] Bendall in 'Crucial bye-election at Ilford North', *SW*, 2 December 1977; *Ilford Recorder*, 23 February 1978.
[134] J. M. Marcelle, 'Cabman's letter to Margaret Thatcher', *SW*, 6 April 1979.
[135] e.g. Monty Schiman on Thatcher's support for the death penalty, *SW*, 4 May 1979.

reflecting real material interests and calculations that had developed over a period of at least twenty years. The transformation of Conservatism was also critical: paternalistic, welfare Toryism had cut little ice with these undeferential individualists, but Thatcher did speak to them. One ironic implication was that cabbies' commitment to Toryism was more ephemeral than would have been a conversion based upon Pooterism or embourgeoisement: in 1997 New Labour won both Ilford seats.[136] Study of groups like these makes the 'Thatcher moment' easier to understand.

[136] Indeed, Labour reclaimed Ilford South in 1992 and recorded a near-twenty-point swing against Bendall in Ilford North.

CULTURES

8

Middle-Class Wanderers and Working-Class Professionals: The British and the Growth of World Football 1899–1954

Tony Mason

> I don't care a brass farthing about the improvement of the game in France, Belgium, Austria or Germany. The FIFA does not appeal to me. An organisation where such football associations as those of Uruguay and Paraguay, Brazil and Egypt, Bohemia and Pan-Russia, are co-equal with England, Scotland, Wales and Ireland seems to me a case of magnifying the midgets. If central Europe or any other district want to govern football let them confine their powers and authority to themselves, and we can look after our own affairs.[1]
>
> (Charles Sutcliffe, FA Councillor and Vice President of the Football League in 1928)

Young men from the British Isles played a significant role in the growth of football in locations far beyond these islands. This essay will not only explore some of the most important ways in which they did it but also examine the reaction of the British to the rapid progress made by foreign football both on and off the field. The irascible statement of one of the most senior administrators in English football in 1928 that Fédération Internationale de Football Association (FIFA) membership was 'magnifying the midgets' reflected both powerful feelings of football superiority from the four countries who had been first in the field, and the sporting expression of a widely shared culture of national greatness. This essay will argue that while insularity was an important presence at the formal level of the national associations and leagues responsible for the running of the sport in the four home nations, at the more informal level of individuals and

[1] *Topical Times*, 14 January 1928 quoted in Pierre Lanfranchi and Matthew Taylor, *Moving With the Ball: The Migration of Professional Footballers* (Oxford, 2001), p. 46.

clubs, the practice could be somewhat different. Two particular examples of this practice will be examined in some detail here: the tours abroad undertaken by British clubs, usually in the Spring after the close of the British football season, and the work of the British coaches in teaching the game to players both in clubs and national associations abroad. A final section will explore football's role in the Second World War, attempts afterwards to broaden its appeal and the shock to the British game delivered by Hungary.

A VERY BRITISH INNOVATION

'Football can never attain the proud position among the national sports of England which its admirers so fondly look forward to—the cricket of the winter months'.[2] Had the writer lived for another forty years he might have been persuaded differently. By 1905 10,000 clubs were affiliated to the English Football Association. A twenty-club strong First Division of Professional clubs was attracting five million spectators every season and the 1901 Football Association (FA) Cup Final had been watched by a crowd of 110,820. Alongside these developments, a small service industry had sprung up producing a range of products from specialist shirts, shorts, and boots to goal nets. Considerable sums had been invested in the development of grounds providing more and better accommodation for the increasing number of spectators. Football had joined cricket and horse-racing as the main elements in a specialist sporting press and the birth of the Saturday evening sports editions. No newspaper could ignore sport but it was the expanding popularity of football which sold most copies. England, Scotland, Ireland, and Wales supported vigorous football sub-cultures. Several writers have emphasised the importance of association football on the contemporary economic and social environment. What had, in the 1860s been largely a game for the leisured elite had become by 1900 a sport which was 'at the heart of much' British 'male culture'. It even had its own international championship.[3]

Moreover, by 1900 football had begun a rapid expansion overseas and was being taken up by young men in Europe, South America, and parts of the British Empire. The attractions of modern sport seem obvious to the early twenty-first century observer. The inherent unpredictability of the contest and the drama which was often associated with it produced a capacity to create a 'uniquely powerful emotional bond between spectators and participants'. Sport provided clear-cut outcomes in an otherwise complex modern world. It also held out the prospect of change especially in team sports, as the losers of today just might become the winners of tomorrow. In an unjust world, sport was a site where the rules were observed and effort and merit

[2] Anon, *Sporting Gazette*, October 1863. I am grateful to Richard Holt, Dilwyn Porter, and Matthew Taylor for reading an earlier version of this paper.

[3] See esp. Dave Russell, *Football and the English: A Social History of Association Football in England, 1863–1995* (Preston, 1997) p. 30; Matthew Taylor, *The Association Game: A History of British Football* (London, 2008) (esp. chs. 1 and 2) and Tony Mason, *Association Football and English Society, 1863–1915* (Brighton, 1980).

apparently rewarded.[4] Although not a religion, football, with its own collective rituals and symbols, could often function like one. It also had the ability to spread across international boundaries.

Track and field athletics, boxing, and association football especially were part of an international language of sporting modernity in which the language was English. Football in particular was the quintessentially British product. Its reception was part of that wider process by which members of European urban elites were attracted by the cultural and social tenets of Britishness, one of which was a love of sport and vigorous physical exercise. Sport in general and football in particular were seen as playing an important role in the production of physical fitness and efficiency. What were thought to be peculiarly British values of physical prowess and fair play were admired. Football was to benefit from a fashionable Anglophilia among educated and prosperous Europeans and South Americans which included wearing English clothes, giving their sons English names and adopting English sporting terms, sometimes giving their football clubs English names even when the teams contained few English players.

Football was introduced to many parts of the world by British soldiers, traders, industrialists, plantation owners, missionaries, and educationalists. They did not all share the same objectives but most shared the same enthusiasm for the game and often played a part in its early organisation. In Cairo, for example, the High School Club was founded on the initiative of two high-ranking British officials but it was soon widening its membership and changed its name to Nadi-al-Alil National Club in 1907, whose first president was British. In Lagos, Nigeria, from 1910 a match was played every Friday evening between Mr Kerr's European Team and a team from the recently founded King's College. In eastern Nigeria expatriate Scots competed for the Beverley Cup from 1906. Meantime there were frequent football matches on the Gold Coast (Ghana) between British officials and local teams, some of whom took the names of English professional sides such as Bolton Wanderers and Everton. If educated elites were the first to play football in the cities of Europe and South America, young working men soon followed their example. Sometimes employers furthered this process in part for their own ends as in 1894 when Harry Sharnock son of a Lancashire textile manufacturer, encouraged his Russian employees to play football in an attempt to stop them drinking vodka on Sundays.[5]

But it was increasingly an indigenous affair. South America provides an interesting example, particularly Argentina. There, football had been pioneered by young men from the 50,000 strong British community in Buenos Aires who had set up their own schools, churches, newspapers and social and sporting clubs from the 1880s. At the beginning of the twentieth century the championship of their local football league was won eleven years in a row by a team of second

[4] I have benefited here from reading Barbara J. Keys, *Globalizing Sport: National Rivalry and International Community in the 1930s* (London, 2006), pp. 8–9.

[5] Paul Dietschy and David-Claude Kemo-Keimbon, *Africa and the Football World* (Paris, 2008), pp. 50–6.

generation British migrants of whom five were the brothers Brown who had attended the English High School. But the mass immigration of young men from Italy and Spain meant that such a state of footballing affairs could not last. In 1913 Racing won the title with a team wholly made up of recent immigrants. Overseas football retained the rules set up by the British associations and overseen by the British International Football Association Board. But everywhere they were translated into the language of the individual country, although in Argentina football did not become 'futbol' until 1934.[6]

This expansion of football overseas was accompanied by some unforeseen consequences for the British. The young football associations of Europe quickly developed an enthusiasm for international matches. This provided an impetus to establish a forum at which regular meetings could take place. Not unnaturally the newcomers were keen that the pioneers from England should join in. Letters were exchanged and eventually representatives of the football associations of France and Holland went to London where they found trying to interest the Football Association in their project was like 'slicing water with a knife'. So the foreigners went their own way and in 1904 formed FIFA. The English did join in 1906 and it proved useful when a group of clubs committed to an extremist interpretation of amateurism broke away from the FA to set up their own Amateur Football Association. There were several reasons why the AFA had little impact but an important one was that FIFA banned their members from playing with AFA clubs. In 1912 FIFA successfully organised the football tournament at the Stockholm Olympics while still a gentleman's club with no headquarters, nor jurisdiction over the laws of the game and no competitions of their own. By 1914 thirty football associations were affiliated and the process by which football was to become the first global sport was underway.

Significantly, it was a process encouraged rather than hampered by the First World War. Several of those nations directly engaged in the conflict increasingly used sport and particularly football not only in their physical fitness programmes but in schemes of specific military training. Sports were also identified as contributing to the morale of all ranks.[7] Wherever British servicemen went it seems they played football. Over 600 members of the 1st Royal Naval Brigade interned in a camp at Groningen in Holland throughout the War not only organised their own competitions but also played many matches against Dutch teams.[8] The game was also famously played at Ruheleben, a camp near Berlin in

[6] For Argentina see Eduardo P. Archetti, *Masculinities, Football, Polo and the Tango in Argentina* (Oxford, 1999), esp. ch. 2 and Tony Mason, *Passion of the People? Football in South America* (London, 1999).

[7] See J. G. Fuller, *Troop Morale and Popular Culture in the British and Dominion Armies 1914–1918* (Oxford, 1990), and Eliza Riedi and Tony Mason, 'Leather and the fighting spirit: sport in the British army in World War I', *Canadian Journal of History* 41 (2006), pp. 485–516.

[8] Door Gerard Helsma, 'Football in Timbertown, 1914–18. The English camp in Groningen', (Unpublished paper, 1999). See also Peter Seddon, *Steve Bloomer. The Story of Football's First Superstar* (Derby, 1999), pp. 136–42.

which several former British professionals, working as coaches in Austria and Germany, were interned. As for those countries uninvolved in the fighting, such as Argentina, Brazil, Chile, and Uruguay, the development of football was uninterrupted. The first ever regional international championship was organised in Montevideo in 1917. Nothing could stop the forward march of football.

The remainder of this chapter will be devoted to a closer examination of how the British responded to these developments. It is hard to disagree with previous writers such as Beck, Lanfranchi, and Taylor that at the formal level of national associations the response to the growth of football outside the British Isles was characterised by an unsavoury mixture of arrogance and insularity.[9] After the end of the War neither Britain nor her allies wanted to resume football relations with Germany, Austria, and Hungary, the defeated nations. There was also a failure to agree about how amateurism should be defined, with many overseas associations favouring compensation to be paid to players for time lost at work while preparing for matches whereas the British wanted a strict interpretation of expenses. And after the partition of Ireland in 1922, that country had two national football associations which caused confusion abroad and irritation in the United Kingdom. These were serious differences between the home associations and their overseas counterparts but as Lanfranchi and Taylor point out these conflicts masked a more fundamental perceived threat to British footballing autonomy. These foreigners might want to change the laws of 'our' game next! When the home nations withdrew from FIFA in 1928 they emphasised that they wanted to have 'friendly relations' but also that they 'wanted to conduct affairs' in a way that long experience had shown desirable. The recent formation of most affiliated members of FIFA was underlined and this rendered them 'ill-equipped' to deal with the complicated issue of what constituted amateurism. Administrators like Charles Sutcliffe, were more outspoken. FIFA was desperate that England should send a team to the inaugural World Cup in 1930 but the reply of the Football Association to the letter of invitation took up only two sentences. This was the language of an insular and island people who thought that football outside Britain was not the 'real' football but a distorted 'foreign' version of an essentially British game. It was the islanders defining themselves as against Europe, something different, exceptional, and *better*. It would take changes in attitude and personnel among British football's administrators and another World War to shift this stifling insularity.[10] Even then Scotland would not award the international cap for matches against overseas nations until 1970.

But if at the more formal level of national associations, British football's international relations were aloof, among the clubs, contacts were being established and relationships developed which not only contributed to the progress of

[9] See Peter Beck, *Scoring for Britain, International Football and International Politics 1900–1939* (London, 1999), p. 67, and Lanfranchi and Taylor, *Moving with the Ball*, pp. 37–68.

[10] See Lanfranchi and Taylor, *Moving With the Ball*, p. 45 and David Cannadine 'British history as a new subject: Politics, perspectives, and prospects' in A. Grant and K. Stringer, *Uniting the Kingdom* (London, 1995), p. 19.

football in many countries but established lasting friendships among individuals. Most of the remainder of this essay will concentrate on the way this process worked in two of its most important manifestations: the part played by British coaches in the development of football abroad and the role of the overseas tour.

FOOTBALL TOURISTS

In the Spring, the fancy of young British footballers increasingly turned to Europe. *The Times* awoke to the fact that in 1925, 'capable Association teams may now be met in practically every country in Europe and in other countries besides'. On one day that Easter 'the Paulistano' FC of Brazil had beaten a Swiss combination in Berne . . . At Zurich, the 'Young Fellows' FC went down before the champion club of Spain, and 'the Dulwich Hamlet' team were touring Germany, while the Tufnell Park FC had just arrived in Czechoslovakia. Even a team from the Royal Yacht had been meeting opponents all along the coasts of Italy and Sicily.[11]

But *The Times* was at least twenty years out of date. *The Sportsman* had noted in April 1907 that 'year by year tours to the Continent become more and more popular and this Easter the exodus has indeed been remarkable' and mentioned what were probably mainly middle-class clubs from the South such as Civil Service, Crouch End Vampires, Townley Park, and Oxford University AFC.[12] The actual numbers of tours would be difficult to discover but some idea of how many is indicated in 1938 when the English FA noted that they had sanctioned 197 matches abroad across the Easter holidays as well as twenty close season tours.

It is not entirely clear when the first football club left these shores to tour abroad. According to the historian of the Cambridge University AFC that club first crossed the Channel in 1886.[13] Clapton went to play in Antwerp in 1890 and Queen's Park, from Glasgow, made what would be the first of several visits to Denmark in 1898. The Corinthians, the Oxbridge elite of English amateur football, made fourteen tours abroad between their first to South Africa in 1897 and their third to Brazil in 1914. Oxford University undertook their first tour in the Easter vacation of 1899. Thomas Cook's were used to work out the cost of a visit to Prague and Vienna and the tour was authorised on a minimum guarantee of £200 to be handed over in Oxford before starting. In the event a team of twelve players travelled and two matches were played in each of the cities.[14]

But if the Corinthians and the two ancient Universities saw themselves, and were recognised by others, as the elite of amateur footballers there was a

[11] *The Times*, 18 April 1925.

[12] Dilwyn Porter, 'Revenge of the Crouch End Vampires: the AFA, the FA and English football's "Great Split", 1907–1914', *Sport in History* 26 (2006), p. 423.

[13] Colin Weir, *The History of Cambridge University Association Football Club 1872–2003* (Harefield, 1998), p. 136.

[14] See Oxford University Association Football Club, House Secretary's Minute Book, Special Collections MSS, Bodleian Library Oxford (hereafter OUAFC MSS). Dep.d. 822–4.

less well-known club for which touring abroad became its sole purpose and whose aim, gradually realised, was to promote the game overseas. In 1898 a group of Old Boys from the British school in Richmond, Surrey, formed a football team. In the Easter holidays of 1901 a French member helped to set up a trip to Northern France with two matches arranged against teams in Roubaix and Calais. Both groups liked it enough to repeat it the next year. The members of the club were mainly middle-class with occupations such as clerks, solicitors, and teachers. In September 1905 the club was reorganised and renamed Richmond Town Wanderers. Easter and Christmas 1906 saw them in France having made contact with the Amiens Athletic Club and the Racing Club de France in Paris. The club was now going to Belgium and Holland as well as France, often twice a year. Their first defeat was in Leiden, Holland in 1909 and two more followed in Belgium in 1910 including a 9–1 defeat in Ghent. These losses led to the feeling that the club's playing strength should be improved by widening the pool of selection and in 1912 its name was changed to Middlesex Wanderers.

Middlesex Wanderers existed solely with the aim of touring. The club had no regular ground or list of fixtures.[15] It did not play a 'home' game until March 1923 when Ajax of Amsterdam were beaten 4–2 at Ilford. However it tried to recruit the best amateur players and the basic qualification was that they had been good enough to be selected for their county teams. That this would not always be enough to win was illustrated as early as 1912 when the club was invited to take part in the Vienna Festival of Sport along with leading English professionals, Tottenham Hotspur and Arsenal. The Wanderers lost all three games in five days to WAF Vienna, MTK Budapest, and FA Bayern, without scoring a goal.[16] The fact of their never really playing together as a team and developing that crucial understanding known as teamwork must have begun to tell against them. In 1914 the Wanderers took their longest tour to date spending two weeks in Barcelona. After winning the first match they lost the next three after Barcelona had allegedly strengthened their team by including some players from other clubs.

After the War the Wanderers resumed their travels with the Alaway brothers, in many respects the inventors and managers of the club, more determined than ever that football could promote international friendships. R. B. Alaway, an auctioneer by profession, was the Secretary of the Wanderers from 1905 to 1949 and wrote a very evocative book about it entitled *Football All Round the World* (1948). His brother, H. G. Alaway was a career army officer and President of the club from 1905 to his death in 1940. Both were founder members of the club and helped to construct particularly close relations with footballers in Holland and Norway. The Wanderers made eleven visits to Holland between 1909 and 1934. In 1932 their tour was actually labelled 'missionary' by the Dutch, implying that they were still learning about the game from the British. Ten games were played in fourteen

[15] I am grateful for the very good centenary history of the Wanderers, Brian Wakefield with Ian Bevan, *Middlesex Wanderers, Sporting Ambassadors for a Hundred Years 1905–2005* (Richmond, 2005), p. 34.

[16] Wakefield, *Middlesex Wanderers*, p. 19.

days. Two years later the Wanderers were one of three teams invited to celebrate the 40th anniversary of the Amsterdam Football Association.[17]

A similar journey took the Wanderers to Norway in 1935 when 'the club fulfilled its true missionary role by playing several matches throughout the country', actually five in ten days. Sumptuous banquets followed the games and the programme for the match at Arendal in the south of Norway summed up the warmth of the welcome. 'Our visitors today come to us from the homeland of sports—England. They have come to show us how football is played by scholared exhibitors of the game, and we feel convinced that their visit will have importance to the extension and development of soccer in southern Norway in the future.'[18] However there were also signs that the football world was changing. The next time the Wanderers were due to visit Norway in June 1938, the trip had to be cancelled because the Norwegian national team had qualified for the finals of the World Cup in France.[19] When the Wanderers visited Sweden and played Landskronas Bol in 1929, a local paper named the visitors 'middle-class' Wanderers. But it would be wrong to conclude that it was only middle-class amateur teams who had the knowledge, confidence, and contacts to spread the gospel according to association football all over the Continent. Nor was it only the amateurs of the south who occasionally found themselves in exotic locations.

Most clubs in the Northern League were stuffed with working-class footballers with jobs in the local coalmining, manufacturing, and transport industries. Few of them would have been able to make a financial contribution to these visits and the cost of travel and accommodation was usually met by the hosts and the crowds who paid to watch. Bishop Auckland, West Auckland, Stockton, and Crook Town were regular tourists both just before and after the First World War. Crook played three games against F. C. Barcelona in April 1913 before crowds of two, seven and ten thousand winning the first and drawing the other two. Crook was there again in 1921 and 1922 and altogether could boast that they had met Barcelona ten times![20] So many visits was probably due to the fact that Jack Greenwell, an ex-player born in Crook, had gone to coach in Barcelona, married a Spanish girl and stayed.

Middlesex Wanderers was one sign of the ways in which touring had become embedded in the sub-culture of British amateur football. But even more extraordinary is the story of how a small club with only a short history, very little in the way of resources, and playing in the North London Thursday League took its enthusiasm for the game not to Europe or South America but to that wider world in the Middle and Far East. There is some suggestion that the chairman of Islington Corinthians and organiser of the tour may have been inspired by the

[17] Ibid., pp. 40–1.

[18] Ibid., p. 42.

[19] Ibid., p. 45.

[20] Brian Hunt, *Northern Goalfields. The Official Centenary History of the Northern League 1889–1989* (np, 1989), pp. 91, 366.

visit of the Chinese team which took part in the football tournament at the 1936 Olympic Games and had paid for the trip to Europe by playing twenty-eight matches en route which brought them a profit of £3,000.[21]

The tour began in October 1937 but did not end until early June 1938. The bare facts reflect its scope but cannot do justice to the organisational planning and ingenuity that made it possible. It was all done by boat and train beginning in Holland and ending in Montreal, Canada. In between the club played in Switzerland, Egypt, India, Burma, Malaya, Singapore, the Dutch East Indies, Hong Kong, the Philippines, China, Japan, Hawaii, and the United States. The party travelled 35,000 miles and played ninety-five games in eight months of which sixty-five were won and eight lost. Thirty-two matches were played in India in a few days over six weeks. It is something of a surprise that the eighteen playing tourists, a mixture of students, teachers, clerks, a commercial traveller, and a professional cricketer, could get the time off work. It is less surprising that only one member of the team appears to have been married with a family.[22]

Professional teams were also in demand as tourists. By 1900 it was the British professionals who were setting new standards of fitness and skill in football. This made them increasingly attractive visitors to those supporters of the sport abroad. Even in 1922 it was the relatively unfashionable British clubs of St Mirren and Notts County who were invited to open the new Les Corts ground of Barcelona.[23] For the British clubs themselves it was money that was probably the most significant factor. The profits from an overseas tour would pay the summer wages of their players. A director of Everton claimed that their 1909 tour to Argentina and Uruguay made a profit of £300. Swindon Town did even better in 1912 when match receipts for their eight games totalled £8,000. When Newcastle United went to Central Europe in 1911 the players were so generously remunerated that the Football league stepped in forbidding professionals to profit from overseas tours. On the other hand when Celtic had gone in May 1904 the management successfully persuaded their players to forego their wages.

Vienna was a popular destination and before 1914 both Celtic (twice) and Rangers had played there as had Southampton, Tottenham Hotspur, Everton, Blackburn Rovers, and Oldham Athletic. Perhaps the football tour was not as exciting for the professional as it was for the amateur. The journeys abroad of British professionals were not part of their Easter holidays but tagged on to the end of what must have seemed a long season in both England and Scotland. The English First and Second Divisions played forty-two matches from 1919 to 1920, while in Scotland the thirty-four matches of the pre-1914 Scottish First Division increased to thirty-eight in 1920. In 1929 the manager of Arsenal, Herbert Chapman, asked his players if they wanted to accept an invitation to go

[21] A. H. Fabian and Geoffrey Green (eds.), *Association Football*, vol. 4 (London, 1960), p. 461. The only book about the Islington tour is by Rob Cavallini, *Around the World in 95 Games* (Kingston, 2008).

[22] He was Alfred J. Martin who had spent the 1931–32 season playing for Antibes in France. Cavallini, *Around the World*, p. 42.

[23] *Soccer History* 5, (2003), pp. 39–41.

to Argentina at the end of the 1928–9 season. As most of them did not seem keen, the Board of Directors decided not to go. Chelsea went instead. In the same year, the holders of the FA Cup, Bolton Wanderers, were contemplating a tour of Germany. But a majority vote among the players decided against.[24]

And of course not only were the opposition getting stronger but their feeling for the game and their interpretation of the rules could present additional problems. The robust shoulder charge so favoured in Britain was increasingly frowned upon overseas. Goalkeepers especially were becoming a species protected from any physical contact and many countries favoured the use of substitutes, often whether players were injured or not. When Chelsea took Arsenal's place in Argentina in 1929 they found things tough on the field but a social success off it.

Amateur players also had to face up to problems of a rising level of performance among foreign teams. Although there was no sign of any lessening of the hospitality on offer to footballing visitors they too had to work much harder for success on the field. This point is nicely illustrated, and with some telling detail by the contemporary account of the Oxford University footballers' tour to Czechoslovakia and Austria in April 1936 compiled by the team captain.[25]

On their 1899 visit the University footballers had beaten Sportourni Slavia 3–0, the Deutscher Fussball Club 9–0, and two scratch elevens, a Viennese team 15–0 and a combined English and Vienna eleven 13–0. But by 1936 they realised that they were going to be up against some first-class teams and that 'we should have to be in really good condition'. They had even undertaken some preparation in the form of two pre-tour practice matches, beating Woking but losing to Cheltenham Town, who had recently joined the Southern League, and whom they described as 'a strong professional side'.

After a stop and a match in Ghent the party took the sleeper to Prague 'where there was a dense crowd at the station to meet us and we were immediately surrounded, presented to officials, photographed and marched off to our hotel which was really first class'. They were 'keyed-up' for the first match against 'Sportourni Slavia' who were described as the Czechoslovakia League champions.[26] Oxford lost 8–2 after having led 2–1 in the first thirty minutes, but 'we could not keep up the pace'. There were six Czechoslovak internationals in the opposition who were 'extremely fast and controlled the bouncy ball cleverly', while Oxford found conditions very difficult. The Czechs had recently introduced professionalism and had actually beaten a full England side 2–1 in Prague in 1934. Before the match with Slavia, what the captain described as 'seven old gents' who had played against the visiting Oxford team of 1899, 'were presented to us and gave us a very handsome banner'. Thence to Brno where the visitors lost 6–1 and then into Austria where they met a team in Vienna whom the captain

[24] See Neil Carter, *The Football Managers* (London, 2006) p. 58 and *All Sports Weekly*, 18 May 1929. W. Capel Kirby and Frederick W. Carter, *The Mighty Kick, The History, Romance and Humour of Football* (1933; Cleethorpes, 2005), pp. 173–90.

[25] What follows is taken from Oxford University AFC 'Annals Book', OUAFC MSS. Dep.d. pp. 822–4.

[26] If it was this team they later became Slavia Prague.

thought were the only amateurs they saw on the tour. The University lost 3–2. That was a good result when it is considered that six of the Austrian team were selected for the party which competed in the Olympic Games football tournament in Berlin in 1936 where they reached the final before losing 2–1 to Italy. An Englishman, Jimmy Hogan, helped coach them.[27]

The final match of the tour was in Bata's boot factory town of Zlin where they were met by some young Englishmen and given 'an excellent lunch'. But tired and weary by the mixture of travel and tough opposition OUAFC were overrun in the second half and lost 5–1. By midnight the party was back in Vienna and as funds would not run to a sleeping car, had a thirty-hour non-stop journey home. Socially the tour was a 'tremendous success' with their reception everywhere leaving them 'quite overcome by the kindness and hospitality which we had received'. It was the 'actual number of goals scored against us' that was a bit of a disappointment. The grounds were hard, the weather warm and British football boots were rather inappropriate footwear. In 1899 Oxford University AFC were the teachers: in 1936 they were the somewhat overmatched pupils, and their masters had been taught by British coaches.

BRITISH COACHES ABROAD

If the touring teams showed what could be achieved, British coaches helped the local players to achieve it. Both provided a dialogue between British football and the game overseas. Matthew Taylor has identified 101 British coaches employed by foreign clubs or football associations during the thirty years or so after 1910 but it seems likely that this was a low figure.[28] There were relatively few coaching jobs in the English and Scottish Leagues in the first half of the twentieth century. Most clubs employed a trainer to keep the players physically fit and the job of football manager was slow to develop. But on the Continent the game was expanding dramatically and employment opportunities for ex-British players increasing. In 1914 the German Football Association advertised in the British press for British coaches and interviewed them at the Adelphi Hotel, Liverpool. At least twenty candidates turned up including Jimmy Hogan, Fred Pentland, and Steve Bloomer. All three had taken up appointments by the time war broke out.[29] The Referee J. T. Howcroft, who had controlled many international matches on the Continent before and just after the First World War, claimed to have sent at least ten old players to Holland where British coaches were in demand and the pay was good.[30]

27 See Norman Fox, *Prophet or Traitor? The Jimmy Hogan Story* (Manchester, 2003), ch. 13.

28 I should like to thank him for allowing me to read his as yet unpublished paper provisionally entitled *The Pioneers: British Football Coaches Abroad* (2009).

29 Pentland and Bloomer were interned in the Ruheleben camp near Berlin. Hogan worked in Austria and Hungary.

30 *Thomson's Weekly News*, 16 July 1921.

Most worked in northern and western Europe but there were few parts of the world, including North and South America and Britain's imperial possessions, which did not offer these itinerant British workers opportunities. Some of them would spend much of their working lives abroad. Hogan was one who between 1911 and 1939 coached in Holland, Austria, Hungary, Germany, Switzerland, and France. He was in charge of the Austrian team at the 1936 Olympic Games. Others stayed in one country. Fred Pentland worked in Spain for fifteen years between 1920 and 1935, mostly at Bilbao but including two spells at Athletic Madrid. William Garbutt lived and coached in Italy for thirty years and became an 'adopted Italian'. More or less forgotten in England, in Italy he has been celebrated as their first real football manager, staying sixteen years at Genoa, six in Naples, two in Rome, and one at AC Milan. He won the Spanish championship in his one year at Bilbao in 1935–6. He is the reason why all Italian professional footballers since the 1930s have called their manager by the English term 'Mister'.[31] Some British players went coaching during their summer breaks like R. Beanie and J. McDougall of Airdrieonians who worked in Norway in the close season of 1927.[32]

Formal and informal networks facilitated these movements and as we have seen, Holland attracted many former professionals from Britain. The Dutch Football Association employed several British coaches in the two decades or so between the wars including Bob Glendenning, who had played for Barnsley and Bolton before 1914. He described a much more sophisticated system for teaching the game than he had known at home. Players were set both practical and theoretical footballing tests, including one in which a player steered the ball alternatively with the inside of either foot between narrow lines dotted here and there with posts, which had to be negotiated by body swerving.[33]

Coaching practices also developed over time. Walter Bensemann's German team which played against an English FA selection in 1899 tried to kick the ball with their toes rather than the inside or outside of the foot. Nor had they quite understood the importance of keeping the ball low and trying to pass it to an unmarked colleague. But these were early days in the history of German football. Hogan once described his job as manufacturing footballers, but as the basics were absorbed it was a different level of knowledge that needed to be passed on. The idea that coaching was different to training seems to have been only reluctantly accepted by the British. Training was physical preparation and for most British professionals it involved lots of sprints and large numbers of laps around the ground and not much practice with a ball. In November 1919 the editor of the *Athletic News* repeating similar criticisms he had made in 1908, had published a series of articles on the necessity of coaching even the best teams but the only serious reply came from William Garbutt in Genoa who claimed that he never

[31] Pierre Lanfranchi, 'Mister Garbutt: The first European manager, *The Sports Historian* 22 (2002), pp. 44–59.

[32] Scottish Football Association, *Minutes*, May 1926–May 1927 p. 166.

[33] Capel Kirby and Carter, *The Mighty Kick*, pp. 142–4.

received any 'tips' on how to play from any of the trainers of the English professional clubs for whom he had played.[34] Charlie Bell who had coached in several European countries and visited South America was only one of several who thought that once an English player turned professional then he thought that he had nothing to learn. Continental players, on the other hand, had a respect for coaches and wanted to improve with their help.[35] In coaching, the basic emphasis was on control of the ball, passing, movement, and general technique. An emphasis on combining the theoretical with the practical knowledge of football appears to have characterised many of those British coaches who went abroad. Class might have been a factor here. Many early footballers on the continent and in South America were students or middle-class professionals. Looking back over his years as a coach in Europe, Hogan said that he was 'astonished to find the class of men playing football when I first arrived in Holland. And I quickly realised that with such intelligent people it was of no use my giving orders to go out for a kick about or a sprint. I simply went on the field and worked with them. Then it was a case of thinking out little ideas and exercises in shooting, ball control, trapping, heading, combination stunts, and afterwards playing in small sided games with them'.[36]

George Raynor was coach of Sweden's national team from 1946 and was another who favoured a mixture of theory and practice. He thought that British football was marked by an absence of what he called 'constructive talking'. His Swedish squads 'talked and talked and talked' and 'became experts at spotting the weak points and strong points of the opposition'.[37]

Finally it is notable that British coaches were often held in high esteem by the overseas footballing communities in which they practised their trade and were remembered long after their careers had ended. Fred Pentland spent seven years with Athletic Bilbao in two spells during which they won the Spanish League title twice, 1929–30 and 1930–1. He was something of an eccentric who wore a bowler hat on most occasions. A tradition developed among the players of whipping it off his head and stamping on it after victory. In 1959 the club brought him over for what they called a homage. He was awarded the Distinguished Member's medal. After he died in 1962 the club held a ceremony at its San Mames stadium which included a high-kicking dance in front of a small memorial, a ritual reserved only for those who have contributed significantly to the culture. The Dutch FA paid for the renewal and maintenance of the headstone on Bob Glendenning's grave in Britain after his death.[38] We have already noticed how the Austrian Football Association insisted on bringing Jimmy Hogan to their inaugural international with England in 1932 and twenty-one years later, and somewhat mischievously, the Hungarian FA did

[34] *Athletic News*, 8 December 1919.
[35] *Topical Times*, 4 August 1934.
[36] Fox, *Prophet or Traitor?*, p. 56.
[37] George Raynor, *Football Ambassador at Large* (London, 1960), p. 53.
[38] Phil Ball (ed.), *Morbo. The Story of Spanish Football* (London, 2003), pp. 70–2. I owe the Glendenning reference to Alex Jackson.

the same on the eve of their victory at Wembley in 1953. British coaches may have been accorded little honour at home but their role in the development of the game abroad was one to be cherished and memorialised. The British were also pioneers in international coaching. Five of the twenty-two teams who competed in the football tournament at the 1924 Olympic Games and three of those which took part in the 1934 World Cup, both tournaments for which no British football association entered, were prepared by British coaches.

There were sufficient signs in the thirties that British football was no longer invincible. 1929 was a bad year for English football abroad. Leading professional teams such as Newcastle United, Huddersfield Town, and Chelsea were criticised for letting the side down on overseas tours and in the football press there were headlines such as 'The Continental Tours. Does our Football Prestige Suffer?'[39] As the Fascist governments in Germany and Italy began to use sport in general and football in particular as a signifier of national prestige, so English footballers began to appear more vulnerable in international matches.[40] England lost for the first time to a foreign team in 1929 when Spain won 4–3 in Madrid. The pitch was hard, the weather was hot, it was a close-run thing. But through the thirties the England team lost seven times more, in Austria, Belgium, Czechoslovakia, France, Hungary, Switzerland, and Yugoslavia. Moreover they could easily have lost their unbeaten home record to Austria in 1932. Neither Germany nor Italy managed to beat England but both beat Scotland in 1931.[41] By 1939 there was also some evidence that British coaches were not as sought after as earlier, with Austrians and Hungarians taking jobs in France, Germany, and South America. If this was a sign that the British were losing their influence on the football fields of the world, the coming of the war and the period of reconstruction that followed appear to have provided at least a temporary respite.

THE WAR AND AFTER

Football played an important if minor part in the winning of the 1939–45 war. Many professional players were conscripted into physical training units in the Army and RAF. As most of the training was done in Britain this meant that they were not only able to play in the wartime version of league football—and get paid for it—but also to appear in representative matches between the services and a series of some thirty home internationals that were played between 1939 and 1945. Many of the representative matches in particular drew large crowds, contributing significantly to military benevolent funds and war charities. The Secretary of the FA, Stanley Rous was transferred from an anti-aircraft battery in

[39] *All Sports Weekly*, 18 May 1929.

[40] Peter Beck is excellent on the way international football was increasingly seen as international relations by other means. Beck, *Scoring for Britain*, esp. chs. 6–9.

[41] England won 4–3 but Austria played the better football and after the match the FA Treasurer Kingscott said at the banquet that Austria had deserved to win.

Fishguard to London to run the Sports Committee of the Duke of Gloucester's Red Cross and Ambulance Fund, raising over £3 million.

Rous was a sports administrator who enjoyed being at the centre of things. He had met many influential people while serving on sporting pressure groups such as the Central Council for Physical Recreation and the National Playing Fields Association and now in government. He was a cautious progressive who took seriously the growing wartime enthusiasm for reconstruction, his own particular panacea being the achievement of national fitness through sport. He believed strongly in the power of international football to unite people of all classes and cultures and it was no surprise when he guided the British football associations back into FIFA in 1946. He encouraged service sides and civilian clubs to resume tours abroad both as an aid to re-establish football on a badly damaged continent and to provide entertainment for local populations as well as British troops stationed overseas.

Before the war both the English and Scottish FAs had organised occasional Empire tours to the white dominions. After 1945, encouraged by the British Council, the FA began to recognise a wider imperial responsibility by arranging for coaches and referees to visit new members of the Commonwealth in Africa and the Caribbean. It was in these early post-war years that the demand for British coaches, falling in the 1930s, grew rapidly with the FA alone helping at least one hundred to find jobs abroad. In 1947 Walter Winterbottom was appointed its first Director of Coaching followed three years later by a technical subcommittee to study how the game was developing. Touring teams from the Gold Coast, Nigeria, Uganda, and British West Indies all visited the United Kingdom between 1949 and 1953.

It seems clear that Rous identified the period of post-war reconstruction as an opportunity to bring football more into the mainstream of the cultural life of the nation. Like other contemporary activists he believed that the war had changed attitudes. There had always been a middle-class audience for football willing to pay more for a seat in the stands. One way to encourage its growth was to halt the pre-war drift away from the game in the grammar and public schools. Rous was pleased to see scholars such as Percy Young writing about football in a similar way to how Neville Cardus wrote about cricket. He encouraged football to play a prominent part in the Festival of Britain. During two weeks in May 1951 75 matches were played, largely against European opposition. The four home countries played seven international matches and Argentina became the first overseas country to appear at Wembley. When the FA celebrated the 90th anniversary of its foundation in 1953 it co-operated with the Arts Council to stage an exhibition exploring football's relationship with the Fine Arts. It had also arranged home and away matches with Hungary who were the Olympic champions and on a long unbeaten run which had made them favourites to win the World Cup to be played in 1954.

Yet the British seemed not to have noticed that football had been evolving abroad in ways which suggested that the English and Scots were no longer the best players of what was a global game. In 1945 Moscow Dynamo had been unbeaten during a four-match tour of Britain and leading club sides touring overseas found it not only harder to win but harder to avoid defeat. Southampton, for example, lost three out of seven games in Brazil in 1948 and Arsenal five out of six when they visited the same country in 1951. Both were baffled by the speed and ball control of opponents who wore shorter shorts and lightweight boots. In the 1950 World Cup held in the same country, England lost to Spain and the United States, the land without football, and at home had struggled to draw against Yugoslavia, France, and Austria. Barely a month before the visit of Hungary only a last minute penalty had saved them from defeat against a FIFA eleven whose players had not played together before.[42]

The seven months between November 1953 and June 1954 were months of reckoning for English football. Hungary not only became the first Continental team to win in England, but they followed a 6–3 victory at Wembley by scoring 7–1 in Budapest the following May. It was the manner of these defeats which was so startling. The Hungarians were superior not only in craft and skill but also in the more typically 'British' footballing virtues of speed, team work, and finishing. One Hungarian told an English friend in a moment of sorrow rather than triumph after the Budapest match, 'we were amazed when your team took the field. We had always thought of them as gods, masters of football. But they looked old and jaded and their kit was laughable. We felt sorry for you'.[43]

But few in England seem to have thought that the masters of football would lose to Hungary on that dingy November afternoon at Wembley. Even Jimmy Hogan apparently told the *Empire News* that the English players only needed to sharpen up their passing in order to win because 'Hungarians were not natural footballers the way Englishmen are'.[44] And just as with the Moscow Dynamo in 1945, whose football was compared by Sir Godfrey Ince to that of the Corinthians, so there was a lot of talk that the Hungarians had used 'our' skills taught to them by our coaches which 'we' had somehow mislaid.[45]

That it was a British as much as an English failure is illustrated by Scotland's own 1954 moment. Beaten by England in Glasgow in April the Scots were preparing for the World Cup when news arrived of England's 7–1 defeat in Budapest. It was apparently greeted with a painful silence in the Scotland camp. Their own World Cup experience was damaged by the curious decision of the Scottish FA to allow Glasgow Rangers to take its leading players on a tour of the United States while the World Cup in Switzerland was actually in progress. The team manager resigned after defeat by Austria in the first match which was followed by elimination after losing 7–0 to Uruguay. These footballing setbacks caused some thought to be given to whether it was time to consider a Great Britain team to represent these islands in major championships. One of the newspapers

[42] On England v. Hungary in 1953 see *Sport In History* 23 (2003–4) particularly the three essays by Peter J. Beck, Ronald Kowalski and Dilwyn Porter, and Jeffrey Hill.

[43] John Moynihan (ed.), *The Soccer Syndrome* (London, 1987), p. 29.

[44] *Empire News*, 22 November 1953.

[45] See Aubrey Howard Fabian and Geoffrey Green (eds.). *Association Football*, vol. 1 (London, 1960), p.387.

which made this suggestion was the *Glasgow Herald*, a staunchly unionist newspaper in 1954.[46] It is unlikely it would be supporting the idea in 2010.

These British footballing disappointments did not bring with them only bad news. They provided powerful evidence that change was needed in the way players learned to play and that at the summit of the sport more thoughts had to go into the technical aspects of training and coaching. Television made this evidence more widely available and questions began to be asked about the competence of those who ran essentially voluntary British football associations and leagues. The voice of insular conservatism could still be heard. A representative of the management at Arsenal told the *Daily Mirror* not long after Hungary's win at Wembley that Arsenal had their own 'particular methods' of training: 'although they have been modernized they differ very little from the routine carried out nearly fifty years ago . . . It is surely farcical to suppose that English league club players should alter their style of training in order to compete with the individual skills of the Continentals.'[47]

CONCLUSION

Orwell was not keen on sport but he did recognise its growing importance in the modern world. He was also impressed by the fact that the English had not only invented several of the world's most popular games but had 'spread them more widely than any other product of their culture'.[48] Individual British footballers and teams played an initially crucial part in this process. But the largely volunteer administrators who ran football in these islands were reluctant to share control with those overseas who had adopted it with such enthusiasm. Associated with this attitude was a relative neglect of the progress football had made in Europe and South America. Harold Perkin has suggested that losing at organised sports and games prepared the British psychologically just as winning prepared the colonists for decolonialisation.[49] Perhaps football was an exception. It had certainly taken over from cricket as the national game by the early 1950s and its British leadership found it difficult to accept that the British had lost the right to footballing superiority, that England and Scotland had become two football powers among many. Perhaps it mirrors a wider reluctance to engage with Europe. Or it might be, as a frustrated Walter Winterbottom would later say, that 'we are a very insular race. We don't like people teaching us any damn thing'.[50] Perhaps all this only mattered in the small self-satisfied world of football. Yet it is difficult not to agree with Jeffrey Hill that it also has wider

46 *Glasgow Herald*, 28 May 1954.

47 *Daily Mirror*, 14 December 1953.

48 George Orwell, 'The English People' in Peter Davidson (ed.), *Orwell's England* (London, 2001), p. 296.

49 Harold Perkin, 'Teaching the nations how to play: Sport and society in the British Empire and Commonwealth', *International Journal of the History of Sport* 6 (1989), p. 154.

50 Undated interview with Sir Walter Winterbottom, possession of the author.

meanings. 1953–4 provided a moment when many people in Britain, not only England, became aware the world was changing. The fact that other people, from behind the iron curtain as well, could play the people's game better than the people who had invented it was salutary. It was the beginning of a recognition of a need for modernisation.[51]

[51] Jeffrey Hill in *Sport In History* 23 (2003–4), p. 60.

9

Just William? Richmal Crompton and Conservative Fiction*

William Whyte

On 23 March 1954 Miss Olivia Morris of London sat down to pen an embarrassing piece of fan mail. 'I know it sounds silly for a grown woman to say that she has been in love with a boy since she was nine years of age', she admitted; going on to confess that although she was now 39 she was 'still in love' with William Brown, the young hero of Richmal Crompton's *Just William* series.[1] Crompton's private papers contain dozens of similar letters from admirers. They include the heartfelt and heartbreaking thanks of a mourning mother, whose son used to love Crompton's stories—and went on to die on the battlefields of Burma.[2] Alongside this is a no less remarkable letter from Kenneth Tite, politics tutor at Magdalen College, Oxford, who wrote to say of William Brown, that 'if he hasn't saved my life, has had a sufficiently important hand in it to be base ingratitude on my part if I don't write now'.[3]

Amongst this small collection of missives, two or three stand out—and they stand out precisely because they are not personal or private, and do not include any sort of emotional detail. One is from a Swedish fan and was written in September 1965. At first, it declares, the writer had simply found her stories amusing. As he grew up, however, things had changed. 'When I was older', he wrote, 'I discovered a new side in your books. It is a satire upon English middle-class people which is better and more humoristic than anything else I have ever read.'[4] A similar point was made at a similar time by a British writer, who wrote to ask her if 'the "middle-class" background of the *William* series was deliberate or simply due to the fact that this was the background with which you yourself were familiar'.[5] Over a long and successful writing career, Crompton must have

* I am extremely grateful to the participants in the St John's workshop for their sceptical comments on this essay—and especially to Boyd and Mary Hilton for their subsequent criticism. I must also thank Zoë Waxman for advising on earlier versions and Professor Edward Ashbee for granting me permission to quote from Crompton's private papers. Unless otherwise stated all books are by Richmal Crompton.

[1] Roehampton University Library (RUL), Richmal Crompton Archive (RCA), 56 (Fan Letters), Olivia Morris (23 March 1954).

[2] RUL, RCA, 56, Edith A. Ferrett (28 September 1948).

[3] RUL, RCA, 56, Kenneth Tite (17 May 1957).

[4] RUL, RCA, 56, Chister Sjölund (9 September 1965).

[5] RUL, RCA, 56, Frank G. Smith (21 July 1966).

received hundreds, perhaps thousands, of compliments. Her decision to retain these letters and to dispose of so many others is consequently very telling. It reveals an author who saw herself—and was pleased that others saw her—as something more than just a humorist: a woman who was flattered when her fans described her books as 'a series which reflect social history'.[6]

Crompton herself made few claims about her work, acknowledging 'that it is in the "lower ranks" of literature'.[7] She told, she said, 'quiet stories about families and village life'.[8] Yet her admirers recognized that her achievements were greater than this suggests. Her gift was the ability to capture middle-class life as it was actually lived. The people she wrote about, commented one reviewer, 'are, in fact, people exactly like oneself'.[9] 'We know so many people who simply *are* your characters,' wrote the Rural Dean of Oxford in 1957, 'and so many of whom we say "she (or even he) would be just right for one of Richmal Crompton's characters".'[10] Crompton evidently appreciated this analysis—and, for the same reason, it is clear that she would have been pleased by the role she plays in Ross McKibbin's work. All told, she makes three appearances in *Classes and Cultures*: as a best-selling novelist—'a writer, who, in general intelligence and style . . . is in a class by herself'; as 'an acute observer of the mood of the southern middle class'; and—perhaps most importantly—as a 'student of middle-class . . . culture'.[11] This sense that Crompton was a representative of bourgeois England is also captured in his *Ideologies of Class*, where her work is used to illustrate the continuing salience of the old Conservative-Liberal binary for many middle-class voters in the late 1920s.[12]

Ross McKibbin is not the only writer to have noticed this aspect of Richmal Crompton's writing.[13] Literary theorists, literary critics, and her biographers have all noted her interest in class and, in particular, her focus on the middle class. Most interestingly, Alison Light, in a little-noticed footnote, has suggested that Richmal Crompton would 'bear investigation as a species of conservative modernist'.[14] But although these suggestions are intriguing, they have not really been explored to any real length or in any real depth. The question of Crompton's own political perspective, of the ideologies that underwrote her writing, has not really been addressed. Should we read *Just William* as a quintessentially

6 RUL, RCA, 56, R. R. Martin (13 October 1957).

7 Quoted in Kay Williams, *Just Richmal: The Life and Work of Richmal Crompton Lamburn* (Guildford, 1986), p. 150.

8 Quoted in Mary Cadogan, *Richmal Crompton: The Woman behind William* (Stroud, 2003), p. 146.

9 Elizabeth Sturch, *TLS*, 1 April 1939, p. 187.

10 RUL, RCA, 56, R.R. Martin (13 October 1957).

11 Ross McKibbin, *Classes and Cultures: England 1918–1951* (Oxford, 1998), pp. 500–2; 55, n 28; 390.

12 Ross McKibbin, 'Class and conventional wisdom: the Conservative Party and the "public" in interwar Britain', in id., *Ideologies of Class: Social Relations in Britain, 1880–1950* (Oxford, 1990), pp. 259–93, p. 276.

13 See also Peter Hollindale, 'Ideology and the children's book', in Peter Hunt (ed.), *Children's Literature: Critical Concepts in Literary and Cultural Studies* (4 vols.; London and New York, 2006), vol. 3, pp. 101–19, p. 111.

14 Alison Light, *Forever England: Femininity, Literature and Conservatism between the Wars* (London and New York, 1991), p. 239.

English pastoral elegy or as a British version of Hucklebury Finn?[15] Should we see Crompton's books as 'decidedly feudal', or are they actually an attack on contemporary snobbery?[16] Or should we heed the advice of Crompton's niece who warns that any attempt to use her books as historical sources is doomed to failure?[17] This essay will suggest that Ross McKibbin is quite correct to see Crompton as a major source for this period. But it will use her writings in rather different ways and reach somewhat different conclusions.

In particular, it will look at Crompton's work as a whole: drawing on all the books that she published between 1922 and 1970. These fall into two parts. First, there are fifty-two volumes of satirical and comedic short stories—thirty-nine of which are part of the *Just William* series. Then there are forty novels addressing adult themes. Crompton's greatest success was with *Just William*: the adventures of a grubby pre-pubescent, which sold more than 12 million copies. Her greatest enthusiasm however, was devoted to the novels, where Crompton explored the nature of love, life, and individual happiness. By considering the novels and the short stories together, it is possible to uncover a coherent worldview: a Conservatism that differs significantly from the ideology identified by Ross McKibbin. In his seminal essay 'Class and Conventional Wisdom', he revealed an interwar coalition of forces that backed the Conservative Party because of 'a particular notion of the working class and . . . an acute hostility to working-class politics'. It was, he argued, this 'largely negative' set of beliefs that underwrote Tory hegemony in the 1920s and 1930s, mobilizing the middle classes behind the party best able to thwart working-class political power.[18] Crompton, by contrast, reveals a different sort of Conservativism: one grounded not on antipathy to the workers, but a general pessimism about human nature; one that showed confidence in the resilience of the middle class and very little fear that bourgeois values could or would be overturned by socialism.

Crompton's attitudes were the product of experience. Born in 1890, Richmal Crompton Lamburn was the daughter of a schoolmaster who took Holy Orders. She was educated at a private boarding school and read Classics at Royal Holloway before becoming a schoolmistress herself in 1915. She continued to teach until disability and literary success encouraged her to become a full-time writer, which she remained from 1924 until her death in 1969. Hers was a story of social ascent and her fiction followed her life. It deals with the Lancashire of her childhood, the schools and college of her adolescence and early adulthood, and

[15] Ralph Stewart, 'William Brown's world', *Children's Literature Association Quarterly* 13.4 (Winter 1988), pp. 181–4; Betty Greenway, 'William forever: Richmal Crompton's unusual achievement', *Lion and the Unicorn* 26 (2002), pp. 98–111, p. 104.

[16] Philip Hensher, 'Outlaws and Blackshirts', *The Spectator*, 28 August 1999, pp. 28–9; Owen Dudley Edwards, *British Children's Fiction in the Second World War* (Edinburgh, 2008), p. 538. See also Nicholas Grene, '*Just (?) William*: a post-structuralist reading', in Arnold Kettle, et al. (eds.), *KM 80: a birthday album for Kenneth Muir* (Liverpool, 1987), pp. 55–7; Greenway, 'William forever', p. 108.

[17] Richmal Ashbee, 'Foreword', Mary Cadogan, *Just William through the Ages* (London, 1994), pp. 7–11, p. 10.

[18] McKibbin, 'Class and conventional wisdom', pp. 275, 281.

the villages in Kent where she lived as a writer. Crompton's second novel, *Anne Morrison* (1925), is her most self-evidently autobiographical, telling, as it does, the story of a Lancashire girl whose father was an ordained schoolmaster, who attended boarding school and a women's college, and who went on to become a teacher before finding the sort of money that enables her to live in comfort. But all of her work drew upon her life—even (although she was childless) her stories about children. As her niece put it, 'When we read Sexton Blake detective stories, William read Sexton Blake. When we wrought havoc with miniscule balls of sealing wax, William did the same.'[19]

In part, this semi-autobiographical approach to her writing was driven by considerations of time: in addition to the *Just William* stories, Crompton produced two novels a year for much of her career. In part, her emphasis on the domestic, the familial, and the familiar was a product of the environment in which she wrote. All the advice of the time recommended that authors—and especially women authors—should 'write about things they know'.[20] But Crompton's decision to focus on the lives and lifestyles of the middle class was driven by more than mere practicality or simple pragmatism. There was an aesthetic and an ethic at work here too. The authors she admired most had also made a career by anatomising the societies they knew best. These included Proust, Henry James, and—significantly—Ivy Compton-Burnett.[21] Compton-Burnett is significant because she and Crompton shared so much. They were both upwardly-mobile middle-class women, both educated at Royal Holloway, and both are representatives of what Alison Light has called conservative modernism: the 'more intimate and everyday species of conservatism which caught the public imagination between the wars'. Conservative modernism, Light argues, was 'conservative in effect yet was often modern in form, a conservatism itself in revolt against the past, trying to make room for the present'. Ivy Compton-Burnett—with her spare style, her miniaturism, and her attack on nineteenth-century sentimentality, especially the Victorian cult of domesticity—is a perfect example of the ambiguities that Light sought to illuminate. Here was a modernism that was, in many respects, highly traditional in form. Yet here was 'a conservatism which was fuelled, in the first place, by a modernist rather than traditionalist impulse'; a conservatism that 'manifested itself in a language of reticence and understatement'.[22]

Richmal Crompton was not Ivy Compton-Burnett. She was neither as inventive, nor as gifted a stylist. She wrote much more and for a wider readership. She was less subtle and more overtly didactic. Nonetheless, both women shared something of the sensibility that Alison Light has identified. In her writings, Richmal Crompton similarly sought to attack the cosy conventionalism of

[19] Margaret Disher, *Growing up with Just William by his Sister* (London, 1990), p. 92.

[20] Cecil Hunt, *Living by the Pen: A Practical Guide to Journalism and Novel Writing* (London, 1936), p. 217.

[21] Williams, *Just Richmal*, p. 167.

[22] Light, *Forever England*, pp. 11, 59.

Victorian thought. Her novels abound with adultery, illegitimacy, divorce, suicide, child abuse, and homosexuality. In her writing Crompton persistently returned to the nature of modernity: a world of new women, of socialism, and of apparent freedom. Her books, and especially her family sagas, were preoccupied with the passage of time, and her belief that every age is unique. From the first, Crompton was interested in how the problem of human relationships is 'different in each generation and each generation has to solve it afresh'.[23] Her style was also self-consciously contemporary: often criticised for its 'light and slangy' manner.[24] The *Just William* series was also driven by the desire to keep up with the times—indeed, from the first, William was characterised by what one horrified individual called 'a *modern* face'.[25] In the 1920s, this meant such things as attending the British Empire Exhibition and singing popular songs.[26] In the 1940s, this meant Brains Trusts, the Beveridge Report, and the Home Guard.[27] Twenty years later, William was plunged into the swinging sixties, encountering pop stars, student radicals, and the 'science' of opinion polling.[28] Crompton's subjects were thus not only modern—they were meant to be modern. Towards the end of her life, Crompton's papers show her determined to remain up to date, with her reminder to be 'topical' or even 'Topical' repeated again and again throughout her notes.[29]

This self-conscious modernity was, however, always consonant with conservatism: revealing a conservatism of the everyday; defending the private against the public and the individual against the demands of society and the state. It is a point picked up at the end of *Mrs Frensham Describes a Circle* (1942) where the despotic Mrs Tylney—a woman who dominates her family and has devoted herself to voluntary work—is blinded by an incendiary bomb. It is in this damascene moment that she realises that she has 'put emphasis on the wrong things', placing the public world above the private.[30] Authenticity and fulfilment, in Crompton's work, come from freely-chosen relationships created by autonomous individuals. It is these relationships, indeed, that constitute the individual. As one of her characters puts it: 'It's a man's ties—his loyalties, his responsibilities—that give him any reality he has.'[31]

The continuity of this position is evident in two of her most popular novels, *The Odyssey of Euphemia Tracy* (1932) and *Matty and the Dearingroydes* (1956). Euphemia Tracy is the daughter of a parlour maid and a valet. On her father's death, she moves to London and is thrilled to find herself living with impoverished members of the middle class in the Belgravia Ladies Residential

[23] *The Hidden Light* (London, 1924), p. 223. See also *The Thorn Bush* (London, 1928), p. 18; *Family Roundabout* (London, 1948), p. 270.

[24] R. D. Chapman, *TLS*, 6 July 1940, p. 325.

[25] *Just William* (1922; London, 1983), p. 146.

[26] *Still—William* (1925; London, 1984), ch. 6; *William—The Conqueror* (1926; London, 1984), p. 160.

[27] *William and the Brains Trust* (London, 1945), ch. 1, 3, 7.

[28] *William and the Pop Singers* (London, 1965), ch. 1 and 5.

[29] RUL, RCA, I c, Ideas for William Stories (1966–67).

[30] *Mrs Frensham Describes a Circle* (London, 1942), p. 278.

[31] *Steffan Green* (London, 1940), p. 99. See also, *The Ridleys* (London, 1947), p. 185.

Club. With this as her base, she enters the world and quickly finds that her common sense and compassion enable her to resolve other people's problems. A typical scene witnesses her meeting with two left-wing navvies who attempt to educate her politically. 'One of them', Crompton writes, 'began to talk to her about Socialism. She wasn't interested in Socialism, but she was interested—passionately interested—in his wife, who, he said, suffered from continual sore throat.'[32] At least one critic found this hard to swallow, wondering whether such a character 'could ever have behaved with the never-failing sense of values' that Crompton ascribed to her.[33] Nonetheless, it was appreciated by other readers and was effectively reprised fourteen years later in the story of Matty Dearingroyde, another outsider whose love of literature enables her to resolve the difficulties of her extended family. She helps one cousin flee the cruelty of her mother—a woman so involved in public activity that she cannot see the value of private life. She also challenges another cousin, Imogen, who chooses to put her own work as a writer above her love for a man called Christopher, fearing that marriage would compromise her freedom. It is in the letter sent by Christopher to Imogen that the moral of the story—and of Crompton's work as a whole—is made uncompromisingly clear. 'You've denied life', he writes, 'and you're paying the price for denying life. It's human ties and responsibility that go to make a human personality.'[34]

In some respects, Crompton's short stories—and especially the *Just William* series—shy away from such fundamental questions. *Just William*, in particular, began life as a comic turn in *Home Magazine* and soon became a regular feature in the family-friendly *Happy Mag*. These stories were always intended to amuse rather than to instruct: for every one that dissected provincial life, there were two or three about nothing much more than the adventures to be had with William's group of friends, the 'Outlaws'. Nonetheless, there are some striking continuities between these two types of writing. Importantly, Crompton was addressing a similar audience in both genres—for despite its popularity with children, *Just William* was always written for adults.[35] The language, the point of view, the background knowledge required: all these remained those of an adult rather than those of a child. William's world is one full of young politicians who give talks on Proportional Representation,[36] women who admire Fauvism,[37] and country squires who have sold their Romneys, Fragonards, and Girtins.[38] When William's elder brother Robert acquires a car, he turns every conversation round to cars: 'the League of Nations, Epstein's sculpture, the theory of relativity, the situation in the Far East—nothing baffled him.'[39] This is scarcely child-friendly

[32] *The Odyssey of Euphemia Tracy* (London, 1932), p. 79.
[33] Orlo Williams, *TLS*, 28 April 1932, p. 308.
[34] *Matty and the Dearingroydes* (London, 1956), p. 235.
[35] Williams, *Just Richmal*, p. 146.
[36] *William—in Trouble* (1927; London, 1984), p. 180.
[37] *William's Treasure Trove* (London, 1962), p. 132.
[38] *William and the Masked Ranger* (London, 1966), p. 125.
[39] *William—the Pirate* (1932; London, 1985), p. 212.

stuff. Even the post-war William, who was arguably more juvenile in tone and whose relationship with his best friend Ginger increasingly came to mirror that of Anthony Buckeridge's Jennings and his companion Darbishire, was not directly addressed to a non-adult audience. These were stories about children—not stories for children. As Nicholas Tucker puts it, *Just William* was written 'rather in the manner of Saki, another contemporary who occasionally took advantage of the public's reaction against over-sentimental views of children in fiction'.[40]

Not only did all of Crompton's writing address a similar readership, it also dealt with similar settings. Like so many of the novels, William Brown's life was circumscribed by the village within which he lived: a situation with a variegated and variable cast, but a stable set of values and a predictable spectrum of ideas. Characters and vignettes travelled freely between the two genres. They are full of curates with an 'ultra-Oxford accent',[41] and wealthy men who drop their aitches;[42] with army officers who tell endless stories about the Boer war,[43] and women who pass their days in 'an unending succession of social activities', chairing meetings and attending committees.[44] Several stories simply recur—like the account of a shy but dutiful woman who invents fictitious members of a local charity because she is too embarrassed to recruit and too ashamed to admit that she has failed to try.[45] Rather than seeing Crompton's novels and *Just William* as diametrically dissimilar, indeed, it makes more sense to see them as aspects of the same vision: different in genre and in style, but not different in perspective.

Naturally, there were some differences between the novels and the short stories. The license granted to satirical and journalistic writing, in particular, freed Crompton to be far more topical and controversial in *Just William* than she was in her novels. It is those, in fact, that most clearly expose her fiction as distinctively Conservative as well as simply conservative. When she presented William's account of British politics—'there are three sides—Conservative, Liberal and Bolshevist'—Crompton was undoubtedly guying a popular attitude of the time.[46] But it is hard not to feel that it was a view that she had some sympathy with herself. The *William* stories, indeed, show Crompton playing a double game. On the one hand, she mocks the unthinking Tory prejudices of many of her characters.[47] She also makes fun of William's own ignorance of the wider world: his willingness to see Bolsheviks everywhere and his unthinking repetition of his father's own views.[48] She is not above mocking her own

[40] Nicholas Tucker, *The Child and the Book: A Psychological and Literary Exploration* (Cambridge, 1981), p. 117.

[41] *Portrait of a Family* (London, 1931), p. 241; *Still—William*, p. 160.

[42] *The Inheritor* (London, 1960), p. 32; *William—the Rebel* (1933; London, 1985), p. 29.

[43] *Mrs Frensham Describes a Circle*, p. 239; *William's Treasure Trove*, ch. 4.

[44] *Matty and the Dearingroydes*, p. 11; *William—the Showman* (London, 1937), pp. 132–3.

[45] *Linden Rise* (London, 1952), pp. 110–11, 127, 183; *William and the Pop Singers*, pp. 133–4.

[46] 'The job I'd like best' (December 1927), in *What's Wrong with Civilizashun and other Important Ritings* (London, 1990), p. 67.

[47] *William and the Evacuees* (1940; London, 1987), p. 107.

[48] *William—the Good* (1928; London, 1984), p. 242.

enthusiasms: casting a sardonic eye over both the foibles of women novelists and the spiritualism with which she became increasingly interested.[49] On the other hand, however, her stories direct their sharpest ridicule at precisely those targets which Crompton herself found objectionable. She sneers at the silliness of Mosley's fascists, for example, by having William found his own group of 'Greenshirts'.[50] She likewise always ensures that, in the end, the Tories win out—as with her mock election in 'William, Prime Minister' (1929). Here, party distinctions are set out by William's friend Henry, who explains:

> There's four sorts of people tryin' to get to be rulers. They all want to make things better, but they want to make' em better in different ways. There's Conservatives an' they want to make things better by keepin' 'em jus' like what they are now. An' there's Lib'rals an' they want to make things better by alterin' them jus' a bit, but not so's anyone'd notice, an' there's Socialists, an' they want to make things better by takin' everyone's money off' em, an' there's Communists an' they want to make things better by killin' everyone but themselves.

Henry himself stands as a Socialist, and gets into an argument with a small, pious child who declares that his proposal to take other people's money is sinful. His friend Douglas stands as a Liberal—and promises presents to anyone who will vote for him. Ginger, as a Communist, threatens war. And William, who becomes the Conservative candidate because of his admiration for a big game hunter who turns out to be a Tory, wins the election unanimously, as character triumphs over any threats or bribes.[51]

Naturally, Crompton was not always overtly partisan. Before the war, she often downplayed the distinction between Liberals and Conservatives—and in 'William Enters Politics' (1924), she showed William accepting the sage advice of the local Conservative candidate. '"You know," said Mr Cheytor, "I wouldn't bother about politics if I were you. They're very confusing mentally."' Subsequently, Crompton concludes, William decided to look on Liberals and Tories 'with equal contempt'.[52] After the War, party politics was similarly satirized, in the shape of Colonel Masters and Mr Saunders, leaders of the local Conservative and Labour parties respectively. '"They work in harness"', complains one harassed villager. '"They're fighting political apathy. They say that they don't mind which Association you belong to as long as you belong to one or the other."'[53] In the end, Crompton concludes, politics is never as important as real life: a point made in one of her first books, *William—Again* (1923), where she tells the story of a cabinet minister who comes to speak in the village, but is so delighted at the Outlaws' play that he ends up late for his own meeting.[54] Nonetheless, even this conclusion can be seen as classically Conservative—and

[49] *William—the Pirate*, ch. 10; *Still—William*, ch. 7.
[50] *William—the Dictator* (London, 1938), p. 43.
[51] *William—the Bad* (1930; London, 1984), pp. 53, 58–65.
[52] *William the Fourth* (London, 1924), pp. 188, 191.
[53] *William—the Explorer* (London, 1960), p. 139.
[54] *William—Again* (1923; London, 1983), ch. 1.

the practicality and pragmatism of Crompton's Tories does invariably contrast with the foolishness of more progressive characters.

Indeed, even when it is not party political, her satire often has a political edge: as with Crompton's guying of Beveridge—'the Outlaws' Report';[55] or William's decision to set up a National Health Service for pets.[56] At the heart of this was a rejection of utopian social reforms which did not take account of real life. It was this that led Crompton to characterize state-run old people's homes as gilded cages: 'old cats' homes', which forced the elderly poor to live lives that were inappropriate to their needs.[57] It was this, too, that provoked the heavy-handed short story, 'The Weak Spot' (1921). This is an account of Robert's dalliance with Communism, expressed through his membership of the Society of Reformed Bolsheviks and symbolised in his purchase—and secret wearing—of a red tie. The Society of Reformed Bolsheviks is committed to the redistribution of wealth, the equalisation of income, and the freedom of the working classes. Unfortunately, so are William and his friends, who form a Junior Branch and purloin Robert Brown's watch, purse, and bike. Robert consequently abandons Communism, concluding: '"It's all right when you get your share of other people's things, but when other people try to get your things, then that's different." "Ah,"' observes his father, '"That's the weak spot. I'm glad you found it out."'[58]

Idealists of all sorts—from the vicar's wife, with her misguided enthusiasm for the League of Nations, to Miss Euphemia Barney, president of the Society for the Encouragement of Higher Thought—are always ridiculous in Crompton's work, and especially so in *Just William.*[59] Typical of this are the Pennymans, the upper-middle-class life-reformers who appear in a number of stories in the 1930s. They dress in flowing robes, they dance folkloric jigs, and, as Mrs Pennyman puts it, they 'live on vegetables and vegetables only . . . And macaroni. Macaroni that we make with our own hands and spread out to dry in the sun.' Ginger writes them off as 'lunatics'—and so does the village, which prefers to dance the Charleston and to listen to the Blues than to participate in the Pennymans' celebration of Merrie England.[60] When they return, several years later, their League of Perfect Love—devoted to non-violence and to the protection of animals—has more success in persuading the adults to join in, aided by the discovery that Mrs Pennyman is an Honourable. But they cannot convince the village's servants not to kill pests, and the League eventually falls apart when the members come face to face with the horrible reality of William's rats.[61] Similarly, in *William—the Showman* (1937), a Miss Milton suggests that every 'upper-middle-class family' should adopt a poor family. '"Just think of it"', she says; '"Every poor family

[55] *William and the Brains Trust*, ch. 7.
[56] *William's Television Show* (London, 1958), ch. 8.
[57] *William's Treasure Trove*, pp. 94–5.
[58] *William the Fourth*, p. 20.
[59] *William—the Gangster* (1934; London, 1985), ch. 1; *William the Fourth*, ch. 10.
[60] *William—the Bad*, pp. 240, 241, 246.
[61] *William—the Detective* (London, 1935), ch. 7.

under the protection of a well-to-do one. There will be no more poverty. There will be no more class warfare. There will be no more communism or fascism or—or anything."' It is a sufficiently alarming suggestion to provoke the usually demure Mrs Brown, William's mother, to condemn it outright. Predictably, Miss Milton herself is unwilling to take part in her own scheme; and so she leaves Mrs Brown and the other middle-class ladies free to carry on with their previous charitable endeavours.[62]

Agitators are, likewise, invariably absurd when they are not self-interested. Usually, like the protest marchers from 'Newlick University', they are both.[63] Most people, Crompton writes, are more concerned to get on with ordinary life. 'What happens to all those young revolutionaries with which our colleges are always full?' she asks in one novel. 'Do they lose their flaming zeal for reformation in the thrill of their first month's salary?'[64] Even when major political change occurs, it is rarely the result of popular pressure. In a notable exchange, William is counselled against imitating the suffragettes by a woman who was herself a member of the movement. '"I'm very much afraid it's no use,"' she says.

> I marched to London and made speeches at street corners and shouted 'Votes for Women' all over the place, and—well, we'd never have got it if it hadn't been for the war. It was the war that made them give it to us, not anything we did.[65]

As a non-militant suffragist, rather than a suffragette, Crompton had a particular reason for stressing this point. Still more strikingly, she made exactly the same argument—and in almost the same words—in several of her novels. The depressed former suffragette, forced to conclude that the struggle had been 'all rather futile', is, indeed, one of Crompton's stock figures: providing further evidence that even the most high-minded and well-justified of campaigns will fail to achieve its goals.[66]

This repetition not only reveals the way in which a busy writer recycles her material. It also suggests that we should see Crompton's work as the expression of a consistent set of values. But what, in the end, are those values? For Owen Dudley Edwards, the *Just William* stories show Crompton as a Tory radical: a scourge of the establishment, an anti-snob.[67] This is, however, only partially true. Crompton was certainly a Tory. A member of the Conservative Party from 1920 onwards, she described herself as 'true-blue'.[68] She was also a shrewd critic of social convention and of the petty snobbery of English life. Her wiser characters are always those who come to realise 'that there is no vulgarity in an aspidistra,

[62] *William—the Showman*, pp. 122, 123, 132–3. See also, *William Carries On* (London, 1942), p. 186.

[63] *William and the Pop Singers*, ch. 5.

[64] *The Innermost Room*, p. 106.

[65] *Sweet William* (1936; London, 1986), p. 201.

[66] *Steffan Green*, p. 28. See also *Anne Morrison* (London, 1925), pp. 213–19; *The Four Graces* (London, 1929), p. 16.

[67] Dudley Edwards, *British Children's Fiction*, pp. 477, 538.

[68] Williams, *Just Richmal*, p. 144; Cadogan, *Richmal Crompton*, p. 116.

but there is a world of vulgarity in the conventional sneer at it'.[69] Many of her stories likewise conclude with the recognition that 'There's only one vulgarity . . . and that's pretending to be something you aren't.'[70] Nonetheless, Crompton's books as a whole reveal a rather more pessimistic sort of Conservatism than Dudley Edwards has discerned. It is not just that she had a very limited belief in the possibility of human progress—although she did, describing the passage of time as rather like a roundabout, with people going up and down but never really moving forward.[71] Nor is it simply that she had a bleak view of the capacity of people to understand one another—although, again, her description of humans as 'A set of children playing blind man's buff', unable truly to comprehend themselves or each other, suggests that this was a central aspect of her world-view.[72] More importantly, Crompton's views on class and on human nature bear little resemblance to the crusade for 'fairness, and the consequent destruction of privilege' that Dudley Edwards sees in the wartime fiction.[73]

Indeed, far from seeking to overcome privilege, Crompton had a clear belief in stability and rightness of the class system. Its stability, in her view, was guaranteed by two things. In the first place, the common sense of the English working class led them to reject the spurious and superficial attractions of change. The servants at the Hall, for example, wholly disregard William's injunctions that they are 'wage slaves' and refuse to let him free them from their bondage.[74] The housekeeper in *Chedsy Place* (1934) is still more deferential: 'The system in which people knew their places had been in her eyes perfect and unassailable.'[75] Crompton even seems to stress the continuing appeal of feudalism—as in the relationship between the two central characters in *There Are Four Seasons* (1937). The book concludes with a description of Andrew, a gardener, and Vicky, his employer, growing old together. 'He was her liege man', Crompton comments. 'He would willingly and without question have given his life for her. All feudal England lay at the heart of their relationship.'[76] Even at the end of Crompton's career, her confidence in class did not escape her. The manor house in *The Inheritor* (1960) is—like the Hall in *Just William*—inhabited by a working-class couple who have made good. In both sets of stories, however, the parvenus defer to the older families, no matter how impoverished. In *The Inheritor*, feeling 'an almost feudal allegiance' to the original owners, they actually give the house back to them.[77] Ultimately, the extent to which even potentially problematic proletarians are neutralised by Crompton's assumptions is symbolized by the mournful handyman who appears in *Portrait of a Family* (1931). Over tea, the

69 *Roofs Off!* (London, 1928), p. 125.
70 *Blue Flames* (London, 1930), p. 284.
71 *Family Roundabout*, p. 270.
72 *Blind Man's Buff* (London, 1957), p. 235.
73 Dudley Edwards, *British Children's Fiction*, p. 538.
74 *Sweet William*, pp. 126–7.
75 *Chedsy Place* (London, 1934), p. 8.
76 *There are Four Seasons* (London, 1937), p. 316.
77 *The Inheritor*, p. 32.

solicitor Stephen Arnold and the object of his affections, Olivia Mainwaring, look outside:

'Your gardener,' he said, 'looks an embittered man.'
'He is,' she said, joining him at the window.
'He had a Union Jack tattooed on his wrist during the war.'
'But why should that embitter him?'
'Because he joined the Communists since, and, of course, he can't un-tattoo the Union Jack. It's *so* trying for him.'[78]

Even Communists, it seems, cannot efface their essential Englishness, nor escape the reality of working-class dependency.

The stability of the class system did not just depend on the weakness of the workers. In the second place, Crompton pointed to the strength of the middle classes and the institutions which they run. The Church, the schools, and the universities: these institutions were, in Crompton's account, particularly responsible for creating a solid and coherent society. In *William—the Outlaw* (1927) Mrs Brown is gently mocked for her 'vague idea that some mysterious change of spirit came over a boy on entering the portals of a boarding-school transforming him from a young savage into a perfect little gentleman'.[79] But, for Crompton, the truth was not so very far from this. In *Mrs Frensham Describes a Circle* (1942) public school and Oxbridge seem to be capable of effecting remarkable transformations. Herman Stoneberry is a 'typical Jew—short, squat, greasy-looking, with a pronounced Hebraic nose'. His son Simon, however, with the benefit of Harrow and Oxford, is 'fair, good-looking, lackadaisical' and 'typically English in appearance'.[80]

The products of these institutions are natural leaders. In Crompton's first book—*Just William* (1922)—the nature of class is made manifest in the story 'William Joins the Band of Hope'. The leading figure in this temperance crusade is Mrs de Vere Carter, who 'before her marriage . . . had been one of *the* Randalls of Hertfordshire'. On this basis she is able to flatter Mrs Brown into letting William join: '"It's the refining influence of children in *our* class"', as she puts it, '"that the village children need"'. Of course, William's presence amongst the lower orders does not refine them; he leads the 'handful of gloomy children' into a riot. But the irony is that this simply reinforces the inescapability of class difference—and the proof of middle-class superiority. Without leadership, the working-class children cannot even rebel.[81] In one of Crompton's last books—*William and the Pop Singers* (1965)—these assumptions are still in place. When the Outlaws encounter the Argonauts, a somewhat shaky parody of the Beatles, they find the band listless without their singer, Chris:

78 *Portrait of a Family*, pp. 105–6.
79 *William—the Outlaw* (London, 1927), p. 136.
80 *Mrs Frensham Describes a Circle*, p. 71.
81 *Just William*, pp. 115, 117–18, 124.

'He's educated. It was him that made us call ourselves the Argonauts.'
'It's a foreign language,' said Ted.
'Out of his education,' said Johnny.
'He's our leader,' said Pete.
'The brains of us,' said John....
'He's had a classy education and taken classy exams, and sometimes it comes over him that he's wastin' his life singin' pop songs...'[82]

It is noteworthy that for Crompton—who could not bear the Beatles—the idea that even these cultural leaders might have come from the working class on their own seems to have been a wholly alien one.[83] The same was true in her 1957 novel, *Blind Man's Buff*, where the new housing estate was pictured as a place 'with no traditions, no taboos', apparent proof of the end of class—and yet it was also a place which depended on the local vicar for leadership: 'Though they would not have admitted it, they looked to him for guidance.'[84] In Crompton's world, class—and the institutions of a class society—always win out.

In tandem with this confidence in class, however, Crompton's work also engages with a more profound and more troubling issue—human nature itself. She hints—and sometimes more than hints—at a darker and more complex vision: the 'sickening realisation' experienced by a character in her first book, 'of the nightmare depths beneath the clear calm surface of life'.[85] Thus, whilst showing confidence that the structures of civil society were strong and that the hierarchies of English life were permanent, Crompton also recognized the ways in which these structures and hierarchies could be problematic. To some extent, her satire could not have worked had she not done so. It rested upon the subtle and often painful distinctions experienced by the middle classes as they negotiated the complexities of English society: a world in which the gradations of class could be measured in the names of houses,[86] and even by what was planted in the garden.[87] More importantly, Crompton acknowledged the weaknesses and the tensions within the institutions she described. Just as she showed the family as a problematic place for human flourishing—potentially a site of tyranny as well as human love—so the schools, universities, and voluntary societies she explored could also be arenas for cruelty as well as happiness.

For Crompton, no human institution can be perfect, because humans are themselves imperfect. The perfect children of the *Just William* series always reveal themselves to be frauds.[88] The perfect families of her novels invariably fail to live up to expectations; underneath 'the pleasant family gathering, the surface unity' is always an 'undercurrent of strain and uneasiness, of something wrong'.[89] The

[82] *William and the Pop Singers*, p. 28.
[83] Williams, *Just Richmal*, p. 211.
[84] *Blind Man's Buff*, p. 44.
[85] *The Innermost Room*, p. 11.
[86] *William—the Detective*, p. 193; *Leadon Hill* (London, 1927), p. 6; *Roofs Off!*, p. 26.
[87] *Naomi Godstone* (London, 1930), p. 78.
[88] *Sweet William*, ch. 2; *William—the Outlaw*, ch. 3; *William—the Pirate*, ch. 10.
[89] *Matty and the Dearingroydes*, p. 210.

social events she describes are likewise scenes of 'envy, hatred, and malice... jealousy, hypocrisy, lies, lies, lies'.[90] In that sense, all Crompton's writings rest upon an anthropology—an understanding of human nature—and a highly pessimistic one, at that. For whilst Crompton could see the good in individual humans, and even sometimes argue that 'Human nature is God's nature',[91] her view of humanity in the mass was much less attractive.[92] Her books are consequently a sustained meditation on what one character describes as 'The tyranny of the pitiless over the pitiful. It was going on everywhere every minute of every day, like a festering sore at the heart of the world.'[93] Even in the *William* books, the fundamental cruelty of humans is exposed in the vandalism and casual violence dealt out to defenceless animals.[94] Most strikingly still, in a story originally published in 1934, Crompton showed the village experiencing its own miniature version of events in Germany. 'William and the Nasties' tells the story of the Outlaws' decision to stage a Home Counties' pogrom:

> 'They chase out Jews,' volunteered Henry.
> 'Why?'
> ''Cause Jews are rich,' explained Henry,'so they chase 'em out and take all the stuff they leave behind. It's a jolly good idea.'
> 'Yes,' agreed William, 'but we couldn't do that even if we started bein' nasties 'cause there aren't any Jews here.'
> 'Ole Mr Issacs is a Jew,' volunteered Ginger.

As the owner of the local sweetshop, Isaacs is an obvious target, not least because the 'hook-nosed little man' did not like the Outlaws. '"Crumbs!" said William with a deep sigh of ecstasy, as there came to him glorious visions of chasing Jew after Jew out of sweetshop after sweetshop.'[95] Crompton was no more anti-Semitic than most of her contemporaries. The reader is intended to find this shocking—and the fact that the story was not included in subsequent editions of the book suggests that people were indeed shocked. But the story fits easily within Crompton's anthropology. Humans, she argues, are weak: they yield to temptation. '"There probably isn't a single moment in our lives when we aren't—grabbing. We destroy everything worth having by grabbing at it"', declares one ostensibly saintly figure—just before she realises that '"I'm grabbing as hard as any of them."'[96]

This analysis, combining confidence in social stability with pessimism about the fundamental nature of humanity, is, of course, a classically High Tory one. It is also a High Anglican—indeed Augustinian—notion, and it comes as little surprise to learn that Crompton was an Anglo-Catholic.[97] In this Augustinian world, her characters are continually surprised 'when wickedness and goodness

[90] *The House* (London, 1926), p. 135.
[91] *Millicent Dorrington* (London, 1927), p. 115.
[92] *Four in Exile* (London, 1955) p. 90.
[93] *Matty and the Dearingroydes*, p. 217.
[94] *William—the Bold* (London, 1950), p. 111.
[95] *William—the Detective*, pp. 117–19.
[96] *The Gypsy's Baby* (London, 1954), pp. 142, 147.
[97] Williams, *Just Richmal*, p. 154.

got muddled up',[98] and have to learn that 'people could change quite suddenly from being nice about a thing to being nasty. The same people. And the same thing'.[99] No one is entirely pure, no one is entirely good; indeed, 'unselfish people are sometimes much more selfish than selfish people'.[100] The answer to such dilemmas was not, however, political action or social reform: it was religion; the 'Mercy, pity, peace, and love' that her characters come to accept is the only real way forward.[101] True wisdom and real change, in Crompton's books, come from just that—from an acceptance of God and of his providence: his capacity to rectify the worst effects of human sin.[102] Human efforts on their own will always fail: just as the reformers of the *Just William* series and the radicals of her novels are always doomed from the start.

In all this, of course, Crompton echoes the words of more celebrated Conservative thinkers. The Conservative, as Quintin Hogg put it in 1947, 'holds to the Old Faith that man, apart from the grace of God, is not perfectible'.[103] The Conservative, wrote Lord Hugh Cecil in 1912, believes that 'unless there is prospect of such an improvement in human nature as the general substitution of love for self-interest, we may be sure at the outset that no change of social or political machinery will redeem society.'[104] Crompton would have endorsed all these views—indeed, in her books she did just that. It was this analysis that shaped her worldview, and this philosophy that led her to abandon her family's optimistic, even idealistic Liberalism in favour of a rather darker political creed.[105] Nothing she said was original, but it is noteworthy nonetheless: revealing a middle-class, middlebrow Conservatism that was more than just a rejection of working-class politics but also less optimistic about human nature than the radical Tory tradition of the late-nineteenth century.[106] Confident in the continuities of class and in the role of the middle classes in providing social leadership, Crompton illustrates a rather different sort of Conservatism from the 'largely negative' approach identified in *Ideologies of Class.* Instead, she seems closer to the self-confident 'bourgeois' democracy that Ross McKibbin has more recently described: a politics that celebrated middle-class values and was not limited to a negative attack on the workers.[107]

Crompton's work is consequently important as more than just a source for social history. It also grants access to a popular political philosophy. Written by a

[98] *The Old Man's Birthday* (London, 1934), p. 167.
[99] *Quartet* (London, 1935), p. 63.
[100] *Blind Man's Buff*, p. 123.
[101] *Mrs Frensham Describes a Circle*, p. 141.
[102] *Steffan Green*, p. 227; *Wetherley Parade* (London, 1944), p. 247.
[103] Quintin Hogg, *The Case for Conservatism* (West Drayton, 1947), p. 12.
[104] Lord Hugh Cecil, *Conservatism* (London, 1912), p. 91.
[105] Cadogan, *Richmal Crompton*, p. 8.
[106] For which, see Jon Lawrence 'Class and gender in the making of urban Toryism, 1880–1914', *EHR* 108 (1993), pp. 629–52.
[107] Ross McKibbin, '*Classes and Cultures*: a postscript', in Stefan Berger, (ed.), *Labour and Social History in Great Britain: Historiographical Reviews and Agendas* (Essen, 2002), pp. 153–66. See also James Hinton, *Women, Social Leadership and the Second World War: Continuities of Class* (Oxford, 2002).

member of the middle class, for members of the middle class, and about members of the middle class, it reveals a Conservative who was unthreatened by modernity. But this optimism was always tempered: first, by a rejection of social and political reform, and secondly by a highly pessimistic view of human nature. This uneasy balance between optimism about society and pessimism about humanity created its own problems, and perhaps explains why the unsystematic satire of *Just William* was so much more successful than her more ambitious novels. We cannot be sure whether such an analysis was influential. We cannot be certain whether it was understood—the fact that her short stories for mothers came to be seen as ideal children's literature is a caution against anyone speculating on the reception of her work. But we can conclude that for at least some of Crompton's readers, the message resonated. 'Looking back', wrote one admirer in 1954, 'I realize now that I have moulded my own sense of values and beauty on your own standards.'[108] Like the other items of fan mail she retained, Richmal Crompton kept the letter because it reflected her own sense of what her vocation was; not to entertain children, but to educate the middle classes: about society, about life, and about themselves.

[108] RUL, RCA, 56, Catherine E. O'Kane (29 April 1954).

10

The People's Orwell

Robert Colls

'It's a strange thing, don't you think, to put your belief in the people?'[1]

(K. O. Morgan.)

This is the story of how, after years of feeling disaffected and disassociated from his country, George Orwell found at last an England to believe in and, in so doing, changed the study of English politics and culture.

EPIPHANY: WIGAN 1936

On the morning of 23 February 1936, Orwell went down a coal mine near Wigan. He'd been asked by his publisher to report on unemployment in the north and chose Wigan on the strength of an old music hall joke about its 'pier' (it didn't have one), and because one of the journals he reviewed for, *The Adelphi*, had Lancashire contacts. Once upon a time, long ago, when he had been an imperial policeman in Burma, Orwell had used the left-wing *Adelphi* for target practice.[2] Now he was using it to make friends.

Right from the start, coal and cotton workers had been at the heart of the Industrial Revolution. Wigan had plenty of both and, in the 1930s, just as Lancashire had come to stand for industrial England as a whole, so, in a way, coalminers had come to stand for the industrial working-class as a whole. In 1914, they included almost one in ten of the adult male labour force. By 1936 their numbers were down from 1.3 million to just over three quarters of a million, but they remained centre stage. They had been in the thick of post-war industrial struggles, losing decisive battles with coal owners and the state first in 1919 when their case for public ownership was rejected, and again in 1926, when a determined government defeated them in a seven-month lock out which had begun with the country's first and only General Strike. The General Strike didn't last long enough to be considered an industrial struggle, but it did carry serious constitutional implications. The lock out, on the other hand, was an old

1 Private conversation: conference on British and French national identities, Lille, May 2004.
2 'He was always an aggressive critic': Michael Sheldon, *Orwell* (London, 1991), p. 107.

fashioned grind and an old fashioned beating. The miners resumed work and the message was clear: the bosses were back. Three years later, after years of strife and suspicion in the coalfields, the capitalist world went into deep depression, hitting British coal's foreign markets particularly hard. By the time Orwell went down the mine on that morning in 1936, even if Wigan itself was beginning to recover, by common consent the coal industry was in a parlous state.[3]

At this stage in his life (he was 33), Orwell had never been to what posh people like him called 'the industrial districts'. He had never seen a factory chimney, or a pit; had never met working-class people on their own terms in their own streets; had never, indeed, been to the north of England. Victor Gollancz, the publisher, for his part, didn't care where Orwell took himself so long as he produced a northern 'pot boiler' to support Gollancz's most recent business venture, The Left Book Club. Partly cheap book shop, and partly socialist reading group, the intention was a club in every town in order to advance the cause. What cause? This wasn't always clear but Gollancz, a Communist Party sympathizer, possibly member, saw Orwell as his man. Had he not lived with tramps? Had he not inveighed against the 'Money God'? Had not his latest novel, *Keep the Aspidistra Flying*, referred to 'the unemployed of Middlesbrough' as a cause for concern? Well then. Send him up there. Wherever it is.

So here was Orwell on a cold winter morning going down the mine for Unemployment, for Victor Gollancz, and for a 50 quid advance on a book.[4] He had started his journey on 31 January travelling across the Midlands by bus and on foot from Coventry to Birmingham ('frightful'), Stafford to Hanley ('bleak'), and on to Manchester ('beastly'), where he made contact with the men from *The Adelphi* before moving on to Wigan where he stayed for four days at 72 Warrington Lane with the Hornbys, an ex-miner, his wife, and three lodgers, and then for two weeks at 22 Darlington Street with the Forrests, another ex-miner, his wife, and their six lodgers. This house had a tripe shop at the front and, according to Orwell, was insufferably dirty. When a full chamber pot was left under the breakfast table, he packed his bags and left.

All told, Orwell stayed in Wigan for a little under three weeks. By day, he went collecting door to door with the National Unemployed Workers' Movement. One afternoon he watched as men scrambled down the heaps to win small coals from the dirt train passing beneath. On 19 February he went to an NUWM social at the Co-operative rooms in support of Thaelmann's Defence Fund. Orwell was deeply sympathetic to the anti-fascist cause.[5] He was less sympathetic to working-class Wigan. More used to the male hierarchies of public school, imperial police, and left-wing London, he found the looser, more diffuse, not-serious-enough women's democracy of the 'social' (cup of tea, meat pie, and dance: 6d) harder to appreciate. Orwell sat through an evening of 'gaping girls',

[3] M. P. Fogarty, *Prospects of the Industrial Areas of Great Britain* (London, 1945), pp. 32, 216–18.

[4] Peter Davison (ed.), *Orwell's England* (London, 2001), pp. 22–3.

[5] Ernest Thaelmann (1886–1944): leader of the German Communist Party, arrested 1933, executed Buchenwald 1944.

'shapeless middle-aged women', and 'excruciating singing' to conclude that the English had lost their political turbulence.[6] In other words, he looked but did not see; did not see the significance of an occasion which had brought people together, cheaply and convivially, with supper and speeches, in order to raise money they could hardly afford on behalf of a man they'd likely never heard of. For a writer who liked to get his facts straight, Orwell could be quick to judge. He was no better on the men's organizations. He is scathing about the Revd Austin's dismal afternoon talk to the Sheffield Methodist Brotherhood on 'Clean and Dirty Water' on the Tuesday, but doesn't mention the concert party with 'The Jollities' and a 'Dainty Dancer' on the Saturday. In Barnsley, he attends a regional meeting of the Yorkshire Workingmen's Club and Institute Union at Highstone Road, only to make ludicrous criticisms of the delegates, quite on a par with standard middle-class prejudices of the day.[7] He is ignorant of trade union and labour history, thinks the CIU could be proto-fascist, and takes a distinctly high Leninist view regarding the working-class's inability to think or act for itself.[8] As for socialism, Orwell seems to regard it as some sort of middle-class fad.[9] Not that he was the only former public schoolboy intent on misunderstanding the people at this time.[10] Among those who meant well, there was the 'Surrey Appeal for Jarrow', the 'Hertfordshire Campaign for County Durham', and that young gentleman whose faith in civilization was saved by going to see an exhibition of miners' paintings.[11]

After twelve days mooching about Wigan, Orwell went down the mine. He came up never to be the same again. At pains to document the labour process, and always keen to understand basic techniques, at the heart of his description is

[6] Orwell, *Wigan Diary*, Peter Davison, (ed.), *Complete Works* (London, 1998), x, p. 431.

[7] *Wigan Diary*, Davison, *Works*, x, p. 455. Orwell criticized the delegates for their high teas in the same way that Beatrice Webb had criticized the Cooperative Wholesale Society board for their free dinners—'shovelled down': Stephen Yeo, *Who Was J. T. W. Mitchell?* (Manchester, 1998), p. 27. McKibbin explains middle-class hostility to organized labour in *Classes and Cultures. England 1918–51* (Oxford, 1998), p. 56. Orwell attended the Brotherhood talk on Tuesday 11 March and the Club tea on Friday 14 March: Orwell Special Archive, University College London: Wigan note book (A/2).

[8] V. I. Lenin, *What is to Be Done?* (1902; Moscow, 1967), p. 122. *The Road to Wigan Pier*, published in 1937, has little to say on working-class association and fails to mention the aversion of a strike that was a major issue during Orwell's stay there: *Wigan Observer*, 1 February 1936. To be fair, Orwell got most of his journalistic facts straight: Joe Hayes, '"Set Down in Wigan". Orwell in the North', University of Leicester, BA History dissertation, 2009.

[9] Orwell, *The Road to Wigan Pier* (1937; Harmondsworth, 1967), part two. Orwell did not attend to the intellectual life of the working class: Jonathan Rose, *The Intellectual Life of the British Working Classes* (New Haven, 2001); Lawrence Goldman, *Dons and Workers. Oxford and Adult Education since 1850* (Oxford, 1995); and Ross McKibbin, 'Arthur Henderson as Labour leader', in *The Ideologies of Class* (1990; Oxford, 1994), p. 42.

[10] Andy Croft, *Red Letter Days. British Fiction in the 1930s* (London, 1990), chs. 2, 3, 4.

[11] Julian Trevelyan, *Indigo Days* (London, 1957), p. 102. For artists going north: William Feaver, *Pitmen Painters. The Ashington Group 1934–84* (London, 1988), ch. 6. On the adopting counties: John Newsom, *Out of the Pit. A Challenge to the Comfortable* (Oxford, 1936), pp. 83–4. For more ambitious programmes by southern people to adopt northern people, see the chapter in this volume by William Whyte.

a religious vision: the miner crucified.[12] In-bye, he marks the stages of the cross. At the coal-face, all comes to pass in a *chiaroscuro* of back breaking toil. The light is dim. Everyone is on their knees, heads bowed. Orwell is exhausted (pondering his middle-class soul no doubt), while in front of him are the coal fillers—bodies like iron, sweating and shovelling, each bearing the stigmata of his labour. So that we might live, Orwell is at pains to show that they are doing it for us.[13]

It took him four days and the rest of his life to get over this moment. He couldn't straighten up. He could only come downstairs sitting on his bottom. He could hardly walk. And he piled on the usual adjectives—'frightful', 'bloody', 'beastly', and so forth—but going down the mine had been worth a thousand political meetings. He had had to go 900 feet beneath the surface to do it, but at last he had found a people to believe in. Just before Wigan, Orwell had written to his Old Etonian pal Richard Rees to say he was getting into *partibus infidelium.* Now he was a barbarian himself.[14]

Or not. For unlike Burmese villagers, or Parisian dishwashers, or Kentish beggars, or deracinated intellectuals, or all the other people Orwell had known and written about, here was a class he did not know and could not join. How could he speak up for the miners, when they spoke so ably for themselves? How could he champion their labour, when he could not even do a portion of that labour? How could he relate to them without changing who he was? All of a sudden, his fellow countrymen began to look more intriguing. He had trotted into Burmese villages with no one to stop him. He had walked out of Kentish doss houses without so much as a cheerio. He'd been miserable in Southwold and gloomy in Hayes and angry in Hampstead—all without too much trouble. Anyone from Eton could do that. But Wigan was a closed shop. It had its own resources. It had its own culture. In this town, if he could not handle a shovel, he could not support a family, and if he could not support a family what was he doing there? A woman thought he had come from the council: 'I don't want you buggers nosing round 'ere,' she said.[15]

Orwell had been brought up in a world that had seen the winning of empires and the virtue of young men like him as one and the same. But five years in Burma had showed him that he had no virtue. There, he came to see himself as part of an imperial 'racket' set up to rob the poor. As he put it, while the British businessman went through the native's pockets, the British policeman held the nature down. When he resigned from the Imperial Indian Police in 1927, Orwell turned his back on all that in order to plunge into the catastrophic world of the poor and

[12] Gilbert Daykin, *The Miner with Chains*, oils, 1937–38, The Science Museum.

[13] Orwell, *Wigan Pier*, p. 31. He melded trips down the mine in Wigan, Grimethorpe, and Barnsley into a single account. His personal papers give no hint of an epiphany. He says the miners are 'very nice' and the area is 'very interesting' but most of his comment is matter of fact. This is not to say that his religious vision of labour was not real. Orwell was a writer. What he chose to say in a published work mattered most.

[14] Orwell to Rees, 29 February 1936: Davison, *Works*, x, p. 441.

[15] Orwell Special Archive, University College London: Wigan notebook (A/2).

oppressed.[16] One of his earliest attempts to write about them, written in 1928 on Government of Burma paper, catches the mood: 'Scene One: a mean and poverty stricken room'.[17] But after years of living among these people, on and off with tramps on the road, dossers on the rope, casuals in the hop fields, *plongeurs* in the scabrous kitchen of a grand hotel in Paris—he was sorry for them, but had no faith in their powers. Then as now it was quite possible to praise the poor for all sorts of human qualities, but not as makers of the modern world.[18] But after he'd been down the mine, as Richard Rees recalled, he suddenly 'broke into flame'.[19] Here was an empire, an empire of labour no less, to which he could lend his virtue. Here were men more valuable than he. Here were true makers and begetters of the world.[20] Here was a happier England. It was as if the road to Wigan pier had led him north out of London, away from the half-starved misanthropic poet Comstock, hero of *Keep the Aspidistra Flying*, into Lancashire and a dazzling white sequinned Gracie Fields and an all-star cast of black-faced coalminers coming out the cage singing 'Look Up and Laugh!'.[21]

After Wigan, Orwell stayed a few days with contacts in Sheffield before taking the train to Leeds to stay with his sister Marjorie Dakin and her family, where he enjoyed the sweetness and light of life at 21 Estcourt Avenue, Headingley. Then back into the coalfield where he lodged with the Greys at 4 Agnes Terrace, Barnsley. Mr Grey, age 50, coal filler, was a 'short, powerful man' with 'coarse features' and a 'very fatigued look'. Mrs Grey, age 38, Orwell tells us, was a clean and skilful housewife. They had two daughters, Doreen, 12, and Irene, 10, as well as other lodgers, but Orwell appears to have been taken into the family circle. By day he went to meetings and down two more pits, the 'Day Hole' on Thursday 19, and modern Grimethorpe on 21 March. It was at Grimethorpe that he saw fillers at work. In the evening, he and the Greys would sit together, the girls watching him type and he and Mr Grey chatting about life on 2s 2d per ton filled. When Orwell came to describe these evenings there is no doubt that he found comfort here. We have to be careful of Orwell's *Narodnik* tendencies, for his little tableau of a family at rest is as much a literary epiphany as his fillers at work. Yet he had every right to account for his feelings and in later life the girls

[16] David Cannadine sees the British Empire as a system of hierarchical signs intended to teach people their place: *Ornamentalism. How the British saw their Empire* (London, 2001), pp. 137–8.

[17] Untitled play: Davison, *Works*, x, p. 104.

[18] Among the many, Thomas Burke, *The Real East End* (London, 1932), p. 152; Gideon Clark, *Democracy in the Dock* (London, 1939), p. 174; Mass Observation, *Britain* (Harmondsworth, 1939), pp. 142–3.

[19] Gordon Bowker, *George Orwell* (London, 2003), p. 185.

[20] Alberto Cavalcanti's *Coal Face* (GPO Film Unit, 1935) carried a similar message but whereas Orwell's *Wigan Pier* stays near the men who made *Coal Face* (including W. H. Auden, Benjamin Britten, and John Grierson) kept it cold and detached. See A. Vesselo, 'Coal Face', *Sight and Sound*, Winter 1935/6, and Robert Colls and Philip Dodd, 'Representing the nation. British documentary films 1928–45, *Screen*, (1985), pp. 21–33.

[21] Jeffrey Richards, *Films and British National Identity* (Manchester, 1997), p. 255.

confirmed the memoir.[22] Mr Grey's coal filling matches Mrs Grey's home-making: one hard and muscular, the other 'sane and comely'. Happy was the man, Orwell must have thought, who had both. Certainly, he had had neither:

> I should say that a manual worker, if he is in steady work and drawing good wages . . . has a better chance of being happy than an 'educated' man. His home life seems to fall more naturally into a sane and comely shape. I have often been struck by the peculiar easy completeness, the perfect symmetry as it were, of a working-class interior at its best. Especially on winter evenings after tea, when the fire glows in the open range and dances mirrored in the steel fender, when Father . . . sits in the rocking chair . . . Mother sits . . . with her sewing . . . and the children are happy with a pennorth of mint humbugs.
>
> Curiously enough it is not the triumphs of modern engineering, or the radio, or the cinematograph, or the 5000 novels which are published yearly, nor the crowds at Ascot . . . but the memory of working-class interiors . . . that reminds me that our age has not been altogether a bad one to live in. [23]

After leaving Agnes Terrace, Orwell went back to Marjorie's in Leeds and then, on 30 March 1936, he caught the train back to London and never, as far as we know, returned to Wigan or Barnsley again. He had spent 60 days away: seven days travelling, eight days with men from the *Adelphi*, twelve days with his sister in Leeds, two and a half weeks lodging in Wigan, and two weeks with the Greys in Barnsley.[24] After years adrift, at last he had found an England to believe in. Keen to join it, he rented a poor man's cottage in April, got married in June, and dug the garden over the summer. As the Jarrow Marchers made their way south in a blaze of publicity, Orwell sat in deepest Hertfordshire writing *The Road to Wigan Pier*.[25] From now on, all hope lay with the Proles.[26]

SPANISH LESSONS: BARCELONA 1937

He arrived in Barcelona on Boxing Day 1936.[27] Carrying a letter of introduction from the British Independent Labour Party, he made his way to the militia barracks of the *Partido Obrero de Unificacion Marxista*, otherwise known as the

[22] 'It was me father, that, that were me Dad': Irene Goodliffe, née Grey, in Stephen Wadhams, *Remembering Orwell* (Ontario, 1984), p. 65.

[23] Orwell, *Wigan Pier*, pp. 104–5. Contrast the fireside scene at Agnes Terrace with the scene at Marsh Farm in D. H. Lawrence's *The Rainbow* (1915; Harmondsworth, 1977), p. 97.

[24] In the Preface to a Ukrainian language edition of *Animal Farm*, in March 1947, Orwell says he spent 'many months' studying the miners: Peter Davison (ed.), *Complete Works*, xix, p. 87.

[25] The march against unemployment arrived in London on 31 October. Orwell married Eileen O'Shaughnessy, who came from South Shields, in Wallington parish church on 9 June.

[26] Though not one of them was sent a complimentary copy: Eileen Blair to Leonard Moore, 11 February 1937: Peter Davison (ed.), *Complete Works*, xi, p. 11. A Right Book Club followed Gollancz's Left Book Club. It avoided Wigan like the plague: W. S. Shears, *This England* (London, 1937), pp. 638, 642.

[27] He arrived six months after a *putsch* by sections of the army against the elected government, which had just lost Malaga in the south but still held large portions of the country, including Madrid and Barcelona. The Prime Minister was the former Minister of Labour and Marxist rhetorician, Largo Caballero.

POUM, where he signed on as 'Eric Blair, Grocer'.[28] His cue was yet another direct encounter with people to believe in and, paradoxically, another step nearer England:

In the Lenin Barracks in Barcelona, the day before I joined the militia, I saw an Italian militiaman standing in front of the officers' table. He was a tough-looking youth of twenty five or six, with reddish yellow hair and powerful shoulders. His peaked leather cap was pulled fiercely over one eye. He was standing in profile to me, his chin on his breast, gazing with a puzzled frown at a map which one of the officers had open on the table. Something in his face deeply moved me...

'Italiano?'

I answered in my bad Spanish: *'No, Ingles. Y tu?'*

'Italiano'.

As we went out he stepped across the room and gripped my hand very hard. Queer, the affection you can feel for a stranger! It was as though his spirit and mine had momentarily succeeded in bridging the gulf of language and tradition and meeting in utter intimacy.[29]

Orwell spent six months in Spain, mainly on the Aragon front with eighty men and the assorted dogs of a *Centura* of the Lenin Division of the POUM. Not everything was to his liking. It was hardly a free society, nor could it be, but in those first few days he was convinced he had found the real Spain. In Wigan, he had been inspired by a people whose first loyalty was to each other. So it was with the Spanish militiamen. Unlike the English coalminers however, not only were the militiamen loyal, they were armed and loyal. They had saved the Republic from Black Spain, the Spain of the colonels, priests, and landowners. Now it seemed they were going to establish Red Spain, a land fit for workers and peasants. 'The revolutionary posters were everywhere, flaming from the walls in clean reds and blues... Human beings were trying to behave as human beings and not as cogs in a capitalist machine... I recognized it immediately as a state of affairs worth fighting for.'[30] Here began Orwell's first lesson in Revolution.

He saw action twice.[31] Once, early in April, taking part in an advance along the Aragon front, and again, late in April, as Barcelona fell into street fighting between his own militia units and those of the newly formed Republican Guard. While the POUM fought fascists at the front, the Guard had moved in to disarm the POUM. Orwell was astonished. He couldn't help noticing how underfed and poorly equipped his own men looked. He took his rifle, an old Mauser, onto a cinema roof overlooking the *Ramblas* and loitered there looking for a kill. He knew by now how confusing war could be, and how squalid. And though he was not yet in a position to know the full extent of Soviet influence on the

[28] The POUM was founded in 1931 as a left breakaway from the Communist Party of Spain, itself a 1920 left breakaway from the Socialist Party of Spain, founded 1879.

[29] George Orwell, *Homage to Catalonia* (1938; Harmondsworth, 1968), p. 7.

[30] Ibid., pp. 8–10.

[31] Orwell's sector was not as hard pressed as Madrid, where the bulk of British volunteers were fighting in the International Brigades. He remarked in *Homage* that no shell ever exploded within 50 yards of him and that he was 'only involved in hand to hand fighting once'. His commanding officer remembered him as 'absolutely fearless': Wadhams, *Remembering Orwell*, p. 78.

Republic,[32] he resisted those anti-militia stories which he knew by his own experience to be untrue. At the same time, he understood the military limitations of the militias, was never convinced by his own side's Marxist-Leninism, remained an instinctive supporter of the Republic and was still inclined to join its new army (once he had finished fighting it).

Late in May, Orwell was back in Barcelona after another tour of front line duty. This time, however, he was sick and on the run. Contrary to his own claim that enemy snipers couldn't hit a bull in a passage, he'd stood up full length in his trench to catch a bullet through the throat—a high velocity 7mm calibre zip just between the trachea and the carotid artery. Having survived the bullet, and the field hospital that treated him, he returned to Barcelona to find the security forces making more arrests. The POUM's leader Andres Nin and other comrades, including Bob Smillie from Orwell's old platoon, had been arrested and murdered. On 16 June the Republic declared the POUM an illegal organization. Orwell and his wife, who had been working in the ILP offices, were cited as Trotskyite spies. British comrades had been spying on them since May.[33] Orwell went into hiding, sleeping rough by night and avoiding the hotel where Eileen was staying by day. At the same time, he and Eileen badgered the British Consulate for travel visas and took considerable risks lobbying on behalf of imprisoned friends. On 23 June, posing as war tourists, the Blairs took their chance and left Barcelona by train. Three weeks later, a full indictment for High Treason and Espionage was issued against them. Here ended Orwell's second lesson in Revolution.

When they got back home to Wallington, life was quieter. They'd seen Utopia and preferred Hertfordshire. But he wasn't finished. He had got into the habit of seeing Spanish circumstances as potentially English circumstances—a habit that would persist for another three years—and in a stream of essays and reviews he wrote against those on the Left who, as he saw it, had sold the Spanish revolution short.[34] Explaining the importance of what he had seen, and making you see it with him, was emerging by now as the mark of Orwell's writing. *The Road to Wigan Pier* (1937) had been a culmination of earlier styles: first person narrative and third person fact driven to a hard political punch. *Homage to Catalonia* (1938), his Spanish book, brought that style to perfection. The documentary film movement had been trying to do something like this for the past ten years,[35] but no English journalist since Cobbett or possibly Hazlitt had shown such self-possession in their blend of politics and personal experience. Orwell had found his voice and was beginning to find his subject too. He is *both* narrator and

[32] 'Elimination' of the POUM had been announced by *Pravda* in December 1936: Davison, *Works*, xi, p. 32.

[33] David Crook, David Wicks and others: Bowker, *Orwell*, pp. 222–7.

[34] Paul Preston explains Stalin's dilemma in his *Concise History of the Spanish Civil War* (London, 1996), p. 107–8, and Tom Buchanan explains the Labour Party's, in *The Spanish Civil War and the Labour Movement* (Cambridge, 1991), p. 39.

[35] Erik Barnouw, *Documentary* (New York, 1974), pp. 144–8. Bill Brandt's *Northern Pictures* (1937) were remarkably apposite to Orwell's *Wigan Pier* text and appeared in the Left Book Club edition.

narrated; the man who shows you the people, and takes their part. This wasn't politics as politicians knew it; but it was politics all the same.

As for the second Spanish Republic, it certainly contributed to its own downfall; and once it had let the Soviets in, no other country wanted it to survive—according to Paul Preston, not even the Soviets. But in Orwell's eyes, Spain's future still hung in the balance and he felt he could make a difference. Breaking with the political correctness of the decade, he went looking for those who gave out the Communist party line.[36] He cut at those who defended *bien pensant* murder, or looked the other way. He made it clear that Lenin and Stalin and Trotsky and all that crew had nothing to do with socialism as he understood it. He warned that Spain was a rehearsal for bigger wars to come; that the world was heading for totalitarianism; that the intellectuals would betray the people.

As early as 1935, Orwell had been convinced that all was not well on the British Left. *Keep the Aspidistra Flying* purported to show the perversity of Gordon Comstock (his name is a joke after the American birth controller and spouting moralist), and part two of *Wigan Pier* is a raking polemic against what Orwell saw as the perversity of all middle-class left intellectuals.[37] If one wanted a representative sample of what Orwell loathed in left-wing intellectuals (he joked that there weren't any right-wing ones) during these years, one need go no further than his publisher's own Left Book Club Committee. On it sat John Strachey, whose father had owned the *Spectator*; Harold Laski, son of a wealthy cotton merchant; and Gollancz himself, son of an upper crust jeweller. Not a prole between them. All three had gone to expensive schools, and to Oxford; all three were close to the Communist Party, if not actually in it; and all three were sympathetic to the USSR, if not actually resident. Most importantly, they were all familiar if not particularly important figures on the higher slopes of the Labour Party. Strachey, the ideologue, wrote popularizations of Marxism; Laski, the academic, for a time, was master apologist for the Soviet Union; and Gollancz, as we have seen, was an extremely energetic publisher.[38] When Orwell joked that left intellectuals took their opinions from Moscow and their cooking from Paris, he might well have been thinking of these three. But what he found suspicious in them, and depressing in himself, he had found murderous in Barcelona. Spanish lessons bore directly on his apprehension of England. Yes, he was convinced now that working-class people would fight to change society. No, he wasn't convinced yet that the English were up to it. War and totalitarianism were

[36] And the party line went looking for him: see Harry Pollitt's withering review, 'Here is George Orwell, a disillusioned little middle-class boy . . . ' in the *Daily Worker*, 17 March 1937.

[37] Because Orwell started out by seeing all socialists as intellectuals, and over-identified intellectuals as middle class, he tended to overrate middle-class influence in the British Communist Party. According to Chris Wrigley, out of a party membership of 7,909 in 1927, 5,823 were trade unionists, of whom 3,753 were coalminers: *British Trade Unions since 1933* (Cambridge, 2002), p. 9. It seems that most British volunteers in Spain came through Communist Party networks: Lewis Mates, 'Durham and South Wales miners in the Spanish Civil War', *Twentieth Century British History* 17, 3 (2006).

[38] For an example of Laski's slippery apologetics, see his *Communism* (London, 1927), pp. 48–54.

coming and they were 'all sleeping the deep, deep sleep of England, from sometimes I fear that we shall never wake till we are jerked out of it by the roar of bombs'.[39]

As the European crisis worsened through 1938 and 1939, and the dictators prevailed, not only in Germany, Italy, and the Soviets but also in European countries holding themselves rigid from attack, for the first time Orwell began to translate England's sleep into the sleep of a country which, if it was not all that good, nor was it all that bad. The English had been insulated from Continental wars and revolutions, he argued, making them resistant to European vices and virtues alike. Defended by their navy, they were a people who could tolerate things abroad, even by their own hand, which they could not tolerate at home. As for snobbery, ignorance, and class consciousness, they were famous for it. And yet, for all that, Orwell's experiences in Wigan and Barcelona had shown him that the English working class were a free people who, at root, and against the odds, believed that England belonged to them.[40] In a world of lies and mass murder, this was something. For if it was true that his countrymen ruled a quarter of the earth at the end of an imperial bayonet, it was also true that they had built a politics and an identity (the Oxford History of England at that time would have said 'a constitution') that worked.

Like many people in the 1930s, Orwell showed little interest in party politics. The old Radical Liberal alliance that had made all the running up to 1914 had fallen apart.[41] The young Orwell might well have been drawn into this, had it survived. After 1918, the Labour Party had gradually taken its place, but Orwell was not much attracted to Labour either, partly because well into the 1930s he hardly had a politics at all, but also because the two Labour governments of 1924 and 1929–31 were desperately unlucky and not appealing. Up to 1914, it had been the Conservatives who had been driven to the outer edge. After 1931, it was Labour's turn, and they were driven there by the men behind the so-called National governments of 1931 and 1935, the years in which Baldwin's Conservatives succeeded in turning national identity into a politics of no politics. National identity suited the Tories. It was their natural territory after all and they thrived, in McKibbin's words, 'on literature, Englishness, music, rural life, fraternity, religion'.[42] So did Orwell, in a way, though from a different point of view.

As war with Germany got closer, Orwell's Englishness got keener. After Wigan, he had come to value the people more. After Barcelona, he had come to trust politicians less. In 1938 he joined the Independent Labour Party because he agreed with them that the coming conflagration would be an 'imperialist

[39] Orwell, *Homage*, pp. 220–1.

[40] 'One recalls with difficulty that England belonged to the labourers as well': E. P. Thompson, *The Making of the English Working Class* (1963; Harmondsworth, 1968), p. 246.

[41] Most famously rehearsed in George Dangerfield, *The Strange Death of Liberal England 1910–14* (London, 1935).

[42] Ross McKibbin, *Parties, People and the State. Politics in England 1914–51* (Oxford, 2010), p. 56.

war'.[43] At this point, his distrust of the political class was so deep he thought that the prime threat to Britain came not from Nazis in Germany but politicians in Britain. He claimed, in other words, that the fascist threat was home-grown and lay in too much build-up for war, not too little, and maintained this position well into 1939. In January 1939 we find him trying to win support for anti-war 'activities'. In March 1939 we find him criticizing war preparations as the 'fascizing process'. But crucially, on 9 September 1939, six days after war was declared and in the same month that an article by him was published in *Left Forum* blaming the war on 'left-wing jingoes', we find him offering his services to the Ministry of Labour and National Service.[44] Over the next four months Orwell completely changes his mind—so much so that by January 1940 he is telling friends that 'now we are in this bloody war we have got to win it'.[45] In his last minute realization that appeasement was lost and that war was necessary, Orwell was only slightly behind most of the British people.[46] He was late in believing that war should be fought; but only believed it could be *won* in June 1940 when, looking for his brother-in-law Lawrence, late of the British Expeditionary Force, at Waterloo and Victoria stations, Orwell witnessed the jaunty patriotism of the British people and took strength. And so it came to pass that the ILP lost his services, and the Home Guard gained them. Sgt Blair now had a little imperial bayonet of his own and when the bombs finally began to drop, he was ready to use it.[47]

All this was to do with Orwell the patriot politician. But his patriotism, as we have seen, ran deeper than politics. His commitment to country had started two years earlier. He found his people in 1936, and his revolution in 1937. However, neither of these experiences particularly endeared him to himself. Then, in 1938–9, he went away to find himself, and his home, in fictional episodes from the life of a middle-class Londoner called George.

[43] George Orwell, 'Why I joined the ILP', *New Leader*, 24 June 1938, in Sonia Orwell and Ian Angus (eds.), *Collected Essays, Journalism and Letters of George Orwell*, vol. 1 (Harmondsworth, 1970), p. 374.

[44] Letters to Herbert Read, 4 January, 5 March 1939; to Geoffrey Gorer, 20 January 1939; 'Not counting niggers', *Adelphi*, July 1939; *Left Forum*, September 1939: ibid., pp. 414–16, 421, 424, 434–5, 581. Record of Orwell offering his services on 9 September appears in a reply from the Ministry, 8 December 1939, cited in Peter Davison (ed.), *Orwell and Politics* (London, 2001), p. 83. Exactly a year before, Orwell had signed a manifesto in *New Leader* threatening to resist the British war effort. There were fine lines of difference between those who were 'anti-Fascist', those who were 'anti-War', and those who were outright pacifist. There were also those who favoured 'appeasement': Peter Mandler, *The English National Character* (New Haven, 2006), p. 185; Peter Clarke, *Hope and Glory. Britain 1900–90* (London, 1997), p. 198.

[45] Letters to Herbert Read, 4 January 1939; Geoffrey Gorer, 10 January 1940; Humphrey House, attacking 'defeatists', 11 April 1940; and 'Democracy in the British army', *Left Forum*, September 1939: Orwell and Angus, *Collected Essays*, i, pp. 415, 444, 450, 581. In May–June 1940 his war diary records his growing confidence in the people: Peter Davison (ed.), *Complete Works*, xii, pp. 168–84.

[46] McKibbin's Ford lectures characterize May–June 1940 as 'a "high political" crisis which... immediately weakened the predominant Conservatism of the 1930s'.

[47] Having abandoned the ILP anti-war line, Orwell tarried with another perversion, the POUM line about the need for revolution and war to be fought simultaneously: 'The Lion and the unicorn. Socialism and the English genius', in Sonia Orwell and Ian Angus (eds.), *Collected Essays, Journalism and Letters of George Orwell*, vol. 2 (1941; Harmondsworth, 1970), pp. 104–8.

ATONEMENT: THAMES VALLEY 1939

In September 1938 the Blairs sailed for Marrakesh in French Morocco, so that Orwell might recover his health.[48] There he wrote *Coming Up For Air*, the story of George Bowling, an insurance salesman who lives with his wife and children in eponymous West Bletchley, or suburban west London, or 'Metroland', according to its railway developers, taking in Wembley, Harrow, Ruislip, Northwood, and Uxbridge. Like its lugubrious owner, 191 Ellesmere Road is semi-detached. Some might say it was half asleep. Let George explain:

> You know how these streets fester all over the inner-outer suburbs. Always the same. Long, long rows of little semi-detached houses—the numbers in Ellesmere Road run to 212 and ours is 191—as much like council houses and generally uglier. The stucco front, the creosoted gate, the privet hedge, the green front door. The Laurels, The Myrtles, The Hawthorns, Mon Abri, Mon Repos, Belle Vue . . . 'Five to ten quid a week', you'd say as soon as you saw me. Economically and socially I'm about at the average level of Ellesmere Road.[49]

The second best thing about George Bowling is that he doesn't take himself too seriously. When he says he has false teeth, a large mortgage, a job he hates, and a wife who (with good reason) doesn't trust him, we might say that George knows his limitations. When he says that he is a fifteen-stone fat man with a thin man on the inside, then we listen because it is the thin one who is doing the talking. George knows there are better lives to be lived and better countries than England to live them in, *perhaps*, but he makes the best of what he has. When he is told by the Cheerful Credit Building Society that he owns his own home, he knows it belongs to them. When he is told by The Flying Salamander Insurance Company that he is 'salaried', he knows he works for wages like everybody else. When he is told by the government there will be peace in our time, he knows there will be war in his time. War is just round the corner. His corner, in fact:

> Seems a pity somehow . . . I looked at the great sea of roofs stretching on and on. Miles and miles of streets, fried fish shops, tin chapels, picture houses, little printing-shops up back alleys, factories, blocks of flats, whelk stalls, dairies, power stations—on and on and on. Enormous! and the peacefulness of it! Like a great wilderness with no wild beasts. No guns firing, nobody chucking pineapples, nobody beating anybody else up with a rubber truncheon. If you come to think of it, in the whole of England at this moment there probably isn't a single bedroom window from which anyone's firing a machine-gun. But how about five years from now? Or two years? Or one year?[50]

There had been a time when a character like George Bowling would not have attracted Orwell's interest. He would have seen Bowling as too suburban, too soft, too south, too stupid, too white. For George follows the crowd, catches the

[48] In March 1938 he had been admitted to Preston Hall sanatorium, Aylesford, Kent, where he was diagnosed with TB.
[49] George Orwell, *Coming Up for Air* (1939; London, 1990), p. 9.
[50] Ibid., p. 21.

8.21, worries about his weight, reads cheap, eats cheap, bets on the horses, earns his commission and, 'properly speaking, that's the end of my story'. In short, George Bowling is one of the masses, and a good deal of superior people's time and effort in the 1930s went into being superior to people like them. Orwell had done his share. Contrary to John Carey's *tour de force* however, *Coming Up for Air* is on their side.[51] In George Bowling, Orwell takes their part not because he thinks they are more admirable, or brave, or especially insightful, but because he thinks they're ordinary and as such, there's a chance that people like them won't be deceived by intellectuals like him. For Orwell, being on the side of the masses is far more significant than being on the side of statuesque coalminers or Spanish revolutionaries with caps pulled fiercely over one eye. Loving the Republic is easy; it's the masses who take some effort.

The best thing about George Bowling is that he is not deceived. He doesn't like or trust intellectuals, and for Orwell, writing in 1939, this was emerging as the pre-eminent virtue. The knowingness and indeed the littleness of men like Bowling, he seems to be saying, will instinctively see through war as a slogan or a fraud ('Listen son . . . if it comes again, you keep out'), but see it through should it become necessary. Haltingly at first in *Coming Up For Air*, published in 1939 when Orwell still thought war was a fraud, but getting stronger through the autumn of 1939 as appeasement failed, Orwell is reconciled to his class and his country and therefore, in a way, to himself. It's not as if he had any choice. By September 1939 everybody, more or less, knew how things stood. It's a straight fight and the English have got to win. And this time Orwell is on the side of the new English, *his* English—middle class and southern for sure, but also in a way class-less, and open-minded, and not at all like the old governing class, or the professions, or the imperial service class. The new English tend to be technical, but also very bright, sceptical, private, modern, *knowing*.[52] George Bowling isn't quite one of them when Orwell invents him in Marrakesh in the winter of 1938, but he's well on his way. One evening, brooding over the coming crisis, Bowling visits 'old Porteous', one of his more refined acquaintances. '"I'm part of the modern world myself"', says George, '"but I like to hear him talk"'. Sadly, while filling his pipe leaning against the bookshelf, old Porteous has nothing to say. He refuses to talk about Hitler ('This German person?'), and prefers to talk about the past. Who's it to be? Old-south classics master? Or new-south insurance salesman? Orwell knew them both, and it's Bowling he's with. He may be fat, he may be vulgar, and he may be one of the masses, but least he's alive. As Gracie Fields has it: 'He's dead, but he won't lie down.'[53]

[51] John Carey, *The Intellectuals and the Masses* (London, 1992), pp. 39–45. See also Declan Kiberd, *Ulysses and Us: The Art of Everyday Living* (London, 2009), and Orwell's letter to Brenda Salkeld, December 1933: 'Joyce interests me so much that I can't stop talking about him': Orwell and Angus, *Collected Essays*, i, p. 153.

[52] He has more to say about this new technical-managerial class once war breaks out. David Edgerton rescued them from the condescension of posterity in his *England and the Aeroplane* (Basingstoke, 1991).

[53] Frontispiece, *Coming Up for Air.*

One day, tired of West Bletchley and with £17 from the bookie's burning a hole in his pocket, Bowling resolves to go back to Lower Binfield, his childhood home. On the face of it he goes for a spot of fishing, but actually it's more complicated than that because really he is looking to retrieve a sense of belonging. But much to his regret, he finds that the whole of the Thames Valley is being bulldozed and built over: 'might as well have been at Margate . . . swollen into a kind of Dagenham . . . red brick everywhere.'[54]

'Lower Binfield' is Henley-on-Thames, where Orwell was brought up. In the novel, he conceives Henley as just another English town in just another English region. This was (and is) unusual. English topography has generally considered England as a country of regions, or counties, except for the south-east, which has generally been represented as England itself.[55] This was (and is) England *profound*, a land of shaded greens, dark thatched cottages, and the River Thames making its imperial progress to London—the official view, the tourist view, the England foreigners think of.[56] Even radicals saw it like this. J. A. Hobson's *Imperialism* (1902), for instance, saw the whole southern area as the heart of an Imperial Englishness living off its colonial investments, while William Morris's *News from Nowhere* (1890), depicted it as a green and pleasant communist Utopia. In the 1930s the south of England was enjoying its moment of quintessential Englishness, but by making it a region again, and a bulldozed region at that, Orwell de-imperializes it to make it ordinary, ordinary enough to be his own.[57] No great offices of state. No glamorous public schools. No horsey regiments. Not a bishop in sight. If this is the real south of England, Orwell seems to be saying—Henley and Wallingford, Burford Weir and Chamford Hill—then it was my England, a people's England of dusty white roads, wild fennel, and sacks of grain. It's myth of course, as sweet as lardy cake, but England real or England fake, England now or England then, there are times when being undeceived is not enough. *You have got to belong.*

Summer days, and the flat water meadows and the blue hills in the distance, and the willows up the backwater and the pools underneath like a kind of deep green glass . . . peacefulness even in the names of English coarse fish. Roach, rudd, dace, bleak, barbell, bream, gudgeon, pike, chub, carp, tench. They're solid kind of names. The people who made them up hadn't heard of machine guns.[58]

[54] Orwell took a conventional view of modern mass excrescences: see J. B. Priestley, *English Journey* (1934; Harmondsworth, 1977). pp. 10, 26, 41.

[55] 'Evocations of English landscape are often specifically regional, projecting a southern Englishness in the name of the whole': David Matless, *Landscape and Englishness* (London, 1998), p. 17; Robert Colls, *Identity of England* (Oxford, 2002), pp. 241–3, 259–60, 312–16, 329–33.

[56] See for instance, Stanley Baldwin, *On England* (London, 1926)—'the one eternal sight of England' (p.7).

[57] See chapters by Howkins, Doyle, Crump and Brooker, and Widdowson in Robert Colls and Philip Dodd (eds.), *Englishness. Politics and Letters 1880–1920* (London, 1986); Krishan Kumar, *The Making of English National Identity* (London, 2003), p. 224.

[58] The masses not the classes fished coarse: McKibbin, *Classes and Cultures*, p. 356. Orwell, *Coming Up for Air*, pp. 75–6.

Written in Morocco, *Coming Up for Air* is about belonging. Wigan had shown him another country, and when he explored it and tried to catch the eye, he couldn't quite. In Barcelona, he caught the eye immediately, but in the end it was eyes he was trying to avoid. In sprawling West Bletchley and ugly Lower Binfield, though, Bowling feels completely at home: 'I'm vulgar, I'm insensitive, and I fit in with my environment.'[59] He feels he knows everyone and you do too: 'You know the kind of place ... You know the line of talk ... You know the type.'[60] Even when he isn't recognized, he expects to be. England might have changed, and George Bowling with it, but he belongs, and he belongs in the past and present tenses: 'Is it gone forever? I'm not certain. But I tell you it was a good world to live in. I belong to it. So do you.'[61] Orwell would call his next writing project 'Inside the Whale'.

Ever since that Wigan morning in 1936, Orwell had been interested in English connections; in how those who won the coal were connected to the rest, and the rest to the coal. And ever since Barcelona in 1937, he had been interested in transmuted loyalties; how one kind of loyalty could serve different causes. What he had seen in Spain in former English public schoolboys fighting Franco with all their patriotic instincts now in the service of the Republic, he saw in 1940 in the English middle classes at war with Hitler. For the first time in his life, he felt he belonged to the people and seized the moment. Essays flowed on all aspects of English life—from its language and literature to its kippers and dumplings and deepest cultural and political instincts.[62] There had been a time when Orwell had been ashamed of his country.[63] Now that there was a war on, and its people were getting their hold on him, and social democracy was at hand, the next five years would see his finest, most embattled writing.

WHY IS THERE NO MARXISM IN ROSS McKIBBIN?

Ross McKibbin came to England from Australia in 1964, fourteen years after Orwell's death and at a time when the social democratic Englishness Orwell had helped to create seemed ripe for renewal: a new Labour government was in office, the industrial working class remained the largest and in some ways the most confident class, there was less snobbery, more money, and somehow the feeling that everything was open to change.

59 Orwell, *Coming Up for Air*, p. 20. On eye-catching, see Mark Rawlinson, 'George Orwell in Spain', in Annette Gomis and Susana Onega (eds.), *George Orwell, A Centenary Celebration* (Heidelberg, 2005), p. 95.

60 Orwell, *Coming Up for Air*, pp. 152–3, 155.

61 Ibid., p.31. This was addressed to his readers, though he never saw himself as writing for the people of Wigan or Barnsley. On 'landscape citizenship' as translations of Orwell's tangible south: Matless, *Landscape and Englishness*, p. 62.

62 His trust in the people put him squarely in the nationalist camp: Mandler, *National Character*, chs. 1, 2.

63 Orwell, *Wigan Pier*, p. 66; Pilgrim Trust, *Men without Work* (London, 1938), pp. 28–9.

McKibbin started writing a history of the Labour Party, a subject that had not interested Orwell even though it should have done.[64] Since the 1950s, there had been a change in the writing of history in Britain. The profession had moved left with a new kind of scholar, the committed Marxist, and a new field of vision, social history.[65] Soon, the new universities were going to be filled with students reading histories and sociologies of class.

In his first book, *The Evolution of the Labour Party*, published in 1974, McKibbin stuck close to political history. His later essays, however, took on a wider cultural and social purview and his *Ideologies of Class*, published in 1990, gathered the best of that work together in a single volume. Chapter one asked the question, 'Why was there no Marxism in Great Britain?' while other chapters included working-class gambling, the social psychology of inter war unemployment, work and hobbies, and the culture of poverty.[66] All of this would have enthralled the great man. Peter Ghosh calls them 'a complete statement of a historian's perspective and of a historical world'.[67]

McKibbin's next book, *Classes and Cultures 1918–51*, published in 1998, spread the net further, spanning Orwell's entire adult life and taking in just about every aspect of that life and a few other aspects besides, including ballroom dancing and football.[68] McKibbin's last eight pages shadow the argument as set out in Orwell's 'The Lion and the Unicorn'.[69]

George Orwell wrote about the English people in original and realistic ways. Starting with the major essays of 1940–1—'Inside the Whale', 'Charles Dickens', 'Boys' Weeklies', 'The Lion and the Unicorn', 'The Art of Donald McGill', 'Rudyard Kipling'—and running through to 1945 with the incomparable *Animal Farm* and into 1946 when he was turning out lesser, quicker, but still richly identifying works such as 'Moon Under Water' and 'A Nice Cup of Tea', Orwell showed the Left, and not only them, first how to see, and then how to think about the English people.[70] His 'Politics and the English Language' (1946) tried to think about what the English think with; so did 'Such, Such Were the Joys' (1946–8), a childhood memoir. These works completely eclipsed all that had gone before in the name of the study of English culture, particularly books by the Leavises, and moved the study of English politics into completely new territory. All post-war writers about England stood on the shoulders of this achievement. Richard Hoggart's pioneering *The Uses of Literacy* (1957), for instance, is impossible to imagine

[64] 'Voting Labour implied allegiance to certain working class traditions and not necessarily to any political ideology': Ross McKibbin, *The Evolution of the Labour Party* (Oxford, 1974), pp. xiv–xv.

[65] Simon Gunn, *History and Cultural Theory* (Harlow, 2006), p. 15.

[66] 'The British workman went his own way': Ross McKibbin (ed.), *Ideologies of Class. Social Relations in Britain 1880–1950* (Oxford, 1990), p. 116.

[67] See Ch. 2.

[68] McKibbin's writing is a master-class in how to write about politics as advised by Orwell: 'Politics and the English language', *Horizon*, April 1946.

[69] Except the very narrow difference that McKibbin concluded that socialism was wide but not deep in English civil traditions (*Classes and Cultures. England 1918–1951* (Oxford 1998), p. 535), while Orwell concluded that it went deeper than people knew ('The lion and the unicorn', Ibid., p. 133).

[70] See my *The Englishness of George Orwell*, forthcoming.

without Orwell, and Hoggart acknowledged his debt.[71] Why then did so many others on the Left not acknowledge, and even actively abuse, Orwell's achievement?

The *marxisant* 'New Left' that broke through in the 1960s with important studies of working-class politics and culture, was particularly hostile, and it is difficult to know why. Sometimes behind rather codified New Left language lay Old Left sympathies, as for instance in Raymond Williams's influential 1971 essay, or his chapter in *Culture and Society*.[72] The trouble with Orwell, Williams concluded, was that he misunderstood the real nature of socialism because he misunderstood the Soviet Union; and that he misunderstood the Soviet Union because of his psychological condition.

Nothing could be less true. Orwell was a self-conflicted man who needed utmost clarity in order to keep himself in order. If his psychological condition had been deliberately feeding a political habit, he would have been the first to admit it; as indeed, like all honest writers, Orwell did admit such things. Far more to the point, Orwell was not wrong about the Soviet Union. Considering he had never visited that country, his *Nineteen Eighty Four* (1949) is remarkable. For he understood how, when private lives are undermined, public life is destroyed. He understood too, that in such a place there comes a point when 'society' (favourite word of socialists, and that on which all their hopes depend) disintegrates.[73] Orwell was never persuaded, unlike many left intellectuals of his generation were persuaded, that the Soviet Union resembled a civilized, or a socialist, or even a social, state. In this regard, Old Left intellectuals around the Communist Party could never forgive him for being so wrong (as they saw it), while New Left intellectuals around the universities, who owed him so much, could never forgive him for being so right.[74] E. P. Thompson left the Communist Party in 1956; the year in which he said he commenced reasoning. He of all people should have acknowledged the People's Orwell. Instead, Thompson brooded over Orwell's support for the North Atlantic Treaty Organization, and even dreamed up a new term of abuse for him and people like him. For a time, it was left to Orwell's friends to best understand his work.[75]

For his part, at a time when every young historian was coming under the spell of E. P. Thompson, McKibbin simply concluded that here was a man he did not know how to learn from.[76] McKibbin went his own way. He did not see his own

[71] Nicholas Wroe, 'The uses of decency', *The Guardian*, 7 February 2004.

[72] Raymond Williams, *Culture and Society 1780–1950* (1958; Harmondsworth, 1968), p. 281; Raymond Williams, *Orwell* (London, 1971), pp. 5, 7–63, 73, 91.

[73] Orlando Figes, *The Whisperers. Private Life in Stalin's Russia* (London, 2007). For an insider's account of life in the party in the early 1950s—'grim . . . depressing': Doris Lessing, *Walking in the Shade* (London, 1997), p. 106.

[74] Christopher Norris (ed.), *Inside the Myth* (London, 1984). Orwell's doughtiest defenders are two former Trotskyists: John Newsinger, *Orwell's Politics* (Basingstoke, 1999), and Christopher Hitchens, *Orwell's Victory* (London, 2002).

[75] Richard Rees, *George Orwell* (London, 1961), p. 53; George Woodcock, *The Crystal Spirit* (London, 1967), p. 251.

[76] Ross McKibbin, 'Did my question ever change?', British History Seminar, St John's College, Oxford, 25 May 2006.

generation of Marxist historians as a model, any more than he saw George Orwell as a model. He had colleagues who were Marxists, like Tim Mason, and he was an honoured if somewhat reserved member of Raphael Samuel's history workshop celebrations, but just like Orwell, whatever the personal fraternity along the way, Ross McKibbin followed his own social democratic road. Redemptive, or rhetorical, or millenarian Marxism was not for him. He preferred the Oxford school of industrial history, which preferred a fact to a theory, as he preferred trade union practices, especially Australian trade union practices, which preferred a job to an ideology. Like Orwell, McKibbin remained grounded in ordinary life, a life both men believed could be made more agreeable by the interventions of the state.[77] Both men also struggled with similar questions—on class, on Marx, on democracy, on Americanization, on literature and society, on how to understand large, non-institutional conglomerates of thought and feeling. Above all, neither man lost their faith in the good sense and talent of ordinary people.[78] In that, perhaps, and in the force of his writing, McKibbin has more in common with Orwell than he imagines.

[77] Oxford 'school'—H. Phelps Brown, *Growth of Industrial Relations* (London, 1959), and Hugh Clegg, Alan Fox, and A. F. Thompson, *A History of British Trade Unions since 1889*, 3 vols. (Oxford, 1998). On Australian labour traditions see: Bernard Attard, 'Andrew Fisher and the collapse of Labor', *Labor History* 68 (1995), and Ross McMullin, *The Light on the Hill* (Melbourne, 1991), p. 446.

[78] 'It is never a good idea for the left to set itself in stark opposition to the values of ordinary people': Michael Walzer, 'George Orwell's England', in G. Holderness et al. (eds.), *George Orwell* (Basingstoke, 1998), p. 188.

11

Love, Romance, and the National Health Service

Joseph McAleer

Seventy years ago, George Orwell tossed an observation about 'disposable' reading matter into the primordial intellectual mix and its ripples are still being felt today, inspiring historians to pay closer attention to popular culture. Looking at twopenny weekly story papers for adults and children, Orwell surmised that such publications exist only if there is a definite demand for them. Therefore, their content can reflect the mindset of the readers, in this case the lower-middle and working classes. The newsagent's shop is a valuable resource, Orwell wrote:

> Probably the contents of these shops is the best available indication of what the mass of the English people really feels and thinks . . . To what extent people draw their ideas from fiction is disputable. Personally I believe that most people are influenced far more than they care to admit by novels, serial stories, films, and so forth, and that from this point of view the worst books are often the most important, because they are usually the ones that are read earliest in life.[1]

Historians of popular culture have agreed, mining the pages of novels and magazines for contemporary views and opinions. For example, Ross McKibbin demonstrates Orwell's theory in his analysis of A. J. Cronin's blockbuster novel *The Citadel* (1937),[2] which revealed a medical system crippled by politics and the class system, as seen through the eyes of the lead character, a new kind of 'medical hero'. 'At [the novel's] base are the demoralized GPs who, however skilful, cannot rise above the system which either abuses them or they abuse. They have become purveyors of useless mixtures and prehistoric medicine,' McKibbin writes.[3] *The Citadel*, he adds, was a runaway bestseller (rated in some reading surveys as second in sales only to the Bible) because it represented medical reality and, therefore, resonated with readers. Not surprisingly, two years after the novel

[1] See George Orwell, 'Boy's weeklies', in Orwell, *Decline of the English Murder* (London, 2009), pp. 32, 64; first published in *Horizon*, March 1940.

[2] Ross McKibbin, 'Politics and the medical hero: A. J. Cronin's *The Citadel*', *EHR* 123 (2008), pp. 651–78.

[3] Ibid., p. 660.

was published, a Gallup Poll found 71 per cent of respondents in favour of hospitals becoming a 'public' service.[4]

McKibbin admits that 'the founding of the National Health Service (NHS), for good or ill, swept away the medical system whose existence was *The Citadel*'s raison d'être.'[5] But popular fiction based in the medical world endured. After the Second World War, the NHS inspired a new kind of popular novel that was more supportive and sympathetic of the emerging health care system. In this chapter, echoing the techniques of both Orwell and McKibbin, we will explore the connection between the NHS and the new 'Doctor–Nurse' novels first published by Mills & Boon in the 1950s, and how romantic fiction reinforced a positive view of the NHS among middle- and working-class readers. In a departure from the past, Mills & Boon authors brought their own work experience as nurses to bear in crafting a more realistic, sometimes gritty background for their love stories. While the traditional elements of the Mills & Boon 'formula' are intact—escapism, the 'Alpha-man' hero, the desire for marriage and security, the happy-ever-after ending—the almost fanatical endorsement of the medical profession is striking. The message sent, and met with approval by adoring readers, was this: nurses are heroic and selfless; doctors are larger than life; the delivery system works; and hospitals are places of romance as well as healing. The NHS could not have asked for a better endorsement.

MILLS & BOON

The legendary bookseller Christina Foyle once declaimed that there were only three publishing houses that had become household names, and which readers asked for by name in a bookshop or library: Penguin, Batsford, and Mills & Boon.[6] Indeed, Mills & Boon is one of the most successful publishing houses in British history. Its origins were humble: a Mr Mills and Mr Boon, two under-appreciated employees from Methuen, striking out on their own in 1908. For two decades they led charmed lives, publishing a wide variety of books. Mills & Boon was a profitable little firm until 1928, when Mills died, suddenly. With his main source of capital gone, Boon was at a crossroads: sell the firm, or specialize in the one category of fiction that was growing at an exponential rate: romantic novels.

The demand for light, escapist fiction was fuelled between the wars by the circulating, twopenny libraries such as Boots and W. H. Smith and mirrored the growth of the cinema and the wireless. Boon made a fateful decision in the 1930s to become a 'library house'. It made his fortune, and Mills & Boon, the 'books in brown' with brightly-coloured dust jackets and a self-proclaimed 'guarantee of good reading', became a leading example of marketing and branding. Succeeded by his two sons, John (a born publisher) and Alan (a natural editor), Mills & Boon

[4] Ibid., p. 665.
[5] Ibid., p. 674.
[6] Christina Foyle, Address to the Royal Society of Arts, London, 1953.

remained family-owned until 1972, when it was acquired by a Canadian publisher, Harlequin Books. Harlequin took the brand global during the paperback revolution. Today, Harlequin-Mills & Boon is the world's largest publisher of series romance fiction, with 110 new titles a month by 1,100 authors in 28 languages.[7]

From the Mills & Boon archives we can test Orwell's theory that people are what they read, and that publishers consciously tried to lead their readers in a specific direction. Correspondence between editors and authors, and between Mills & Boon and the women's magazines (which purchased serial rights to novels), indicate that this genre was carefully crafted and managed. Mills & Boon's intentions were not sinister (as Orwell would have suspected); rather, they felt a responsibility to their loyal readership to maintain a solidly middle-class moral worldview that maintained the status quo.

However, what makes Mills & Boon even more interesting to the historian is the firm's admission that, at the end of the day, they had to sell books. They were pioneers in the art of market research, always contacting their loyal readers (who on average consumed ten books a month), and tweaking their editorial policy accordingly. For example, as the 1950s fade and the Swinging Sixties arrive, the novels become more and more permissive. 'In general, we operated the way the tide flowed', Alan Boon, the renowned Mills & Boon editor, recalled. 'We had a lot of readers' letters saying, "I like this" or "I like that". That would influence our decisions.'[8] With an eye on sales, and maintaining the loyalty of readers, the firm was willing to adapt. 'The Mills & Boon romance is not something that is static', Boon added. 'We shall continue to be successful if we believe in what we publish, sell books at a reasonable price, packaged nicely, and which answer in an attractive way the requirements of women's biological instincts.'[9] It is Mills & Boon's desire to satisfy its readers while embracing change that makes the firm a good test of Orwell's theory. The novels, moreover, can be a useful prism for the historian of attitudes and concerns towards, in particular, the medical service and profession, as McKibbin's analysis has shown for an earlier literary period.

POSTWAR READERS

The shift in style of the Mills & Boon romance in the 1950s reflected social and cultural changes after the Second World War. Wartime consolidated Mills & Boon's readership. Paper rationing meant that every book that was printed was sold, and wartime heightened the demand for light romances. Mass-Observation reflected the mood when interviewing a middle-class woman from Chelsea in 1943: 'Well, I like a nice sentimental love-story, something that makes you feel really absorbed. When I get hold of one I really like, I don't believe I'd notice the

[7] See Joseph McAleer, *Passion's Fortune: The Story of Mills & Boon* (Oxford, 1999).
[8] Alan Boon (d. 2000) was interviewed by the author in London in 1986.
[9] Ibid.

sirens. I don't like anything highbrow or unpleasant. I don't like books that make you feel life's worse than you think.'[10]

But the perceived emancipation of women during the war meant that the Mills & Boon heroine had to become more independent, as interested in her work and personal advancement as she was in nabbing a husband. Maurice Paterson was editor of *My Weekly*, the fourth most popular women's magazine in Britain in the 1940s and 1950s, behind *Woman, Woman's Own,* and *Woman's Weekly.* The women's magazines were a testing ground and a revenue source for Mills & Boon. Paterson observed:

> In 1940, the women you met were domestic animals. They were brought up to make the meals, do all the work, and think nothing of it. But the girls who came back from the war, who'd been in the services, factories, hospital nurses, some had been abroad—they weren't. That was your start of feminism. They weren't prepared to put up with being cut-off-from-this and you-shouldn't-do-that. They still wanted to get married, but they looked for a man who had the same kind of opinions as themselves.[11]

Boots also noticed the change, in one of its 'Literary Courses' for Boots 'Booklovers' Library' employees in 1949: 'Women to-day are quite capable of taking care of themselves, so that instead of attracting the attention of the hero by their helplessness, they usually meet and win him through a joint interest in some occupation. It becomes a juxtaposition of secretary-marries-boss, nurse-marries-doctor, land girl-marries-farmer, etc.'[12]

Hence, in the 1950s editorial policy shifts at Mills & Boon. There is a new emphasis on the independence of the heroine. She has a career, and it is important to her. Never before had Mills & Boon paid so much attention to the heroine's work life. And in the 1950s, one career that stands out in their novels is the hospital worker. For these workers, two branches of romance emerge: If the heroine is a nurse, she winds up marrying the doctor, and happily sacrifices her career (marriage meant a departure from the hospital). But if the heroine is a doctor herself, she marries a colleague, and they plan their future as a joint practice—in more ways than one.[13]

[10] 'Reading' 8/F (18 October 1943), Mass-Observation Archive, University of Sussex.

[11] Maurice Paterson (d. 1990) was interviewed by the author in Dundee in 1987.

[12] Boots Booklovers Library, 'First literary course: light romances and family stories and westerns', 1949; The Boots Company PLC Archives, Nottingham.

[13] Mills & Boon's decision to cultivate Doctor–Nurse romances in the 1950s would change the course of the firm's history. For it was these 'nurse books' exported to Canada that caught the attention of Mary Bonnycastle, whose family owned a small Toronto-based printing company called Harlequin Books. Bonnycastle urged her family to forge an alliance in a new venture to print paperback editions. The first was a Doctor-Nurse title, *The Hospital in Buwambo*, by Anne Vinton (1957). Twenty years later, Harlequin would purchase Mills & Boon.

THE NEW GENRE

In 1949, the new National Health Service employed more than 500,000 people in England and Wales, making it one of the world's largest employers. Over the next 25 years, the number of hospital doctors and nurses more than doubled. 'Women have become well recognised as an important part of our medical services, and their work opens up a special field of interest', Boots told its library workers.[14]

It is no wonder that Doctor-Nurse romances blossomed in the 1950s. 'Because of National Health Service developments, more people are more health-conscious, and use the medical and nursing services more', observed Elizabeth Gilzean, a registered nurse and one of Mills & Boon's new authors. 'They see doctors and nurses as actors on a stage. To read about their private lives is as big a thrill as going round to the dressing rooms to meet stage heroes off duty.'[15] J. D. Davidson, managing editor of women's magazines for D. C. Thomson, including *My Weekly* and *The People's Friend* (which serialized Mills & Boon novels, a significant source of revenue), agreed. He wrote to Alan Boon, 'I have a theory that fiction must never disturb the faith and trust a woman feels for doctors and/or nurses. Women are in their care more often than men, and are more emotional towards them, giving them an aura.'[16]

'Everyone likes books about doctors and hospitals and nurses', Mills & Boon stated in its catalogue, cleverly published in the back of every book and featuring a special medical romance section by the mid-1950s. In 1953, Alan Boon told his authors that Christina Foyle had given another stamp of approval; in her address to the Royal Society of Literature, she announced, 'One almost never failing ingredient for a successful novel was a doctor.'[17] By 1957, nearly a decade after the founding of the NHS, fully one-quarter of romance novels published by Mills & Boon were Doctor–Nurse romances. 'In those days', Boon recalled, 'there was a tremendous demand for medical books. Anything we could get in with a doctor of something.'[18]

Existing Mills & Boon authors were encouraged to try their hand at a hospital romance. In 1953 Boon wrote to author Marjorie Moore (who joined the firm in 1935), 'You never let us have a hospital flavour in the title, and I know it is something rather difficult to achieve. If you can achieve this, however, it is a definite asset to sales. Titles of this sort which we have used at times in the past are: HOTEL DOCTOR, CALLING NURSE GRANT, JESS MAWNAY—QUEEN'S NURSE'.[19] Two years

[14] Boots Booklovers Library, op. cit.

[15] 'The clinical cult', article submitted for publication to the *Birmingham Post*, n.d., 1959, Harlequin-Mills & Boon Archives (referred hereafter as H-M&B), Richmond.

[16] H-M&B, 18 June 1958.

[17] H-M&B, Alan Boon to Jean Macleod, 26 May 1953.

[18] Alan Boon interview, op. cit. Sales figures for Mills & Boon titles are hard to come by. However, in May 1960 Alan Boon gave author Alex Stuart a progress report on her 'best-sellers' in the Canadian market, all Doctor-Nurse books: 'SURGERY 37,000, GARRISON HOSPITAL 35,000, SHIP'S NURSE 42,000, BACHELOR OF MEDICINE 26,000.'

[19] H-M&B, 15 June 1953. In 1956, Alan Boon asked another veteran author, Valerie K. Nelson, to try a hospital background, and was pleased with the results: 'We think that STAFF NURSE should be good "Box Office".' H-M&B, 17 August 1956.

later, he coaxed author Jan Tempest, another veteran since the 1930s, to pick up the scalpel: 'People seem to like to read about doctors and hospitals, even though they are not so keen on coming into contact with them for reasons of health.'[20]

New authors brought work experience and considerable pride to the genre. Many hailed from the Birmingham area, which happened to be one of Mills & Boon's biggest markets. Kate Norway (who also wrote as 'Erica Bain' and 'Olive Norton') told her local writers' circle there was money to be made. 'There is a certain poetic irony in the fact that what was for generations a notoriously underprivileged profession—nursing—is now, best-sellers apart, about the most lucrative line in fiction,' she wrote.[21] Norway told Alan Boon about the twopenny library near her home in Sutton Coldfield. The librarian told her, 'My dear, they don't look at the names! They send the children with a note asking for "two more nurse books" or "a couple of Mills and Boons I haven't had"—and as long as there's a nurse and a doctor on the cover they lap them up.'[22]

As Mills & Boon mined the hospitals for revenue in the 1950s, they won support from an unlikely ally: television. Many had proclaimed the death of reading with the rise of television, but not in this case. *Emergency-Ward 10* started on ITV in 1957 and became one of the first TV soap operas. It mirrored the Mills & Boon style in following the private lives of doctors and nurses amid a realistic hospital background. Alan Boon tied his novels directly to the popular programme, writing to the editor of *Woman's Illustrated* in 1957, 'We are aware of the current interest in hospital series like the EMERGENCY-WARD 10 television series which have an extremely authentic and detailed hospital background.'[23]

Emergency-Ward 10 was more than a television show; it was a public service. It was praised by the British Medical Association for easing people's fear of hospitals, and by the Minister of Health, Enoch Powell, for reminding the public of the importance of immunization.[24] Not so Mills & Boon, which experienced a lack of official praise, which irked the firm somewhat. In 1957, author Lilian Chisholm asked Alan Boon for his usual donation of books for Christmas for her hospital library. Chisholm worked on the committee of the St John & British Red Cross Hospital Library Department, which gave out more than 11,500 books, 'a large percentage' of which were Mills & Boons. 'It beats me how long-term patients can bear to read about hospitals, however glamourised, whilst they are enduring the actual background in grim reality—but one can never fully account for human nature, can one?' Chisholm wrote.[25] Alan Boon was pleased, noting that popularity 'is a sound indication that we are all working on the right

[20] H-M&B, 1 February 1955.

[21] 'The clinical cult', op. cit.

[22] H-M&B, 19 October 1956.

[23] H-M&B, 1 November 1957. Three years earlier, Alan Boon alerted his authors that *Woman's Illustrated* was known to be 'very "hospital story" conscious' and eager to see serials with doctors and nurses. H-M&B, 1 June 1954.

[24] See Mike Spadoni, 'Emergency-Ward 10', *Television Heaven* (July 2003), posted on www.televisionheaven.co.uk/ward.htm.

[25] H-M&B, 23 August 1957. 'Demand for these books in every hospital represented was quite beyond all hopes of supply', Chisholm wrote on 17 November 1958.

lines'. He added, with a touch of envy, 'I feel that the situation is a little tantalising. With such a demand, how nice it would be if the Government were to give the hospitals a grant so that they could buy our books.'[26]

EDITORIAL POLICY

The new Doctor–Nurse series posed special challenges for Mills & Boon editors, apart from the usual vetting for proper behaviour and conduct in line with the firm's strict moral code (in the 1950s this meant no premarital sex, for example). The names of doctors and hospitals were checked against official medical directories and changed accordingly, to prevent libel. 'We have found the name of GARTON in the Medical Directory, and have therefore invented a name of our own—DENNABY', Alan Boon told Jean Macleod of her latest, *The Wild Macraes,* in 1948. 'We are making the necessary changes in the MS.'[27] In 1958, Boon asked new author Anne Vinton about a secondary character in her novel, *Night Sister at St Aubyn's:*

A reader reports to me about NIGHT SISTER that—'Dr. Hughes comes on to a ward fairly drunk'. With an eye to the law of libel, we should alter either the incident or change the name—preferably the latter. Would Mrs. Vinton like to suggest a surname not in the Medical Register?[28]

Medical details and situations, no matter how minor, had to be checked carefully for fear that an incorrect diagnosis or procedure would be published. Editors in this case were nit-picky. For example, Valerie K. Nelson's 1956 novel, *Bid Me Love You,* was called out:

Page 125. Sister's statement that no one but the surgeon could give a particular injection sounds most odd. Perhaps no one could *prescribe* it, but even if it was intra-venous (as suggested by its very rapid effect) a hospital staff should provide plenty of people able to carry out the administration. Where were all the anaesthetists, for instance? I'm sorry if I seem hypercritical, but honestly the whole of the hospital part is unconvincing.[29]

Later in the manuscript, the editor inquires, 'Virginia flings herself on her knees by Andrew's bed and proceeds to talk to him for a considerable time. Hospital beds are very high, and kneeling by them is not a good way to establish communication with a patient.'[30] Indeed: the scene was rewritten in the published novel: 'Andrew was sitting in a big chair by the window, and he turned his handsome red head to look at the door. Virginia's wide eyes devoured his face.'[31]

[26] H-M&B, 26 August 1957. [27] H-M&B, 15 January 1948.

[28] H-M&B, 24 September 1958. After the novel was published, Vinton wrote to Alan Boon about the rather impressive dustjacket: 'Don't take this too seriously, but isn't the heroine on the dust cover of Night Sister rather formidable? My husband said "Mon Dieu!!" in English and wondered if the lady had never heard of uplift brassieres.' H-M&B, 21 March 1959.

[29] H-M&B, 20 October 1955.

[30] Ibid. [31] Valerie K. Nelson, *Bid Me Love You* (London, 1956), p. 128.

In *Bachelor of Medicine* (1956), Alex Stuart, a pathologist by training, erred on the side of caution in expanding her medical descriptions from the women's magazine serial version, as she informed Alan Boon:

> I have gone more precisely into the nature of the operation (for radical excision of a carcinoma of the head of the pancreas) than I did in the serial, in which I *suggested* a different operation (total gasterectomy). I changed this because it could be done more effectively and with greater medical exactitude. You may not like all the added medical terms but I honestly don't think I've used them too much for the lay reader and I am obsessed by the fear that a professional reader may take me to task for (in a romantic story) unavoidable technical errors of omission.[32]

In 1959 Mills & Boon advised veteran author Jean Macleod to bend to the wishes of *Woman's Own* and remove the diagnosis of 'hysterical paralysis' from her latest serial, as she had deemed it an 'incurable condition'. Macleod, like many authors, relied on friends in the medical profession for advice. 'I shamelessly asked all three to dinner', she informed her editor. 'We had a long session on hysterical paralysis and were in most hearty agreement by the time we parted . . . we agreed that it should come out.'[33] Joan Bryant, the Mills & Boon editor, was pleased:

> Between ourselves, I feel they have been making a huge fuss about very little, particularly as medicine and surgery are in such a state of activity that what is incurable one day may be just a fortnight's discomfort the next. I'd be surprised if the B.M.A. really committed themselves to a word like 'impossible'—'unlikely' is *quite* strong enough for anyone who doesn't want to look like a fool eighteen months hence.[34]

Some procedures, however, were absolutely taboo, even into the next decade. In 1966, Alan Boon scolded one Doctor–Nurse author for allowing the word 'abortion' in a conversation between doctors:

> If you are looking for the biggest possible gross, it is advisable for you to see that jarring episodes or mentions do not occur in the text—the mention of abortion, for example. This genre of story has sometimes been described as cosy, escapist if you like, and while we feel that gradually more can go, it is still desirable to steer clear of what is sometimes called kitchen sink.[35]

[32] H-M&B, 14 December 1955. [33] H-M&B, 28 April 1959.

[34] H-M&B, 30 April 1959.

[35] H-M&B, 7 July 1966, Alan Boon to Nora Sanderson regarding *Junior Nurse on Ward Seven.* Boon's use of the term 'kitchen sink' may have referred to the harsh realism of the 'kitchen sink dramas' which permeated British culture in the late 1950s and 1960s, perhaps starting with John Osborne's play, *Look Back in Anger* (1956). In this letter, Boon also offered a primer on what not to write, in order to appease the editors at Harlequin Books in Canada, which purchased the lucrative paperback rights to Mills & Boon novels: 'They require a fairly straightforward love story . . . which, above all, can be read by young Canadian girls in their teens without any words or incidents occurring which might be considered to strike a jarring note . . . the very mention of the word "abortion" would worry our Canadian associates from the point of view of what they feel their teenage girls should read . . . they do not like heroines to be in love with married men, or married heroines in love with other men, or unhappy married situations, and no touching on differences of colour.' But certain violence was, apparently, tolerated if central to the dramatic plot. In *Junior Nurse on Ward Seven*, for example, a pyromaniac stalks the hospital, setting fires and causing injury.

As the demand for hospital stories increased, Mills & Boon delved into its archives, resurrecting the handful of titles from the 1930s and 1940s that were set in hospitals. In 1954, 'Joan Blair' (the penname of two authors) was asked by Alan Boon to update *Sister of Nelson Ward*, first published in 1937, for re-publication. 'The chief trouble, as expected, is that the introduction of the National Health Service has made some changes in hospital management and terminology,' they said. The long list of corrections included: 'Page 219. Must mention penicillin, discovered since book was written.'[36] For *Love and Sister Lorna*, first published in 1939, 'Blair' announced, 'We made as few alterations as possible, and have not, for instance, changed Probationer to Student-nurse, because it would involve so many corrections, often very awkward ones. We both think that in old-fashioned teaching hospitals, the word probationer still survives, and see no reason why we shouldn't say that it does in ours!'[37]

Similarly, in 1957 Alan Boon asked Anne Vinton about NHS changes in her latest novel, *Doctor Immacula*:

> Another query concerns the heroine's father, a doctor with a country practice. He dies and bequeaths the practice to a young doctor, his partner. The query is whether this is possible under NHS regulations. Our reader feels that villagers and farmers must, on the whole, be N.H. and not private patients, and we shall be glad to hear what you feel about this.[38]

Vinton, a registered nurse, reported that, yes, he could inherit the practice, although there was no guarantee his patients would remain with him.

Mills & Boon depended on the women's magazines for serial revenue and a good shop-window. The serial debuted before the novel was published; as an abridged form, it was a teaser for women to head to the library or bookshop to read more. As such, the magazine editors yielded great influence on storylines. Without exception, they upheld the medical profession as sacred—if they were not always keen on graphic details.

In 1958, J. D. Davidson, managing editor of women's magazines for D. C. Thomson, criticized Elizabeth Gilzean's manuscript, *On Call, Sister!*:

> From our point of view, Mrs. Gilzean is perhaps *too* knowledgeable about medical matters!... Her knowledge, and her obvious enthusiasm for nursing, tend to let medical exactness swamp her actual 'story.' A big section of the reading public appears to lap up the swift progress of an operation: but there must be just as large a section which finds it too strong meat. As far as we are concerned, romance, human relationships and emotions must come first.[39]

Gilzean replied, 'He had the typical male reaction to medical scenes—far more medical students faint in theatre than ever a nurse'.[40] Similarly, author Betty Beaty (who would help to establish another new Mills & Boon series, the pilot-air hostess romance) took up the advice of Winifred Johnson, editor of *Woman's*

36 H-M&B, 21 January 1954.
37 H-M&B, 28 May 1954.
38 H-M&B, 23 August 1957.
39 H-M&B, 18 June 1958.
40 H-M&B, 19 June 1958.

Weekly, to write a hospital serial. 'Although I had never written one, nor indeed ever read one, I embarked boldly and foolishly', she recalled. 'I came to grief. My hospital had a typhoid epidemic, and I did a minor thesis on drains and the bugs that lurked therein. Miss Johnson returned the manuscript immediately and said it was no good. Back it came by return of post, with Miss Johnson's epic words— "My girls are interested in young men, NOT in drains".'[41] In 1954, Johnson rejected Marjorie Moore's latest for one important reason: 'I don't think readers would find a heroine who so disliked hospitals sympathetic.'[42] The storyline was changed.

The Doctor–Nurse romance, by nature more realistic in tone, allowed once-taboo subjects like race relations to enter the canon. In Anne Vinton's *Caprice in Hospital Blue* (1957), the heroine, Caprice 'Priss' Clandon, defends Nurse Kamba from Nigeria, the only black nurse at St Luke's Hospital in Oldsborough. Dorothy, a young patient, is initially intimidated by her:

> 'It's—it's that black nurse. She—I'm frightened of her.'
>
> Priss quite understood. Many children on their first visit to the hospital had never before been in close contact with an adult African.
>
> 'You'll be boasting about knowing Nurse Kamba before you go home', Priss promised. 'She only looks after very special patients, like you, and she expects everyone to be brave. You see, she's a chief's daughter in Nigeria—that makes her almost a princess.'[43]

Problem solved. Vinton also pushed the boundaries on sex and lovemaking. 'Romance was the key word', she recalled. 'The lady was always a virgin. There was no actual sex, only the promise, and I was once blue-pencilled for allowing my couple to marry and actually enjoy the first night experience of pure love. Alan Boon told me it wouldn't "go down" in Ireland, so I had to do a retake on that.'[44]

The Irish market for Mills & Boon romances was large and important. Although separate sales figures for the Irish market are not available, it is obvious from archival evidence that it was a significant source of revenue for Mills & Boon, and any attempt to upset the market made the firm jittery. Alan Boon included a stock paragraph in letters to several writers who crossed the firm's moral line. For example, he wrote to Constance M. Evans in 1958:

> Eire objects strongly to divorce, bedroom scenes, or attempted seduction appearing in novels, even if in the context the comment is unfavorable to such. We have to be very careful indeed about seeing that there are no complaints about the novels in this important market. At the present time all our novels are accepted without question as being certain to satisfy their requirements, and it is our policy to maintain this. The possibility of being banned in this market is a very serious matter. . . .One of our travelers has recently spent 17 days in Eire touring the country and speaking to librarians throughout the length and breadth of their

[41] Betty Beaty was interviewed by the author in Slindon, Surrey, in 1996.
[42] H-M&B, 24 September 1954.
[43] Anne Vinton, *Caprice in Hospital Blue* (London, 1957), p. 24.
[44] Anne Vinton was interviewed by the author in Amersham in 1995.

land, and he, in his report, has emphasized the utmost importance of suiting the market in the way I have described. [45]

Evans submitted, but replied, 'Don't go telling me that in Ireland people are all so good and so ignorant of the facts of life! I've known several Irishmen, and they didn't give me that idea!' [46]

THE CAREER

What did women take away from reading Mills & Boon's Doctor–Nurse romances in the 1950s, besides a strong moral code and the sanctity of marriage? A close analysis of the novels shows that the firm, led by a new stable of authors, was determined to support the medical profession and the new NHS by allowing an unprecedented amount of opinion and endorsement in the light-hearted romance. Specifically, the novels sell nursing as a noble career choice (with the ultimate prize of a doctor husband, of course); salute the few women doctors out there in a burst of quasi-feminism in a male-dominated system; and even suggest patience with the emerging NHS as old hospitals and procedures struggled to change and adapt.

Nursing, for whatever its faults, challenges, and sheer exhaustion, was presented in Mills & Boon romances as the most worthy and noble of professions. Authors, having been there themselves, pulled no punches as to the toughness of the work and the severity of Matron. At the end of the day, the hard work was worthwhile, almost akin to a sacred vocation, as Kate Norway suggested to Alan Boon in 1959:

You get the same atmosphere with any profession where skilled people, with a sort of 'closed-shop' knowledge and training, do a job in a uniform which sets them apart. For example, I've often thought that there was room for more books about nuns. Like nurses they have a vocation in which not everyone can share; they live in a tight community that is essentially feminine and has an inner life into which the reader itches to be initiated. There's a mystery about it, the attraction of the unknown.[47]

The nobility of the nurse was always presented. In Elizabeth Gilzean's novel, *On Call, Sister!* (1958), Elizabeth Sheldon is Theatre Superintendent at St Hilary's Hospital. She fancies the surgeon, Graham Ross, the man 'with the rugged manners to go with the rugged good looks'. She has a reflective moment at the end of a busy day:

Tonsils, teeth, abdominal cases, an abscess, intussusception, appendix—what a medley made up the quota of patients that passed through their hands. Each a problem, each a human being wanting to be made whole again, each bringing its troubles to the theatre door to leave them with consciousness on the threshold. Elizabeth sighed a little. What a

[45] H-M&B, 19 November 1958. [46] H-M&B, 21 November 1958.
[47] 'The clinical cult', op. cit.

tremendous responsibility was theirs that they, each and every one of the theatre staff, should give of their best at any hour of the day or night, without fear or favour, without thought of self.[48]

Similarly, in *Sister Grace* by Marguerite Lees (1958), the title character runs the children's unit as a latter-day Joan of Arc: 'As Grace took a shower and dressed, she had the feeling she was putting on armour . . . She was the sister in charge of an important block of the hospital, and she stepped now like a queen into her own domain.'[49]

Any doubts associated with the profession were dispelled outright. However unrealistic this may have seemed, Mills & Boon would have no truck with criticism of nursing. In Norrey Ford's *Nurse with a Dream* (1957), Jacqueline Clarke begins work at St Simon's Hospital in Barnbury. She's unsure at first, but is given a pep talk by her mate, Bridget:

'We all swear to give up nursing at least twice a month, but I dunno—it grips you, Jacky. You see, beyond the pettiness and the aching feet and chapped hands, there's a purpose. Wait till you've helped to bring your first baby into the world, or saved a mother who would have died but for you, or seen a child walk who might have been a cripple. I can type and I know I could get a job as a typist to-morrow, with more money and less work and responsibility—but I'd hate it after a week. It would be such an aimless existence, working for nothing but a pay-packet.'[50]

Jacqueline is soon converted—so much so, that when her farmer-cousin Guy proposes to her, and says she needs to quit her job immediately, she rebels:

'All my life I've wanted to be a nurse—why should I give it up?'

He sulked, like a small boy, his handsome face dark and angry. 'As if a woman's career mattered, when she has a chance of marrying!'

She stared, unable to believe he had made such a preposterous statement.[51]

This being Mills & Boon, Guy is jettisoned, and Jacqueline is swept off her feet by the dashing surgeon Alan Broderick. Love conquers all, until their kisses are interrupted by an emergency call, on the penultimate page of the novel:

'This is how it will be—always. Our tenderest, our most important moments—humanity will barge in and interrupt. Are you prepared for that? Will you always understand—and know that I love you best and dearest; that you are of all beings most important to me?'

'After to-day—yes, I will. I'll always say, "Lord, he whom Thou lovest is sick"—and I won't resent your leaving me, because I know you will come back.'[52]

48 Elizabeth Gilzean, *On Call, Sister!* (London, 1958), p. 89.
49 Marguerite Lees, *Sister Grace* (London, 1958), p. 9.
50 Norrey Ford, *Nurse with a Dream* (London, 1957), p. 76.
51 Ibid., pp. 101–2.
52 Ibid., p. 187.

THE DOCTOR-HERO

All of the requisite qualities of the Mills & Boon hero were apparent in the doctor. He is the 'Alpha-man'; if not the most prominent surgeon on staff, then the one with the most promise and heart to get ahead. In 1950 Mills & Boon editor Joan Bryant rejected a manuscript from Ann Cameron because the doctor-hero was less than dominant: 'His medical career seems to be far from distinguished. This of course is not at all fashionable at the moment.'[53] Ross McKibbin's description of the doctor-hero conceived by A. J. Cronin is applicable here: 'The medical hero is more central to the human condition than other young men: he not only is a personal symbol of modern technology but also stands for human relationships at their most sensitive and vulnerable.'[54] Similarly, Betty Beaty noted that the most successful Mills & Boon romances took place where the hero and heroine faced danger and vulnerability on a daily basis: a hospital or, in Beaty's specialty, an airplane.[55] Anne Vinton, a trained nurse, had also seen her share of real-life hospital drama. 'You don't want to have a coal miner as a hero, or for that matter a carpenter,' she said. 'You're looking for somebody in a position. The best position is a doctor. I got all sorts of ideas from doctors and nurses. A doctor is a bit more glamorous and [has] more sense of humour. Nurses were noble.'[56]

Mills & Boon doctors were always larger than life and physically impressive. In Vinton's *Caprice in Hospital Blue* (1957), Nurse Caprice runs into her old acquaintance, Dr Rex Dinwall: 'She saw his Viking blondness bearing down on her. He was tanned and his excellent teeth flashed into a wide grin which made her think of an advertisement for dentrifice.'[57] In Marjorie Moore's *Unsteady Flame* (1953), Sir Richard Aylmer is 'the adored surgeon, almost a demi-god . . . He's treated more as if he were a matinee idol than a surgeon' at St Jude's Hospital.[58] In Moore's next novel, *Sister Nairn,* the title character looks longingly at the star surgeon's large and dexterous hands as he operates: 'Unconsciously her eyes would stray to Mark Serely's gloved hands as they delicately probed the wound.'[59]

The hero shares the heroine's nobility. In the Mills & Boon world, Harley Street is disdained in favour of public service to the common people in the NHS. In Alex Stuart's *Master of Surgery* (1958), Ann Royston, at age 24, is a former ballerina turned junior house surgeon at St Martha's Hospital. She fancies medical student

[53] H-M&B, 13 July 1950.
[54] McKibbin, 'Politics and the Medical Hero', p. 670.
[55] Beaty interview, op. cit.
[56] Vinton interview, op. cit.
[57] Vinton, *Caprice in Hospital Blue* (London, 1957), p. 60.
[58] Marjorie Moore, *Unsteady Flame* (London, 1953), p. 21.
[59] Moore, *Sister Nairn* (London, 1954), 17. Alan Boon praised this novel as one of Moore's best Doctor–Nurse attempts, writing to her in 1953 about 'your sure touch with the hospital background, the heroine, . . . [and] the patient with the rabbit bone'. H-M&B, 26 March 1953. Of the latter, Sister Nairn swoons when Dr Mark heroically saves an elderly probationer, extracting the remains of his lunch.

Michael, but he fails his exams and runs off to sea. His Harley Street brother tries to swoop her up. But Michael returns as a national hero—performing an appendectomy aboard a fishing trawler in the North Sea—and passes his exams. He tells his selfish brother, 'You can keep your M.S. and your Fellowship, Nick—and your surgery. I just want a plain M.B. and a nice, quiet country practice under the Health Service . . . where all I'm expected to do is diagnose measles and mumps and deliver the occasional baby.'[60]

NURSES AND DOCTORS

Remembering that Mills & Boon novels were managed, with constant market research as to what the readers would tolerate and what would offend, it is significant in the 1950s Doctor–Nurse romances to find an independent spirit and outspokenness that borders on feminism and, in many cases, challenges the status quo. Here were nurses proud of their abilities and not afraid to speak their mind. Here, too, was the emergence of the female doctor, meeting her doctor-hero as an equal. Only 10 per cent of qualified doctors in Britain in the 1950s were female, but on the bookshelves they were taking over. One could dismiss this as part of the escapist fantasy, but the authors regarded this as an aspiration for their readers and wish-fulfilment. Not surprisingly, the Mills & Boon 'Medical Romances' of today are all Doctor–Doctor romances.[61]

Most of the doctor-heroines have it in their blood. In Anne Vinton's *Doctor Immacula* (1958), Dr Immacula 'Mac' Hayes comes from a long line of Westmorland physicians: 'She had not allowed her sex to turn her away from medicine, and had not only taken an M.D. in her stride during her sojourn in Edinburgh, but had added another diploma to her name after a further year of work under a Professor of Pathology.'[62] Her beauty, however, was a disadvantage: 'Mac was as pretty as a wax doll, with her blue eyes and golden hair. The trouble was that this tended to prevent people from taking her seriously as a doctor. So she was delighted to be offered a job in a Sudanese hospital by a man who seemed willing to regard her as a useful colleague and nothing else.'[63] Before long, Mac does look for something else—Dr Roy Victor Kingsland of the Hospital for Tropical Diseases. When Mac faints, Roy examines her and professes his love: 'She couldn't help looking up into the dark eyes as the stethoscope traveled over her chest and lingered under her breast. "I can't find anything there

[60] Alex Stuart, *Master of Surgery* (London, 1958), p. 81.

[61] Interestingly, in 1922, when Mills & Boon was a general publishing house, the firm published *The Woman Doctor and Her Future* by L. Martindale, MD, Honorary Surgeon at the New Sussex Hospital for Women and Children in Brighton, staffed entirely by women doctors. 'We cannot doubt that the Woman Doctor of the future will give to the scientific world gifts of a value we cannot yet measure, and a service to humanity illimitable in its fearlessness and devotion', Martindale wrote (p. 153).

[62] Vinton, *Doctor Immacula* (London, 1958), p. 6.

[63] Ibid., p. 7.

to account for the trouble," he said at last.'[64] Alex Stuart, writing as 'Barbara Allen' in *Doctor Lucy* (1956), is even more forthright about her profession. At Melfield General Hospital in Yorkshire—'catering for the needs of a large industrial town'—Dr Lucy Grey follows in her father's footsteps, facing obstacles daily:

> There still remained a prejudice against women in medicine; they were regarded as vulnerable beings who might at any time throw up their careers in order to marry. Really good women surgeons were few and far between because, temperamentally, they were believed to be unsuited to surgery, they were mistrusted by their male colleagues and in particular by their male teachers, condemned out of hand as being too emotional, too lacking in the single-minded dedication which surgery demanded. But *she* wasn't, Lucy thought.[65]

In the end, fellow surgeon Paul Brandon accepts Lucy as an equal: 'Lucy, I want you for my wife, you know—on any terms. Any terms at all.'[66]

In Anne Lorraine's *White Coated Girl* (1955), Anne Caxton is the only female doctor at Manderfield's Hospital: 'Anne Caxton, who had so bravely and confidently told the world that her work came first, and would always be of prime importance in her life!'[67] A nurse rises to defend Dr Anne in the face of prejudice from a patient:

> 'Mind you, I don't hold with women doctors myself, do you? As my husband says, women was made to marry and have children, not waste their time learning something that can be done far better by men.'
>
> The nurse opened the door.
>
> 'As long as there are women in the world like you', she said evenly, 'we'll need all the women doctors we can get, believe me! Good night.'[68]

Anne falls for the resident surgeon, Dr James Thrapston. In the end, it is happily-ever-after as a partnership, offering a new dimension to the Mills & Boon reader's dream of companionate marriage:

> 'Let's go together, my dearest. That's how I want it to be, always—Doctor Anne, my wife.'
>
> 'You mean—I needn't give up Manderfield's Hospital?' Anne asked wonderingly, her eyes brimming with tears of happiness. 'I can have Mandy's *and* you? It seems too much to ask of life, James.'
>
> He kissed her again, and his hands on her shoulders were strong yet gentle.
>
> 'But that's the way I want it, Anne, my darling', he told her. 'And one day, if you agree, we'll make the clinic dream come true, together.'[69]

Of course, only the doctor-heroine was expected to continue working. Nurse heroines happily abandon the careers they so vigorously defended as soon as the

64 Ibid., p. 161.
65 Barbara Allen, *Doctor Lucy* (London, 1956), p. 12.
66 Ibid., p. 185.
67 Anne Lorraine, *White Coated Girl* (London, 1955), p. 173.
68 Ibid., p. 10. 69 Ibid., p. 188.

engagement is announced. The expectation, however, is that the heroine will support her doctor husband through thick and thin as a loyal companion. In Anne Lorraine's *Emergency Nurse* (1955), Nurse Gina Delham falls for Dr Simon Brayford, casualty physician at Barneford Hospital. She's happy to just work with him; he wants more:

> 'How many times do I have to tell you I no longer want you as an assistant, Gina? What I am looking for now is a partner in every sense of the word—somebody who will love me, and work with me, and live with me.' ...
>
> She lay very still, her being flooded with a great joy. She felt as if her heart were beating in her throat, and there was a wonderful warmth over her whole body.
>
> 'Simon', she said at last, in a gentle voice. 'Simon, my darling—I'd like to take that job, if you still want me?'[70]

THE NATIONAL HEALTH SERVICE

Mills & Boon authors were encouraged to use their experience in nursing to provide a setting that was more realistic and descriptive than in most romance novels to date. This seemingly was what the readership wanted. Most intriguing are the descriptions of hospital life in transition under the new NHS. In 1948 there were 2,800 hospitals in Britain; two-thirds of these were more than fifty years old.[71] Coping with old and outdated facilities was a way of life not ignored by authors, while new hospitals were greeted like rays of sunshine.

In *Sister Nairn* by Marjorie Moore, the transition between old and new was evident at St Anselm's Hospital: 'Like many of the older hospitals, St Anselm's had spread far beyond its earlier boundaries, and now the original façade was dwarfed by the extensive modern wing which had sprung up at its side.'[72] At Melfield General Hospital in Yorkshire, setting of *Doctor Lucy*, NHS benefits are apparent in the detailed description of the facility:

> The hospital, being extensively rebuilt, was on very modern lines—two main wings, broadly divided into medical and surgical, with the Theatre Block as a self-contained unit in the centre and on the first floor ... Residents' and nurses' quarters were separated from the main building by a wide paved square, with covered-in passage-ways for the convenience of the staff, and the Obstetric Block—again a separate unit—formed one side of the square, in the centre of which a well-kept lawn, edged with flower-beds, made a pleasant splash of colour against the grey stone of the buildings which hemmed it in.[73]

Mary Burchell's 1955 novel, *Hospital Corridors,* was set in Montreal. English Nurse Madeline Gill arrives at Dominion Hospital from All Souls Hospital in Yorkshire. There she is attracted to Nat Lanyon, 'one of the most brilliant

[70] Anne Lorraine, *Emergency Nurse* (London, 1955), p. 188.

[71] See Brian Watkin, *The National Health Service: The First Phase: 1948–1974 and after* (London, 1978), and John E. Pater, *The Making of the National Health Service* (London, 1981).

[72] Moore, *Sister Nairn,* p. 5.

[73] Stuart, *Doctor Lucy,* p. 19.

surgeons attached to the Dominion'. Burchell's novel is interesting in contrasting the advancements of the Canadian hospital system with its British counterpart. All Souls, Madeline admits, is a 'rather old-fashioned, shabby bulk'. But she discovers that hospitals, whatever their condition, share a common mission:

> Under this splendid roof [at Dominion] the same rhythm of activity went on. The same fears, the same hopes, the same drama. Here life was ushered in and death held at bay as long as possible. The outer shell might be different, but the spirit—the flame of service which burnt steadily within it—was the same.[74]

Madeline has beautiful accommodations at Dominion, unlike her 'rather ugly little room' at All Souls: 'It never occurred to her that in this hospital she would have anything different from the standard high white bed and the utilitarian furniture which seemed to be all part of hospital life.'[75] Canadian Nurse Eileen is amused by Madeline's excitement, especially her amazement that only two nurses share a bathroom—unheard of back home:

> 'Back in England nursing is treated in a rather Cinderella-ish sort of way, isn't it?' she said.
>
> National and local pride immediately impelled Madeline to make some defence of the situation.
>
> 'No, I wouldn't say that exactly. It's a respected profession, and although most improvements quite rightly go to the patients first, I do know that in the more modern hospitals great efforts are made to improve the nurses' quarters and conditions too. But most of our big teaching hospitals are old, you know. It's only when you're building an entirely new place, starting from scratch, that you can have anything as lovely—and enlightened—as this.'
>
> 'Well, I guess you're right', her companion conceded.[76]

In Marguerite Lees's *Sister Grace*, the author vents her opinions on how best to proceed with hospital development and changes. The title character runs the children's unit at the hospital. Despite the fact that this is escapist entertainment, Lees takes advantage of a captive audience to express her views:

> [Grace] had listened to learned discussions between the consultants about improvements in the future; but if they had asked her—a course which wouldn't have occurred to them—about her own views, she would have said boldly that instead of bigger and better and brighter hospitals, she could foresee children being nursed, when this was possible at all, in their own homes by visiting nurses and doctors. No emotional uprooting whatever! And how much less risk of cross-infections![77]

In the end, Grace, like a true Mills & Boon heroine, chucks it all for a future with Dr Mark Halcott, the pediatric doctor, who proposes: 'If you give your notice to Matron right now, we can be married at Christmas. We'll put in right away for one of the new medical staff flats.'[78]

[74] Mary Burchell, *Hospital Corridors* (London, 1955), p. 25.
[75] Ibid., p. 27. [76] Ibid., p. 28.
[77] Lees, *Sister Grace*, p. 11. [78] Ibid., p. 192.

In *Nurse with a Dream* by Norrey Ford, tensions are evident between the old and the new, and private patients are looked upon with disdain in the NHS hospital. Nurse Jacqueline Clark is initially repelled by the hospital's main ward, unattractively called Lister Ward: 'It was a bleak, old-fashioned ward with high windows and walls in a sickly green. Thirty old women occupied the high-enamelled beds, each wearing a pink bed-jacket in a hue which clashed violently with the scarlet blankets.'[79] She prefers night duty in the Private Patient's Block, 'separate from the main building, lighter, more modern, and alleged to be easier on the nurses' feet':

> The private patients were much like those in the wards, with the same fears, hopes, courage or the lack of it. Some would suffer any inconvenience rather than trouble the nurses; others were impatient, inconsiderate, rude—just as on the wards. The difference was that here the inconsiderate patient had a bell, and used it.[80]

But Jacqueline has an awakening, when a private patient raises her ire, demanding that she sneak her a sleeping pill outside of doctor's orders. With her refusal, Jacqueline strikes a blow for the egalitarian nature of the NHS:

> 'I'm a special friend of Mr. Broderick. He was very anxious about me, and says I'm to have every attention. I nearly died, you know.'
>
> Jacqueline turned at the door. 'We give every attention to every patient, Miss Lovell, whether they pay or not. If you nearly died, so did a number of other people in here . . . I shall do my duty as I've been taught to do it.'[81]

CONCLUSION

The launch of the National Health Service in 1948 brought revolutionary change to Britain—and not simply in the way people received medical care. The NHS renewed interest in all aspects of the medical profession, as more and more people came under its care. This was absorbed into the culture, which in turn reflected and promoted the new industry.

A case in point is Mills & Boon. The rise of the 'Doctor–Nurse' romance in the 1950s coincided with the NHS and, in fact, helped to promote and reinforce it. Mills & Boon authors, most of them former nurses, were ambassadors for the system and would tolerate no criticism of it. Unlike the sustained attack on the contemporary medical system by A. J. Cronin in his pre-war novels, the Mills & Boon 'medical books' are universally supportive of a system that was growing in popularity. Given Mills & Boon's own admission that their novels were carefully vetted so as not to offend a loyal readership, and deliberately reflected their readership's values and opinions, Mills & Boon romances offer proof of George Orwell's theory. As such, they are a useful source for historians of attitudes and

[79] Ford, *Nurse with a Dream*, p. 7. [80] Ibid., p. 146. [81] Ibid., p. 148.

influences of the period, as Ross McKibbin has shown in a very different historical period.

To the firm, a commitment to accuracy and realism was considered good business sense. 'The tremendous appeal of these books lies, we are convinced, in the authenticity of their settings,' Mills & Boon told Kate Norway in 1959. 'Their hospitals are *real*, and details of the most minor treatments are presented with real-life accuracy.' [82] Norway concurred, 'Our readers are just a little bloodthirsty—in a perfectly nice way, of course!'[83]

[82] H-M&B, 17 June 1959. [83] 'The clinical cult', op. cit.

12

Being His Own Rabbit: Geoffrey Gorer and English Culture*

Peter Mandler

Social historians of modern Britain inevitably and increasingly rely on the social sciences for the raw material with which they as historians work—as witness the two best single-author syntheses we have, Jose Harris's *Private Lives, Public Spirit*, which uses social science to portray the self-images of the age, and Ross McKibbin's *Classes and Cultures*, which uses social-scientific accounts and surveys for direct reportage on behaviours and practices.[1] It's a safe bet that the syntheses of the second half of the twentieth century, when they come, will make even more use of social-scientific sources. Already there has been, recently, in the work of Mike Savage, Selina Todd, and Angela Davis, growing awareness of the way in which social science has since the Second World War come to provide some of the everyday language of self-awareness not only for elites, as suggested in Harris's work, but for the mass of the people.[2]

The more we mine social science the more we need to fathom it—that is, to incorporate its own history into our own. In this chapter I offer a tentative fathoming of the now much-cited work on English culture of Geoffrey Gorer. Gorer presents a significant case-study because his work on the English, carried out mostly in the 1950s, centred presciently on topics that are now more interesting to historians than they were then to contemporaries—that is to say, he wrote not on sociological themes such as work, community and class, but on

* I am very grateful to Mathew Thomson for sending me his unpublished paper on 'Geoffrey Gorer and the "Social Science" of Modern Sexuality', to Deborah Cohen for more than one helpful reading of drafts of this paper, and to the audience at the Oxford symposium in April 2009 for a boisterous discussion.

[1] Jose Harris, *Private Lives, Public Spirit: A Social History of Britain 1870–1914* (Oxford, 1993); note esp. p. 37, where Harris's chosen themes are warranted by reference to 'contemporary social theorists' whose observations of these themes were 'incorporated . . . into a general sociology of the modern world'; Ross McKibbin, *Classes and Cultures: England 1918–1951* (Oxford, 1998).

[2] Mike Savage, *Identities and Social Change in Britain Since 1940: The Politics of Method* (Oxford, 2010); Selina Todd, 'Affluence, class and Crown Street: reinvestigating the post-war working class', *Contemporary British History* 22 (2008), pp. 501–18; Angela Davis, 'A critical perspective on British social surveys and community studies and their accounts of married life, *c.*1945–70', *Cultural and Social History* 6 (2009), pp. 47–64.

cultural and psychological themes such as love, sex, marriage, parenting, death, attitudes to religion and the supernatural, to law and order, and to 'Englishness'. The tempting usefulness of this data has, however, to be treated with caution due to the very idiosyncrasies that caused Gorer to stand out from his contemporaries. It is not only that Gorer was as much a literary intellectual as a 'scientist'—in that, he differs little from well-known and rightly respected figures such as Richard Titmuss, Michael Young, Richard Hoggart, or Raymond Williams. But, outside the mainstream of sociological thought, Gorer was more of a loner, and also, as a determinedly uninstitutionalized man of leisure, freer to frame his own questions (and his own answers) unscrutinized. That alone gives us a reason to scrutinize him.

I

Geoffrey Gorer was born in 1905, the son of a wealthy Jewish antiques dealer who went down with the *Lusitania* in 1915, leaving a widow and three sons free to live lives of relative ease. He went to Charterhouse and Cambridge, where he read classics and modern languages. Like many sensitive young intellectuals coming to maturity in the Slump, his keen personal and aesthetic sensitivities were wounded by the misery and ugliness he perceived around him. The Puritan tradition, modern urban life, and the grim homogeneity of the mass-produced society had, he felt, conspired to make England 'the most hag-ridden and almost the ugliest country (architecturally) in the world'.[3] Where some might have retreated from this horror into an aesthetic or literary redoubt, Gorer was moved to address it, either for selfish reasons—'I cannot myself be happy when surrounded by unhappiness' was his self-diagnosis in 1935—or out of guilt, as his friend Margaret Mead thought, and as was common enough among privileged young Cambridge graduates in the early 1930s.[4]

Gorer had already developed a clear diagnosis of the problem of English culture—which was only a special case in the bigger problem of Western culture more broadly—by the time his first book, on the ideas of the Marquis de Sade, was published in 1932; it was the diagnosis that would, essentially, frame his approach to the English throughout his life. His twin guides were, as for so many of his generation, Freud and Marx. From Freud he took the fundamental psychodynamic assumptions—that the driving forces in humans were sex and death, that these forces could not be denied but had to be expressed in some form, either constructively or destructively, and that modern civilization was predicated on the repression of these forces, leading to neurosis and occasional catastrophic outbreaks of destructiveness. But in the spirit of the 1930s he saw

[3] Geoffrey Gorer, *Bali and Angkor, or Looking at Life and Death* (London, 1936), pp. 56–7.
[4] Geoffrey Gorer, *Nobody Talks Politics* (London, 1936), p. 215; Gorer, *Bali and Angkor*, 101; Margaret Mead to Geoffrey Gorer, 15 July 1942 (photocopy): Jane Howard Papers, Columbia University, Box 37.

Freud as essentially a pre-war figure with 'an unjustifiable pride in European civilization'.[5] From Marx, therefore, he took the critical view that modern civilization was *not* inevitable or even desirable, but could be transformed—through the late 1930s he still believed in a socialist revolution[6]—to provide constructive outlets for these pent-up psychic forces.

Gorer's idiosyncratic refinement of these ideas about human motivation sheds further light on his own motives in approaching English culture. Although the most natural and most constructive psychodynamic outlet is sex, Gorer's personal view was that sex, 'though pleasant', provided 'no such lasting ecstasy and final solution' as the likes of Freud and D. H. Lawrence would have us suppose. Another effective outlet is what he would come to see as 'mastery', which could be destructive (expressed as aggression) or could be guided into constructive channels, including mastery over objects and ideas. Gorer's compulsion to diagnose others' unhappiness could be seen as a constructive form of 'mastery over' others by means of intellectual work, one which fit with his inherited gentlemanly sense of *noblesse oblige*. Or, as Margaret Mead put it in a kinder moment, 'he is happy and he is a deviant, and so it is the 90 per cent of the world who are different and unhappy and should have things fixed up for them'.[7]

Whatever his motives, the combination of a strong antipathy to the society in which he grew up and a personal mission to address its ills through close study presented a paradox: how to study his society without being contaminated by it? How, to use a phrase that would recur much later in his life, to 'study at a distance', especially to study something into which he had been born and, presumably, by which he had been shaped? So first, he had to run away.

For most of the 1930s and 40s, Gorer restlessly cast about for ways and means to study (and, ultimately, to cure) the ills of his home culture without becoming too personally implicated in them. At first he dallied in Paris, Berlin, and Florence with a literary, political, and largely homosexual crowd; tried and failed to become a man of letters; then almost on a whim he essayed quasi-ethnographic, quasi-touristic expeditions to West Africa and Southeast Asia. In Bali for the first time he glimpsed utopia—the Balinese, he felt, had found the near-perfect formula for eliminating 'fear, guilt and duty' (the three predominating neuroses of his own civilization) by channelling their energies into the constructive outlets of sex, art, and 'creativeness of any sort'.[8]

[5] Geoffrey Gorer, 'Notes on the way', *Time & Tide*, 23 May 1936, p. 752.

[6] Geoffrey Gorer, *Hot Strip Tease and Other Notes on American Culture* (London, 1937), pp. 20–4.

[7] Gorer, *Bali and Angkor*, 104; Geoffrey Gorer to Margaret Mead, 27 Jan. 1939; Margaret Mead to Gregory Bateson, 9–10 Jan. 1936: Margaret Mead Papers, Library of Congress, B5, S1; and see also Geoffrey Gorer, *Himalayan Village* (London, 1938), pp. 448–9; Geoffrey Gorer, *Exploring English Character* (London, 1955), p. 292.

[8] Gorer, *Bali and Angkor*, 52; Mead to Gorer, 20 Aug. 1936; Gorer to Mead, 5 Sep. 1936; Mead to Gorer, 1 Oct. 1936; Gorer to Mead, 16 Oct. 1936: Mead Papers, B5. This important exchange, occurring while Mead was on her own field trip to Bali, also crystallizes a lot of the psychological differences between Mead and Gorer which I have skipped over here.

Towards the end of 1935 he moved on to America in order to try an approach to something more like his own culture (without being too much like it), and here he had a stroke of luck—an encounter that would change his life, both personally and intellectually, with the anthropologist Margaret Mead. At the moment of his arrival in New York, Mead was unfortunately about to go off on an extended field trip—to Bali, as it happened—with her future husband Gregory Bateson, but in a torrid month she managed to induct Gorer into the mysteries of her discipline (and possibly into the mysteries of heterosexuality) before handing him on to colleagues for further training. From them he appropriated two significant new bodies of doctrine to fit into his existing schema. The first was the sub-discipline of anthropology that Mead and her lover and mentor Ruth Benedict had pioneered, 'culture and personality', which taught that a culture—in practice, any culture, from a simple, homogeneous one like the Samoans to a complex, modern one like the Americans—had a distinctive 'personality' (a psychological 'pattern') that could be related to every little detail of their social and cultural practice, as exemplified in Benedict's *Patterns of Culture* (1934). The second was a loose congeries of ideas which has come to be known as 'neo-Freudianism', embracing a range of psychoanalytically minded thinkers such as H. S. Sullivan, Karen Horney, Erich Fromm, and Erik Erikson who like Gorer accepted Freud's basic account of the psychic architecture but emphasized the culturally specific ways in which individuals developed and adapted. Gorer's principal introduction to these ideas came through Mead's friend at Yale, John Dollard, and Gorer spent much of the next few years in and out of Yale learning neo-Freudian techniques and undergoing psychoanalysis himself by Earl Zinn. Together these two bodies of knowledge made Gorer feel more like a scientist, and they gave him a set of tools to pursue his life's work, which he admitted to Mead (then in Bali) was 'predominantly concerned with my own culture, and the remedy of our present discontents'.[9] He could now see that each culture—the Balinese, the Americans, the English—had a distinctive psychological 'pattern', inculcated and maintained through a variety of socialization processes, and thus that their distinctive psychological woes could be treated, not by a socialist revolution (or at least not by a revolution that was merely socialist), but by alterations to those socialization processes. At Yale he learned to focus on the ways in which aggression in modern society was born out of the frustration of the main drives, and how this systematic frustration was internalized by the system of rewards and punishments delivered principally by parents (and as one neo-Freudian approach suggested principally in infant training in the first two years).

Undoubtedly Gorer got carried away by the scientific claims especially of Dollard and the Yale psychologists. He had long admired science, but from afar, and besides these ideas seemed to offer a series of brilliant simplifications—technical fixes—which he might apply to his cultural preoccupations. Not only

[9] Gorer to Mead, 17 Feb. (1937): Mead Papers, B5.

was a culture like a personality, but any one individual personality could be taken as a microcosm of the culture; complex, modern cultures were more or less like simple, homogeneous ones in this respect; all cultures developed their personality-types through learning processes and the most important of these were concentrated in infancy; infant learning determined how people responded to the challenges of their culture and on this ultimately rested their character, indeed their happiness.

Thus armed he was inclined to run amok, alarming Mead. Almost immediately after his initiation by Mead, Benedict, and Dollard, he laid out his programme. 'It seems to me certain that our culture is at present working very badly', he wrote in November 1936.

> A thorough examination of our own culture would, I think, be extraordinarily useful because it would show those institutions and habits which influence the formation of various social attitudes, and might suggest alterations which would modify those which are most undesirable because of the aggression, frustration or anxiety that they produce. I believe, for example, that there might possibly be shown to exist a connection between a puritanical attitude towards sexual acts, a fear of impotence, and a cultural emphasis on hoarding; or between a sharp differentiation in the desirable behaviour of small boys and girls and the incidence of homosexuality and a fear of loneliness which manifests itself in various ways.[10]

This manifesto came from the preface—'rather pretentious', he admitted—to an anthropological study of burlesque theatres in New York City that he had scribbled down in a few excited months in mid-1936, as 'a sort of preliminary canter for the work which I foresee and want to do of investigating our own culture'. It was published to Mead's horror as *Hot Strip Tease*, which she was sure would destroy his academic credentials before he had even acquired any.[11] He toyed with the idea of settling down at Yale and undertaking 'a fairly novel survey of American culture as manifested in adolescents—Growing up in New Haven, if you like'.[12] Another idea was to rush back to England and attempt 'some field work in Bermondsea [sic], the poorest and toughest quarter in London, which has a practically homogenous isolated culture with some very odd features in the best Margaret style (odd ways of treating infants, peculiar marriage ceremonies and so on)'.[13]

Finally, much to Mead's relief, he decided on doing some real old-fashioned anthropological fieldwork and hooked up with an expedition to the Himalayas, where he spent a few months in the spring of 1937 living amongst the Lepchas of Sikkim. Still, he warned her, he would never be 'an ethnologist pur sang . . . I am putting myself into the "ethnological situation", less perhaps to find out about the Lepchas than to try and find out what it is like to be an ethnologist . . . In

[10] Gorer, *Hot Strip Tease*, pp. 17–19.

[11] Gorer to Mead, 16 Oct. 1936; Mead to Gorer, 4 Dec. 1936; Mead to Gorer, 13 Oct. 1937: Mead Papers, B5.

[12] Gorer to Mead, 29 May 1936; Mead to Gorer, 20 Aug. 1936: Mead Papers, B5.

[13] Gorer to Benedict, 23 Oct. 1936: Ruth Benedict Papers, Vassar College, Box 28.

short, I am trying to find out "by being my own rabbit" what is the value of ethnology for extrapolating into our own culture.'[14] Nevertheless placing himself in the 'ethnological situation' did him a world of good. He came back in a calmer state, though also, he claimed later, physically maimed by his Himalayan ordeal. *Hot Strip Tease* had evidently triggered some last regrets for the life of the arts, but he had got over that. '[H]orrified at the way I had behaved', he apologized for 'a good deal of silliness' in that book, and promised that henceforward he would keep his intuitions 'rigorously within bounds'.[15] The account of his fieldwork, *Himalayan Village*, is certainly by far the most well-rounded and rigorous piece of anthropological writing he attempted. It is the closest he came to the ethnographic approach to 'culture and personality' that makes *Patterns of Culture* so satisfying. It helped that the Lepchas, like the Balinese, seemed to him a happy people free of frustration and aggression. However, his explanation for this was that due to their isolation and the terrible challenges of their mountainous kingdom they had had to channel all of their psychic energies into 'wresting a livelihood from their environment'. Again he asked himself, what relevance their situation could possibly have to our own culture? In conditions of plenty where psychic energy was likely to build up rather than be let off, how could 'the excess of personal and national aggression' be handled? '[W]ill it be necessary for us too to view our neighbours impersonally, to tone down all the contrasts in personality, talent and achievement which have resulted in the greatest glories as well as the greatest horrors of our society? Or is there another solution?'[16]

II

These questions were given far greater urgency by the darkening international situation in which *Himalayan Village* was published in 1938. Gorer never showed any interest in 'primitive' peoples again.[17] Not even Mead and Bateson insisted on that any longer. Their own efforts after their return from Bali turned increasingly to applications of 'culture and personality' to questions of international relations, addressing precisely the problem of how to relieve 'the excess of... national aggression' that Gorer had raised. Oddly, however, it was Mead and Bateson, rather than Gorer, who focused on the English—taking the Anglo-American relationship as their paradigm for intercultural communication and using their anthropological understandings of both cultures to explain how and

[14] Gorer to Mead, 17 Feb. 1937: Mead Papers, B5.

[15] Gorer to Mead, 17 Apr. 1937: Geoffrey Gorer Papers, University of Sussex, Box 91; Gorer to Mead, 20 Oct. (1937): Mead Papers, R8.

[16] Gorer, *Himalayan Village*, pp. 448–51.

[17] He admitted to Mead that his aversion to another field trip in the non-Western world was not only physical—'I don't fancy the idea of undertaking another one emotionally or scientifically'. Gorer to Mead, 18 Nov. 1938: Gorer Papers, Box 91.

why Anglo-American relations improved or deteriorated. For this purpose, Mead used her own relationship with Gorer as well as Bateson to test propositions.[18] But while Mead always kept both sides—the English and the American—in full view, Gorer had become temporarily fixated on the Americans. He took a trip to the American South with Dollard, accepted an assignment from the Rockefeller Foundation to study Hollywood, and then established himself at Yale. Whereas Bateson left behind Mead and their infant daughter to return immediately to England when the war broke out, to offer his services to all and sundry as an analyst of culture, Gorer instead brought over his dependent mother and settled her in New Haven where he could continue to cultivate his psychological science at a safe distance from home.

By this stage Gorer's repeated insistence that he was really only interested in his own culture begins to sound disingenuous. In truth he had been running away from England ever since he came down from Cambridge—Paris, Berlin, Africa, Asia, now America. He associated England with unhappiness and boredom and, while claiming to be seeking a fix, was still maintaining his distance. His standard justification was that '[u]nfortunately the hardest of all cultures to investigate is our own. We are so much part of our own culture that it is impossible to be objective about it. Even the most revolutionary thinkers are inevitably culturally limited.'[19] Mead took almost the opposite view—you had to feel truly comfortable in a culture to understand it—and in a rare outburst she once accused Gorer of being too much motivated by hatred and guilt about his own culture to be constructive.[20] Before their meeting he had admitted, 'I dislike the company of those I feel to be my inferiors,' which should have further queried his qualifications as a participant-observer.[21] For Gorer America provided that safe distance; it was, he wrote in *Hot Strip Tease*, 'rather like an image of Europe seen in a distorting mirror (with recognisably the same objects but seen from a new angle, and in completely different proportions, so that one views them with fresh eyes)'.[22]

In fact Gorer remained in the States throughout the war, where he formed part of a network assembled by Mead of workers in various government agencies, all devoted to applying the 'culture and personality' techniques to the study of friendly and enemy cultures. Gorer's first job was in the Office of War Information—where, uncoincidentally, he worked for Mead's brother-in-law Leo Rosten—and with Mead and others he gaily attempted a series of 'rapid, diagnostic sketches' (what they called 'culture cracking') of the personality patterns of Greeks, Burmese, Germans, and, especially, the Japanese. In this latter work on the Japanese he became notorious for his overestimate of the significance of toilet training in forming the adult Japanese character: 'early and

[18] I discuss Mead's and Bateson's work on the Anglo-American relationship in 'Margaret Mead amongst the natives of Great Britain', *Past & Present* 204 (2009), pp. 195–233.

[19] Gorer, 'Notes on the way', p. 753.

[20] Mead to Gorer, 15 Jul. 1942 (photocopy): Jane Howard Papers, Box 37.

[21] Gorer, *Bali and Angkor*, p. 40.

[22] Gorer, *Hot Strip Tease*, pp. 5–6.

severe toilet training', he argued, imposed conformity in the culture but stored up huge amounts of frustration which accounted for 'the overwhelming brutality and sadism of the Japanese at war'.[23] Gorer leant much more heavily on neo-Freudian analyses than did other anthropologists and even other psychologists in war service. Towards the end of the war he moved from OWI to a Political Warfare post at the British Embassy in Washington. There he supported H. V. Dicks's psychoanalytic theses on the peculiar dualism of the German character—'The German alternately commands and kowtows'—which argued that the German was divided between twin desires to submit to the father and to rescue the mother.[24] Similarly his principal contribution to Mead's wartime work on Anglo-American relations was to play up the themes of differences in child training and homosexual seduction.[25]

Working in tandem with Mead these tendencies were kept under control by her greater concern for the different forms of socialisation and by her greater tact about the use of psychoanalytic language. After the war, as they gradually pulled apart, Gorer lost this control. Crises came with two books that he struck off quickly in the style of the wartime sketches, on the American national character (written in 1946–7) and the Russian (written in 1947–8). The former, despite Mead's wishful attempt to see it as 'written with real gentleness and lack of bitterness or rancour of any kind', got American backs up by portraying the American conscience as 'predominantly feminine' and 'the clinging mother' as 'the great emotional menace in American psychological life'.[26]

This approach reached its zenith in Gorer's book on the Russians, which adumbrated the notorious 'swaddling hypothesis'—that Russian character was closely connected to infant swaddling and feeding on demand. The storm of controversy into which this swept Gorer (and, to her despair, Mead as well) destroyed whatever tenuous credibility his neo-Freudian approach—now scorned as 'diaperology'—had once had in official circles. Even Mead, though she defended Gorer valiantly in public, was dismayed by his overuse of neo-Freudian language and possibly by what she saw as his playing up to the 'mother-blaming' atmosphere in popular culture.[27] The 'swaddling controversy'

[23] Geoffrey Gorer, 'Themes in Japanese culture', *Transactions of the New York Academy of Sciences*, 2nd ser., 5 (1943), pp. 106–24.

[24] Gorer to Lt. Col. G.R. Hargreaves, War Office, 27 Apr. 1945, and Dicks's memoranda attached: Gorer Papers, Box 32.

[25] For the former, see Margaret Mead, 'Facilitating Anglo-American relationships: a case study in the application of anthropological methods to understanding between peoples', n.d., 15–16: Mead Papers, E155, and Margaret Mead, *And Keep Your Powder Dry*, (1942; New York and Oxford, 2000), esp. pp. 88–100; for the latter, Margaret Mead, 'Formulation of triangular relationship to reconcile Anglo-American incompatabilities', 5 May (1944), and subsequent commentary; Mead to Bateson, 20 May 1944: Mead Papers, M24, R3.

[26] Mead to Benedict, 3 Aug. 1947: Mead Papers, R7; Geoffrey Gorer, *The American People: A Study in National Character* (New York, 1948), pp. 56, 64.

[27] Mead to Gorer, 19 Dec. 1950: Gorer Papers, Box 91; see also Lois W. Banner, *Intertwined Lives: Margaret Mead, Ruth Benedict, and Their Circle* (New York, 2003), p. 436. I discuss the 'swaddling controversy' at greater length in 'One world, many cultures: Margaret Mead and the limits to Cold War anthropology', *History Workshop Journal* 68 (2009), esp. pp. 158–61.

coincided with a crisis in Mead's and Gorer's relationship, and after a period of enhanced intimacy immediately after the war (when she and Bateson had separated), such that they had contemplated marriage, they now settled into a more distanced relationship as old friends.[28] Gorer was on his own—and, finally, thrown back onto the English.

III

At the war's end, Gorer had returned reluctantly to live in England: he bought a country house in Sussex where he ensconced his mother and built up a world-class rhododendron garden, and aimed to rebuild for himself a reputation as a social scientist, on home turf. Conditions in those chill austerity years were not conducive to a cheerful view, even had Gorer been inclined to take one. In 1949, still handicapped by his feeling that out of subjectivity or squeamishness he was ill-equipped to study the English, he tried out some tentative theses in the pages of Cyril Connolly's *Horizon*. Like the Lepchas, the English appeared to him to be a people almost devoid of overt signs of aggression. Unlike the Lepchas, however, he did not believe them to be happy—quite the contrary. Whereas the Lepchas had avoided frustration by venting their psychic energies through sexual activity and the struggle for subsistence, the English must have disposed of their energies otherwise. Unlike the Lepchas, they did not discharge themselves by sexual activity—astoundingly, the reverse, they showed little or no sexual appetite. Thus a tremendous act of repression seems to have been required, manifested first in the middle and upper classes—by around the mid-nineteenth century—and then, a generation or two later, by the working classes. As a result, the English were stifled, private, secretive, and inarticulate. Worst of all, they were shy and lonely. Though atomization was a feature of all modern, mass-produced societies, it had reached an apex amongst the English due to their programmed horror of aggression—they shunned sociality because they feared not only aggression in others, but also the aggression they knew was stored up in themselves.[29] Despite his disclaimers, Gorer seemed to have a pretty good idea of what the English were about—what he did not know was how they got to be that way. What were the psychological mechanisms, of the kind that he had learned to search for at Yale, that explained this unique (and uniquely unhappy) solution to the problem of controlling aggression in modern society? And how could he find out without getting any closer than he absolutely had to?

The *deus ex machina* appeared in the autumn of 1950, when Gorer was approached by the editor of the *Sunday People*, the second most popular Sunday

[28] In an undated letter, possibly late 1951 or early 1952, she traced the deterioration of their relationship to 1949, and by the date of another, 20 Jul. 1950, they had already put things on hold: Mead Papers, B6, R8.

[29] Most of this diagnosis appears in Geoffrey Gorer, 'Notes on the British character', *Horizon*, Dec. 1949, 369–79. Some of the elements were already present in 1938, when he was integrating neo-Freudianism into his initial hypotheses from the de Sade period.

newspaper in Britain after the *News of the World*, about doing an anthropological study of the English. He had had similar approaches sporadically since the 1930s and had always rebuffed them, out of his own inhibitions but also for lack of funds. His inhibitions, as we have seen, had weakened. There was also now a much more powerful incentive both for him and the newspaper, in the runaway commercial success of the Kinsey Report in America. As a result the newspaper was willing to pay for a survey and statistical analysis similar to Kinsey's. Gorer and Mead had been highly critical of Kinsey, who had encroached on their turf, at the same time draining it of cultural and indeed psychological meaning, with his flatly biological statistical measurements of type and number of sexual 'outlet'. Gorer saw the chance to out-Kinsey Kinsey—to devise a questionnaire that would assess meaning as well as practice, across a wider range of topics than simply sex—and thus, at last, to test his propositions about the English character without engaging too intimately with any real English people. At the same time a statistical survey would answer criticisms of his and Mead's previous work that it was based only on 'a free exercise of feminine intuition unhampered by either facts or frequencies'.[30]

Partly on Mead's advice, Gorer designed the questionnaire very tightly around his already established hypotheses about the English problem: eleven questions asked about aggression, 22 about impulse control, 15 about shyness and loneliness, and 14 about infant and child training. Again, very deliberately, respondents were not given much opportunity to respond in an open-ended way, but provided with 'forced choices' aimed at providing either a clear positive or a clear negative to Gorer's hypotheses. In short, as Mead's assistant Rhoda Metraux pointed out, 'you give a very rigid frame and you do not get anything you did not start out with, but you do get data on that'.[31] To be fair to Mead, she urged him in writing up the results to add some vivid ethnographic detail about 'streets and houses and shops and chapels' to lend verisimilitude to the sketch of the character pattern, as Ruth Benedict's work did, but that was precisely the kind of close encounter that Gorer had avoided all his life. As he admitted in the published version, *Exploring English Character*, 'I know very little of England', had hardly ever been north of Oxford, indeed had 'no variety of personal experience, even of personal vision, to supplement, or replace, the non-existent sociological studies'.[32] What he did have was a verdict on his hypotheses, based on over 10,000 completed questionnaires received from readers of the *People*—or so it seems. A close reading of *Exploring English Character* shows how Gorer was able to confirm his hypotheses whatever the data. His hypothesis that the English had channelled very little of their psychic energy into their sex drives was born out

[30] Ralph Linton's review of the American edition of Gorer's *The Americans* in *Scientific American*, May 1948, pp. 58–9.

[31] Gorer to Mead, 31 Oct. 1950, 16 Nov. 1950: Mead Papers, B6, S6; Mead to Gorer, 13 Nov. 1950: Mead Papers, B6; Mead to Gorer, 9, 19 Dec. 1950: Gorer Papers, Box 91; Rhoda Metraux to Gorer, 15 Nov. 1950: Mead Papers, B6.

[32] Mead to Gorer, 28 May 1952; Gorer to Mead, 9 Jun. 1952: Mead Papers, B6; Gorer, *Exploring English Character*, p. 2.

almost entirely by reference to the finding of a high premium placed on virginity before marriage, betokening 'a low interest in sexual activity, compared with most of the neighbouring societies' (although he had no evidence on neighbouring societies).[33] He ignored the parallel finding that the English placed what would seem to be a high estimate on 'the importance of sexual love inside marriage'—55 per cent answered 'very important' and 36 per cent 'fairly important'.[34] Similarly, although the fact that only 4 per cent of the English reproach themselves for 'lust' is taken to support his argument about low sex drive, the fact that over half reproach themselves for 'anger' is *not* taken to falsify his argument about low aggression, but only to demonstrate 'self-consciousness about the expression of anger'.[35] To assess shyness Gorer asked a set of disparate questions about family, neighbours, and friends as well as directly about shyness. He got hardly any useful information about neighbours or friends, except the finding that the longer people lived in one place the more close friends they had nearby, which nevertheless he took to mean that 'the English appear exceptional in the length of time it takes them to knit new bonds'.[36] About shyness itself he found that most people think shyness natural in the young, that they were themselves exceptionally shy when young, but that as they grew older they became less shy. These findings led him to conclude that 'most English people' think they feel 'excessive shyness', even though in answer to a direct question only 15 per cent of men and 10 per cent of women characterized themselves as shy. About loneliness his results amounted even more clearly to a flat contradiction, providing a very large pool of evidence about the richness of associational life in post-war Britain. Before the survey he had been very impressed by the 'Peckham experiment' which seemed to him to attest to widespread loneliness, simply because of 'the apparent unwillingness of something like half the population' to use the Peckham Health Centre. Despite the overwhelming evidence of high levels of sociability in his own survey, he continued to assert as a fact the loneliness of the urban working class 'as illustrated by the Peckham experiment', and on the basis of his findings about shyness deemed it 'specifically English'.[37] In fact his own survey showed that on a given Saturday night in January 1950 barely 7 per cent of the population spent it alone; the only negative spin he could put on this

[33] Ibid., ch. 8. Even so, 43 per cent admitted to 'a real love affair' outside marriage, and this did not count all of the many respondents who admitted to pre-marital sex with their future spouses. Gorer found this alleged misreading of his 'purposefully vague' question a sign of 'strict views of sexual morality', though what is being recorded is pre-marital sex. Ibid., pp. 86–7, 287.

[34] Gorer explained this away by arguing that it was the importance of marriage itself, not sex inside marriage, that was being emphasized. Ibid., pp. 94, 138, 161, 288, and chs. 8–10 *passim.* I am not making the counter-argument, that Gorer's data suggests a high level of sexual energy, nor denying that English sexual codes in the 1950s might be more restrictive than some others. I am simply pointing to the fact that many different interpretations—especially psychological interpretations—might be placed on Gorer's data, and that his interpretive bias ran along very narrow channels.

[35] Ibid., p. 284.

[36] Ibid., pp. 51–5, and ch. 4 *passim.*

[37] Ibid., pp. 21, 65–6. He did admit that the presence of large numbers of family members within walking distance had 'modified' his views about loneliness. Ibid., p. 46.

finding was that 'considerably more people spent the evening with their own family than would have chosen to do so'.[38]

Gorer therefore confirmed, or pretended to confirm, nearly all of his previous 'assumptions' about the English national character, including the assumption that there was such a thing, undivided by class. In trying to explain how this national character had come about, and why it took the form that it did, naturally he paid attention to 'very widely shared patterns' of infant and child training which could explain psychological homogeneity despite all of the superficial sociological differences. Satisfyingly he concluded that an 'absolute moral value' was placed on early toilet training, a value 'so highly charged with emotional and moral values that [the English] are incapable of learning from experience'. This and the total suppression of childhood aggression by paternal authority were taken to explain the adult pattern of 'impulse control'. Impulse control was achieved by toilet training, deprivation of privileges, and restraint, and with relatively little recourse to rewards, and it was implanted deep in the psyches of all English by the 'incorporation of some aspects of the dominant figure or figures of authority in childhood' into the 'super-ego'.[39]

Nevertheless, having evidently learned something from the fate of the swaddling hypothesis, Gorer provided in addition a less static and more historical narrative to explain the English pattern of impulse control. As he had suggested in *Horizon* in 1949, the English elite and their rural dependants had long exhibited these peculiar characteristics—at least since the Puritan revolution—but the urban masses had not, being instead notorious across Europe for their 'truculence', 'their readiness to fight and to endure', and with 'sufficient aggression for every possible event'. Over the last 150 years, however, these class distinctions had been gradually erased by the inculcation of 'strict conscience and self-control' in the masses, principally, Gorer now suggested, through the agency of the police. The remaking of the popular psyche would not have been possible if the police had only acted as a suppressing force. It was crucial to Gorer's argument to show that the image of the policeman had been internalized 'as a model of conduct . . . the ideal model of masculine strength and responsibility', 'incorporated into the personality'. Though he did not spell this out, the natural corollary of this causative argument is that early toilet training, paternal discipline, and so on then spread to the working classes *because* they fit into a pattern already established by the introjection of the policeman into the superego. Nor did he spell out a further step in the argument, which he made in private to his friend W. H. Auden. When Auden objected that 'I have the typical approval of the English police but I don't think that in our kind of upbringing they played a psychological role', Gorer completed the circle by which repression had moved from the middle to the working to the upper classes:

[38] Ibid., p. 72, and ch. 5 *passim*. 'Considerably more' meant 36 vs. 25 per cent. Understandably, Gorer did not dwell on loneliness in the conclusion, though he did stick with shyness.

[39] Ibid., pp. 162–9, and chs. 11 and 12 *passim*.

I don't think the police influenced the ego ideals of the upper middle/upper classes directly, but did have an enormous influence on the working-white collar groups, and so indirectly on the people who raised the upper/middle/upper; I spent most of my earlier years, in measurement of time, with nurses, governesses, grooms, gardeners rather than with my parents; and the ideals of conduct they inculcated had I think something of the policeman background.[40]

Thus Gorer had finally solved the problem that had been vexing him since his youth, the diagnosis of the unhappiness and grim homogeneity that had made the English the most 'hag-ridden' people in the world. There remained the puzzle as to where all of that 'unconscious energy' that was so effectively repressed *went.* Gorer concluded oddly that much of it went on its own suppression, which might account, he thought, 'for the slowness which so many respondents think typically English, the sloth—the procrastination or laziness'. They were simply tired out from all that self-control. And still they were fearful of their own aggression and of others, leading to shyness, loneliness, and a host of minor symptoms that most psychiatrists would pronounce neurotic. Nevertheless, it was axiomatic to Gorer that suppression of all that 'unconscious energy' should lead to frustration and thus to the inevitable outbreak of aggression, and so he made good-faith attempts to find some 'constructive' outlets that would explain their relative contentment. In his own case, and that of the English elite, he knew, energy devoted to mastery over ideas and people led to incredible feats of creativity and derring-do. The masses had to make do with humour (often based on 'insult and humiliation'), vandalism, and occasionally war to let off steam; mastery they could exhibit only in their care of pets and in the cultivation of their gardens. While in truth he could not admire this solution—what a waste of psychic energy, to be devoted to its own annihilation rather than to sex or art—he had to admit that it *had* proved a solution to enduring problems of civilization of a kind that Freud had not envisaged. He closed his book by revealing that his principal reaction to the questionnaires had been, 'What dull lives most of these people appear to lead!', but he was careful to append, 'What good people!', too.[41]

IV

These grace notes cushioned the reception of *Exploring English Character.* It triggered a less hostile reaction in England than *The Americans* had in America. Perhaps because it chimed with a certain kind of post-war disappointment in the masses amongst the intelligentsia, the most positive responses came from the likes of Cyril Connolly, Elizabeth Bowen, V.S. Pritchett, and the reviewers for

[40] Auden to Gorer, 9 Jul. 1955; Gorer to Auden, 15 Jul. 1955: Gorer Papers, Box 78.
[41] Gorer, *Exploring English Character*, pp. 288–93, 303.

the *TLS*, the *Spectator*, the *Listener*, and the *Economist*.[42] Overall, however, the tone adopted by most reviewers was playful and mildly sceptical, especially of the psychoanalytical elements to the argument, and in many ways the book was a flash in the pan, without lasting impact. I have argued elsewhere that the book arrived on the scene too late, just as public opinion was turning against the whole idea of a 'national character' and towards a more individualistic idea of personality; also, of course, turning against the self-image of repression towards new models of liberation, as signalled by the Angry Young Men. The social-scientific establishment was naturally the most hostile, especially in America, on methodological and sociological grounds.[43]

One might conclude from this pattern that Gorer fit neatly into an elite subculture defined by its aesthetic and literary values that continued to dominate the British scene at the expense of democratic and social-scientific influences more evident in America. It is certainly true that it was easier to laugh Gorer off as a 'cavalier English gentleman' in America than it would be in England.[44] But such a contrast would be too easy, and in some obvious respects false. Gorer *did* claim social-scientific authority. Though he pretended to be above such language, undoubtedly he enjoyed the way in which the *People* trumpeted his findings: 'A Great Scientist Has Found out the Truth about the English'.[45] A lot of the criticism was aimed at puncturing *his* scientific pretensions, but not science itself. Richard Mayne's critique in *Time & Tide*, for example, objected to 'the familiar heads-I-win-tails-you-lose argument beloved of psychoanalysis', but took this circularity as 'only another argument for the academic endowment of properly conducted research'.[46] Within the BBC, similarly, there were those who defended Gorer on the grounds that he was bold and amusing, but others who thought the BBC should turn instead to real professionals such as Cyril Burt or Melanie Klein.[47] Ultimately, the 'culture and personality' approach proved no more enduring in the US than in the UK, and Mead and Gorer both moved away from their strongest neo-Freudian claims after the anticlimax of *Exploring English Character*.

For Gorer did learn from his mistakes. Just as he had downplayed toilet training after the swaddling controversy, so he further downplayed neo-Freudianism and indeed the whole 'culture and personality' will-o'-the-wisp after

[42] Cyril Connolly, 'The national character', *Sunday Times*, 10 Jul. 1955; Elizabeth Bowen, 'English lips unsealed', *Tatler*, 3 Aug. 1955; V.S. Pritchett, 'John Citizen', *New Statesman*, 21 Jul. 1955; (H. F. Carlill), 'National Gallery', *TLS*, 12 Aug. 1955; J. D. Scott, 'Not Passion's Slave', *Spectator*, 1 Jul. 1955; *Listener*, 21 Jul. 1955; *Economist*, 13 Aug. 1955.

[43] Peter Mandler, *The English National Character: The History of an Idea from Edmund Burke to Tony Blair* (New Haven and London, 2006), esp. pp. 210–13.

[44] David Riesman, 'Comments on Dr Kluckhohn's Paper', *Human Development Bulletin*, 6th Annual Symposium, University of Chicago (1955), p. 67.

[45] 'The Gorer Report: A great scientist has found out the truth about the English', in *The People*, 5 Aug. 1951.

[46] Richard Mayne, 'New stereotypes for old', *Time & Tide*, 16 Jul. 1955.

[47] Isa Benzie to George Barnes, 11 Dec. 1946; Barnes to Harman Grisewood, 28 Jan. 1947; Benzie to Grisewood, 12 Feb. 1947: BBC Written Archives Centre, RCONT1, Geoffrey Gorer, Talks, File 1: 1946–62.

Exploring English Character. In the late 1950s and early 1960s he made his peace with the sociological mainstream in Britain and instead of challenging the salience of class offered psychological commentary on the class-based studies that then predominated. He became close friends with Peter Willmott and acted as a psychological consultant to Willmott and Young's Institute of Community Studies from 1958, sometimes providing a useful check on the tendency of that school to romanticise the working-class community. After Gorer's sympathetic critique of *The Uses of Literacy* Richard Hoggart admitted that he had de-emphasized sex to avoid alienating middle-class readers. At the same time, Gorer opened himself up to signs of social and cultural change that he could no longer ignore. His review of *The Uses of Literacy* rightly worried that Hoggart had 'exaggerated the passivity of the working classes' and not seen the constructive, 'Dionysiac' potential of rock 'n' roll.[48] His two later social surveys, both funded by the *Sunday Times*—on death and mourning in 1965, and on sex and marriage in 1969—were austerely statistical, much more like Kinsey than Gorer could ever have admitted, largely eschewed psychoanalytical language, and acknowledged changing attitudes to sex and greater communicativeness overall. All of this made Gorer a less controversial figure in his later years than he had been in the early 1950s. Out of the glare of publicity, however, he had not lost his mischievous taste for neo-Freudianism. In his last major statement about 'English national character', in 1967, he admitted that the working-class character had changed *again* since 1945, with an evident lessening of shyness and anxiety and the rampant growth of hedonism. Why? Simply because, he speculated, the younger generation had for the first time in history been amply fed as children, resulting in 'a genuine diminution of anxiety, of which fear and experience of hunger was such a large component'. Burgers and chips were the new police.[49]

Gorer's own, almost always tacit admissions about the over-simplifications of *Exploring English Character* can serve as a partial guide to our conclusions about how we as historians should approach it. As his later work accepted, any study of the psychological makeup of the English could not assume anything like the cross-class homogeneity that the 'culture and personality' school so dogmatically required, and would need to consider psychological sub-cultures (and not only those based on class). Gorer was very hostile to some rival studies in this mode which had suggested gross differences between middle- and working-class psychology. He tore into the most famous of these studies—Madeline Kerr's *The People of Ship Street* (1958)—as having nothing to do with English culture (the

[48] Gorer to Mead, 1 Mar. 1957: Mead Papers, B6; Geoffrey Gorer, 'Dionysus and the welfare state' (1957), and 'The perils of male hypergamy' (1957), in *The Danger of Equality and Other Essays* (New York, 1966), pp. 105–11, 242–7; Richard Hoggart to Gorer, 21 Mar. 1957: Gorer Papers, Box 86; Gorer's relations with Willmott and the ICS can be traced in Gorer Papers, Box 45. See also a late attempt to put a high valuation on class identity as part of the culture pattern in 'The vicissitudes of English identity over time and empire' (1970), with Willmott's critique, in Gorer Papers, Box 54/3.

[49] Geoffrey Gorer, 'English character in the twentieth century', *Annals of the American Academy of Political and Social Science* 370 (1967), pp. 80–1.

people in question being Irish—'feckless, violent, intermittently criminal . . . unhygienic, dishonest and stupid') even though she had taken pains to accommodate them into Gorer's scheme as the bottom 10 per cent that his study had slighted. Though his later work accommodated greater diversity, *Exploring English Character* is profoundly vitiated by its dogmatic insistence on homogeneity, to the extent that even the residuum he tried to reduce to a mere one per cent.[50] Where there was evidence of psychological diversity, especially along class lines, his interpretation systematically underplayed it. Even Mead's work on the English had tried to exploit class difference to explain the peculiarly English mode of communication—exhibitionism by the upper orders, spectatorship by the lower—but Gorer never showed much interest in such an analysis, which would have inserted him into English society rather than allowed him to remain outside, a 'deviant', looking in.

As I have tried to show, a great deal of the interpretation in *Exploring English Character* was predetermined by Gorer's assumptions both about what the problems were and about how they had been generated. This was made easier by the design of the questionnaire that aimed, as Metraux had suggested, only to get out what it put in. About half of the questions about attitudes offered 'forced choices', where the options were phrased by the questioner. A number of the remaining questions were themselves phrased in ways that meant something specific to Gorer but not necessarily to his respondents. The question, 'Do you think English people fall in love the way you see Americans doing it in the films?', was Gorer's means of demonstrating that the English (unlike the Americans) didn't believe in 'love at first sight'. His respondents might just as easily have meant that they differed from the Americans in some other way, or that they differed from people in films whatever their nationality.[51] However, even in the case of fairly open-ended questions, where a (small) space was left for the respondent to provide open-ended answers, Gorer's processing and coding permitted him to find the answers he was looking for. A recent study by Jessica Fogarty has examined the coding of Gorer's key question about the police and found that this coding conflated the statements of psychological identification with the police that Gorer prioritized with other approving statements varying from a belief in their effectiveness to a belief in their necessity.[52] A recoding exercise on a large sample reveals that only 11 per cent of respondents adverted directly to the character of the policeman on which Gorer placed so much emphasis. Fogarty further suggests that the positive responses to the police in this survey portray a complex web of conflicting views of ideal and reality, very much predicated on the particular post-war moment of anxiety over crime during which the survey was undertaken. In fact popular idealizations of the

[50] Gorer's *TS* review of B. M. Spinley, *The Deprived and the Privileged*; Gorer's *TS* review of Madeline Kerr, *The People of Ship Street*: Gorer Papers, Boxes 74, 75.

[51] Gorer, *Exploring English Character*, p. 84.

[52] Jessica Fogarty, 'English attitudes to the police, 1947–62', University of Cambridge BA dissertation, 2008. I am very grateful to Jess Fogarty for permission to cite this unpublished work.

police may reflect a much keener awareness of the differences between ideal and reality than Gorer—or later surveys that incorporate his findings, such as McKibbin's—were prepared to accept. McKibbin was, rightly, surprised by Gorer's findings, given that (as he writes) in most working-class communities 'the police were thought to be agents of an intrusive authority', and the only explanation he can find is Gorer's. People were prepared to overlook their own social experiences, writes McKibbin, because they had 'strongly internalized those norms for which the police were thought to stand. That was one way aggression was controlled, as puritanism controlled and partly civilized an aggressive sexuality.'[53] Closer scrutiny of Gorer's own data suggests that people may have accepted the police for more utilitarian purposes—that is, to control crime—and that any idealization of the police may have reflected a desire for something better in fact than they knew from their own experience. Certainly there is no *prima facie* reason to assume a collective delusion, still less one generated by a psychodynamic imperative to control aggression.

My conclusion is not that all social-scientific surveys are rotten to the core. To the contrary—Gorer's survey was unusual in being so blithely overdetermined, not only in its conception but in its fine structure, by his long-standing preoccupations and by the remorseless oversimplification of his neo-Freudianism. That is why it is particularly important to understand the aetiology of *this* study. 'Being your own rabbit' is always perilous, but in this case it was rendered profoundly unreliable by Gorer's deep if under-articulated conviction that, though he was not in fact a rabbit himself, still he already knew everything there was to know about rabbits (and most of what he knew he didn't like). Thus I think McKibbin understates the case when he suggests that 'the biases are probably no more serious than that of any survey which questions people about their sexual behaviour'.[54] There remain 10,000 questionnaires in the bowels of the University of Sussex library, compromised by Gorer's framing of them but still offering a treasure trove of information on psychological topics not easily accessible by other means. All they require is for us to be better historians than Gorer was a social scientist.

53 McKibbin, *Classes and Cultures*, pp. 329–30.
54 Ibid., p. 296 n. 2.

POLITICS

13

The Cultural Politics of Tory Socialism: *The Clarion* in the Labour Movement During the 1890s

Gregg McClymont

The history of the early Labour movement's political culture is in part the history of an uneven contest between Liberal and Conservative traditions. Liberalism predominated politically in the preference for the Liberal Party over the Conservative Party (if forced to choose), and culturally in an emphasis on (among other things) peace rather than war, free trade rather than protection, self-improvement rather than paternalism, and puritanism rather than hedonism. Martin Pugh's ambitious essay asserts that the Labour Party eventually embraced significant aspects of the Tory tradition,[1] but David Howell's restrained conclusion remains the more persuasive. In his history of the Independent Labour Party he defined as 'Tory socialism' a bundle of related political and cultural affinities—romanticism, economic and cultural nationalism, hedonism—and suggested they were a 'suppressed alternative' in the Labour movement, incompatible with the resolutely Liberal-Radical inclinations of the majority of Labour movement activists, but attractive to significant Labour institutions and personalities, including Robert Blatchford's *Clarion* movement.[2]

In this essay I want to look in more detail at *The Clarion*'s Tory socialism; or at least, at one aspect of it: hedonism.[3] Ross McKibbin believes the Tory tradition

[1] Martin Pugh, 'The Rise of Labour and the Political Culture of Conservatism, 1890–1945', *History* 87 (2002), pp. 514–37. Also his recent return to these themes: Martin Pugh, *Speak for Britain! A New History of the Labour Party* (London, 2010), esp. ch.1.

[2] David Howell, *British Workers and the Independent Labour Party, 1888–1906* (Manchester, 1983), pp. 373–88. For studies which locate Blatchford and the Clarion movement closer to Radical Liberalism than Tory socialism: Logie Barrow, 'The Socialism of Robert Blatchford and the Clarion 1890–1918', University of London Ph.D. thesis (1975), pp. 480–1, and *passim*; Chris Waters, *British Socialists and the Politics of Popular Culture, 1884–1914* (Manchester, 1990); Martin Wright, 'Robert Blatchford, The Clarion Movement, and the crucial years of British socialism, 1891–1900', in Tony Brown (ed.), *Edward Carpenter and Late Victorian Radicalism* (London, 1990), pp. 74–100, 78.

[3] The other dimensions of *Clarion* Tory socialism have been addressed recently by historians. On romanticism: Deborah Mutch, 'The *Merrie England* triptych: Robert Blatchford, Edward Fay and the didactic use of *Clarion* fiction', *Victorian Periodicals Review* 38 (2005), pp. 83–103. On

has been written out of Labour's history to an extent which risks distorting the historical record.[4] What follows is a modest contribution to the writing back in of the history of Tory socialism. The focus is the triumvirate who owned, edited, and wrote *The Clarion* newspaper: Blatchford, A. M. Thompson, and E. F. Fay.[5] Deborah Mutch has recently discussed their libertarian attitude to drink;[6] I want to examine the *Clarion* men's broader affinity with the hedonistic aspects of working-class recreational culture. Specifically, the essay explores the origins of their hedonism, the forms in which it was expressed, and its limits. The absence of Nonconformity from their lives (although Blatchford had a chapel background) was likely significant in the genesis of their often exuberant socialism; geography too, since they lived and worked in London and Manchester, cities where the puritanical political culture of Lib-Labism was weak.[7] Social class was probably another factor in explaining their distance from puritanism, at least in the case of Thompson and Fay, who came from the upper middle classes.[8] But I want to emphasize their common experience of work.

Blatchford's (though he had previously worked elsewhere, including the army), Fay's, and Thompson's trade was sporting newspaper journalism. This was a world far removed from the often rule-bound and ordered workplace of late nineteenth-century industrial workers.[9] Culturally it had much in common with the Edwardian service sector as described by Ross McKibbin: 'that vast and unnumbered race who worked for themselves or others on a catch-as-catch-can basis . . . a jaunty and attractive individualism was essential to their lives . . . their occupational world of chance and quick-wittedness was in many ways absolutely opposed to collectivist politics.'[10] In the rather similar workplace culture of sporting newspapers lay, I think, roots of the hedonism that characterised the

nationalism see, for example: Paul Ward, *Red Flag and Union Jack: Englishness, Patriotism and the British Left, 1881–1924* (Woodbridge, 1998); Kevin Morgan, 'Militarism and anti-militarism: socialists, communists and conscription in France and Britain 1900–1940', *PP* 202 (2009), pp. 221, 228.

[4] Personal conversations with the author over a number of years; but see also McKibbin's argument that Labour's attitude to the constitution has been 'Tory' rather than 'Liberal': Ross McKibbin, *Parties and People. England 1914–1951* (Oxford, 2010), pp. 198–9.

[5] Blatchford's older brother, Montague, was also a founding owner-employee of *The Clarion* but his influence was more limited.

[6] Deborah Mutch, 'Intemperate narratives: Tory tipplers, Liberal abstainers, and Victorian British Socialist fiction', *Victorian Literature and Culture* 36 (2008), pp. 471–87.

[7] Gareth Stedman Jones, 'Working-class culture and working class politics in London 1870–1900: notes on the remaking of a working class', reprinted in *Languages of Class. Studies in English Working-Class History* (Cambridge, 1983), pp. 179–238; Peter Clarke, *Lancashire and the New Liberalism* (Cambridge, 1971), parts 1 and 2.

[8] Thompson's father was a *rentier* and the family (though English) lived in Germany and France; Thompson's brother became a successful stockbroker: A. M. Thompson, 'Dangle', *Here I Lie. The Memoirs of an Old Journalist* (London, 1937). Fay and his brother were privately educated—the latter going on to Cambridge: Robert Blatchford, *The Bounder: The Story of a Man by his Friend* (London, 1900), pp. 3, 6–10.

[9] On the rule-bound and disciplined work environment of railway workers, for example, see David Howell, *Respectable Radicals. Studies in the Politics of Railway Trade Unionism* (Aldershot, 1999), esp. pp. 3–5.

[10] McKibbin, *The Ideologies of Class: Social Relations in Britain 1880–1950* (Oxford, 1990), p. 4.

Clarion men. These origins are discussed in the first section. The second section discusses the transfer of this exuberant culture to *The Clarion.* The third section discusses the extent to which their hedonism was myth as well as reality. *Clarion* socialism was not always exuberant; Blatchford, in particular, the dominant figure, possessed a significant puritanical streak. While this aspect of his character lessened over time, the *Clarion* triumvirate preferred to deny that puritanism had ever played a role in their movement. The limits of their version of history are discussed in the third part of the essay. My conclusion notes that cultural politics of the kind discussed in this essay emerged again after 1906, insofar as attacks on the puritanism of the Parliamentary Labour Party were one way in which dissatisfaction with its tactics and strategy was articulated before the First World War.

THE CULTURE OF THE SPORTING NEWSPAPER

Fay and Thompson were professional sporting newspaper journalists. Thompson began his career as theatre critic for the (Manchester) *Sporting Chronicle* and recalled in his autobiography the cultural milieu he entered; late Victorian popular theatre was denounced by puritans as 'an annexe of the brothel'. Thompson expressed a strong dislike of this puritanism: 'Samuel Smith, member [of parliament] for the enlightened city of Liverpool, proclaimed his conviction that "all plays" and "all novels" are works of the Devil . . . Imagine it, youths and maidens of to-day, the dull and stupid world, the dead-alive, lacklustre, toad-in-a-hole existence of this sanctimonious prig's ideal.' He claimed his Continental upbringing—in Germany and France—had given him an aversion to British respectability. Sabbatarianism was sour and crabbed and he welcomed its historical retreat: 'Sunday picnics on the Thames are as gay, and almost as sober, as on the Seine . . . Young people . . . are allowed to hear good music. They are even permitted to dance. And civilized food may be bought even in the most expensive restaurants. The Entente Cordiale has had its triumphs.'[11] He was a hedonist: 'As a boy in Paris . . . I acquired a habit which refuses to be rude to a bottle of good claret. I don't brag . . . Frankly, I am rather ashamed of it, and swear off occasionally to prove to myself that I am not a slave of a vice . . . But just as I come within sight of the martyr's crown, I feel so smugly virtuous, so disgustingly self-satisfied, that I have to backslide to regain my self-respect.' Thompson insisted that alcohol, cigars, and good food made life worth living.[12] Abundance was central to Thompson's socialism. He believed in a life 'easy and comfortable' with no one working for more than six hours a day.[13] Thompson's 'profession' enabled him to practise what he preached. His fellow drama critics were huge drinkers with great stamina, and when Thompson was not in the pub with them,

[11] Thompson, *Here I Lie*, pp. 251–2, 13–15, quote at 15.
[12] Ibid., pp. 121, 170.
[13] Ibid., p. 85.

there was *The Sporting Chronicle* itself: 'It was the genial and not infrequent habit of my own proprietor Mr Hulton [to take me out for a drink].'[14] The paper was a betting sheet which had 'began by issuing a single sheet of racing news . . . in public houses'.[15] Tipsters were the most important employees, 'white-bearded patriarchs to whom the Turf had been for many years what the theatre is to an actor, or Parliament to a professional politician. I never heard them talk of anything but horses.'[16] Thompson avoided betting, but otherwise embraced this culture. The *Chronicle*, wrote Thompson's son, 'taught him to drink whisky and not to back horses, and introduced him to the fretful, fascinating, behind-the-scenes world of Manchester sporting and dramatic life. He took, as his first wife, a barmaid.'[17]

Fay's cultural politics were more exuberant still. Blatchford recalled his first encounter with Fay in the office of the London sporting newspaper *Bell's Life* during 1884: 'shabbily dressed, untidy and not quite sober . . . he asked me to have a drink with him . . . His utterance was rapid, and quite half he said was in the manner of soliloquy, indistinct, half audible.' His verbal style 'mix[ed] slang and poetry, profanity and ethics, racing talk and shrewd criticisms of Shelley, Dickens, Milton, and Bret Harte.'[18] Blatchford was fascinated by Fay's hedonism. 'He loved all the good things of life . . . He loved boxing and the drama, football and Milton, Rabelais and Cardinal Newman . . . He loathed self-righteousness and detested respectability.'[19] Abhorrence of the latter certainly appeared to run deep in Fay. Cleanliness was not next to godliness rather it was a puritanical imposition. 'The curse of Cromwell on their brooms and scrubbers', pronounced Fay of the women who cleaned his rented rooms. Fay's respect for order grew over time,[20] and, indeed, the wider development of his character under Blatchford's influence (and vice versa) was a recurring theme of Blatchford's biographical study of his friend: 'He was not free from intellectual pride, had even imbibed a little Cambridge caste prejudice, and through many years of wild bachelor life and a close intimacy with the racecourse had not grown in grace . . . Before we started the *Clarion* he was often dull, melancholy and discontented [by his] idle, aimless life.'[21] Fay's conversion to socialism made him happier; as such, it possibly increased his hedonism. Blatchford latterly defined him as 'a Christian epicure', who 'liked the lion's share of the wine and the best cuts,' and usually encouraged his dining companions to foot the bill.[22] 'I am

[14] Ibid., p. 259.
[15] Ibid., p. 41.
[16] Ibid., p. 45.
[17] Laurence Thompson, *Robert Blatchford*, p. 28. For a recent study of Hulton and his newspaper empire see: Steve Tate, 'Edward Hulton and sports journalism in late-Victorian Manchester', *Manchester Region History Review* 20 (2009), pp. 46–67.
[18] Blatchford, *The Bounder*, pp. 30, 35.
[19] Ibid., pp. 123–4.
[20] Ibid., p. 159.
[21] Ibid., pp. 28, 43. Fay's brother had attended Cambridge.
[22] Ibid., pp. 174, 126–7.

a low beggar and I like low company,' Fay always insisted;[23] in character and temperament he appeared to have close affinities with the 'catch-as-catch-can' world of chance and quick-wittedness.

Fay's style was an enlarged reflection of the culture of the sporting newspaper. 'Bell's Life was given over to mirth, good fellowship, old port', claimed an early journalist biographer of Blatchford's,[24] and he recalled its jocularity, spontaneity, and disorder himself. The paper was often put together at the very last moment. 'We went to press at 1.20 am . . . at 1am . . . Smiling and expectant we strolled up for orders [from the editor]. Thus, dictating his racing article and clipping original par[agraphs] for general sport at the same time, would this truly great man steer, work, and captain his ship off the rocks night after night in the space of half an hour.'[25] It was perhaps no surprise, then, that 'One night the editor fell asleep half-way through the racing article, and waking up went on with the boat-race . . . we read next day how "Flyaway, if he could hold his place to Tattenham corner, would simply romp away from the Oxford crew, who, fast as they were, showed little signs of staying"'.[26] Blatchford also illuminated the way in which the worlds of the sporting newspaperman and the 'unrespectable' working classes interacted. He recalled being assigned 'to visit the low-class boxing shows in the East End' with orders to produce 'a lurid article . . . Next morning there arrived [at the office] a deputation of East End artists with flat noses and prominent ears', keen to take issue with the author of the piece. The *Bell's* editor defused the situation by offering to shout the boxers a drink. 'There was some shuffling of feet, then a hoarse voice spoke: "Lor lumme, Guvnor, you're a real old sport." After which the editor led forth his men in triumph.'[27]

In 1886 the ownership of *Bell's Life* changed hands and Blatchford switched to Hulton's new *Sunday Chronicle*, which he described as a 'semi-sporting organ' which did not aspire to the dignity of an editorial and gave itself no highbrow airs.[28] Blatchford's 'As I Lay A-Thinking' articles, which began in 1889 under the by-line 'Nunquam' made his journalistic name. During 1890 he announced his conversion to socialism. The Labour Church's John Kenworthy rhapsodized, 'While parsons were anathematising us, and the "respectable" papers denouncing us, this sporting journalist, writing in a wicked Sunday paper devoted to horse-racing and prize-fighting, rose up to bless the righteous cause'.[29] Blatchford's biographer, Laurence Thompson, provided a more secular assessment, but one which similarly emphasised Blatchford's reach beyond the culture of Lib-Labism.

[23] Ibid., p. 160.

[24] A. M. Neil Lyons, *Robert Blatchford. The Sketch of a Personality. An Estimate of Some Achievements* (London, 1910), p. 73.

[25] Blatchford, *My Eighty Years*, pp. 177–8.

[26] Blatchford, *The Bounder*, p. 33.

[27] Blatchford, *My Eighty Years*, pp. 178–9.

[28] Ibid., p. 184.

[29] *The Weekly Times and Echo*, 29 July 1894, quoted in Mike and Liz Sones, *An Introduction to Robert Blatchford and the Clarion Newspaper* (Harrow, 1986).

> To expand Carlyle's parallel between newspaper and church Blatchford set out to become, not an archbishop or a bishop, nor even a respectable rural dean, but a new John Wesley, or perhaps better still, a new apostle to the Gentiles... he sought his converts... among... the don't-knowers of the Gallup polls, the men who do not vote nor attend union meetings, but who must somehow be reached if democracy is to work. Blatchford failed to reach most of them; but no-one since has succeeded half as well.[30]

By the end of 1891 Blatchford's relationship with the *Chronicle* proprietor had deteriorated significantly. The *Clarion* men always claimed that Blatchford's socialism antagonized Hulton, but there may have been other issues involved. Blatchford and Thompson had expended time and money producing their own comic opera and it is possible they were neglecting their newspaper responsibilities.[31] Whatever the exact circumstances, Blatchford was quickly followed out the *Chronicle* door by Thompson and Fay. Blatchford summed up the trio's time in this world pithily and appropriately hedonistically: 'We had big salaries, pleasant work, an eightpenny income tax and sound whisky at 3s. 6d. a bottle.'[32]

THE CLARION'S HEDONISM

The first issue of *The Clarion* appeared in Manchester on 12 December 1891. Circulation quickly settled around 30,000; geographically the paper's readership was biased towards the North. Its influence was greatest in these early years. Owned and written by Blatchford, Thompson, Fay (and Blatchford's brother Montague) *The Clarion*'s content and style reflected the triumvirate's sporting newspaper background. Theatre was prominent in the early editions,[33] football briefly, and cricket especially. The tone was genial. As Blatchford's first leading article announced, 'We... beg our serious friends to remember that truth may lie under a smile as well under a frown, and to our merry friends would say that a jest is none the less hilarious when it comes from the heart. The policy of *The Clarion* is a policy of humanity.'[34] Jocularity was integral to this manifesto, and with Fay on board it rarely seemed forced or contrived. The 'roistering, buoyant Playboy of the Movement',[35] Fay played one-on-one cricket with John Burns MP, 'chose as his umpire a member of the Social Democratic Federation (SDF) (who by now hated Burns) and had Burns given out first ball, a fast bumper, bottom before wicket. Burns retaliated by hitting Fay in the pit of his immense stomach and secured a similar decision from his umpire, a member of Battersea Liberal and Radical Association. That, with its political implications, filled three columns'. Likewise Fay's popular walking tours of the British outdoors: carrying a thousand

30 Laurence Thompson, *Robert Blatchford*, p. 49.
31 Ibid., p. 77. Judith Fincher Laird and John Saville, 'Robert Blatchford', *Dictionary of Labour Biography*, vol. 4.
32 Blatchford, *My Eighty Years*, p. 191.
33 Thompson, *Here I Lie*, p. 116.
34 Laurence Thompson, *Robert Blatchford*, p. 82.
35 Thompson, *Here I Lie*, p. 81.

yellow sticky labels promoting *The Clarion* he set off in 1893 on a search for appropriate advertising space. 'Readers took up the game with more enthusiasm than discrimination . . . and had to be advised to exclude tombstones, carriage doors, the gates of "villa residences", church porches, and hotel looking-glasses.' Fay's speciality became a rudimentary kind of travel writing/food tourism. His walking tours were full of eating and drinking, and of the search for suitable nourishment and rehydration.[36]

However, it was not all fun and games. The paper had a didactic aspect, which separated it from sporting newspapers, and which was evident in the paper's omission of horse racing and betting. 'We took the view that it would savour of incongruity to combine our appeal to the people's sanity with direct incentives to the opposite,' Thompson explained.[37] He was himself very hostile to betting and gambling; his father, a *rentier* and speculator, committed suicide after a huge loss on Spanish consols.[38] 'Blatchford apparently believed that if John Smith of Oldham . . . were told the plain truth in simple language, he would waste no more time on racing.' Thompson added that this was wishful thinking on their part: 'Our actual experience had not encouraged belief in this democratic John Smith with his unsatisfied longing for high thinking and his susceptibility to pure reason.'[39] An early advertisement emphasized that the socialist weekly was 'Free from all pandering to the gambling spirit, as to the morbid love of the prurient and horrible.'[40]

The workplace culture of *The Clarion* was otherwise exuberant. Hedonism and spontaneity, lubricated by alcohol, were prominent. Fay was to the forefront. R. B. Suthers, a significant journalist in the Labour movement, who early in his career served as *Clarion* office boy, remembered meeting Fay to 'convey the instructions of the Board that he report forthwith for Stalybridge, and write one of his brilliant accounts of a football match'. Fay agreed but insisted that '"I must have lager, and plenty of it. Where can I get lager [?]".' Suthers took him to the Cathedral Hotel: 'He rushed up the steps, and was in the bar drinking a large one before I was through the door. I stood there, wondering at his Metropolitan manners. He put down the glass and said, "Another one, please, missy." And then, noticing me under his walking stick, added, "And a small lemon for the boy."'[41] Charles Touchstone, a *Clarion* contributor remembered entering the office for the first time. 'After a most uncomfortable pause, the big man [Fay] said, '"My boy, I hope you are not one of those measly teetotalers?" I replied that "I hoped I wasn't". "Then come and have a glass of wine with me . . . I have been

36 Ibid., pp. 118–19; Robert Blatchford, *The Bounder: His Book* (London, 1895), pp. 63–97, and *passim*.
37 Thompson, *Here I Lie*, p. 123.
38 Ibid., pp. 5, 31–2, 45–50.
39 Ibid., pp. 128–9.
40 The advert was titled 'What *Clarion* Readers say of the *Clarion*' and found on many early *Clarion* publications.
41 R. B. Suthers, *The Clarion*, 6 December 1912 (Coming of Age Supplement).

here two hours, and not one of [my colleagues] has had the common politeness to ask if I had a mouth." '[42] It seems appropriate that Blackpool, mecca of working-class hedonism, hosted an early *Clarion* works day out. This apparently was one of Fay 'happiest days'.[43] Yet his extravagant irregularity also had less savoury ramifications. Fay was its London agent in the early days, not perhaps the ideal job for one whose attitude to money was anarchic.[44] 'Being often in a condition when his next meal depended on the collection of an account', Fay 'resorted to compromises which a strict accountant would not have tolerated.'[45] On one occasion, having failed to come to a suitable arrangement with a London newsagent, Fay beat him, 'spat upon him, and left him'.[46]

MYTH AND REALITY

Cultural politics featured prominently in Labour movement memories of *The Clarion.* Jimmy Middleton, Arthur Henderson's successor as General Secretary of the Labour Party, suggested in 1923 that 'Labour is not so well on the way to the Socialist state that it can lightly let go the plain talk and cheerful fellowship which gave *The Clarion* its influence in the old days.' Fred Montague MP, in the wake of Labour's ejection from office in 1931, recalled the influence of Dickens on this 'a merry lot of literary vagabonds... A common taunt of intellectually snobbish critics was that we proposed to cycle or dance ourselves into the Socialist commonwealth.'[47] Harry Snell, London County Council leader and Labour leader in the Lords provided the introduction to Thompson's 1937 autobiography. 'Arid minded high-brows thought it was trivial', he recalled, 'their genial assaults upon sanctified shibboleths and political myths, and their saucy criticism of both personalities and institutions... [was] a crusade for a more excellent way of living.'[48] Margaret Cole, activist as well as historian, wrote a decade later that 'It was full of stories, jokes, and verses—sometimes pretty bad verses and pretty bad jokes... it carried Morris's gospel of fellowship through the industrial areas in homely terms... it made Socialism seem as simple and universal as a pint of bitter.'[49]

The Clarion's greatest influence lay in the period before the Labour movement was compromised by the exigencies of electoral politics, and the paper was consistent in its commitment to the educationalist rather than the legislative

[42] Blatchford, *The Bounder*, pp. 115–17.
[43] Ibid., p. 163.
[44] Ibid., pp. 164–5.
[45] Suthers, *The Clarion*, 6 December 1912.
[46] Blatchford, *The Bounder*, p. 127; *The Bounder: His Book*, pp. 21–4.
[47] *The Clarion*, February 1932 (it was a monthly by this stage).
[48] *Here I Lie*, pp. xi–xii. Quoted also by Stephen Yeo, 'A new life: the religion of Socialism in Britain 1883–1896', *History Workshop Journal* 4 (1977), pp. 5–56, here p. 8.
[49] Margaret Cole, *Makers of the Labour Movement* (London, 1948), p. 195.

route to socialism.[50] Activist portraits of *The Clarion*'s geniality might therefore be seen as oblique criticism of the contemporary Labour movement's renunciation of a more exciting and carefree 'religion of socialism',[51] or, more generally, as a way of avoiding difficult questions raised by the legislativist trajectory of the movement after 1900. Also (as in Snell's case), an emphasis on *The Clarion*'s cultural politics provided a means of avoiding difficult questions about its own decline. Not that these portrayals were mythical; my argument so far has been that hedonism, imported from the sporting newspaper, was important to the culture of *The Clarion* and its leading men. At the same time, myth-making is integral to the construction of political parties' histories,[52] and the *Clarion* triumvirate themselves were very eager to explain their estrangement from the Labour movement in cultural terms.

A significant thread in Blatchford's and Thompson's autobiographies is the unbending puritanism of Hardie's ILP. Furthermore, it is perhaps the central theme of the Blatchford biography written by Thompson's son, Laurence. Blatchford's oft-quoted letter to A. M. Thompson summarises the *Clarion* position:

> I was always a Tory Democrat and you a French Democrat . . . The Labour Leader people were Puritans; narrow, bigoted, puffed up with sour cant. We both disliked them, because we were both Cavaliers. They were nonconformist, self-righteous ascetics, out for the class war and the dictation by the proletariat. We loved the humour and the colour of the old English tradition. You know it was so . . . You have often seared them with your scorn. I am glad the Labour Party is defeated because I believed they would have disrupted the British Empire. I dreaded their childish cosmopolitanism.[53]

Romanticism, Nationalism, and Hedonism—Blatchford's declamation recalled each aspect of Tory socialism. Particular emphasis was placed on the latter, however: 'French Democrat' is an allusion to Thompson's distance from puritanism, a heuristic device which, as we have seen, Thompson pursued in his own autobiography. The *Clarion* version made much of Blatchford's first meeting with Hardie. Hardie, having been told that Blatchford consorted with undesirables, mistook their meeting place for an illicit brothel and turned tail: '"I offered him the warmest welcome that I ever gave to another man, and he held out a hand like a cold toad, and ran away."' The venue did indeed belong to a theatrical friend of Blatchford's, but there was, 'no reek of whisky, no women sitting on men's knees. Hardacre was not a brothel-keeper, nor anything but

[50] Barrow, 'The socialism of Robert Blatchford', *passim*; Logie Barrow, 'Determinism and environmentalism in socialist thought', in Raphael Samuel and Gareth Stedman Jones (eds.), *Culture, ideology and politics* (London, 1982), pp. 194–214.

[51] Yeo, 'A new life', *passim*. The journalist and Labour parliamentary candidate G. T. Garratt captured something of the party's cultural shift as it moved closer to power after 1918, noting with regret the ILP's increasing 'self-righteousness, and a dulling of all sense of humour': G. T. Garratt, *The Mugwumps and the Labour Party* (London, 1932), p. 39.

[52] Jon Lawrence, 'Labour—the myths it has lived by', in Duncan Tanner, Pat Thane, and Nick Tiratsoo (eds.), *Labour's First Century* (Cambridge, 2000), pp. 344–66.

[53] e.g. Laurence Thompson, *Robert Blatchford*, p. 230.

one of the naughty boys and girls, who was often drunk, was not quite respectable in his morals, but who was enormously generous to the unfortunate of his profession.'[54] Hardie's discomfort in this hedonistic environment is hardly surprising and, on the *Clarion* view, it was the beginning of a gradual estrangement. A. M. Thompson recalled his initial encounter with Hardie.

> I said, perhaps rather flippantly, that our people did not take enough delight out of themselves . . . and jokingly submitted that a Labour Party Movement need not be a hard labour Party. Hardie looked pained . . . He replied to the effect that the Labour Movement was too serious for frivolities, and the rebuke of his glance signified that jesting was not respectable.[55]

Thompson remained aligned to the Labour movement throughout the interwar period and his autobiography made some concessions to the developing mythology of Hardie. The 'dour severity of a Scottish Covenanter' was hardly attractive, but 'his scorn of snobbery, his simplicity, his incorruptible disinterestedness—were just the qualities required in a Parliamentary pioneer of a working-class party'.[56] Laurence Thompson, writing after the Second World War, and confronted with the sanctified Hardie, made further concessions. The *Clarion* men's references to 'poverty and sacrifice' after their departure from the *Chronicle* were 'mockery' to a man who, in his whole life, never made the four pounds a week which was briefly their starting salary on *The Clarion*.[57] Thompson also stressed that Blatchford's character was unsuited to the responsibilities of the role played by Hardie as Labour pioneer. Blatchford's bonhomie, his emphasis on pleasure, could become an alibi for his dislike of the serious political work of organisation and agitation. 'The Covenanters alleged—and sometimes rightly alleged—that the Fellowship thought only of enjoying itself.'[58]

Laurence Thompson nonetheless accepted the thrust of his father's and Blatchford's accounts—the divide was cultural in character and Hardie and his followers bore the greater responsibility: 'The ILP [Independent Labour Party], drawing much strength from nonconformity, drew also its weaknesses—the grim, dour attitude of Chosen People, of Scottish Covenanters on bleak hillsides, scorning all who were not as they, concerned too often to save their own souls and complacently regarding the faint odour of roasting sinner as a burnt offering to their virtue.' The ILP lacked *The Clarion*'s humanity, its 'closeness' to the unrespectable working classes.[59] Fay, in his *Clarion* journalism, 'met tramps and nigger minstrels, drunkards, down-at-heel music hall singers and cheapjacks in the Caledonian Market, all the world of failures and frauds and human weakness so far outside the corrugated iron walls of the North Country chapels, and taught

[54] Ibid., pp. 70–1.
[55] Thompson, *Here I Lie*, p. 98.
[56] Ibid., p. 98.
[57] Laurence Thompson, *Robert Blatchford*, p. 138.
[58] Ibid., pp. 132, 159; Yeo, 'A new life', p. 48.
[59] Yeo emphasized this aspect of *Clarion* socialism, 'A new life', pp. 28–9.

his readers that these too were men and women who if pricked would bleed, if starved would die, if loved would love.'[60]

The *Clarion* men claimed the Social Democratic Federation [SDF] as a kindred spirit in this cultural conflict with the ILP.[61] Fraternal relations between the SDF and *The Clarion* were aided by the ploughing of complementary political and geographical furrows; the SDF focusing on the economics of socialism, *The Clarion* on literature and art, the SDF being London-centred and agitational, *The Clarion* more northern and fraternal.[62] But a shared conviviality was also stressed on both sides: '*Clarion* and . . . *Justice* [the SDF newspaper] could box one another's ears and the staffs enjoyed a drink together afterwards.'[63] A. M. Thompson recalled of the SDF leader H. M. Hyndman: 'In my encounters with him, in a Soho restaurant and in his retreat in Hampstead . . . Hyndman passed the loving-cup with a bonhomie that was frequent and free.' His attendance at a *Clarion* festival was likewise fondly recalled: getting into the swing of things, and expressing appropriate glee, Hyndman 'enjoyed himself like a schoolboy at a picnic!'.[64] These affinities were also reflected in Hyndman's memoirs. He praised Blatchford as 'the single greatest Socialist communicator' and criticized wryly his increasing distance from the political fray: 'In his daily life he is the laziest white man who ever sat on the top rail of a fence. He will sit for hours smoking in silence, like a Red Indian chief puffing at his calumet . . . It is the same with him by his own fireside, even in company with that whisky and water he pretends to like.' Hyndman noted approvingly the conviviality of the *Clarion* movement, whose members were 'undoubtedly Socialist in all their aspirations, and contrive in the meanwhile to get a great deal of fun out of life'.[65] On the other hand, the personal affinity between Hyndman and the *Clarion* men is not easily reduced to hedonism alone. Blatchford might describe Hyndman as 'Old blowhard' in the knowledge that he would laugh it off, but Laurence Thompson noted that George Bernard Shaw and the strikingly puritanical John Burns were also among those that Blatchford could 'hit hard . . . without bitterness'.[66]

The Clarion and Burns remained on good terms into the early Edwardian era. It was as a *Clarion* pamphlet that Burns published his austere manifesto for the working classes, *Brains better than Beer or Bets* in 1902. The connection to Burns

[60] Laurence Thompson, *Robert Blatchford*, p. 120.

[61] Ibid., pp. 164–5. See also the quasi-official history of the Labour Party published in 1925 which suggested that Hyndman and Blatchford's dislike of Hardie was 'personal' rather than about 'public or party policy.' Herbert Tracey (ed.), *The Book of the Labour Party*, vol. 3 (London, 1925), p. 114.

[62] See e.g. J. H. Watts's synthesis of the two traditions in an early *Clarion*, 19 January 1892.

[63] Laurence Thompson, *Robert Blatchford*, p. 138.

[64] Thompson, *Here I Lie*, pp. 97–8.

[65] H. M. Hyndman, *Further Reminiscences* (London, 1912) accessed at [http://www.marxists.org/archive/hyndman/1912/further/ch15.html]. The 'closeness' between Hyndman and Blatchford is noted in the SDF's official history, H. W. Lee and E. Archbold, *Social Democracy in Britain* (London, 1935), pp. 167–80.

[66] Laurence Thompson, *Robert Blatchford*, p. 138.

is suggestive of puritanical aspects of Blatchford's political style and identity. The *Clarion* version portrayed Blatchford as a puritanical young man rapidly broadened and humanized by his experiences in the army and on sporting newspapers. In the trenches, claimed Laurence Thompson 'he developed a sense of humour, and that streak of puckish irresponsibility'.[67] But Blatchford confessed that on his arrival at *Bell's Life* he remained 'rather strait-laced, inclined to a certain unforgiving or self-righteous Puritanism'.[68] For Neil Lyons, *Clarion* journalist and friend of Blatchford, the work culture of the sporting paper was the significant source of change: 'The jolly, careless, "Irish" atmosphere, the breezy methods . . . must have taught much to R. B. who had been schooled and nurtured in the stuffy air of chapel and amid the cast iron laws of the barrack-room and the soul-mangling devices of mill and workshop.'[69] Blatchford did not immediately cast off every one of his puritanical inclinations. His attacks on the luxury and idleness of the wealthy[70] included an extraordinary denunciation of the kind of 'young swells' whom Stedman Jones has identified as coming to the defence of London music halls under attack from Mrs Ormiston Chant's Social Purity campaigners during the 1890s:[71]

> You wicked, clever, knowing young rascals . . . Allow me to hold up a mirror wherein you may see your weak, dissipated foolish faces in all their native ugliness . . . You don't even know that you are asses . . . You have . . . accomplished nothing but folly, dissipation and villainy . . . Mind I am not preaching a teetotal sermon. I think good claret and good cigars good things to have. I can conceive that under some circumstances 'a quart of ale is a dish for a king' but let us have the truth about these things . . . You are the rich harvest of the pander and the plunderer. You are the goose that lays the golden eggs for the harlot and the sharper . . . You are cynics too; you believe that every man has his price . . . Your wit is an echo of the music hall song and the pantomime libretto; the rinsings of the muddiest and foulest minds of an age of dirt and duncedom.[72]

Blatchford's care in distancing himself from teetotalism notwithstanding, this was puritanical sermonizing. Barrow concluded that Blatchford during his *Clarion* years was 'inclined . . . not necessarily toward conservatism, but surely towards traditionalism'. A number of examples were offered. First, his definition of culture began with the necessity of self-control. Second, work was lauded for its disciplinary value—Blatchford defending Samuel Smiles in this respect. Third, Blatchford claimed to be an idealist throughout this period—he was committed to the agency of 'altruism'.[73] Fourth, he was a defender of the nuclear family. Fifth, there was his moralistic denunciation of *Dorian Gray*: 'Writers of

[67] Ibid., p. 10.
[68] Blatchford, *The Bounder*, p. 28.
[69] Lyons, *Robert Blatchford*, pp. 74–5.
[70] Robert Blatchford, *Impressionist Sketches* (London, 1897), 'The curate's dream', pp. 88–95.
[71] Stedman Jones, 'Working-class culture', p. 233.
[72] Robert Blatchford, *The Nunquam Papers. Reprinted from The Sunday Chronicle* (London, 1891), 'To the rakes of modern Athens', pp. 48–58.
[73] His commitment to 'altruism' might suggest a positivist influence too—idealism and positivism being compatible.

such trash as is offered in the modern erotic novel ought to be set to work to wash the streets and be fed on a diet of oatmeal, porridge and skim milk.'[74] *Merrie England*, Blatchford's common-sense and hugely popular explanation of socialism promoted 'Frugality of body and Opulence of mind'—he wanted to raise the culture of the masses. Neither drink nor tobacco nor betting was available in the utopia Blatchford presented in his *News from Nowhere* style novel *The Sorcery Shop*.[75] Lyons, whose literary specialism was a form of working-class urban realism,[76] criticized the novel: Blatchford 'expects too much from his fellow craftsmen—when he asks him to consider seriously ideals which eliminate wine and tobacco'.[77] Blatchford always claimed that disapproval of waste had initially led him down the socialist path,[78] and a collection of his post-Labour movement journalism included an attack on the wastefulness of the idle rich, admiration for the restraint and self-control of the Scots and English national characters, and an indictment of Wilkins Micawber from *David Copperfield*: 'That kind of sloppy, loafing, disreputable person does not appeal to me as funny . . . In real life such human jellyfish are intolerable.'[79]

A possible means of approaching the complexities of Blatchford's cultural politics is to suggest that he gradually disinherited his mother's (puritanical) legacy. Robert's relationship with his mother was difficult on his own account.[80] Blatchford's parents had been provincial jobbing actors, but his mother had reacted violently against this peripatetic, irregular, unrespectable lifestyle following his father's early death. She was determined that her sons gain a steady trade.[81] Blatchford's move into sporting newspaper journalism, his immersion in the theatrical world, his writing of a comic opera with Thompson and his cousin Clarence Corri, each could be seen as a renunciation of his mother's quest for respectability. 'Nunquam' responded emphatically to criticism of these activities as 'trivial', challenging his *Sunday Chronicle* readers: 'Have I not [insisted] from the first day I began to write . . . that one of the great wants of the people was the want of amusement and pleasure? Have I not told you a hundred times that the people want cheering more than they want improving? Is not the first line of my creed, "The object of life is to be happy"?' Blatchford went on to distance himself entirely from conventional mores, insisting that 'The wicked are more agreeable and interesting. They generally know more than the righteous and . . . are always a lot more charitable . . . I don't see how a man who never did wrong . . . can be considered a complete specimen . . . It is human to err, and the more humanity a

[74] Barrow, 'Robert Blatchford', pp. 70–1, 243–47, 252–3, 472, citing *The Clarion*: 15 April 1893, 30 January to 13 February 1897, 21 August to 4 October 1897, 14 May 1898.

[75] Laurence Thompson, *Robert Blatchford*, p. 111. Yeo, 'A new life', p. 17.

[76] Thompson, *Here I Lie* (1937), p. 134.

[77] Lyons, *Robert Blatchford*, p. 117.

[78] See e.g. Blatchford's interview in the *Ashton Under Lyme Herald*, 28 May 1892.

[79] Robert Blatchford, *As I lay a-thinking: some memories and reflections of an ancient and quiet watchman* (London, 1926), pp. 276, 123, 114, 181.

[80] Blatchford, *My Eighty Years*, pp. 1–6.

[81] R. C. K. Ensor, 'Blatchford, Robert Peel Glanville (1851–1943)', rev. H. C. G. Matthew, *ODNB*.

man has the more he is liable to err.'[82] Half a lifetime later Blatchford was still asking 'What's the use of being always sensible and always correct. It does us good to do silly things sometimes; it takes the conceit out of us.'[83]

Blatchford defended music hall on this basis—it was among the acceptable leisure pursuits in *Merrie England*.[84] He told a sceptical Thompson that, 'I think you are rather hard upon the music hall audience . . . beware how you scorn them . . . many of them be hard headed, practical workmen, sensible fellows in their way; useful fellows—even better still good fellows . . . A good man is more desirable and commendable than a clever man.'[85] Blatchford opposed Local Veto unambiguously during his brief Bradford ILP candidature in the early 1890s, long having left behind his teetotal years.[86] Periods of heavy drinking appeared to become part of his life.[87] As a prospective parliamentary candidate Blatchford had been equally brisk in responding to a reverend who had asked him to clarify that the love for woman which 'Nunquam' expressed in print was 'spiritual' rather than physical. 'No . . . I used the word love in every sense in which it can be employed.'[88] Indeed, his admiration for the female form was a notable aspect of his anti-puritanical cultural politics: 'It annoys me to hear a parcel of yeaforsooth prudes snuffling about immorality. God's whiskers! Are they sterile and manless, or are they only hypocrites? When I see a red-faced burly paunchy person holding forth on masculine chastity I wonder. I do. I marvel. Don't these freaks love women, then; or are they only liars?'[89] Lyons's biography, published in 1910, emphasized Blatchford's hedonism: 'R. B. shines forth even more brilliantly as a gossip and playfellow . . . no pastime [is] too useless for his amusement. I have sat for hours by his side on the sea-shore shying stones at a bottle . . . I have lain on my chest throughout a summer's day and shot at postcards and clay pipes with an air gun in strenuous competition.'[90] Lyons insisted that Blatchford was temperamentally a Tory—he was suggesting that Blatchford's attitudes reflected animal spirits rather than intellectual calculation.[91] The picture was therefore complex but Blatchford's ratio of hedonism to puritanism appeared to increase over time.

1906 AND BEYOND

The 1890s were the zenith of *The Clarion*'s influence as newspaper and social movement. Fay's death in 1896 was a significant blow. With him went some of

[82] Laurence Thompson, *Robert Blatchford*, p. 68.
[83] Blatchford, *As I lay a-thinking*, p. 181.
[84] *Merrie England* (London, 1894), pp. 17–18.
[85] Laurence Thompson, *Robert Blatchford*, p. 43.
[86] Ibid., p. 76. See Blatchford, *As I lay a-thinking*, p. 299, for a later era Blatchford attack on prohibition.
[87] Laird and Saville, 'Robert Blatchford', *DLB*, vol. 4.
[88] Laurence Thompson, *Robert Blatchford*, p. 76.
[89] Ibid., p. 170; also pp. 19, 228–9. A reader of Blatchford's 'Nunquam Dormio' column in *Bell's Life* for the years 1883 to 1886 is left in no doubt of his fascination with women.
[90] Lyons, *Robert Blatchford*, pp. 182–3.
[91] Ibid., pp. 10, 186–8.

the hedonistic exuberance that had characterized *Clarion* socialism. But it was never just about Fay. Blatchford and Thompson also endorsed a cultural politics which was in ethos closer to the hedonism of the wider (i.e. non-Labour movement) working classes. Blatchford in particular was not consistent in his application of this cultural politics. It sat uneasily with his competing impulses to educate and improve the masses. He could be strikingly puritanical. Nonetheless, for all his complexities, *The Clarion* during the 1890s attempted to construct a socialism more aligned to working-class culture. In doing so, Blatchford, Thompson, and Fay exposed the distance at which the wider Labour movement often stood from this culture.

The tension was manifest following the emergence of the Parliamentary Labour Party in 1906. The stolidity and respectability of the twenty-nine Labour MPs, their respect for the procedures of the House—manifest in an unwillingness to engage in un-parliamentary forms of protest—and, more widely, their obvious sympathy with Liberalism, encouraged a backlash among more radical sections of the Labour movement. The debate was a profound one, which exposed different conceptions of the Labour movement's nature and purpose. But among the lines of attack opened up by the Parliamentary Labour Party (PLP)'s closeness to the Liberal Government, was a cultural one. Nonconformity and puritanism were common to both, but neither belonged in the Labour movement, which, argued critics of the PLP, should be as distant from Liberalism as it was from Conservatism. Victor Grayson was the symbolic leader of opposition to Lib-Labism following his sensational victory in the Colne Valley by-election of 1907.[92] He subsequently became the de-facto political editor of *The Clarion*. Yet the *Clarion* version of history dwelled not on their shared belief in socialism and in extra-parliamentary agitation, but rather on Blatchford's and Grayson's cultural affinities and the distance at which this placed them from the puritanical Labour leadership. Grayson,

> treated Blatchford with an affectionate, leg-pulling respect... He made Blatchford laugh... he fitted neatly into Blatchford's circle, where the men and women enjoyed charades and comic recitations and silly family jokes, and were deeply earnest about their socialism. There is in *The Clarion* an article by Blatchford explaining how he and Grayson were late for a meeting. They missed their train, he said, because they became fascinated by the finger-shadows Grayson was making on the refreshment-room blind... The Movement with its customary charity said they were drunk. Yet it happened to be unadorned truth.[93]

True or not, the kind of cultural cleavages discussed in this essay were increasingly evident after 1906. This was because they overlapped, unevenly, with the political division between the PLP-ILP-trade union alliance on the one side, and on the other, socialist forces represented by (among others) *The Clarion*

[92] David Clark, *Colne Valley: Radicalism to Socialism* (London, 1981); Duncan Tanner, 'Ideological debate in Edwardian labour politics: radicalism, revisionism and socialism', in Eugenio Biagini and Alistair Reid (eds.), *Currents of Radicalism: Popular Radicalism, Organized Labour and Party Politics in Britain 1850–1914* (Cambridge, 1991), pp. 271–93.

[93] Laurence Thompson, *Robert Blatchford*, pp. 203–4.

and the SDF. Ben Tillett's (in)famous attack on the PLP mixed political and cultural critique in a fashion representative of the 'socialist' position: one might even call it Tory socialist in its hostility to Liberalism and Nonconformity.[94] Certainly, Labour's cultural orientation was a source of some tension as the Labour movement considered its future direction in the years before the First World War.

[94] Ben Tillett, *Is the Parliamentary Party a Failure?* (London, 1909 [1st edn, 1908]). See also Leonard Hall's introduction to Leonard Hall et al., *Let us Reform the Labour Party* (Manchester, 1910).

14

'The Plague Spots of London': William Joynson-Hicks, the Conservative Party, and the Campaign against London's Nightclubs, 1924–29

James J. Nott

Between 1924 and 1929, a campaign was launched to try and close down or 'clean up' London's nightclubs and nightlife. Seen as symbolic of a new age of moral decline by their detractors, nightclubs were raided, closed, and fined, and revellers harassed by the Metropolitan Police. The campaign was spearheaded by the Conservative Home Secretary, William Joynson-Hicks, and the Chief of the Metropolitan Police, Thomas Horwood. But the Bishop of London, the churches, and various morality pressure groups were also key protagonists. The issue was further amplified by the sensationalist reporting of the popular press, whose editors were keen to boost their readership with lurid 'human interest' stories. Hannen Swaffer, editor of *The People* wrote with particular relish in February 1925:

> The bogus night club is a pest house that should be shut. It is a centre for the spreading of disease . . . It is certainly not the sort of freedom for which nearly a million British soldiers died, but a hovel of unbridled licence, a scandal that cries aloud to high Heaven, and a perpetual shame, a mockery, a crime.[1]

Such histrionics were not unique. Moral policing (and moral panic) had been frequent in London during the late nineteenth and early twentieth century. By the 1920s there had already been numerous campaigns against pubs, cinemas, music halls, and attempts to regulate other aspects of 'immorality' throughout Britain. Historians have demonstrated how, in this period, an alliance of progressive politicians was championing the use of the state to 'improve people,' and took increasingly punitive and morally coercive measures to achieve their end, often opposed by those on the right.[2] Within this context then, the nightclub

[1] *The People*, 8 Feb. 1925.

[2] See Stefan Petrow, *Policing Morals: The Metropolitan Police and the Home Office, 1870–1914* (Oxford, 1994); Chris Waters, 'Manchester morality and London capital: the battle over the Palace

campaign of the 1920s is of particular significance, because it is an example of moral policing and state regulation of individual morality from the right, rather than the left. The Conservative government of 1924 to 1929 was prepared to use the full force of the state to regulate morality.

This essay will ask, as a campaign of moral policing coming from the right, what does the nightclub campaign tell us about the nature of popular Conservatism, the party's relationship with the state, and the place of 'Jix' (as Joynson-Hicks was known) within that party? At first sight, the campaign seems to sit very oddly indeed with a dominant view of pre-war popular Conservatism which portrays the party as one which championed the pleasures of life against the moral reform of the Liberals. The period from 1880 to 1914 was extremely significant in the construction of this populist Conservative public image. As Jon Lawrence has identified, under Salisbury, a popular libertarianism was espoused which was a shrewd reaction to a change in the position of the Liberal Party.[3] Traditionally the Liberals had opposed state interference with individual freedom, but by the end of the nineteenth century there was a shift in this position, caused by changed economic and social circumstances and the influence of the 'New Liberalism' of the 1890s. The Conservatives moved to pick up the mantle of personal liberties and individual freedoms as the Liberals appeared to be dropping it. Lawrence argues that a popular and populist brand of urban Toryism arose between 1880 and 1914 specifically contrived around a critique of late Victorian Liberalism, which had at its centre an attack on coercive moral reform. In particular, the apparent 'right'/'left' conflict over the issue of state regulation of individual morality at this time was exemplified by the respective stances of the Liberals and Conservatives in the growing battle against the music halls and pubs. The Tories deliberately championed these features of urban popular culture in order to distinguish themselves from the 'moral reforming' of the Liberals. The nightclub campaign appears to reverse this trend.

Furthermore, Joynson-Hicks's stance also seems to fit very oddly with much of his party's rhetoric about the state following the First World War. During the 1920s, in the new era of 'mass democracy', one of the key demarcation lines drawn between Labour and Conservative was their attitude towards state intervention. In the propaganda of Baldwin's party, Labour stood for a huge, menacing, unaccountable bureaucratic state; Conservatives for a small, 'liberating' state, balanced by the maintenance of personal freedoms and private property. Countering the ideology of the large, interfering state became increasingly important to Conservatives and party pamphlets produced during the 1920s illustrate this. For example, writing in 1924, Edward Wood—later Lord

of Varieties' and Susan Pennybacker, '"It was not what she said but the way in which she said it": The London County Councils and the music halls', in Peter Bailey (ed.), *Music Hall: The Business of Pleasure* (Milton Keynes, 1986); Chris Waters, 'Progressives, puritans and the cultural politics of the Council, 1889–1914', in Andrew Saint (ed.), *Politics and the People: The London County Councils* (London, 1989); Jon Lawrence, 'Class and gender in the making of urban Toryism, 1880–1914', *EHR* 208 (1993), pp. 629–52.

[3] Lawrence, 'Class and gender'.

Halifax—argued that the Conservative Party's love of individualism and liberty 'explains our reluctance to see the moderate enjoyment of things not wrong in themselves restricted by legal prohibitions'.[4]

So, how can Jix's campaign be squared with these positions? There are two explanations. First, party attitudes towards the state and moral regulation were by no means clear-cut—a variety of traditions existed within the Conservative Party. Indeed, the Conservatives were traditionally a party under whose banner a particularly diverse range of opinion existed. Furthermore, as Martin Francis has highlighted, the Conservative Party's relationship with the state in particular was a complex one.[5] Whilst observing that 'the Conservative Party has long been a blend of paternalist and libertarian traditions', he refutes the idea that it was always naturally more libertarian than paternalist. On the issue of moral regulation, in particular, as Stuart Ball has shown, during the early twentieth century, the Conservatives' respect for the past and its traditions meant that morality and politics were inextricably linked.[6] Thus, at the same time that Lawrence's popular Conservatism was defending the right of pleasure seekers, the party was also deeply concerned with public morality. For example, as David Cannadine and Alex Windscheffel have shown, radicals on the right were deeply critical of those members of their own party who became embroiled in financial and personal scandals.[7] Personal morality was important to the party.

Secondly, the nightclub campaign also sheds new light on the career of Joynson-Hicks, and his position within the Conservative Party. Although Jix's role has been dealt with briefly by other historians, notably Ronald Blythe and Martin Francis, this chapter offers a much fuller examination of one of his most notorious and high-profile acts of moral policing.[8] I examine the religious and political philosophy behind Joynson-Hicks's actions, and locate these actions within the broader context of the Conservative Party's philosophy. I believe that Joynson-Hicks was not just a rogue eccentric, but an—albeit extreme—example of an important school of thinking regarding morality within the Conservative Party. Significantly, the nightclub campaign allows us to focus on the nature of Conservatism in the 1920s, at a critical time of political realignment. As historians have shown, the 1920s was a pivotal period in which the Conservative Party successfully revitalised itself in the face of the challenges of mass democracy, the rise of Labour, and the dislocation caused by the Great War. After a decade of electoral disappointment, the 1920s saw a rebirth of popular Conservatism under Stanley Baldwin. I will argue that 'morality' and 'respectability' were central to

[4] Edward Wood, *Conservative Beliefs* (London, 1924), p. 70.

[5] Martin Francis, '"Set the people free?" Conservatives and the state, 1920–1960', in Martin Francis and Ina Zweiniger-Bargielowska (eds.), *The Conservatives and British Society, 1880–1990* (Cardiff, 1996), pp. 58–77.

[6] Stuart Ball, *The Conservative Party and British Politics 1902–1951* (London, 1995), p. 27.

[7] See David Cannadine, *Aspects of Aristocracy: Grandeur and Decline in Modern Britain* (London, 1995) and Alex Windscheffel, *Popular Conservatism in Imperial London, 1868–1906* (London, 2007).

[8] See Ronald Blythe, *The Age of Illusion: England in the Twenties and Thirties, 1919–40* (London, 2001), and Francis, 'Set the people free?'.

this Baldwinite Conservatism. This chapter therefore locates the nightclub campaign firmly within the context of the cultural politics of Baldwin's Conservative Party. It will highlight the role which 'morality' played in the Conservative Party's new cultural identity and will add to the body of historical opinion which emphasises the non-economic ways by which the Conservatives sought to distinguish themselves from Labour and the Liberals.[9]

THE COMPLAINANTS

The 'Nightclub Problem' exercised a wide range of people in Britain during the 1920s. The campaign involved a coalition of different interests rather than a coherent lobby, and included groups with often-contradictory motives and objectives. The first, and most vocal, were the 'moralists'—those groups which were strongly opposed to nightclubs on moral grounds. By the 1920s, there was a strongly entrenched morality lobby in England, and it had successfully agitated for state intervention on a number of issues. Between 1870 and 1914, sections of this lobby had achieved much closer regulation of prostitution, gambling and drinking, through successful campaigns targeting the Home Office and—in London—the Metropolitan Police.[10] Such bodies as the Public Morality Council (PMC), National Vigilance Association (NVA), and the British Social Hygiene Council, actively campaigned to prevent immorality, working in railway stations and ports to prevent 'traffic in women and children', and monitoring public parks, nightclubs, and other places of amusement.[11]

The churches played a leading role in these morality campaigns. The Church of England, the Roman Catholic Church, and the Free Churches all contained majorities who were alarmed at perceived declining moral standards and falling church attendance following the war, fearing that they were 'losing the war against impurity'.[12] Dominant amongst those clergy who opposed accommodation with the new post-war morality was Arthur Winnington-Ingram, Bishop of London from 1901 to 1939. He involved himself in many high-profile campaigns on moral matters, and chaired the PMC, which contained representatives from all the major Christian denominations as well as Jewish representatives.

[9] See Martin Pugh, *The Tories and the People 1880–1935* (Oxford, 1985); Ross McKibbin, 'Class and conventional wisdom: the Conservative Party and the "public" in inter-war Britain', in *Ideologies of Class: Social Relations in Britain, 1880–1950* (Oxford, 1990); David Jarvis, 'The shaping of the Conservative hegemony, 1918–1939', in Jon Lawrence and Miles Taylor (eds.), *Party, State and Society: Electoral Behaviour in Britain since 1820* (Aldershot, 1997); Neal R. McCrillis, *The British Conservative Party in the Age of Universal Suffrage: popular conservatism 1918–28* (Columbus, 1998); Philip Williamson, *Stanley Baldwin: Conservative Leadership and National Values* (Cambridge, 1999).

[10] Petrow, *Policing Morals.*

[11] See The Women's Library (WL), London: 4NVA/1/1/07, NVA minutes.

[12] Lambeth Palace Library (LPL), Lambeth: Davidson 428, f. 44, 10 May 1918.

It worked closely with the police to close down brothels, clean up public parks, and oppose 'offensive' plays and birth control propaganda.[13]

There was also a very receptive ear for the morality lobby in government during the period 1924 to 1929. The Home Secretary William Joynson-Hicks was a Conservative firmly in favour of active state regulation of morality. The extent of Jix's illiberalism is well documented. David Cesarani has highlighted his racist, xenophobic, and anti-Semitic beliefs, and positioned him as part of the 'ultra-right' in Britain.[14] Ronald Blythe described him as a 'mid Victorian busybody' who 'had no humility and too much to say'.[15] More recently F. M. L. Thompson has described him as 'the most prudish, puritanical and protestant Home Secretary of the twentieth century . . . a stern late Victorian Evangelical'.[16] Joynson-Hicks was indeed a vociferous and devoted campaigner for Christian values—so much so that his biographer called him a religious crusader.[17] He was vice-president of the World's Evangelical Alliance which called for interdenominational unity in order to maintain the influence of Christianity in international life. He was also president of the National Church League from 1921, as well as treasurer of the Zenana Bible and the Medical Missionary Society. Like Winnington-Ingram, he wanted a revival of godliness and religious observance at home and abroad.

Jix was also firmly in favour of using the state to intervene in matters of morality. For example, he attempted to stem 'the flood of filth coming across the Channel' by banning the books of D. H. Lawrence, Radclyffe Hall's *The Well of Loneliness*, works on birth control, and hundreds of other publications, as well as stopping the production of a number of plays which he found offensive. He ordered the investigation of parks after dark and increased the number of prosecutions for obscenity. A teetotaller (he had signed the pledge at the age of 14), he supported calls for the tighter regulation of pubs and alcohol, and was an active member of the Church of England Temperance Society.

Jix had clear views on protecting the public from 'indecency', and for ensuring its moral well-being; and his actions were underpinned by a strong ideological framework. In 1929 in his pamphlet, *Do We Need A Censor?* he remarked:

> The government has a general responsibility for the moral welfare of the community, which is traceable partly perhaps to the peculiar relationship existing between the Church and the State, and partly also to the duty inherent in all Governments of combating such dangers as threaten the safety or well being of the State.[18]

[13] See London Metropolitan Archives (LMA), London: A/PMC/98/1–15: Public Morality Council Annual Reports.

[14] David Cesarani, 'William Joynson-Hicks and the radical right in England after the First World War', in Tony Kushner and Kenneth Lunn (eds.), *Traditions of Intolerance* (Manchester, 1989).

[15] Blythe, *Age of Illusion*, pp. 33, 42.

[16] F. M. L. Thompson, 'Hicks, William Joynson-, first Viscount Brentford (1865–1932)', *ODNB*.

[17] H. A. Taylor, *Jix—Viscount Brentford* (London, 1933), p. 67.

[18] William Joynson-Hicks, *Do We Need A Censor?* (London, 1929), p. 10.

Using the language of the social hygiene movement, Jix considered it the duty of government to protect the population from acts of 'public indecency,' believing that: 'It is as much a crime against the community to commit an act of public indecency as to commit a theft.'[19] Jix was also not afraid to take a clear interventionist role to protect the moral health of the nation and to control acts of public indecency. His thoughts about the function of the police here were clear:

> Just as the police, who are agents of the Secretary of State—himself an agent of the Government—arrest and prosecute a person who is reasonably suspected of having committed a burglary or a murder, so it is the duty of the police—again as agents of the Home Secretary—to prosecute for acts of public indecency.[20]

The full power of the state, then, was to be used to maintain the moral well-being of the nation. His analysis of moral and national decline, and his solutions to both, thus echoed those of many churchmen and morality campaigners.

Although his evangelicalism and authoritarian nature made him unusual in the extent to which he was prepared to press for action, Jix was not alone in wanting 'decency' and 'morality' to be upheld. The Conservative government was also active in overseeing the nation's morals in other spheres. The Cinematograph Act of 1927 and the growth of film censorship under the British Board of Film Censors, for example, were driven by strong moral concerns. Similarly, in 1928 the party conference at Great Yarmouth passed resolutions demanding firmer control of the BBC and censorship of 'controversial' material on air, both political and moral.[21] The Calvinist Lord Reith's governance of the BBC, with its strong moralising tone, was completely in line with that of the Conservative Party at this time. Significantly, Stanley Baldwin was also a man inspired by a deep religious faith, having considered ordination before he turned to politics. Indeed, in 1926, he lamented the lack of religious belief amongst people, 'Today the world seems more irreligious than at any time in the Christian era. Irresponsibility, pleasure-seeking and prodigal luxury abound.'[22] Furthermore, as Philip Williamson has noted, and as discussed in detail below, one of Baldwin's most 'striking' characteristics was his public enunciation of a religious conception of politics during this time.[23] Both are vital to understanding the nightclub campaign.

The third group concerned with nightclubs were those sections of the police force, magistrates, lawyers, and others who were concerned with their legal

[19] Ibid., p. 6.
[20] Ibid.
[21] Conservative Party Archive: National Union of Conservative and Unionist Associations: Annual Party Conference Reports: Gt. Yarmouth, 27 Sept 1928.
[22] Stanley Baldwin, *On England and Other Addresses* (London, 1971), pp. 195–6.
[23] Philip Williamson, 'The doctrinal politics of Stanley Baldwin', in Michael Bentley (ed.), *Public and Private Doctrine: Essays in British History Presented to Maurice Cowling* (Cambridge, 1993), pp. 202–3.

position. Again, there were a variety of positions taken on the issue: many magistrates, for example, were alarmed at the tactics used by the police and thus opposed the campaign. Equally, there were those who were alarmed by breaches of licensing laws, and illegal gambling and prostitution in clubs. In particular, the police were central to the success of any moral campaign and by the 1920s the Metropolitan Police already had a long history of policing morality. They were used by successive governments, Liberal and Conservative, under direction from the Home Office, to experiment with various methods of social control. Whilst Petrow argues that Metropolitan Police Commissioners were 'not the lap-dogs of moral authoritarians', he also points out that some at the centre were often willing and active participants in these moral campaigns.[24] The Chief of the Metropolitan Police at the time of the nightclub campaign, Sir William Horwood, was one such enthusiast for moral policing. Horwood was convinced of the necessity of 'hands on', rather than 'hands off', policing methods. He believed that the Metropolitan Police should be involved in controlling and regulating behaviour that many believed was a matter of private conscience.

COMPLAINTS AGAINST NIGHTCLUBS

Why were nightclubs considered to be especially dangerous? Described by Joynson-Hicks as 'The Plague Spots of London', for those groups opposed to them, they caused several specific concerns.[25] First, they were linked with sexual immorality. Second, there was a strong association made between nightclubs and drug abuse. Related to this, nightclubs were seen to have intimate links with the criminal underworld. Finally, there were cultural reasons for disapproval—most notably the link between nightclubs and black, American 'jazz' music—which added to their 'disreputable' image.

Observers suggested that most of the clientele, especially men, attended nightclubs in order to pick up sexual partners. The journalist Sydney Moseley wrote that, 'Nine men out of ten who frequent night haunts do so to indulge a physical craving. The question of sexual passion is crucial.'[26] Even though it seems likely that Moseley was exaggerating, many of the larger nightclubs in central London definitely exploited this factor. Attractive female 'hostesses' were employed by many establishments. Officially they were there to act as waitresses; to dance with patrons; to talk and to entertain those who entered alone. Yet nightclub hostesses were much more than just this. They were chosen deliberately as bait to draw in male patrons. Hostessing could be a lucrative business, with some women earning up to £80 a week—a fortune when a kitchen maid could earn as little as £2 a month. Furthermore, it is clear that many such hostesses *did* also provide sexual

[24] Petrow, *Policing Morals*, p. 295.
[25] *The Times*, 18 Nov. 1925, p. 11.
[26] Sydney Moseley, *The Night Haunts of London* (London, 1920), p. 116.

services and it was this activity that was perhaps key to the poor reputation many nightclubs had. The NVA were particularly interested in this issue and they monitored nightclubs and dance halls for potential irregularities, believing that thousands of women a year were being lost to the so-called 'White Slave Trade'.[27] The police also claimed that prostitution flourished in some nightclubs: in a case brought against one club—'Daltons'—in 1920, they claimed to have counted 292 'prostitutes' leaving those premises during their operational surveillance.[28]

It is hard to establish whether these girls were indeed prostitutes—how could the police accurately deduce this information just by observing people coming and going? Nevertheless, these were not the only links that nightclubs had with sex. The association of nightclubs with the new dances of the 1920s meant that they were part of a wider attack on 'immorality'. These social dances were deliberately formulated as dances for couples. They required close bodily contact between men and women—and thus increased the opportunities for sexual contact between the two. The foxtrot, for example, introduced to Britain in 1914, required that dance partners held each other close and tight. The vitality and free expression of new dances, such as the 'Shimmy' and the 'Charleston', was also a cause of concern. Such dances were equated by critics with dangerously uncontrolled sexuality and eroticism. Writing in *The Times* in September 1922, J. D. McAughton, a member of the Scottish District of the British Association of Teachers of Dancing, described the new dances as simply 'hugging to music' and concluded that they were degrading, indecent, immoral, and deliberately sensual.[29] Unsurprisingly, the morality lobby went further still. A member of the clergy, presiding over a meeting of the Maidenhead Preventive and Rescue Association in March 1919, for example, strongly condemned the new dance craze as 'one of the most degrading symptoms of the present day', a sign of a 'very grave disease which was infecting the country'.[30] Frederic Spurr, in *The Christian Use of Leisure* in 1928 argued that: 'In the public dancing places, where miscellaneous crowds gather and mingle, the greatest danger lies.'[31]

Increasingly such critiques were addressed specifically to women. They were the most ardent fans of dancing and they flocked to the new nightclubs. To their opponents, nightclubs were regarded as the 'wrong sort' of places for young women to frequent—specifically because they were encouraging women to behave in an 'un-ladylike' fashion. In June 1924, the *Sunday Chronicle* printed the views of one woman on the new craze for dancing in nightclubs:

> These women cannot know how revolting they appear, as they shuffle around the room with striding legs too far apart, rigid bodies and fixed staring eyes. They are so closely

[27] WL, London: 4NVA/3/1, F. Sempkins, 'Traffic in women and children', n.d.

[28] *Empire News*, 11, 18 Jan., 2 Feb. 1920 cited in Marek Kohn, *Dope Girls: The Birth of the British Drug Underground* (London, 1992), p. 122.

[29] *The Times*, 21 Sept. 1922, p. 8.

[30] *The Times*, 15 Mar. 1919, p. 7.

[31] Frederic Spurr, *The Christian Use of Leisure* (London, 1928), pp. 55–6.

clasped by the men that free movement is impossible. Yet only a few years ago girls, among themselves, unanimously condemned the partners who didn't keep their proper distance. They drew a sharp line between dancing and embracing. They didn't give to the casual stranger that which they reserved for a chosen man.[32]

Gender was an important dimension in another aspect of the nightclubs' tainted reputation: illegal drugs. For according to journalists, drugs were an essential feature of London's new nightlife—especially for women. In 1923, Sydney Felstead regarded the problem as widespread, affecting 'thousands of women'. He explained: 'How easy is the path to temptation! Midnight suppers and early morning dances, bodily lassitude and sleeplessness, all be banished by "dope".'[33] Although the scale of the problem was relatively small—with an average of 65 cocaine prosecutions a year between 1921 and 1923—the press became fascinated by cases of drug addiction, especially as they often concerned young women connected with the nightclub world.[34] Stories of 'Cocaine Girls' filled the newspapers. In March 1922, for example, Freda Kempton, a 23-year-old nightclub dancer and cocaine addict, committed suicide by drinking cocaine.[35] Her story was the kind of tragedy which Fleet Street's editors loved. It caused a public outcry and the *Daily Express*, keen to make the most from the episode, launched its own campaign against drugs.

The newspapers and the authorities were not only interested in the victims of drugs, but also in the suppliers. Some of the seedier clubs in central London were owned by members of the criminal underworld. Such people saw the provision of drugs as a legitimate sideline, and a particularly profitable one at that. In 1923, for example, cocaine, smuggled into the country from Germany and Holland retailed at about £240 per ounce, representing a 1000 per cent profit for smugglers.[36] Two of the most notorious leaders of the drugs world in London in the 1920s were a Chinaman called 'Brilliant Chang' who styled himself as London's 'Dope King', and the Jamaican, Eddie Manning.[37] Both had connections to nightclubs, using them to sell their drugs and target new users. Manning, in particular, used violence as an intrinsic part of his operation, utilising guns, razors, knuckledusters, and coshes on a regular basis. This, in turn, attracted organised crime. The Police clearly had an interest in monitoring nightclubs in order to suppress the growing problem of gang violence and extortion and the fact that many of these gangs were of foreign descent made them even more disreputable to many.

Racism was a further factor in the condemnation of nightclubs. They were deeply suspicious because they were so closely associated with black, American 'jazz'. Indeed, the explosion in interest in this music in the immediate aftermath

32 *Sunday Chronicle*, 24 June 1924, quoted in Jim Godbolt, *A History of Jazz in Britain* (London, 1984), pp. 32–3.

33 S. T. Felstead, *The Underworld of London* (London, 1923), pp. 264, 283.

34 Kohn, *Dope Girls*, p. 168.

35 Arthur Tietjen, *Soho: London's Vicious Circle* (London, 1952), p. 25.

36 Felstead, *Underworld*, pp. 268–9.

37 See Robert Fabian, *London After Dark* (London, 1954).

of the war was one of the key catalysts for the expansion of nightlife in general. Jazz's 'blackness' inevitably caused considerable debate. The composer Constant Lambert parodied the 1920s reaction to jazz in Britain, with its 'crusty old colonels', 'choleric judges', and 'beer-sodden columnists' complaining of jazz as 'swamp stuff', 'jungle rhythms', and 'negro decadence'.[38] Jazz was regarded as 'primitive', yet such primitivism was not benign. It was seen as a serious threat to white culture and civilisation. Moreover, the fear of Americanisation was taken very seriously in the post-First World War period—'jazz bands', cocktails, and nightclubs were symbolic of America's cultural power. For those concerned with the perceived moral decline of Britain since the end of the Great War then, nightclubs offered plenty of reasons for disquiet.

THE CAMPAIGN

Campaigns against nightclubs did not start with Joynson-Hicks, they started with Winnington-Ingram. The first regulations governing 'improper' conduct in nightclubs had been introduced during the First World War. The Clubs (Temporary) Bill of November 1915 allowed for official registration and regular police inspection of nightclubs, together with measures to 'prohibit the harbouring of any undesirable persons'. It was part of a larger crackdown on drinking and drunkenness which was seen to be affecting Britain's capacity to wage war against Germany. Winnington-Ingram played a key role in getting the legislation enacted, and his experience in that campaign informed the lobbying of the 1920s.

With the lifting of most wartime regulations in 1920, however, control of nightclubs reverted to the 1910 Licensing Act, which provided very limited powers for their supervision. Under compliance with the Act, which was concerned with controlling alcohol, it was possible for anyone to register a club at a police court or petty sessional court on the payment of five shillings. No authority had the power to determine whether premises should be registered as a club or not, and the police had no right of entry except by search warrant. In cases of wrongdoing, clubs could only be temporarily suspended and the fines imposed were usually negligible compared to the profits to be made from running clubs. In 1921 a new Licensing Act restricted nightclubs no more effectively than had the Act of 1910. Nightclubs flourished.

Their growth, and the concerns about them, increased the pressure for some form of new legislation that could administer and control nightclubs more effectively than the Licensing legislation. The morality lobby now began to pressurise the authorities, seeking to control what it considered to be a serious social problem. The Public Morality Council, for example, actively monitored nightclubs, presenting evidence to the police and pressing for prosecutions.[39]

[38] Constant Lambert, *Music Ho! A Study of Music in Decline* (London, 1934), pp. 201–2.
[39] LMA, London:A/PMC/148.

As a result, in January 1921, a Parliamentary Committee was established to inquire into the question of nightclubs. The report of the committee, issued in April 1922, confirmed the suspicions of critics. It concluded that a large number of nightclubs and dancing resorts were conducted 'in a manner seriously detrimental to those who frequent them'.[40] The committee urged that 'a drastic remedy' was needed to deal with the problem and, within months of the report being issued, the Home Secretary, Edward Shortt, mooted plans to introduce a Bill in the new session of Parliament designed to give the police greater control over the regulation of nightclubs and increased penalties which could be imposed by the magistrates for breaches of the law.[41] The Bill, however, was stalled and never introduced.

Parts of the legal profession were also in favour of a change in the law, but not all agreed about which direction to take. At their third annual general meeting in October 1924, the Magistrates Association condemned the growing 'nightclub evil' in London and attacked existing laws which gave the police authority to oversee the problem. The following year they called for the control and registration of nightclubs to be given to the bench of magistrates in any given area.[42] They too were unsuccessful in effecting any change.

The election of a new Conservative government, and the appointment of Joynson-Hicks as Home Secretary in November 1924 gave the campaign for tighter regulation the receptive ear in government which it needed. Sensing that their moment had come, the morality lobby sought an audience with the new Home Secretary at the earliest opportunity. In January 1925, a deputation organised by the Public Morality Council, the Charing Cross Vigilance Society and the Temperance Council of Christian Churches, visited the Home Secretary and Sir William Horwood to discuss the subject of London nightclubs. The delegation pressed Jix to deal with the matter 'finally and adequately'. The Bishop of London, who headed the deputation, and was instrumental in its organisation, wanted a return to the regulation of the 1915 Bill. His condemnation of nightclubs was unequivocal.

The Bishop's sentiments chimed happily with the new Home Secretary's. Indeed, Jix had set in motion plans for new legislation almost immediately on taking office. He told the press in January 1925 of the necessity for new police powers:

> The police are fighting the night club evil with one arm tied behind their back. They are helpless at present. They cannot get evidence except by acting the despicable part of a spy. But we are now preparing to introduce legislation which will purge London of this horrible blot on the city's life.[43]

The draft Nightclubs Bill—the result of correspondence between Jix, Thomas Horwood, and Sir John Anderson, the hard-line Presbyterian permanent

[40] *The Times*, 29 Apr. 1922, p. 12.
[41] *The Times*, 26 Apr. 1922, p. 14.
[42] *The Times*, 27 Jan. 1925, p. 11.
[43] *Evening News*, 26 Jan. 1925.

secretary to the Home Office—represents a blueprint for direct state interference in an area of public life which had clear moral implications.

In terms of its scope, the Nightclubs Bill was designed for the registration, inspection and regulation of nightclubs. For the first time in law, a nightclub was defined as: 'A club . . . the premises occupied by which are habitually used or intended to be used for the purpose of dancing at night.'[44] Under the new Bill, all nightclubs would have to be registered and issued with a license. Local authorities, police, and local residents were to be allowed to object to the annual renewal of licenses on various grounds—the conduct of members and proprietors; the admittance of non- members; the safety of premises; as well as the conduct of dancing. Thus, those who conducted their businesses 'improperly' could have their licenses revoked and not be allowed to trade. Premises could be barred from operating as a nightclub for anything from one to five years. Furthermore, offending nightclub owners were liable to imprisonment with or without hard labour for up to three months.

In order to assess whether licenses could be renewed, nightclubs were to be open to regular inspection. The Chief of the Metropolitan Police would have a right to enter at all times, day or night, using force if necessary, should he suspect wrongdoing. A search warrant was no longer required. On entering, the police would have the right to take the names and addresses of all present and seize all business papers related to the club. Those obstructing such inspections would be subject to fines and/or imprisonment. Finally, further regulation would be made to eliminate the worst aspects of nightclubs. There were thus specific provisions made to target prostitution and gambling, with heavy fines and imprisonment for those found guilty.

The Nightclubs Bill mirrored the sort of regulation that had been imposed on music halls in the late nineteenth century as progressives in local government had tried to create a form of 'rational recreation' out of a hearty, non-deferential, bawdy form of entertainment. Significantly, this new act came not from local authorities but from central government, not from progressives, liberals, or socialists, but from the Conservative Party.

However, having drafted a Bill to present to parliament, in May 1925 Jix announced that he would not proceed with it due to insufficient time in the parliamentary session. The precise reasons for this apparent climb down are hard to fathom. There seem to have been a number of pertinent factors, however. On the one hand, the lack of clear evidence to prove systematic problems with the running of nightclubs was a major difficulty. Joynson-Hicks told campaigners that although numerous prominent clubs in Central London and Soho had been under police surveillance for several years, it was difficult for the police to gain evidence of wrongdoing due to various devices employed by clubs to keep them out.[45] Many nightclubs locked doors, using 'spy holes' to monitor guests, and others installed electric alarms in order to give warning of ensuing police raids.

44 The National Archives: Public Record Office, Kew: PRO:HO:472038/15a, 6 Feb. 1925.
45 TNA. Kew:PRO:MEPO:472038/2, letter TH to WJH, Dec. 1924.

As a result, evidence of bad behaviour was quickly hidden. The number of convictions up to 1925 was minimal—between 1 December 1922 and 30 November 1925, only 115 clubs in the Metropolitan police district had been entered by a search warrant. From these, 107 convictions had been obtained, with 69 premises being temporarily disqualified and fines and costs totalling just over £15,000 being imposed.[46] Joynson-Hicks thus argued that he had insufficient evidence to conclude that such places were immoral.

There were also problems over the definition of a nightclub which made the exact framing of the legislation difficult. Creating an appropriate definition caused the lawyers considerable headaches. No doubt there were some political constraints too. Joynson-Hicks was mindful of the fact that the members of the 11,000 nightclubs made up a considerable number of voters and that offending legitimate clubs, especially those with a prominent aristocratic or political membership, was a sensitive issue. Moreover, by mid-1925 a series of other much more pressing concerns were mounting on the Home Secretary's in-tray; among them striking miners and communist agitation.

This halted the legislation, but not the campaign against nightclubs. Jix was frustrated that his Bill had not been given a reading. He had not, however, given up on his crusade. On 17 November 1925, Jix received a second deputation from the PMC, including representatives of the Bishop of London; the London County Council; the National Council of Women; the London Council of Social Service; the Social Welfare Department of the Methodist Church; the Jewish Association for the Protection of Women; the YMCA; the Church of England's Men's Society; the NVA; and the British Social Hygiene Council. The PMC presented a dossier of evidence from surveillances it had been carrying out on nightclubs in London and Jix urged them to write to Conservative Members of Parliament and Peers, to press for legislation.[47]

Meanwhile, despite a lack of legislation, Joynson-Hicks intensified the use of police to 'clean up' the nightclubs, and raids became increasingly common. From 1924 to 1927 sixty-five nightclubs were prosecuted in the West End, with sixty-two of them struck off the register of clubs and closed down.[48] In 1927 twenty-two clubs were raided in the Metropolitan area, and all were closed as a result.[49] In 1928 thirty-three clubs were prosecuted.[50] The usual *modus operandi* for gaining evidence of wrongdoing was to send in undercover officers posing as nightclub patrons, who would join the club and attempt to order alcohol after permitted hours. Officers also looked for evidence of drunkenness and disorder, prostitution and gambling. This in itself was a controversial policing method, sanctioned by Horwood and Jix.[51] Once sufficient evidence was gained, police would obtain search warrants and enter the premises, taking samples of drinks,

[46] TNA, Kew:PRO:MEPO:312969/291269, 3 Dec. 1925.
[47] TNA, Kew:PRO:MEPO:472038/52, 25 Nov. 1925.
[48] TNA, Kew:PRO:MEPO:312967/291269, letter TH to WJH, 18 May 1928.
[49] TNA, Kew:PRO:MEPO:312967/291269, 24 Nov. 27.
[50] TNA, Kew:PRO:MEPO:312967/291269/11A.
[51] TNA:PRO:MEPO:4720378/73, 14 March 1928.

and other evidence, and taking down the names of all of those present, with the warning that they could be summoned. In May 1928, for example, the police took the names and addresses of 150 people during raids on the Manhattan and the 43 Clubs.[52] Sometimes they even arrested those present *en masse*. In February 1925, following a raid on the Cursitor Club, one hundred people were put in cells overnight at Bow Street, many of them girls still in fancy dress.[53]

At the height of this campaign, the police raided nightclubs indiscriminately, regardless of their size or conduct. Raids were often planned to coincide with one another, for maximum impact. In November 1925, for example, seven West End nightclubs were raided within 50 minutes in the early hours, by uniformed officers of the Tottenham Court Road police station.[54] In 1928 Jix authorised the use of the Flying Squad to carry out these raids, thus heightening the tension further. High-profile raids on fashionable venues such as the Kit-Kat Club, which was frequented by the Prince of Wales, frightened many club-goers. They were intended to do so. Joynson-Hicks was determined to make life as difficult as possible for nightclubs, their patrons and owners—clear evidence of a willingness to enforce this morality campaign by those in government.

One of the most famous victims of this campaign was Mrs Kate Meyrick, nicknamed London's 'Nightclub Queen'. Meyrick's establishments were regularly raided, extensive fines levied, and she was repeatedly imprisoned. In all she was given five prison sentences; one sentencing magistrate arguing in June 1928 that, 'Punishment must be such as may be calculated to deter her and discourage others from committing the same type of offence.'[55]

Such active moral policing seems to have had a substantial impact on the nightclub business. In 1928 the press ran a number of stories pointing to the emptying of nightclubs in the wake of frequent police raids. The *Daily Mail* observed:

> Friday night, the busiest night of the week for nightclubs in London, proved yesterday to be one of the slackest on record. The police raids have so frightened members . . . that attendances have been very poor. The dance floors usually crowded were last night occupied by just a few couples and tables round the rooms were empty. There is a general feeling of uneasiness that further police raids are imminent and members were staying away lest they be caught during any of them.[56]

Indeed, it seems that the new tactic of high-profile raids might have succeeded in breaking the nightclubs, if it had not been for a scandal that was to rock the heart of the Home Secretary's campaign and question the integrity of the police force. The behaviour of the police force was under particular scrutiny at this time due to a press-led campaign against what they considered to be a heavy-handed approach from the police in harassing innocent citizens. Despite the report of the Macmillan committee on the conduct of the management of the police,

[52] *Daily Mail*, 26 May 1928. [53] *The People*, 8 Feb. 1925.
[54] *The Times*, 18 Nov. 1925, p. 11. [55] *Daily Herald*, 23 June 1928.
[56] *Daily Mail*, 26 May 1928.

which cleared the police of all but one of the allegations made against them in the newspapers, their reputation continued to suffer. Furthermore, in May 1928 the police were accused of brutality during an interrogation.[57] Questions were asked in Parliament, and in August 1928 Jix was minded to establish a royal commission to examine police powers and police methods.

The final nail in the coffin for Horwood's and Joynson-Hicks's campaign came in 1928, when the so-called 'Goddard scandal' erupted. Sergeant George Goddard was one of a number of officers who had monitored nightclubs, and had received several commendations for his behaviour in suppressing disorder in such places.[58] However, in 1928 he was accused by a fellow policeman of accepting bribes from the owners of nightclubs to save themselves from police investigation. In 1929 Goddard was found guilty on all counts, and was sentenced to eighteen months imprisonment with hard labour, and a fine of £2,000. The case sent shock waves through the country, and seriously undermined public confidence in the police. Jix was forced to replace Horwood with General Lord Byng as metropolitan commissioner of police. The nightclub campaign collapsed.

CONCLUSION

So, were Jix and his campaign eccentric oddities, or do they tell us something important about political ideas within the Conservative Party? Certainly, many Conservatives considered the campaign, and Jix himself, as an eccentric oddity. Beaverbrook, for example, described him to Mackenzie King as 'a man who is thought a fool by his colleagues, a fine fellow by the private member, and a romantic hero by the chairman of the local Conservative Association'.[59] Moreover, the Nightclubs Bill that Jix wanted was not supported by his party, and failed to reach the statute book. This suggests that Jix wanted a solution to this problem that most in his party did not. The questioning of the *methods* utilised by the police during the campaign also suggests that libertarians within the party were worried. For example, whilst broadly in agreement with the aims of Jix's campaign, in 1925 Lord Apsley, Conservative MP for Southampton, criticised the methods used during nightclub raids. Describing the method of undercover police officers pretending to be nightclub patrons as 'a somewhat un-English proceeding', Apsley objected to such underhand means.[60] Similarly, writing in the *Daily Express* in February 1925, for example, Michael Walsingham attacked Joynson-Hicks's interfering and hectoring actions, warning that he was alienating Conservative voters who expected such things of socialists, but not of their own:

[57] Taylor, *Jix*, 211–15. [58] *Daily Telegraph*, 20 Dec. 1928.
[59] Thompson, 'Hicks, William Joynson'.
[60] Parliamentary Debates (Commons), 180, 28 Feb. 1925, 2119–20.

> The Home Secretary is making the Government profoundly unpopular among its own supporters throughout the home counties, not because they ever go to nightclubs, but because they object to a combination of Puritanism and police... they can hardly believe it. They still have a pathetic faith... that the Tory cause is the last refuge of the rights and liberties of the individual and the people. This faith the Home Secretary... (is) rapidly undermining.[61]

But against this, we should also remember that not a single motion was tabled at a party conference or local association, nor a single question asked by Conservative MPs in the Houses of Parliament, which criticised the *direction* of the campaign against nightclubs throughout the 1920s. Moreover, Baldwin himself did nothing to rein in his Home Secretary. According to Leo Amery, Baldwin once said of Jix, 'he may have said many foolish things but rarely did one.'[62] Indeed, in Baldwin, Jix found a kindred spirit in relation to issues of morality. Though they were often dealing with a party that wasn't as committed to this sort of 'Puritanism' as themselves, Baldwin and Jix were leading a party which placed considerable emphasis on morality.

I believe that there are three aspects of 1920s popular Conservatism in particular which help us to understand that Jix's nightclub campaign was not very much out of step with the dominant direction of the party, even if its methods were. First, the Conservative Party based its appeal on a strong sense of 'morality', derived from strong religious beliefs, particularly from its leader, Stanley Baldwin. Indeed, the Conservatives made a deliberate appeal to religious sentiment in the country and aimed to become the main 'Christian' party. Second, and related to this, the party wished to present itself as defenders of 'conventional morality', championing 'middle-class values', especially in relation to the role of women and the centrality of the family. Finally, the Conservative Party also wished to present itself as the defenders of the interests of the 'common man and woman', against the excesses of those at the margins of society, top and bottom.

An appeal to 'morality' was a key part of Baldwin's appeal to the electorate during the 1920s. As Williamson has stated, Baldwin 'tapped and stimulated the forces of a morally conservative and religious nation'.[63] Significantly, public morality had been the issue that first brought Baldwin to political prominence, in his principled stand in 1922 against Lloyd George's honours and Marconi scandals. His concern with the moral reputation of his party was considerable. Yet there was much more to Baldwin's morality than just a concern to transform the reputation of government and politics. As Bill Schwarz has noted, 'the language of constitutionalism' espoused by Baldwinite Conservatism was one derived from the strong sense of morality which Baldwin, like Jix, believed to lie at the centre of the British character.[64] In 1924 he stated that 'Moral values are

[61] *Daily Express*, 26 Feb. 1925.
[62] Thompson, 'Hicks, William Joynson'.
[63] Williamson, 'Doctrinal politics', p. 208.
[64] Bill Schwarz, 'The Language of Constitutionalism: Baldwinite Conservatism', in *Formations of Nation and People* (London, 1984).

the foundation of a country's greatness. If moral values flourish in our common life, all will be well with the nation.'[65]

Moreover, it is clear that one aspect of Baldwin's electoral strategy was to make a deliberate appeal to the spirituality of the nation and to the 'religious vote'. This tactic was a good one, for it is easy to overstate the extent to which religious issues had ceased to matter in British politics. Significantly, the 1920s offered real electoral potential, as the denominational disputes that had characterised pre-war politics declined, offering the possibility of an 'electoral realignment of large parts of religious and moral opinion'.[66] Not only did Baldwin consolidate the Anglican vote, but he also attracted increasing numbers of Non-Conformist voters. Williamson claims that these votes were important to Conservative Party electoral success, especially in former Liberal strongholds in south-western and eastern England, and in Scotland. The nightclub campaign of moral policing would certainly have appealed to these voters—as we have seen, some of the key groups pressing for action were non-conformists in the morality lobby. It also seems possible that the emphasis on morality was part of an attempt to take former Liberal votes, and to occupy the ground formerly occupied by the Liberal Party vis-à-vis morality. More obviously, the emphasis on morality was helping to transform, as Williamson puts it, 'the party of the Church of England' into a party of 'the majority of religious opinion'.[67]

Yet the appeal to morality was central to other aspects of the Conservatives' electoral strategy too. In particular, morality was a key part of their appeal to the middle class, 'general public' via a defence of the status quo. As Maurice Cowling first argued, during the 1920s Conservative leaders mobilised numerous sections of society in defence, not only of established institutions, but also of established conventions and habits, in the name of order and stability.[68] Thus, just as Baldwin aimed to 'slow down the pace of change' politically, he also aimed to restore conventional morality. As we have already noted, the post-war era was widely supposed to have brought about serious threats to that morality, in addition to a host of other pre-war certainties. In the face of these challenges, as McKibbin argues, the Conservative Party aimed to became 'the party of bourgeois propriety and dignity'.[69] Jix for one, was firmly behind such an alignment. Talking about the raids he launched on public parks, for example, he justified his interventions as necessary to the defence of mainstream values:

Let there be no mistake . . . If the police were to cease for forty-eight hours to patrol and enforce public decency in our parks, they would become places where it would be impossible for a man to take his daughters for a walk . . . I for one am not prepared to

[65] *The Times*, 12 Feb. 1924, cited in Williamson, 'Doctrinal politics', p. 188.
[66] Williamson, 'Doctrinal politics', p. 205.
[67] Ibid., p. 206.
[68] Maurice Cowling, *The Impact of Labour 1920–1924: The Beginning of Modern British Politics* (London, 1971).
[69] McKibbin, 'Class and conventional wisdom', p. 281.

accept that position . . . I would go further and say that if the law were not in existence, it would be necessary to enact one.[70]

That the nightclub campaign attacked apparently 'deviant' behaviour should then come as no surprise within this context. The Conservative Party made 'conventional morality' a key plank of its appeal throughout the 1920s, and it was also closely linked with the party's attack on socialism and with its concerns about women.

Morality was another way by which the Conservatives could distinguish themselves from Labour. Thus, as Neil McCrillis has shown, in the early 1920s a number of scare stories were spread by the press and the Conservative Party which linked socialism to an attack on conventional morality. Conservative Party pamphlets contained horror stories from the Soviet Union of free love, bestial orgies, rape, and even the 'nationalisation' of women, whereby Revolutionaries used women like 'breeding animal[s] on a stud farm'.[71] Jix, a strident anti-communist notorious for pursuing left-wingers rabidly, keenly supported such attacks. It was argued by other Conservatives that the 'hidden' socialists and radicals within the Labour Party were hoping to bring the same attitudes to Britain.

Furthermore, within the Conservative Party there was widespread concern about the apparently increasing lack of respect for femininity and motherhood in post-war society as a whole. The behaviour of 'flappers' was of particular concern, as young females were seen as particularly vulnerable to the influence of socialists, and, as we have seen, the behaviour of free-spirited young women in nightclubs was a very clear symbol of supposedly changing gender boundaries.

As well as invoking a threat that needed to be defended against, morality was a key part of the Conservative strategy of appealing to women voters. David Jarvis has shown that the Conservative reaction to the changing position of women in society was to champion a slightly modified, but essentially traditional, female role with home and family life central to their appeals.[72] They emphasised women's childbearing, nurturing, and civilising tasks, associating traditional gender roles with sociality stability. In particular, they wanted to create women as 'responsible citizens' and looked to the older female electorate to set a firm example to the younger. Neil McCrillis's study of the Women's Unionist Organisation (WUO) claims that after 1918 these Conservative 'women became . . . the matrons of society, crusading for greater morality and spirituality at home and in society'.[73] They campaigned for the home and family, maternity and health care, housing, and local government and were increasingly active in

[70] Joynson-Hicks, *Do We Need*, p. 7.

[71] McCrillis, *British Conservative Party*, p. 76.

[72] See David Jarvis, 'Mrs Maggs and Betty: the Conservative appeal to women voters in the 1920s', *Twentieth Century British History* 5 (1994), pp. 129–52; David Jarvis, 'The Conservative Party and the politics of gender, 1900–1939', in Francis and Zweiniger-Bargielowska, *Conservatives*, pp. 172–93.

[73] McCrillis, *British Conservative Party*, pp. 71–2.

morality campaigns. Even before 1918, they had demanded action on brothels and gin palaces and after the war the WUO played a key role in the passage of the 1923 Intoxicating Liquors Act, which prohibited alcohol consumption by minors. It also pressed the government in 1923 to pass the Dangerous Drugs Act. Thus, a concern with the position of women in society and an appeal to female voters based on morality were key aspects of popular Conservatism in the 1920s. It appears to have been a highly successful tactic, McKibbin describing the Conservative lead among women in the 1920s as 'huge'.[74] Both explain the party's willingness to see action taken against nightclubs.

There was also a populist aspect to Conservative claims to represent mainstream morality, which was important within the context of the nightclub campaign. Baldwin refuted the idea that Labour was the natural home of decent working men and women. As McKibbin has shown, the Conservatives successfully isolated the organised working class from the rest of the working class, by portraying them as sectional, aggressive, greedy, and un-English. Yet Williamson argues that in addition to the negative ideological stereotypes that McKibbin highlights, Baldwin used a range of positive ones in relation to the working class—he celebrated the commonsensical, decent, self-reliant, contented working man and woman.[75] He wanted to create a populist political language that would compete with socialism, and it was one that emphasised 'decency' and 'respectability'. As Martin Pugh has noted, the encouragement of 'working class respectability' was a long-standing feature of Conservatism, and it took on new urgency with the arrival of universal suffrage.[76] Courting working-class notions of respectability and decency was thus central to Conservative strategy.

In addition, Baldwin believed that ostentatious displays of wealth and pleasure-seeking were detrimental to social cohesion. Jix echoed these sentiments, promoting a self-image of hard work, clean living, and self-control to act as a role model for others. An indication of Baldwin's feelings on the matter come from his 1925 warning that the 'vulgar luxury which flaunts itself in London' formed the 'best propaganda [for] revolutionary doctrine'.[77] In this context, an attack on the supposedly bohemian activities of nightclub goers makes perfect sense. The clientele of nightclubs were not respectable working- or middle-class citizens, they were those at the margins—upper-class socialites and lower-class criminals. In the public's eye, they were seen to share common traits—excessive drunkenness, gambling, vice, and a lifestyle of idleness. Within this context the Joynson-Hicks campaign makes more sense. The excesses of nightclub owners and their clientele were shown in sharp contrast to the behaviour of 'normal', family-loving Britons. In attacking these people, and these traits, the Home Secretary could

[74] McKibbin, 'Class and conventional wisdom', p. 285.

[75] Williamson, 'Doctrinal politics', p. 195.

[76] Martin Pugh, 'Popular Conservatism in Britain: continuity and change, 1880–1987', *Journal of British Studies* 27 (1988), p. 255.

[77] Speech given in Aberdeen, 5 Nov. 1925, cited in Williamson, *Stanley Baldwin*, pp. 214–15.

claim to be protecting the law abiding, respectable 'ordinary' man and woman to whom the party wanted to appeal.

Just as the shift in the language of popular Conservatism that Lawrence identifies in Edwardian Conservatism was the result of the party's response to the changing character of Liberalism and the emergence of Labour politics, then the shift of the 1920s was also a reaction to party realignment in the face of franchise extension. The Tories sought to occupy the middle—or rather the middle-class—ground. They were seeking to occupy the political place left vacant by the Liberals and to position themselves vis-à-vis Labour. They sought a wide electoral alliance based around their traditional supporters, and the emerging middle and aspiring 'decent' working class. The nightclub campaign shows that the issue of 'morality' and 'respectability' were a vital part of this revitalised popular Conservatism. Only within this context can Joynson-Hicks's campaign be fully understood.

15

Arthur Henderson: An Evolving Liberal Internationalist among Labour Little-Englanders

Martin Ceadel

In his penetrating article on 'Arthur Henderson as Labour Leader' Ross McKibbin observed that, although during his party's first thirty years he seemed 'to have a centrality shared by no other man', in 'almost every way the labour movement developed against his wishes'.[1] Yet, as McKibbin would surely have pointed out had he not forsaken the life of Henderson for the social underpinnings of British politics, in foreign affairs, where the long-serving party secretary preached liberal internationalism to his colleagues, he got much of his own way. This is implicit in Mary Agnes Hamilton's, F. M. Leventhal's, and Chris Wrigley's biographies, which, despite an absence of personal peccadilloes to keep their pages turning, are of the highest standard, and is explicit in Henry Winkler's seminal studies of Labour's international policy.[2] Building on these accounts, the present essay shows how foreign affairs brought Henderson not only a measure of reconciliation between his ideological Liberalism and his institutional Labourism but a reputational breakthrough from party functionary to world statesman, whilst perhaps also contributing to an under-recognised political miscalculation in August 1931. It also questions some recent accounts of Labour's foreign-policy attitudes by tracing the evolutionary process whereby Henderson's liberal internationalism first disentangled itself from and then confronted the tenacious little-Englandism that many Labour activists favoured in the form of radical isolationism, war resistance, or pacifism.

Born in 1863, the young iron moulder, trade unionist, Wesleyan lay preacher, and Liberal activist discovered analogies between the industrial relations to which

[1] Ross McKibbin, *The Ideologies of Class: Social Relations in Britain 1880–1950* (Oxford, 1990), pp. 42, 64.

[2] M. A. Hamilton, *Arthur Henderson* (1938); F. M. Leventhal, *Arthur Henderson* (Manchester, 1989); Chris Wrigley, *Arthur Henderson* (Cardiff, 1990). H. Winkler, 'Arthur Henderson', in Gordon Craig and Felix Gilbert (eds.), *The Diplomats 1919–1939* (Princeton, 1953), pp. 311–43; 'The emergence of a Labor foreign policy in Great Britain, 1918–1929', *Journal of Modern History* 28 (1956), pp. 246–58; *Paths Not Taken: British Labour and international policy in the 1920s* (Chapel Hill, 1994).

he initially devoted himself and the international relations in which he ultimately specialised: each was a conflict-prone sphere in which arbitration should be applied and law introduced. Henderson's political patrons, Sir Joseph Whitwell Pease, Robert Spence Watson, and Jack Pease, were Quakers who successively presided over the Peace Society in the period 1881 to 1914. And one of his closest adult friends, the Revd Henry Carter, became Methodism's leading pacifist.[3] Unsurprisingly, Henderson became a *pacificist*, condemning the 'iniquitous' Boer War and attending peace meetings,[4] though he never went as far as pacifism. In other words, he believed that war could and should be abolished by reforming either the international system or the states that composed it, but that until this was achieved, military force was legitimate for defensive and progressive purposes.[5]

In 1903 Henderson metamorphosed from Barnard Castle's Liberal agent into its Labour Representation Committee MP. He switched parties not because of an intellectual conversion but because his trade union changed its affiliation. In domestic politics, of course, his success as a Labour politician contributed to the demise of the Liberalism with which he remained personally comfortable. But in the international sphere it ultimately helped the liberal variety of *pacificism* hold its own against the radical and socialist versions. A fusion of Cobdenite confidence in the integrating power of commerce with Gladstonian trust in an emerging public law of Europe, liberal *pacificism* was always internationalist in orientation, though prior to 1914 it rarely called for a world organization. By the early twentieth century it was being queried by radicals convinced that economic interests could push Britain into war, as could a diplomatic and imperial elite that concocted political entanglements for its own professional satisfaction. Radical *pacificism*'s remedy was thus democratic control within little England rather than regulation of inter-state relations. At the political margin, moreover, a few socialists were beginning to insist that capitalism itself caused war, which meant that neither liberal nor radical remedies were adequate: a socio-economic transformation was needed; and in the meantime any attempt to fight should be challenged by a general strike, a policy that became known as war resistance. Socialist *pacificism* was internationalist in its aspiration that war be resisted multilaterally, though little-England to the extent that it was prepared to go it alone if concerted action proved impossible. It was, however, only rarely advocated in Britain prior to the Bolshevik revolution: most early advocates of

[3] Leventhal, *Arthur Henderson*, p. 5; Hamilton, *Arthur Henderson*, pp. 67, 218; M. Ceadel, *Pacifism in Britain 1914–1945: The Defining of a Faith* (Oxford, 1980), p. 68. Henderson was never as close as McKibbin suggests (*The Ideologies of Class*, pp. 45–6, 52) to Fred Maddison, secretary of the International Arbitration League, the former Workmen's Peace Association: the official of the Friendly Society of Ironfounders who helped Henderson had similar views but was Joseph Maddison. Where better than a *Festschrift* to correct so uncharacteristic a slip?

[4] Wrigley, *Arthur Henderson*, p. 71. *The Times*, 20 March 1909, p. 6; 20 May 1909, p. 9.

[5] The pacifism–*pacificism* distinction originated in A. J. P. Taylor, *The Trouble Makers* (London, 1957), p. 51 n., and was developed in Martin Ceadel, *Thinking about Peace and War* (Oxford, 1987).

socialism in domestic politics, such as Ramsay MacDonald, adopted an essentially radical approach to international relations.

Prior to the First World War these strands of *pacificism* were differentiated only by the clearest-minded of progressives. Henderson's occasional statements about international affairs constituted an eclectic blend of liberal engagement with and radical detachment from European affairs, though he consistently opposed a general strike against war. When Europe succumbed to conflict in 1914, he at first preferred radical detachment, joining Keir Hardie in demanding 'vast demonstrations against war in every industrial centre' on 1 August, and speaking at Labour's peace rally in Trafalgar Square the following day.[6] Admittedly, he did not intervene, other than to make a procedural complaint, in the Commons debate of 3 August, during which Sir Edward Grey won over most doubting Liberals, including that doughty parliamentarian William Pringle, who in consequence made the liberal internationalist declaration: 'We who hold to Liberal tradition, and still honour Mr Gladstone's ideas, are bound in a conflict of this kind to range ourselves on the side of international morality against the forces of blood and iron.' But Henderson undoubtedly approved of MacDonald's radical-isolationist criticism of the foreign secretary for failing to show 'that our country is in danger'.[7] His invitation to join the Neutrality League had not arrived in time; but on 4 August he assured its organizer, Norman Angell, that 'it would have given me the greatest pleasure to have associated with you'.[8]

This debate about British intervention gradually exposed the fault lines between liberal and radical *pacificism.* The former, exemplified by Pringle, was engaged and pro-France. It soon found an outlet in calls for a league of nations, a project taken up initially by loyal Liberals, who, having supported British intervention, were looking to justify the propaganda claim that theirs was a war to end war. By contrast, radical *pacificism,* exemplified by MacDonald, was detached and pro-Germany. It subsequently expressed itself through the Union of Democratic Control (UDC), set up privately on 10 August by MacDonald and Angell along with C. P. Trevelyan, who had resigned as a junior minister when Britain intervened, and E. D. Morel, a long-standing conspiracy theorist in respect of Anglo-French diplomacy. Ostensibly, it merely called for foreign policy to be carried on publicly, through an international council, and with popular consent. Implicitly, however, it accused Britain of contributory negligence in respect of the war, which made it highly controversial once the *Morning Post* revealed its existence on 10 September. The UDC's populist defiance, which contrasted with the league movement's elitist timidity, enthused Liberal and more especially Labour dissidents. The divide between liberal and radical *pacificism* thus became political-sociological as well as intellectual.

[6] Wrigley, *Arthur Henderson,* p. 70.

[7] *Hansard,* 65 HC cols. 1853–4, 1830, 1880.

[8] Arthur Henderson to Norman Angell, 4 August 1914, cited in Marvin Swartz, *The Union of Democratic Control in British Politics during the First World War* (Oxford, 1971), p. 148n.

Instinctively rather than consciously, Henderson inhabited both camps. Germany's violation of Belgium turned him into a resolute supporter of the war: he became chairman of the Labour Party when MacDonald resigned, and, as its first-ever minister, accepted conscription. He embraced internationalism, endorsing a 'congress of nations' in January 1915[9] and again after President Wilson's conversion turned a league into a practical post-war possibility.[10] Yet Henderson was also one of the UDC's 'first supporters',[11] and joined its general council knowing it had become a contentious body.[12] Moreover, he 'rejoiced' at the overthrow of the Tsar, although it encouraged those calling for a negotiated peace, as the UDC now was: in particular, the International Socialist Bureau proposed a conference at Stockholm that enemy leftists would attend as well as allies and neutrals. The war cabinet dispatched Henderson to Russia, where his discoveries of June–July 1917 about its fragile morale decisively affected British politics. Previously an opponent of the Stockholm conference, he now concluded it was essential to keeping the Russians at war.[13] Discovering, in Wrigley's words, 'a new and fulfilling role, that of the international man . . . a major politician who looked beyond merely national considerations' and who also appreciated the importance of the international labour movement,[14] he quit the war cabinet in August when it rejected the Stockholm proposal. (His replacement, G. N. Barnes, was, incidentally, an even more committed internationalist, being chairman of the League to Abolish War, a society founded in May of the previous year to promote an international organisation with its own military force.[15])

Thereafter Henderson joined MacDonald in reuniting Labour's pro- and anti-war wings on the basis of UDC policies. Even so, inspired by an unusual combination of realism and idealism, he kept his party committed to a league of nations too. Realism was to the fore when he stated soon after America's entry into the war that 'a League of free peoples' could 'provide the necessary guarantees for the security of the world against aggressive military action'.[16] Idealism was evident in a short book he compiled in December 1917, which insisted that the international court of justice to be created as part of the league's machinery should apply not only international law but the principles of equity, thereby tackling even 'non-justiciable disputes, i.e. disputes which cannot be covered by international jurisprudence but which can be settled by moral law'. In addition, to reassure the UDC, he linked internationalism organically with democratisation: 'The coming of world democracy . . . involves international co-operation

[9] McKibbin, *Ideologies of Class*, p. 51.

[10] *The Times*, 12 December 1916, p. 9. See also 16 January 1917, p. 7.

[11] H. M. Swanwick, *Builders of Peace, Being Ten Years' History of the Union of Democratic Control* (London, 1924), pp. 34–5.

[12] Swartz, *The Union of Democratic Control*, pp. 147–8.

[13] J. M. Winter, *Socialism and the Challenge of War: ideas and politics in Britain, 1912–18* (London, 1974), pp. 243–55.

[14] Wrigley, *Arthur Henderson*, p. 120.

[15] Martin Ceadel, *Semi-detached Idealists: the British Peace Movement and International Relations, 1854–1945* (Oxford, 2000), pp. 231, 234.

[16] *The Times*, 21 May 1918, p. 5.

and goodwill.'[17] Likewise a pamphlet he wrote during 1918 argued that a true league

will bring foreign policy under the control of popularly elected assemblies resolved to maintain the sovereign rights of peoples. It implies the suppression of secret diplomacy and the development of Parliamentary control over Cabinets. It will mean that a vigilant watch will be kept over the activities of Foreign Ministers, diplomatists, and the agents of international finance. It involves full publicity for all agreements between States. It will render powerless for further mischief the evil influence of the armaments trusts which are so largely responsible for the awful tragedy in which the world is at present engaged.[18]

By contrast, Gilbert Murray, an Asquithian academic who was emerging as a leader of the league movement, not only denied that diplomacy could dispense with secrecy but insisted: 'The principle that will solve the problem of war is not Democracy but Internationalism.'[19]

Although a League was duly created at the Paris peace conference, its limitations and association with the Treaty of Versailles upset even its fan club, the League of Nations Union (LNU). Henderson himself complained on 17 November 1919:

The League at present is not an all inclusive League of Nations; it is a coalition of victorious powers. If that League is to do its proper work . . . it will have to cease to be a coalition of victorious powers and become an all-inclusive League of the Peoples. Another thing that we look to the League of Nations to set about, and that as speedily as possible, is a revision of the Peace Treaty.[20]

Two months later, he appeared at a meeting organised by the Widnes branch of the LNU alongside Lord Robert Cecil, a maverick Tory ex-minister who now devoted himself to the internationalist cause. Cecil artfully wooed the largely leftist audience by presenting the League as the best instrument for improving relations with Soviet Russia. Henderson returned the compliment by stating that 'the Labour Party regarded Lord Robert as an ally. When the time came they would find him on the floor of the People's Parliament as the champion of revision of the League'.[21] But in fact Cecil soon decided that to talk the League down in this way would simply play into the hands of the nationalist right. The LNU permanently changed tack, putting a positive spin on the achievements of the flawed and struggling new institution at Geneva.

Between the peace settlement and the 1924 Labour government, the UDC outgunned the LNU, its hostility to the League and its uncritical admirers being

[17] Arthur Henderson, *The Aims of Labour* (London, n.d), pp. 39–40, 78–9. (The preface was dated 22 December 1917.) For the generality of league thinking, see Martin Ceadel, 'Supranationalism in the British peace movement during the early twentieth century', in Andrea Bosco (ed.), *The Federal Idea*, vol. 1: *The History of Federalism from the Enlightenment to 1945* (London, 1991), pp. 169–91.

[18] Reprinted in Viscount Grey et al., *The League of Nations* (London, 1919), pp. 108, 110.

[19] Ibid., p. 138.

[20] *Hansard*, 121 HC col. 697.

[21] *The Times*, 14 January 1920, p. 9.

endorsed by the growing minority of socialist *pacificists*. Its attitudes permeated *Control of Foreign Policy: Labour's programme*, a party pamphlet of 1921 that did not mention the League but insisted that 'irresponsible autocracy and oligarchy are still today firmly entrenched in the Foreign Office in Downing Street', and claimed that a Labour government would 'dispense at once with all professional Ambassadors and Ministers'.[22] When MacDonald became Labour leader again the following year, he consistently refused the honorary presidency of the LNU that came with the position, accentuating this snub by agreeing to be a vice-president of the by-then moribund Peace Society instead.[23] (On becoming prime minister, moreover, he was to instruct his private secretary not to 'bring to his notice any letter containing any mention of the League of Nations Union'.[24]) Both Britain's near-involvement in war during the Chanak crisis of October 1922 and France's controversial occupation of the Ruhr in January 1923 further increased radical-*pacificist* sentiment.

Henderson did not challenge UDC negativity during its heyday, but increasingly sought to balance it with positive policies. His early years as a trade union official had taught him the importance of active conciliation and compromise. And his recent efforts first to salvage the Second International and then to establish the Labour and Socialist International required him to engage diplomatically with his European counterparts. By contrast, as Mrs Hamilton noted, Philip Snowden always manifested 'a dangerous measure of post-war ILP [Independent Labour Party] hostility to France' because he lacked either trade union or Continental experience.[25] One of Henderson's favourite sayings was that 'Labour has its international organisation, international ideals and an international following', as he put it in the Commons.[26] His pamphlet *Labour and Foreign Affairs*, written late in 1922, used almost identical language to explain the party's conviction that 'international competition and hostilities must be superseded by international co-operation and friendship'. Admittedly, the pamphlet declared in UDC-friendly fashion that 'the conception of the League of Nations has been perverted' by being turned into 'an instrument of Allied policy', and that the League 'should play a part in the revision of frontiers'. Moreover, it humoured socialist *pacificists* by attributing all international tension to 'the ambitions of imperialism and the operations of capitalism'. But its main argument was liberal internationalist: the Covenant had to be strengthened by making arbitration compulsory and providing collective defence. And, though rejecting 'the friendship of one country at the expense of the probable enmity of another', it aspired to 'the friendliest of relations with France'.[27] When in the Commons on 19 February 1923 Morel's call for a top-to-bottom revision of Versailles stung Cecil into accusing Labour of failing to 'recognize the

[22] Labour Party, *Control of Foreign Policy: Labour's Programme* (London, n.d. [1921]).
[23] Ceadel, *Semi-detached Idealists*, pp. 195, 255.
[24] D. S. Birn, *The League of Nations Union 1918–1945* (Oxford, 1981), p. 51.
[25] Hamilton, *Arthur Henderson*, p. 316.
[26] *Hansard*, 160 HC col. 710 (19 February 1923).
[27] Arthur Henderson, *Labour and Foreign Affairs* (London, n.d. [1922]), pp. 1, 6, 9, 10, 11–13.

importance of friendship with France', Henderson professed surprise at Cecil's accusation, and, while making clear that his party 'cannot support any French Government which chooses to act as the military dictator of Europe', claimed it was 'neither pro-German or anti-French' but resolutely pro-League.[28]

By then, Henderson championed what he came to call 'the tripartite system of arbitration, national security, and reduction of armaments'.[29] All liberal internationalists did so; and all agreed that the compulsory arbitration of every dispute (which the League Covenant had not required) could alone objectively identify aggression (as the refusal to arbitrate). Yet they differed over the relationship between security on the one hand and disarmament and revision on the other. Those at the realist end of the liberal internationalist spectrum, like Lord Robert Cecil and the LNU leadership, believed that security, particularly for France, had to be provided before disarmament could be attempted, and that, again to avoid antagonizing France, revision of the peace settlement had to be deferred indefinitely. Henderson was at the idealist end, however, being convinced both that disarmament could be agreed as part of the same package that delivered security, and that treaty revision could not be ignored even in the short term. So, although dismissive at the June 1923 party conference of an 'absurd and futile'[30] ILP attempt to commit Labour to vote against the service estimates, Henderson joined his colleagues in opposing the Draft Treaty of Mutual Assistance that Cecil proposed to the League Assembly in September 1923: this was an up-front security scheme designed to encourage France to disarm in due course. In a speech at Burnley the following February, moreover, Henderson demanded treaty revision, which was tactless because MacDonald, by then both prime minister and foreign secretary, was seeking French co-operation for a reparations settlement. Lacking a parliamentary majority, this first Labour government enjoyed policy flexibility only in external affairs, where it could rely on crown-prerogative powers and largely ignore the Commons—a paradoxical predicament given that its UDC inheritance demanded parliamentary control of foreign policy. Moreover, MacDonald was keen to exploit his reputation as a peacemaker, now belatedly an asset. Henderson must have known that his revisionist remarks would appear anti-France, something that he normally tried to avoid: indeed, in another irony, during the second Labour government his and MacDonald's positions would be reversed, with Henderson being more concerned than his prime minister about Gallic sensibilities. His Burnley speech was too forceful to be merely the result of simple deference to conference resolutions, as Mrs Hamilton loyally suggested.[31] He was almost certainly venting his anger at MacDonald's attempt first to exclude him from the cabinet and then to palm him off with the inappropriate War Office before conceding the less-than-ideal Home Office.

[28] *Hansard*, 160 HC cols. 685–7, 708–14.
[29] *The Times*, 13 October 1924, p. 8.
[30] Labour Party, *Report of 23rd Annual Conference* (London, 1923), pp. 232–3.
[31] Hamilton, *Arthur Henderson*, pp. 239, 268.

But although the oddity of this fact has passed unnoticed, Henderson slipped his departmental leash to spend six weeks in Geneva formulating the replacement for the Draft Treaty of Mutual Assistance that became known as the Geneva Protocol. Its 'vital principle', as Mrs Hamilton noted, was 'that pooled security becomes operative after, and only after, all-round disarmament'.[32] Addressing his constituents the following month, Henderson explained that, whereas Cecil's proposal 'would lull the nations into a false sense of security—security of a military kind', his own alternative would provide sanctions only as 'a last resort. They were not necessarily sanctions of a military character. The need for them might never arise. The moral, judicial, and arbitral determinations would, in his judgment, practically restrain any state from going to war. Military, naval, and aerial measures were the last of the sanctions to be applied.' Henderson also pointed out that unlike Cecil's remedy, his 'did not stereotype and fix the present political system of Europe' but implicitly allowed for territorial revision.[33] Yet continuing isolationist doubts meant that Henderson's Geneva Protocol had yet to be endorsed by the Labour cabinet at the time of its fall.

With hindsight, however, the protocol's formulation marks the moment at which the UDC's hold over progressive opinion slipped.[34] The 1924 Labour government had discovered that little-Englandism alone could not resolve the Franco-German quarrel. The UDC lost its dynamo when Morel died two weeks after Labour left office. By the logic of adversary politics the rejection of the Geneva Protocol by the incoming Conservatives, who toyed with a military pact with France before opting for the fudge of Locarno, caused Labour to become its posthumous admirer: for example, Sir Oswald Mosley, who as a Labour MP chaired the National Peace Council in the mid-1920s and took an interest in such issues, came to regard the protocol as 'the greatest instrument of international peace ever devised'.[35] Finally, the reduction of the Liberals to minor-party status weakened the socialist-*pacificist* objection that the 'policy of the League of Nations was the policy of Liberalism and not of Socialism'.[36]

Admittedly, the General Strike of May 1926 complicated matters briefly: the next Labour conference carried by acclamation a resolution calling on workers to resist 'any threat of war, so-called defensive or offensive',[37] which Fenner Brockway, an ILP stalwart and former conscientious objector, had proposed, and Arthur Ponsonby, a leading member of the UDC who had subsequently become a pacifist, had seconded. This was unmistakeably an expression of little-Englandism. At this point Henderson, now fully aware of the internationalist-isolationist divide, tilted decisively towards the former. Previously, Labour's main foreign-policy advisers had been former radical politicians recruited via the UDC; but

[32] Ibid., p. 248.
[33] *The Times*, 13 October 1924, p. 8. See also *Hansard*, 182 HC col. 295 (24 March 1925).
[34] As noted by Swartz, *The Union of Democratic Control*, p. 221.
[35] Ceadel, *Semi-detached Idealists*, p. 250. Labour Party, *Report of 28th Annual Conference* (London, 1928), p. 187.
[36] Labour Party, *Report of 25th Annual Conference* (London, 1925), p. 253.
[37] Labour Party, *Report of 26th Annual Conference* (London, 1926), p. 255.

Henderson turned instead to two young, pro-League, and socialist academics, Hugh Dalton and Philip Noel Baker. Their joint efforts ensured that the 1928 party programme, *Labour and the Nation*, emphasised that the party 'holds that the whole structure of peace and of a foreign policy of co-operation must be built firmly on the foundation of the League of Nations'. This document did not propose to revive the Geneva Protocol, but embraced the Optional Clause and the General Act of Arbitration, Conciliation and Judicial Settlement, claiming that in conjunction with the other provisions of the League Covenant they would 'abolish war, and thus provide a complete solution of the vital problem of national security in Europe'.[38] By then the UDC was in disarray: in 1928 it was accused of having 'no coherent policy' by Ponsonby and another long-standing activist, Helena Swanwick, who both resigned when it refused to repudiate all international sanctions.[39]

Labour successfully played the League card in the 1929 election, which took place just after the tenth anniversary of the armistice had produced an outburst of anti-war literature, by which time the LNU had entrenched itself in civil society as a partial substitute for a decayed Liberal Party and an attenuated protestant nonconformity. In the second Labour government Henderson could not be denied either the Foreign Office or the right to appoint not only Dalton and Noel Baker as his junior ministers there but also Cecil as an in-house adviser and League delegate. Despite his hectoring style Henderson's purposiveness appealed to his officials at home and opposite numbers abroad. At The Hague in August he secured a compromise over the Young Plan after Snowden's little-England intransigence had almost wrecked it. At the League's tenth Assembly in September, with his copy of the Covenant ever-present in his pocket, Henderson was the dominant figure, with the supreme advantages of not only representing a great power and being a practised negotiator but of believing in his brief. As he put it on returning home: 'On the paramount questions of arbitration, security, and disarmament, the British delegation has, I venture to say, spoken with the voice of conviction.'[40] Shortly afterwards he received a remarkable ovation from the 1929 party conference after declaring: 'We are out to end war. We are out to end the waste and folly of competitive armaments which the nation still maintains.'[41] Contemporaries recognised the enhancement of his reputation: the June 1930 edition of Egon Wertheimer's *Portrait of the Labour Party* noted that had he 'died before the setting up of MacDonald's second Cabinet . . . he would not have been a figure in the political history of Great Britain. His work at the Foreign Office changed all this—almost at one blow'. Previously 'regarded in the Labour Party as a somewhat matter-of-fact and even bureaucratic person, as a man lacking in imagination and vision', and moreover as someone whom MacDonald could

[38] Labour Party, *Labour and the Nation* (London, 1928), pp. 44, 46.
[39] Ceadel, *Semi-detached Idealists*, p. 266–7.
[40] Hamilton, *Arthur Henderson*, pp. 322–3, 332.
[41] Labour Party, *Report of 29th Annual Conference* (London, 1929), p. 210.

always master, he had shown himself on becoming foreign secretary to be 'a man with ideas of his own, able to display personal initiative'.[42]

By then the economic depression was destroying such chance as multilateral disarmament ever had. Though at the 1930 League Assembly Henderson reaffirmed his 'profound belief' that 'nothing can make our peoples truly secure until a Treaty of General Disarmament has been made', he admitted: 'The pace is slow, and the peoples of the world are growing impatient and doubtful of our good faith.'[43] Yet his response was to encourage that impatience and doubt. When in January 1931 a world disarmament conference was finally summoned for February of the following year, he told a rally: 'If the people want disarmament, they can have it. If they will exert their will, they can compel results... I hope you will show the Governments that however far they may be ready to go their people will be behind them.'[44] His desire to egg the public on was already evident in the desire to create 'an organization, under F[oreign] O[ffice] control, to instruct the British public in "the arts of peace"', which, as he later privately admitted, was one of his unfulfilled goals as foreign secretary.[45] He presumably took this line in the belief that a Labour government would make a bold initiative at Geneva and therefore need the political protection of a supportive electorate; but it stoked up excessive popular hopes. In a notably optimistic Burge Memorial Lecture delivered in May he 'with the voice of faith' expressed the belief that 'our generation may yet succeed in wiping out the scourge of international war'. Yet by then he had dropped both his early expectations that the League could represent 'peoples' rather than governments and his former reservations about its constitution, claiming instead: 'Twelve years after their labours were accomplished, we can say without doubt or hesitation that the authors of the Covenant laboured well.'[46] It was unsurprising that his lecture was published by the LNU as a pamphlet. That same month Henderson accepted the presidency of the world disarmament conference; but although it was an honour to be regarded as the obvious candidate, and he was experienced at multi-tasking, this additional responsibility was probably a mistake. It required impartiality, so Henderson would have been in a difficult position if also running British disarmament policy, as he then expected to be.[47] The conference needed bold national inputs more than good chairmanship.

By increasing his self-confidence and his irritation with MacDonald's and Snowden's residual UDC attitudes,[48] the foreign secretaryship may have made Henderson more intransigent during Britain's August 1931 financial crisis, with

[42] Egon Wertheimer, *Portrait of the Labour Party* (2nd edn.: London, 1930), pp. 291–2.

[43] Cited in Hamilton, *Arthur Henderson*, pp. 337–8.

[44] *Headway*, March 1931: supplement, 1.

[45] Gordon Martel (ed.), The Times *and Appeasement: The Journals of A. L. Kennedy, 1932–1939* (Camden 5th Series, vol. 15: Cambridge, 2000), p. 33 (entry for 16 April 1932).

[46] Arthur Henderson, *Consolidating World Peace* (London: LNU pamphlet no. 301, July 1931), pp. 17, 21, 31.

[47] F. P. Walters, *A History of the League of Nations* (London, 1960 edn.), p. 502.

[48] David Carlton, *MacDonald versus Henderson: The Foreign Policy of the Second Labour Government* (New York, 1970), pp. 200–11.

disastrous consequences. Having previously as a minister accepted policies required by his government but hated by his party (such as conscription in 1916), he now blocked cuts in unemployment benefit sought by MacDonald and Snowden yet opposed by the labour movement.[49] The administration's resultant collapse produced a National Government dominated by the Conservatives, thereby depriving Henderson of influence over British disarmament policy at a crucial moment. It also reduced his authority over the party: although he replaced MacDonald as leader, his defeat in the October general election meant that George Lansbury had to act for him in the Commons; and with Ponsonby taking over in the Lords, Labour was led in both houses by outspoken pacifists as, lurching leftwards to Henderson's alarm, it sought socialist purity even in foreign policy.

Just as the burden of presiding over an ill-starred conference was added to that of curbing Labour's leftism, his long-standing gallstone problem flared up. Visiting Geneva in May 1932 Ponsonby found him 'terribly changed by his illness', and concluded that 'he ought not to be Leader of the Party *and* Chairman of the Disarmament Conference'.[50] Soon after telling Labour delegates in October 1932 of his disappointment 'at the meagre results of the Disarmament Conference' in its first eight months and being rebuffed over domestic tactics,[51] Henderson resigned the party leadership. He could thereafter concentrate on disarmament, but by February 1933 was adjudged 'desperately tired' by a visitor to Geneva.[52] A month later he considered formulating his own scheme, but desisted when MacDonald belatedly offered one of his own.[53] Frustrated at France's and Germany's incompatible demands, he admitted privately to the National Peace Council that 'it almost baffles me how we can bring together these two Powers'.[54] Yet he persevered, his 'guileless and naïve dragging out of the conference' annoying Beatrice Webb, who complained that he 'absurdly overrates the binding value of *signed documents*'.[55] She had a point: had his efforts somehow conjured up a disarmament agreement, it might have had no more substance than the Kellogg–Briand Pact of 1928, to which he attached more importance than now seems warranted. Even so, he could have prevented Germany winning the propaganda battle over disarmament's inevitable failure: that the National Government was to be so spectacularly worsted by Hitler in this regard was the more remarkable for the fact that its policy throughout the conference was more favourable towards Germany than towards France.[56]

[49] Philip Williamson, *National Crisis and National Government: British Politics, the Economy and Empire, 1926–1932* (Cambridge, 1992), pp. 310–17, 429–31.

[50] Entry for 24 May 1932: Ponsonby diary (transcript), private collection.

[51] Labour Party, *Report of the 32nd Annual Conference*, p. 232.

[52] Beverley Nichols, *Cry Havoc!* (London, 1933), pp. 144–5.

[53] T. R. Davies, *The Possibilities of Transnational Activism: The Campaign for Disarmament between the Two World Wars* (Leiden, 2007), p. 140.

[54] Minutes, NPC, 28 September 1933: British Library of Political and Economic Science.

[55] Cited in Wrigley, *Arthur Henderson*, pp. 181–2.

[56] According to Carolyn Kitching, *Britain and the Geneva Disarmament Conference* (Basingstoke, 2003), p. 203.

By summer 1933 Henderson was alarmed at British progressivism's response to Hitler's accession to Germany's chancellorship. Admittedly, because Nazism so obviously outranked Britain's diplomats and arms traders as a threat to peace, radical *pacificism* did not revive. Almost its only champion now was Helena Swanwick, who was to kill herself when war came. But there were upsurges of both pacifism, which Henry Carter now embraced, and war resistance, to which UDC co-founder Trevelyan was converted. In July Henderson issued a pamphlet, *Labour's Foreign Policy*, which acknowledged the new unpopularity among his colleagues of the League Covenant and Locarno on the grounds that by 'their terms this country is committed to "intervene in other people's quarrels" whether its own interests are involved or not'. It combined a justification of these commitments with an emphasis on the fact that others, notably the Kellogg-Briand Pact and the Optional Clause, restricted Britain's freedom to declare war.[57] Henderson thus proposed a Peace Act that would enshrine all such obligations in domestic law; and to revive his influence with party members he returned to parliament at a by-election on 1 September. Even so, Labour's conference at Hastings on 4 October passed by acclamation a resolution 'to take no part in war' that made no distinction between intervention in support of international law and intervention in contravention of it. Its proposer was Trevelyan, who declared: 'Individual resistance will not be enough to stop war in the rising tide of patriotism and fear. We who remember know that only by united resistance, politically and industrially organized, is there any chance of rulers who are bent on war listening.'

Labour's leaders ducked confrontation, as in 1926, and attempted education and deviousness instead. After patronising Trevelyan's resolution as the expression of a worthy pro-disarmament sentiment, Henderson made a left-wing case for liberal internationalism: 'The League of Nations was set up largely in response to the pressure of the Labour and Socialist Movement, and under the influence of Socialist thinkers. Its fundamental idea is precisely that for which we Socialists stand.' He also highlighted the proposed Peace Act, and insisted on 'the duty to boycott a peace-breaker'—a euphemism for collective security tailored to the ethos of the labour movement. This pro-League rhetoric had a short-term effect on Sir Stafford Cripps, a former moderate who since 1931 had become the leader of Labour's left. Previously teetering on the brink of war resistance, Cripps now urged that Henderson's speech be published as a pamphlet.[58] The party leadership also smuggled through a commitment to an international police force, buried deep in a long composite resolution, which ultimately enabled it to claim that Trevelyan's motion must logically have applied only to wars undertaken in contravention of the Covenant or similar obligations. But before it could do so, isolationist sentiment received a further boost when, a mere eight days after Labour's delegates left Hastings, Hitler pulled Germany out of the disarmament conference and the League.

[57] Arthur Henderson, *Labour's Foreign Policy* (London, 1933), pp. 10, 13, 20.
[58] Labour Party, *Report of 33rd Annual Conference* (London, 1933), pp. 186, 190–1.

In 1934, however, as little-Englandism eventually ebbed, Henderson and his aides won their party over to collective security, albeit by optimistically claiming that economic and naval pressure alone would normally suffice. Asked by the chairman of the LNU's Birmingham Central Youth Group whether support for the League required rearmament, Noel Baker thus insisted that it was 'a travesty of the argument for collective security to suggest that increased armaments are now required to enable Great Britain to play her part in collective guarantees'.[59] They also implied that Labour had never lapsed from its liberal internationalist faith. In his last conference speech, at Southport in October, Henderson thus claimed:

> At Hastings there were two resolutions that were carried. Some people seem to have forgotten that there were two and not one only. . . . Neither resolution contradicted nor invalidated the other, nor was ever intended to supersede the foreign policy by which the Labour Party has been guided for many years, and which we can say a serious attempt was made to apply by both the minority Labour Governments.

He argued that the party had 'very soon found there was a sense in which it was difficult to separate the question of war resistance from the wider question of preventing war by organizing peace' and that reliance on war resistance alone placed excessive demands on organised labour's industrial wing, whereas 'the Trade Union Movement alone should not be expected to bear the responsibility for stopping war'. He also reiterated the League's leftist credentials, arguing that the 'founding of the League was a revolutionary break with the tradition of international anarchy', and that peace could be achieved only 'by applying the Socialist principle of co-operation'. This time Henderson's efforts were backed up by Ernest Bevin, who, having got war resistance out of his system during the 1920s, had quickly taken Hitler's measure. After the socialist pacifist Wilfred Wellock had condemned collective security while professing loyalty to the League despite its being 'largely a broken institution', Bevin insisted that 'to support the League of Nations, as Mr Wellock does this afternoon, and not back it with power in certain eventualities, seems to me like a man joining a Union on condition that under no circumstances will you ever ask him to strike'.[60]

Labour's internationalists also secured the adoption of a new party programme, *For Socialism and Peace*, which made a strong commitment to a 'collective peace system'. The public was now ready for this message, as was to be revealed by the extraordinary success of the LNU's 'Peace Ballot' and the entrenchment in English usage of 'collective security' during spring 1935.[61] Having received the Nobel Peace Prize in December, when he surrendered the party secretaryship, Henderson celebrated with *Labour's Way to Peace*. Though claiming that the 'principles of Labour's foreign policy have not varied since the

[59] L. Haigh to Philip Noel Baker, 29 September 1934, and reply, 30 September 1934: NBKR 4/498.

[60] Labour Party, *Report of 34th Annual Conference* (London, 1934), pp. 153–8, 167, 170–1.

[61] Martin Ceadel, 'The first British referendum: the peace ballot, 1934–5', *EHR* 95 (1980), pp. 810–39.

world war', it confirmed the extent to which his own views had in fact been transformed during that time. In acknowledging the 'good people of liberal views, including many in the Liberal Party' who a decade previously 'were instinctively reacting against what they held to be the plain indisputable wrongs which the Treaties of Peace had perpetrated upon the defeated nations', Henderson (or his ghost writer) now asked: 'Could they have re-drawn the map as easily as they believed? Could they have found new frontiers which would have been approved by the universal conscience as self-evidently just?', and gave resoundingly negative answers. Moreover, whereas in 1917 he had wanted an international court to apply 'moral law', he now condemned as wholly fanciful the demand for a 'Court of Equity', 'a body of men . . . with the power to decree such changes in the territorial or other established rights of states as seemed good to them'. He had come to emphasise 'the realistic nature of the Covenant' and to mention the LNU no less approvingly. Although he continued to call for arbitration and disarmament, he now gave priority to the need 'to make a reality of the method of pooled defence by putting the whole power of the British Empire behind the League in exchange for other countries doing the same'. His claim that 'the roots of war lie deep in the private profit-making system of production' was perfunctory by comparison both with his assertion 'Our international faith is the soul of our Socialism' and with his final call for the youth of the world to join in 'the endeavour to bring into being the great Federation of the World as the visible embodiment of the Brotherhood of Man'.[62] The previous year the Hampstead branch of the party had unsuccessfully tried to expunge the phrase 'Brotherhood of Man' from *For Socialism and Peace* and replace it with 'international solidarity of the workers'.[63] Henderson's last political testament thus concluded on a defiantly liberal internationalist note.

His terminal illness began just as public support for collective security peaked in Britain at the start of the Abyssinian crisis: he lived to see Ponsonby resign the leadership in the Lords, Bevin force Lansbury's replacement by Attlee, and the League apply sanctions, albeit mild ones, against Mussolini. His death on 20 October 1935 spared him the discovery that much enthusiasm for the League had been of a fair-weather variety, even in his own party. But had he lived to learn that collective security could be achieved only by the rearmament of Britain and the encirclement of Germany, he would surely have bitten the bullet. His support for the First World War and subsequent opposition to war resistance suggest that he would have stood shoulder-to-shoulder with Bevin and Citrine in the Churchillian camp.

Despite a possible miscalculation in 1931 Henderson had been, in Michael Hughes's felicitous phrase, 'a practical utopian'.[64] Without him his party lacked a parliamentary heavyweight to give realism an internationalist and labourist

[62] Arthur Henderson, *Labour's Way to Peace* (London, 1935), pp. 48, 51–4, 78, 97, 109, 111.
[63] Labour Party, *For Socialism and Peace: The Labour Party's Programme of Action with Amendments & C. Proposed by Affiliated Societies* (London, September 1934), p. 11.
[64] Michael Hughes, *British Foreign Secretaries in an Uncertain World, 1919–1939* (Abingdon, 2006), p. 97.

spin, and so risked relapsing into foreign-policy negativity. For example, although Cripps had been hauled back largely by Henderson from the brink of war resistance in 1933, he was soon persuaded that 'the League of Nations composed of Capitalist Governments cannot end war' and that 'a blind reliance on the League of Nations as the sole weapon is to endanger peace'.[65] What Cripps described as 'the definite recession to Liberalism of the Labour Party'[66] caused him to reject League action against Mussolini as a quarrel among imperialists. In October 1936 Cripps even denied that it 'would be a bad thing for the British working class if Germany defeated us'.[67] The ideological purchase such a view then had within Labour's ranks meant that in 1937, when the parliamentary party stopped opposing arms estimates, it abstained rather than voted in favour; and Attlee felt obliged to endorse 'the general proposition that there is no agreement on foreign policy between a Labour Opposition and a Capitalist Government'.[68] Even after the gallant struggle of the Spanish Republic against its Francoist insurgents persuaded Cripps that not all military causes were capitalist-imperialist, and that he should support a 'peace front' of Britain, France, and the Soviet Union against fascism, he continued to prefer war resistance as long as the National Government remained in office. Cripps believed, in other words, Britain should pursue a little-England policy until its left came to power, and only then join a peace front. Fortunately for Labour, such absurdities were wiped from the public mind by the military crisis of 1940, the political importance of which McKibbin has recently stressed in his Ford Lectures.

Some recent historians have used 'internationalism' too loosely. Rhiannon Vickers has described it as the 'underlying basis' and 'overriding principle' of Labour's twentieth-century foreign policy, though she also claimed oxymoronically: 'Internationalism is an impulse that can be used to prescribe non-intervention in the pursuit of peace.' John Shepherd called Labour's first prime minister an 'instinctive internationalist'—evidently a considered phrase as it had appeared in his and Keith Laybourn's study of the first Labour government. And Caspar Sylvest classified MacDonald's and Morel's thinking as 'isolationist (liberal) internationalism' and Ponsonby's as 'pacifist internationalism' before more reasonably placing Henderson's and Angell's in a box marked 'pragmatic (liberal) internationalism'.[69] But though indeed anti-militarist and supportive of

[65] Stafford Cripps to Konni Zilliacus, 4 September 1934 (copy): NBKR 2/20, Churchill College, Cambridge.

[66] Stafford Cripps to Konni Martin: 25 September 1935: Kingsley Martin papers, Sussex University.

[67] Cited in Keith Middlemas, *The Diplomacy of Illusion: the British government and Germany 1937–39* (London, 1972), p. 106.

[68] C. R. Attlee, *The Labour Party in Perspective* (1937), p. 227.

[69] Rhiannon Vickers, *The Labour Party and the World*, vol. 1: *The Evolution of Labour's Foreign Policy, 1900–51* (Manchester, 2004), pp. 5, 193–4. Paul Corthorn and Jonathan Davis (eds.), *The British Labour Party and the Wider World: Domestic Politics, Internationalism and Foreign Policy* (London, 2008), pp. 29, 59–60. John Shepherd and Keith Laybourn, *Britain's First Labour Government* (Basingstoke, 2006), p. 131. For a subtler account see John Callaghan, *The Labour Party and Foreign Policy* (Abingdon, 2007).

the labour movement's transnational institutions, MacDonald, Morel, and Ponsonby, like Cripps, Snowden, and Swanwick, cannot helpfully be called internationalist to the extent that they pursued the little-England policies of radical isolationism, pacifism, or war resistance. This label implies a willingness to stand by international commitments, as Henderson, for all his optimism about transcending inter-state conflict, came to see more clearly than many of his colleagues.

16

An Ideology of Class: Neo-Liberalism and the Trade Unions, *c.*1930–79

Ben Jackson

In his classic paper 'Why was there no Marxism in Great Britain?', Ross McKibbin identified the relative class neutrality of the British state as one important historical impediment to the British working class embracing a radical 'rejectionist' political party. In particular, McKibbin noted that by the late nineteenth century the governing ideology of British class relations was such that

> the state was more or less compelled to withdraw from the sphere of industrial relations. Any attempt to give the market generally or bargaining in particular a legal or punitive framework infringed the understood basis of the state's stability: such a framework would have required the recasting not simply of employer-employee relationships but of the idea of the nation itself.

The result, McKibbin continued, was that 'the British unions were given a freedom of action unique in Europe and (as far as I know) in the world, unencumbered by law or opinion.' The 'market' was therefore excluded from 'politics', but in a fashion that weakened the hand of employers. As McKibbin noted: 'If, for example, one of the most dogmatically individualist of the Charity Organisation Society's ideologues, Helen Bosanquet, could see virtue in the propensity of the British working man to enrol in trade unions and co-ops then, one might say, all was lost.'[1]

This broadly accommodationist stance towards trade unions endured as ideological common sense for much of the twentieth century. But it had been tested to destruction by the 1980s, when a new set of industrial relations arrangements were put in place that excluded the 'market' from 'politics' in

Earlier versions of this chapter were presented at the 'Classes, Cultures and Politics' workshop at St John's College, Oxford in April 2009; the History of Recent Economics conference at Antwerp University in June 2009; and the Politics Seminar at Manchester University in October 2009. I am grateful to Roger Backhouse, Beatrice Cherrier, Kevin Morgan, Jonathan Quong, Zofia Stemplowska, Jim Tomlinson, the editors of this volume, and the participants on each of those occasions for very helpful feedback. The Institute of Economic Affairs and Lord Tebbit kindly granted permission to quote from private papers.

[1] Ross McKibbin, 'Why was there no Marxism in Great Britain?', *Ideologies of Class* (Oxford, 1990), pp. 27–30.

a fashion that decisively weakened the hand of the unions. This chapter examines the attitude of the post-Bosanquet generation of individualist ideologues to organised labour and their role in legitimising this late twentieth-century shift in the governing ideology of British industrial relations. It charts the history of the neo-liberal right's opposition to trade unionism, from neo-liberalism's earliest years as a subterranean movement against the collectivist politics of the 1930s and 1940s to the intellectual formation of Thatcherism in the 1970s. The chapter's focus is not exclusively British: it investigates a transatlantic intellectual network that explicitly sought to prescribe economic rules that were of universal validity, and there is a sense in which it forms a case study in the 'Americanisation' of British post-war politics.

Although the chapter is chiefly intended as a piece of intellectual history, it does have one further aim. In addition to giving a historical account of neo-liberal thinking about trade unions, the chapter also identifies some significant silences and ideological closures in this theorising. It will be my contention that these silences and closures tell us something about the underlying, less formally articulated social priorities of neo-liberal theorists and, not to put too fine a point on it, the interests that their theories served.

LAYING THE FOUNDATIONS: W. H. HUTT AND HENRY SIMONS

The leading exponents of neo-liberal doctrine did not think that there was much to be learned about trade unions from consulting the works of earlier, nineteenth-century liberal economists or even the works of classical economists such as Adam Smith who they otherwise revered. Nor did they harbour any illusions about the toxicity of their views for the liberal intelligentsia and the political classes alike. 'Questioning the virtues of the organised labour movement is like attacking religion, monogamy, motherhood, or the home', noted one (American) neo-liberal in 1944.[2] Long before Margaret Thatcher took her immediate Conservative predecessors to task for their consistent appeasement of the labour movement, free-market economists began their analysis of trade unionism by firmly rejecting the sentimentality and woolly thinking that they felt had led earlier liberals to accommodate a legitimate role for workers' combinations within their political economy.

Two early works gave a first approximation of the neo-liberal case. One was W. H. Hutt's *The Theory of Collective Bargaining*, published in 1930 and, significantly, republished in Britain in 1975 by the Institute of Economic Affairs (IEA).[3] Hutt studied at the LSE under Edwin Cannan, and worked for Ernest Benn's publishing company, before moving to South Africa for the bulk of his

[2] Henry Simons, 'Some reflections on syndicalism', *Journal of Political Economy* 52 (1944), p. 1.

[3] It was also republished in the United States in 1954 by the Free Press, a conservative publishing house.

career as a professional economist. He was an opponent of apartheid, the development of which he associated with the determination of white trade unionists to exclude non-white workers from skilled work.[4] Hutt was a stalwart member of the Mont Pèlerin Society, the elite international discussion group convened by Friedrich Hayek from 1947 onwards to revive market liberal ideas, and a leading contributor to the Society's deliberations on industrial relations. Hutt's book was not only a critique of the accommodationist stance taken towards workers' combinations by earlier generations of economists; it was also an explicit rejection of the labour history of the Webbs and the Hammonds that had valourised the rise of trade unionism. Sportingly, Hutt's preface suggested that readers who had not yet tackled the Webbs' *Industrial Democracy* should read four of its key chapters before diving into his own text.[5]

The second early statement of neo-liberal disquiet about trade unionism was developed independently by Henry Simons in a 1944 article entitled 'Some reflections on syndicalism'.[6] Simons was based at the Chicago Law School for most of his career and along with colleagues such as Frank Knight and Aaron Director formed the earliest cohort of the 'Chicago School' of economics. He was, of course, a critic of the New Deal. Although his career was cut short by an early death in 1946, his piece on trade unionism was considered to be a seminal and courageous intervention by his free market allies. The influence of both Simons and Hutt was long-lasting—it can be seen in Hayek's *Constitution of Liberty* (1960), for example—and their works continued to be cited by British popularisers of the case against trade unionism well into the 1980s.[7]

Hutt and Simons conceptualised unions as monopolies which sought to control the labour supply in order to charge a price for labour in excess of its competitive level. In making this case, they explicitly rejected two arguments for unions that had persuaded earlier liberal economists to offer at least conditional support for workers' combinations. First, Hutt and Simons argued that unions

[4] W. H. Hutt, *The Economics of the Colour Bar* (London, 1964). See too *The Theory of Collective Bargaining* (London, 1975 [1930]), pp. 11, 14, for an early statement of this view. Hutt's reflections on the development of his individualist philosophy during his time in Britain and South Africa can be found in his unpublished 'Autobiography, Copy 2', typescript, 10 August 1984, W. H. Hutt Papers 11, Hoover Institution Archives, Stanford University (HIA). Hutt also cited the 1926 General Strike as a catalyst for his opposition to trade unionism: W. H. Hutt to S. Petro, 17 October 1979, Hutt Papers 67.

[5] Hutt, *Theory* [1930], p. viii. The preface containing this injunction was dropped from the 1975 edn. All other references to this book are to the 1975 edn.

[6] The article was originally drafted in 1941: Simons, 'Reflections', p. 1 n.1.

[7] See e.g. Samuel Brittan, 'How to end the strike-threat system', *Financial Times*, 5 September 1974; Samuel Brittan, 'The political economy of British union monopoly', *The Three Banks Review* 111 (1976), p. 7; Samuel Brittan, 'How British is the British sickness?', *Journal of Law and Economics* 21 (1978), pp. 263–5; Ralph Harris, 'Are trade unions really necessary?', *The Free Nation*, 23 July 1977, p. 7; Ralph Harris, 'Bullock's basic blunder', in Brian Chiplin et al., *Can Workers Manage? IEA Hobart Paper 77* (London, 1977), pp. 103, 106; *Trade Unions: Public Goods or Public Bads? IEA Readings 17* (London, 1978), pp. 25–6, 52; C. K. Rowley, 'Institutional reform to tame union power', *Economic Affairs* 7 (1986), p. 10; Arthur Shenfield, *What Right to Strike? IEA Hobart Paper 106* (London, 1986), pp. 29–38; Charles Hanson and Graham Mather, *Striking out Strikes, IEA Hobart Paper 110* (London, 1988), pp. 27–9.

could not be justified on the grounds that they enabled workers to receive competitive wage rates that they would otherwise be unable to obtain as a result of the monopsonistic power of employers to bargain down wage rates to sub-competitive levels. In their view, unions did not equalise the bargaining power of labour and capital, since the owners of capital were in principle as vulnerable to competition as workers—employees enjoyed considerably greater choice and mobility with respect to employment opportunities than the supporters of unionisation traditionally insinuated. This meant that at a fundamental level they rejected the idea that the labour market was characterised by monopsony or that labour suffered from any special sort of disadvantage because it had less of a reserve to fall back on than the owners of capital.[8]

Second, Hutt and Simons argued that unions could not be justified on the grounds that they raised the wages of labour at the expense of capital. Instead, they claimed, unions were formed by particular groups of workers in order to exclude other workers from their trades and hence to benefit their own sectional interests by acquiring higher wages relative to other workers. While particular groups of employees could increase their incomes in this way, the overall effect of trade union action was to reduce employment in a particular industry, since the union mark-up on wages priced some workers out of a job. This increased the pool of labour available for lower-wage non-union jobs, and therefore drove down wages in these low-paid sectors of the economy. As a result, said Hutt and Simons, the monopoly gains reaped by union insiders should not be seen as improving the position of labour as a whole but rather as increasing unemployment and income inequality, since union members were simply advantaging themselves relative to the genuinely low-paid members of the working class. As Simons put it, unionism 'enables an aristocracy of labour to build fences around their occupations, restricting entry, raising arbitrarily the costs and prices of their products, and lowering the wages and incomes of those outside, and of the poor especially.'[9] Hutt and Simons also argued that unions facilitated collusion between certain groups of employers and workers—bilateral monopoly—to the detriment of the consumer. Increased prices were the outcome, and since the majority of consumers were workers, they argued that this too served to undermine working-class living standards. In the 1975 edition of his book, Hutt quoted a journalist's observation that the latest wage agreement concluded in the US steel industry resembled 'a Viking blood oath between union and management to go to commit piracy on the high seas'.[10]

Hutt and Simons levelled one further objection at trade unions. They were both appalled by what they regarded as the unacceptable coercion and violence used by trade unions to enforce their interests. Strikes, boycotts, closed shops, and other trade union tactics were, in their view, the use of private coercive power

[8] Hutt, *Theory*, pp. 3–33; Simons, 'Reflections', pp. 1–2, 6–7. Compare with e.g. A. Marshall, *Principles of Economics* (1920; London, 8th edn., 1961), pp. 559–69.
[9] Simons, 'Reflections', p. 12.
[10] Hutt, *Theory*, pp. 66–73, quote at p. 102; Simons, 'Reflections', pp. 2, 15.

to impose an economic settlement on other workers, employers, and consumers in a way that threatened the state's monopoly on the use of violence. 'Labour monopolies', said Simons, 'enjoy an access to violence which is unparalleled in other monopolies', rendering governments 'impotent' and enabling unions to 'deal with scabs in ways which make even Rockefeller's early methods seem polite and legitimate'. Unions therefore presented an unparalleled challenge to the liberal state: 'they are essentially occupational armies, born and reared amidst violence, led by fighters, and capable of becoming peaceful only as their power becomes irresistible.'[11] The use of metaphors comparing unionism to legalised piracy and banditry were widespread in both these texts, for what was most infuriating to Hutt and Simons was that industrial relations legislation in Britain and the United States respectively had actually been designed to facilitate coercive union action: the 1906 Trade Disputes Act and the 1935 Wagner Act were prime examples of the political appeasement of the unions that they deplored. Interestingly, however, neither Hutt nor Simons mentioned any specific proposals for legislative reform. By the time Hutt's book was reissued in 1975, he was less reticent. 'Ideally', he wrote in a new epilogue, 'what is needed for the emancipation of labour is the enactment of the principle underlying the British Combination Acts of 1799 and 1800 adapted to the 1970s.'[12]

UNIONS AND THE POST-WAR SETTLEMENT

The analysis of Simons and Hutt was ignored by economists and policy-makers alike in the 1930s and 1940s, but their arguments provided a framework for later neo-liberal thinking about trade unions as the free-market critique of the post-war settlement took shape in the 1950s and 1960s. The serious work of developing neo-liberal economic discourse got underway in this period in sympathetic university departments, in the Mont Pèlerin Society itself, and in its associated think-tanks located across the world. A central theme of this discourse as it emerged from these diverse institutional locations was a deep anxiety about the enhanced power enjoyed by organised labour as a result of the post-war boom and the social democratisation of policy-making in the industrialised economies.[13] The most important interventions in this vein were probably those made by Hayek himself, but Hayek's work should be contextualised within the wider network of market liberal economists and publicists who built on the theoretical foundations laid by Hutt and Simons: figures such as Gottfried Haberler, H. Gregg Lewis, Fritz Machlup, Sylvester Petro, and many others.[14]

[11] Simons, 'Reflections', pp. 7, 21. [12] Hutt, *Theory*, p. 119.

[13] For a valuable account of how this neo-liberal discourse about trade unionism was hammered out within the Mont Pèlerin Society (MPS) in the 1950s, see Yves Steiner, 'The neo-liberals confront the trade unions', in Philip Mirowski and Dieter Plehwe (eds), *The Road From Mont Pèlerin: The Making of the Neo-Liberal Thought Collective* (Cambridge, Mass., 2009), pp. 181–203.

[14] A useful list of relevant works by these authors is cited in F. A. Hayek, *The Constitution of Liberty* (Chicago, 1960), pp. 505–6, n.8. Important examples included: Jacob Viner and Fritz

These authors agreed with the case already elaborated in the 1930s and 1940s, namely that unions were coercive monopolies that harmed workers, consumers, and employers alike, and enjoyed unacceptable legal privileges that allowed them to commit acts of violence and intimidation. But the neo-liberal analysis of trade unions in the 1950s and 1960s also pushed the discussion forward by introducing three innovative lines of argument.

First, Hutt and Simons had been clear that their arguments against trade unionism formed part of a general critique of all forms of monopoly, whether corporate or trade union, and were not intended as arguments against income redistribution per se. Rather, they favoured an anti-monopolistic liberalism that would sanction significant legal regulation of the size of corporations and the use of taxation and state-guaranteed minimum incomes to ensure that economic inequality was narrowed. Such policies, they argued, could effectively redistribute without distorting market mechanisms and price signals in the way that trade unions did.[15] However, a striking feature of the neo-liberal thinking on trade unionism that emerged after the War was that these qualifications largely disappeared. The attention of market liberals became almost entirely focused on the problems posed by organised labour—organised capital was hardly mentioned—and the redistribution of income was increasingly regarded as morally suspect and economically counter-productive. As Hayek remarked:

> I believe I have myself in the past used the tactical argument that we cannot hope to curb the coercive powers of labour unions unless we at the same time attack enterprise monopoly. I have, however, become convinced that it would be disingenuous to represent the existing monopolies in the field of labour and those in the field of enterprise as being of the same kind.[16]

Whether or not Hayek was correct to characterise his earlier equation of labour and corporate monopolies as 'tactical', it is clear that there was indeed a shift in emphasis in neo-liberal thinking after the War: they now saw unions as posing a much more serious threat than large corporations, and they felt increasingly less inclined to concede that underlying distributive injustices would nonetheless

Machlup, in *Wage Determination and the Economics of Liberalism* (Washington DC, 1947); David McCord Wright (ed.), *The Impact of the Union* (New York, 1951); Sylvester Petro, *The Labor Policy of a Free Society* (New York, 1957); E. H. Chamberlin, *The Economic Analysis of Labor Power* (Washington DC, 1958); P. D. Bradley (ed.), *The Public Stake in Union Power* (Charlottesville, 1959); Hayek, *Constitution*, pp. 267–84; W. H. Hutt, *The Strike-Threat System* (New Rochelle, NY, 1973). On the role of the American Enterprise Association, a free-market think-tank, in fostering some of these studies, see Kim Phillips-Fein, *Invisible Hands: The Making of the Conservative Movement from the New Deal to Reagan* (New York, 2009), pp. 65–6.

[15] Henry Simons, *A Positive Program for Laissez-Faire* (Chicago, 1934), pp. 26–30; his 'Reflections', pp. 5, 19; W. H. Hutt, *Plan for Reconstruction* (London, 1943), pp. 5–19, 60–2, 165–85; W. H. Hutt, 'Trade unions and the price system', paper for MPS conference, Seelisberg, 1949, MPS Papers 6/6, HIA, p. 3. For further discussion, see Ben Jackson, 'At the origins of neo-liberalism: the free economy and the strong state, 1930–47', *Historical Journal* 53 (2010), pp. 129–51.

[16] Hayek, *Constitution*, p. 265.

require redress by other means if the unions were disarmed.[17] The reasons for this shift were complex, but essentially neo-liberal theorists had come to believe that the interests of organised labour had been significantly advanced during the 1930s and 1940s, leaving business embattled in the face of unprecedented pressure from the state and trade unions. As Haberler put it, 'in our times industrial "monopolies" and "oligopolies" do not have the same power, strength and iron discipline that many unions have developed in many countries.'[18] Meanwhile, neo-liberal economists had become increasingly sceptical, on both theoretical and empirical grounds, of how far corporate monopolies posed a genuine threat to market competition and individual liberty. New economic theories of monopoly and revisionist studies of the history of industrial organisation made the problem of corporate monopoly seem considerably less urgent.[19]

The second post-war innovation in the neo-liberal theory of industrial relations concerned the relationship between trade unions and inflation. Hutt and Simons, writing at a time of deflation and crisis, had not given this relationship much attention. As the putative role of strong unions in promoting inflationary wage settlements became central to economic policy debate after 1945, neo-liberals began to develop their own analysis of inflation. The place of trade unions in this analysis was not straightforward, since neo-liberals were committed to the monetarist insight that inflation was a monetary phenomenon and should therefore be controlled by reducing the rate of growth of the money supply. On the strict interpretation of this view, union wage bargaining was irrelevant to the overall price level in the economy. However, this apparent implication of monetarist doctrine did not deter certain leading neo-liberals from attributing co-responsibility to the unions for the inflation they detected creeping inexorably upwards over the course of the post-war boom.

The inflationary power of trade unions, such neo-liberals argued, stemmed directly from the economic theory of Keynes, and in particular from what they regarded as a political fudge at the heart of *The General Theory*. As Hayek put it, Keynes started

from the correct insight that the regular cause of extensive unemployment is real wages that are too high. The next step consisted in the proposition that a direct lowering of

[17] As Yves Steiner has observed, in the 1950s one strand of opinion within the MPS, predominantly continental European in origin, was slightly more sympathetic to trade unionism than the subsequently dominant Anglo-American strand of neo-liberalism. I am not convinced that the difference between the two sides was as great as Steiner suggests, but we are nonetheless in agreement that, by the end of the 1950s, this difference in emphasis had been resolved by the ideological victory of the Anglo-American analysis of unions: see Steiner, 'Neo-liberals confront the trade unions', esp. pp. 183–8, 195–6.

[18] Gottfried Haberler, *Inflation and the Unions* (London, 1972), p. 34.

[19] W. G. Nutter, *The Extent of Enterprise Monopoly in the United States 1899–1939* (Chicago, 1951); J. F. Weston, *The Role of Mergers in the Growth of Large Firms* (Berkeley, 1953); Aaron Director and Edward Levi, 'Law and the future: trade regulation', *Northwestern University Law Review* 51 (1956), pp. 281–96. For further discussion, see Rob Van Horn, 'Reinventing monopoly and the role of corporations', in Mirowski and Plehwe (eds.), *Road From Mont Pèlerin*, pp. 204–37.

> money wages could be brought about only by a struggle so painful and prolonged that it could not be contemplated. Hence he concluded that real wages must be lowered by the process of lowering the value of money. This is really the reasoning underlying the whole "full employment" policy, now so widely accepted.[20]

Keynes, like other liberal economists before him, was therefore portrayed as capitulating before organised labour by incorporating into his economic theory a political judgement about the undesirability of upsetting the trade unions. Although Keynes was well aware that unemployment was caused by wage rigidity, argued Hayek and his colleagues, he deemed it inexpedient to tackle the root cause of the problem and was forced instead to prescribe an inflationary expansion of the money supply so as to lower the real value of wages instead.[21] However accurate this was as an interpretation of Keynesian economics, it illustrates that, in Hayek's view, union wage bargaining on its own was not inflationary. What was inflationary was the combination of union wage bargaining and full employment policies, since an inflationary expansion of the money supply was regarded as the practical up-shot of the use of fiscal policy to reduce unemployment. Without a government commitment to full employment, Hayek suggested, unions receiving wage settlements in excess of the competitive level would simply cause unemployment and deflation.

This complex argument ultimately divided neo-liberals over whether, in the light of monetarism, unions could legitimately be said to 'cause' inflation. A helpful summary of this dispute was provided by Arthur Shenfield, a key contributor to the work of the IEA, in his 1974 presidential address to the Mont Pèlerin Society. Shenfield noted that within the Society it was agreed that inflation was a monetary phenomenon:

> But we have not reached agreement on the whole process. On the one side are the Friedman-Powellites, for whom monetary expansion is the whole story. On the other side are those who ask why our politicians debauch the currency, and answer that they fear unemployment. Since, apart from frictional and temporary labour market dislocations, unemployment is almost wholly caused by unions, they are part of the causal chain . . . On this view, they do not cause inflation, but they deter the politicians from terminating inflation.[22]

As Shenfield observed, Milton Friedman was the leading advocate of an account of inflation that left the unions out. Friedman shared the broader neo-liberal critique of trade unions, although he was mildly sceptical about whether unions had a significant impact on unemployment, inequality, and inefficiency in the United States since union density in the labour force was in his view too low to

[20] Hayek, *Constitution*, p. 280.

[21] For a summary and endorsement of this analysis, see Richard Cockett, *Thinking the Unthinkable* (London, 1995), pp. 42–5; for a firm rebuttal of this characterisation of *The General Theory*, see Peter Clarke, *The Keynesian Revolution in the Making 1924–36* (Oxford, 1988), pp. 274–6, 324–7; Peter Clarke, 'Serial evangelists', *London Review of Books*, 23 June 1994, p. 12.

[22] Arthur Shenfield, 'The English disease', presidential lecture to the MPS, Brussels, 1974, F. A. Hayek Papers 86/14, HIA, p. 9.

have a very large effect.[23] This empirical reservation aside, Friedman maintained that it was a serious theoretical mistake to depict inflation as the result of organised labour. As he argued following a trip to Britain in 1974:

I have been dismayed, even in my few days in London, at the widespread support of 'union bashing' as a way to attack inflation. Unions do much harm, primarily by restricting the employment opportunities available to the more disadvantaged of your citizens. But they do not produce and have not produced inflation. On the contrary, one of the unfortunate effects of inflation has been to strengthen unions. Blaming unions for inflation leads to wrong policy, to evasion of the real problem and, even more tragically, to weakening the political fabric of your society.[24]

Friedman therefore explicitly differed from the view taken by other leading figures in the movement, notably Hayek and Haberler. Those engaged in popularising neo-liberal ideas were keen to find a formula that might reconcile the two sides. Ralph Harris, Director of the IEA, had earlier suggested to Friedman that both sides might agree on the following formula: 'trade unions may be regarded as the *active* agents of inflation so long as the government *passively* stands ready to supply whatever increase in money may be thought necessary to secure full employment at ruling wage rates.'[25] Friedman replied that this statement was untrue with respect to inflation in the United States, although he politely allowed that it was possible that the British case might be different.[26] But, as we have seen, when Friedman later visited Britain, he was publicly emphatic about the irrelevance of unions as agents of inflation even in the British case. He articulated this more emphatic view at greater length at an IEA seminar during his visit, at which he defended a clear 'Friedmanite' line against the 'Hayekian' position expounded on that occasion by Peter Jay and Samuel Brittan.[27] In retrospect, the differences between the two sides seem rather narrow: neither side denied that inflation stemmed from the expansion of the money supply or that trade unions were on the whole economically damaging. But it is interesting that British neo-liberal publicists were keen to portray the inflationary threat of organised labour in the starkest possible terms and were willing to depart from their most eminent American adviser to do so.

In addition to down-playing the importance of corporate monopolies and grappling with the causes of inflation, the third post-war innovation in the neo-liberal theory of industrial relations was a greater readiness to propose concrete

[23] Milton Friedman, 'Some comments on the significance of labor unions for economic policy', in McCord Wright (ed.), *Impact of the Union*, pp. 204–34.

[24] Milton Friedman, letter to the editor, *Economist*, 28 September 1974, p. 4. For a fuller exposition of Friedman's reasoning, see his 'What price guideposts?', in George Shultz and Robert Aliber (eds.), *Guidelines, Informal Controls and the Market Place* (Chicago, 1966), pp. 17–39.

[25] Ralph Harris to Milton Friedman, 26 February 1973, IEA Papers 296/11, HIA, emphasis in original.

[26] Milton Friedman to Ralph Harris, 8 March 1973, IEA Papers 296/11.

[27] *Inflation: Causes, Consequences, Cures, IEA Readings 14* (London, 1974), esp. pp. 25–50, 56–8, 89–104.

reforms aimed at reducing union power. While Hutt and Simons had shied away from examining how to solve the problems they diagnosed, and were implicitly fatalistic about the prospects for reform, later debates featured more practical consideration of what was to be done. The main burden of this discussion was that a significant state-led restructuring of the labour market would be required to contain unions' monopoly powers. A range of legal remedies were debated, including the prohibition of picketing in numbers; the abolition of closed and union shops (for example by the use of 'right to work' laws in the United States); the prohibition of secondary action; the removal of social security entitlements from workers on strike; and the removal of the right of unions to make contracts that would subsequently bind those who did not voluntarily delegate such authority to the union.[28] Some of the fiercest critics of the unions, such as Hutt, took this analysis much further by arguing for the abolition of the right to strike itself by returning to the principles that underpinned the Combination Acts. This was never a widely supported proposal in these circles. As a half-way house, some support did exist for removing the right to strike from workers in essential services, a category that was sometimes construed as co-extensive with virtually the entire public sector.[29] In the 1980s, the IEA even published pamphlets with titles such as *What Right to Strike?*[30]

More popular in neo-liberal circles were two other radical proposals: that unions, like corporations, should be subject to anti-monopoly legislation (with a view to abolishing industry-wide unions); and that union legal immunities should be removed to render unions liable for damages in civil law. These points, especially the latter, were not initially flagged up particularly clearly—in *The Constitution of Liberty*, for example, Hayek rather cryptically remarked that 'the responsibility for organised and concerted action in conflict with contractual obligations or the general law must be firmly placed on those in whose hands the decision lies, irrespective of the particular form of organised action adopted.'[31] But by the 1970s the neo-liberal analysis of trade unions had become more apocalyptic in its predictions and its prescriptions accordingly much starker. Hayek now plainly advocated that the union legal immunities established in the Trade Disputes Act should be revoked. He wrote to *The Times* in 1980 to argue that the British government should call a referendum to obtain permission 'to rescind all the special privileges which have been granted to the trade unions by

[28] See e.g. Petro, *Labor Policy*, pp. 235–47; Sylvester Petro, 'Free employee choice as a basis of labor policy', paper to MPS, Princeton, 1958, MPS Papers 12/5; Hayek to Friedman, 15 December 1957 and Friedman to Hayek, 16 January 1958, both in Hayek Papers 73/40; Hayek, *Constitution*, pp. 278–9; H. Hazlitt, 'The dark side of the unions', paper to MPS, Munich, 1970, Hayek Papers 86/7, p. 7; Haberler, *Inflation*, pp. 45–50; Shenfield, 'Trade unions and the law', paper to MPS, Spain, 1979, Hayek Papers 88/4.

[29] Charles Hanson, 'Trade union reform: Tebbit's next step', *Economic Affairs* 4 (1983), p. 19.

[30] Shenfield, *What Right to Strike?* (1986).

[31] Hayek, *Constitution*, p. 278. For other examples of these radical proposals, see H. G. Lewis, 'The labor-monopoly problem: a positive program', *Journal of Political Economy* 59 (1951), pp. 277–87; Milton Friedman, *Capitalism and Freedom* (1962; Chicago, 2002), p. 132; Haberler, *Inflation*, pp. 47–8.

law'.[32] Hayek also wrote to Margaret Thatcher and Norman Tebbit, the Secretary of State for Employment, to lobby for this idea. They politely declined to take the matter any further. Tebbit added in hand-writing at the end of his letter: 'I have to say that a step so radical as that which you propose, while it would galvanise the economy, would I fear be so controversial that it would be frustrated in this over-conservative nation.'[33] Finally, since many neo-liberals regarded the combination of trade unions and full employment policy as inflationary, the abandonment of full employment as an objective of government policy should also be seen as a further prong of the neo-liberal strategy to reduce union power.

By the 1970s, then, a detailed critique of the rôle played by unions in the economy had been elaborated by neo-liberals, a critique that contrasted the public interest of individual consumers with sectional producer interests. But the producer interests identified by neo-liberals were, in the later part of our period, almost exclusively those of employees. Employers were only criticised in so far as they failed to be sufficiently firm in their dealings with trade unions. From an initial argument in the 1930s and 1940s that bosses and workers were conspiring in a joint monopoly against the public, neo-liberals moved in the 1950s and 1960s to the narrower claim that workers were conspiring against the public. They made this case on the basis of certain arguments derived from economic theory, in particular that unions drove up prices, reduced productivity, increased unemployment, and increased income inequality; on the libertarian grounds that unions exercised unacceptable coercive power over the individual; and because they thought that granting economic pressure groups significant legal latitude in effect led to the state surrendering its monopoly on the legitimate use of violence. Neo-liberal theory envisaged a society in which individuals would enjoy rich consumer lives, full of market-based choice-making and agency, but exercise little control over their roles in the process of production, which was to be the prerogative of unilateral managerial decision. Even the limited democratisation of economic life envisaged by social democratic advocates of trade unions was, on this account, dangerous. The corporatist vision of a state that proceeded by deliberating over its social and economic plans with relevant interest groups, especially unions, was seen as at best pandering to producer interests and at worst incipiently totalitarian.

NEO-LIBERALISM AND BRITISH CORPORATISM

The neo-liberal critique of trade unions was intended to be universally valid. Neo-liberal theorists and publicists did not really distinguish with any care between the diverse industrial relations regimes that had evolved in different

[32] F. A. Hayek, 'A testing time for monetarism', letter to the editor, *The Times*, 13 June 1980.

[33] Tebbit to Hayek, 29 September 1981; Hayek to Thatcher, 28 August 1979; Hayek to Thatcher, 24 April 1980; Thatcher to Hayek, 13 May 1980; all in Hayek Papers 101/26.

states. In practice, as a predominantly English-language movement, most of their observations were based on an acquaintance with industrial relations in the United States and Britain. And it was in British political debate in the 1970s and 1980s that the neo-liberal analysis made the most dramatic headway. In the United States, the critique of unions had been pushing at an open door throughout the post-war period as a result of the well-known weaknesses in the bargaining position and coherence of the American labour movement.[34] In Britain, the door had to be kicked in. But before the battering ram of the state could be deployed under the Thatcher government, some intellectual headway had to be made among political elites in order to legitimise Thatcherite statecraft. It was here that the works of Hutt, Simons, Hayek, et al. were of particular significance. When read and popularised in Britain in the 1970s and early 1980s, they seemed to crystallise the pathologies of British corporatism. Three aspects of this neo-liberal discourse held a particular political appeal to their avid readers in late twentieth-century British political parties, think-tanks, business organisations, and broad-sheet journalism.

First, the neo-liberal critique of trade unions was easily translated into an analysis of the causes of British 'decline'. Elite opinion in the 1970s and 1980s was famously gripped by the feeling that something had gone badly wrong in Britain's post-war trajectory. The version of neo-liberalism that was popularised in Britain by free-market think-tanks, economists, and journalists directed this mood by attributing blame to various aspects of the post-war settlement but, in particular, to the existence of a potent form of free collective bargaining in the British economy.[35] On this account, successive governments, businessmen, and intellectuals, notably Keynes and his disciples, had abandoned good economic sense in order to appease the unions. This 'Munich mentality', it was argued, had slowly undermined the capacity of the British economy to function efficiently.[36] Shenfield, for example, took the heroically optimistic view 'that there was nothing to prevent post-imperial Britain from remaining Europe's pre-eminent economic power save one malady, the disruptive power of the British unions'.[37] In truth the neo-liberals did not simply offer an analysis of post-war Britain.

[34] On the much earlier potency of the corporate back-lash against trade unions in the United States, see Elizabeth Fones-Wolf, *Selling Free Enterprise: The Business Assault on Labor and Liberalism 1945–60* (Urbana, Ill., 1994); Phillips-Fein, *Invisible Hands*, pp. 87–114.

[35] On the role played by theories of 'decline' in British politics, and in the early justifications for Thatcherism in particular, see David Cannadine, 'Apocalypse when? British politicians and British "decline" in the twentieth century', in Peter Clarke and Clive Trebilcock (eds.), *Understanding Decline* (Cambridge, 1997), pp. 275–84; Michael Kenny and Richard English (eds.), *Rethinking British Decline* (London, 2000); E. H. H. Green, *Thatcher* (London, 2006), pp. 55–6, 71–5; Jim Tomlinson, *The Politics of Decline* (Harlow, 2000), esp. pp. 48–61, 83–99; Jim Tomlinson, 'Mrs Thatcher's macroeconomic adventurism, 1979–81 and its political consequences', *British Politics* 2 (2007), pp. 14–17.

[36] Brittan, 'Political economy', p. 32.

[37] A. A. Shenfield, 'Thatcher's reform of Britain's labour unions' [1989], in Norman Barry (ed.), *Limited Government, Individual Liberty and the Rule of Law: Selected Works of Arthur Asher Shenfield* (Cheltenham, 1998), p. 255; see also his criticism of Baldwin's failure to press home the advantage after the General Strike, at p. 228.

Their indictment reached much further into the past, to the interwar period and even to the passage of the 1906 Trade Disputes Act. They directly challenged a deep-rooted assumption within British political culture, ultimately originating from the Victorian consensus on industrial relations noted by McKibbin, that trade unions were legitimate and, within certain constraints, socially beneficial institutions. The neo-liberal argument, voiced by figures such as Shenfield, was that the legal privileges granted to unions as a result of this social consensus were largely responsible for Britain's economic underperformance since the heyday of the nineteenth century. Although they rarely put this point as starkly as Shenfield, the architects of Thatcherism shared at least some of his historical diagnosis. Keith Joseph went as far as to attribute British economic 'decline' to the constitutional link between the unions and the Labour Party. This, he argued, had enabled obstructive union militants to promote 'a romantic, outdated and economically illiterate socialism which the people of this country don't want and which the people of most other Western countries have firmly rejected'.[38]

The second way in which the neo-liberal theory of industrial relations resonated in British politics was that it resolved a tricky policy dilemma for the Conservative Party. The conventional wisdom among policy elites in the 1970s was that excessive wage claims increased inflation. It was therefore regarded as essential to implement an incomes policy if inflation was to be contained. But such a policy inevitably locked governments into arduous negotiations with trade unions. Moreover, as the exponents of market liberalism observed, a policy focused on wage restraint would further strengthen the position of the unions, since the resentments and comparisons created by such policies were likely to drive more workers to join unions to protect their interests.[39] The neo-liberal analysis, in particular the doctrine of monetarism, had the great political advantage that it cut through this Gordian knot, since it stipulated that union wage demands in themselves did not cause inflation (regardless of whether or not unions were indirectly inflationary by pressuring the state into increasing the money supply). It was therefore entirely unnecessary for governments to become entangled in detailed wage negotiations with the unions. Instead, inflation could be reduced by exerting control over the money supply and abandoning full employment as an objective of government policy. Perceptive strategists within the Conservative Party saw that, irrespective of its economic merits, this offered the strategically appealing vista of a future Conservative government simply bypassing the wage bargaining that had undermined British governments of both parties in the 1970s and had led to the strength of organised labour reaching a new high water-mark.[40]

[38] Keith Joseph, *Solving the Union Problem is the Key to Britain's Recovery* (London, 1979), pp. 5–9, quote at p. 9.

[39] Friedman, 'Some comments', p. 231; Shenfield, 'What about the trade unions?', in Barry (ed.), *Limited Government*, pp. 242–3.

[40] On the evolution of this thinking within Margaret Thatcher's inner circle in the 1970s, see Green, *Thatcher*, pp. 62–4, 109–15. Monetarism had the further advantage of legitimising public expenditure cuts as a necessary component of counter-inflationary strategy.

The third way in which the neo-liberal analysis held a particular political appeal in the 1970s was that it furnished British sympathisers with a language of the public good that could be juxtaposed with the sectional interests pursued by the unions. The idea that unions represented the privileged interests of 'insiders' or 'producers' over 'outsiders' or 'consumers' was used as a rhetorical card that could trump the more conventional discourse of social class. Implicit within this language was a resonant characterisation of the dangers posed to the public good by powerful producer interest groups. An influential version of this idea was placed at the heart of elite political debate in the 1970s by Peter Jay and Samuel Brittan, commentators for the *Times* and the *Financial Times* respectively. The writings of Jay and Brittan in this period were essentially popularisations, as they freely acknowledged, of neo-liberal ideas previously canvassed by counter-cultural figures such as Hayek, Friedman, Simons, and Hutt. Jay's distinctive spin was to formulate an 'irreconcilable quadrilateral', by which he meant four apparently desirable political goals that could not in fact be pursued simultaneously in Britain: free collective bargaining, democracy, full employment, and stable prices. These goals were incompatible, Jay argued, because free collective bargaining inevitably created unemployment by pricing workers out of jobs (for the reasons specified by Hutt et al.), but democratic government was now understood to require the state to pursue full employment, which in turn meant that the state would loosen the money supply and increase inflation. Jay identified free collective bargaining as, in economic terms, the most dispensable of these four goals, but, in keeping with the pessimistic tone of New Right commentary in this period, he also implied that the political power of the unions was such that it was more likely that democracy would go first.[41] Brittan, meanwhile, suggested that 'the pursuit of self-interest by rival coercive groups', in essence the unions, would lead to the steady erosion, and perhaps even the extinction, of British liberal democracy itself.[42] Brittan and Jay were explicit that the problem in Britain was free collective bargaining, not producer interests more broadly construed.[43] Although business organisations could be argued to be as susceptible to these strictures regarding producer interests as trade unions (as Mancur Olson, for example, maintained),[44] this was not the view promoted by

[41] e.g. Peter Jay, 'How inflation threatens British democracy with its last chance before extinction', *The Times*, 1 July 1974; his 'The good old-days of stop-go economics', *The Times*, 5 December 1973; his contribution to *Inflation*, pp. 25–34.

[42] Samuel Brittan, 'The economic contradictions of democracy', *British Journal of Political Science* 5 (1975), pp. 142–6, 150, 155–8.

[43] Unlike the post-war neo-liberal theorists, however, Jay and Brittan accepted that workers suffered from the distributive injustice of low-pay and proposed to address this via alternative forms of redistribution that they thought less likely to create labour market rigidity: workers' co-operatives and an unconditional basic income respectively: Peter Jay, *Employment, Inflation and Politics* (London, 1976); Samuel Brittan, *A Restatement of Economic Liberalism* (London, 1988), pp. 296–301.

[44] Mancur Olson, *The Logic of Collective Action* (Cambridge, Mass., 1965), pp. 141–8; his *The Rise and Decline of Nations* (New Haven, 1982), pp. 143–4. Hayek and Brittan nonetheless drew on Olson to bolster their case against the unions: F. A. Hayek, *Law, Legislation and Liberty*, vol. 3 (London, 1979), pp. 143–4; Brittan, 'How British', pp. 266–7.

neo-liberal theorists, nor was it the line taken by neo-liberal popularisers amid the industrial relations turbulence of the 1970s.

THE NEO-LIBERAL CRITIQUE IN RETROSPECT

The neo-liberal analysis of trade unions was influential in bolstering the intellectual self-confidence of right-wing politicians and activists, particularly in Britain and the United States. Of course, the leaders of the British Conservative Party in the 1970s and 1980s hardly needed to be told by a group of intellectuals that the trade unions posed a serious threat to their political objectives. Nonetheless, neo-liberal ideas framed and deepened their political thinking and furnished them with a powerful rhetoric about the necessity of industrial relations reform. Connoisseurs of historical irony can savour the fact that one of the most important factors in constraining extremism in British politics in the twentieth century—the relative liberalism of the British state in relation to the labour movement—had by the 1970s come to be regarded by powerful elites as the single most important threat to the economy and the constitution. In retrospect, however, the reasoning that led to this conclusion was characterised by significant silences and ideological closures.

In spite of the intellectually assertive, social-scientific character of neo-liberal analysis, it is striking how little empirical evidence was produced to support it. Although neo-liberal arguments were largely derived from economic theory, they generated predictions that were presented as bearing on the effect of trade unions in the economy as it actually existed and not just in a hypothetical model of competitive capitalism. Indeed, neo-liberals did not shrink from making strong empirical claims. The British unions, Hayek wrote, 'have become the chief cause of unemployment' and of 'the falling standard of living of the working class'. Unions, he added, 'are the main reason for the decline of the British economy in general'.[45] Hayek also predicted 'that the average worker's income would rise fastest in a country where relative wages are flexible, and where the exploitation of workers by monopolistic trade union organisations of specialised groups of workers are effectively outlawed'.[46] But these exceptionally strong claims were not supported by a systematic use of empirical evidence. Hayek never explained how he knew that the unions were 'the chief cause of unemployment'.[47] He was not alone. Hutt, for example, provided no data to support his proposal to return to the Combination Laws on the grounds that it 'would raise the material welfare of perhaps 90 per cent of the people'; 'would enormously improve employment

[45] F. A. Hayek, *1980s Unemployment and the Unions* (1980; London, 1984), pp. 62, 52.

[46] Hayek, *1980s Unemployment*, p. 54.

[47] For a persuasive critique of Hayek on this score, see R. Richardson, 'Hayek on trade unions: social philosopher or propagandist?', in S. F. Frowen (ed.), *Hayek: Economist and Social Philosopher* (Basingstoke, 1997), pp. 259–80. As Richardson notes, Hayek's disengagement from empirical investigation was influenced by his intellectual formation within the Austrian school of economics, which had methodological objections to empirical studies of economic phenomena.

security'; and 'would bring about an unprecedented improvement in the quality of human relations.'[48] Exceptionally, the Chicago labour economist H. G. Lewis did undertake detailed empirical work on the impact of unions on the economy. He found that unions raised wages for their members, but thought it likely that as a result unions widened income inequality between unionised and non-unionised workers. However, the conclusions he drew from his data were appropriately scholarly: 'I conclude tentatively that unionism has had a small impact on the relative inequality of wages among all workers. The direction of the effect, on presently available evidence, is ambiguous.'[49]

Overall, though, in the 1970s and 1980s there was a shift in the character of the social-scientific analysis that influenced policy-makers, in particular a move from a broadly institutionalist or historicist understanding of labour markets to one grounded on an ahistorical, a priori analysis drawn from economic theory. It is worth noting that the gradual political acceptance of the legitimacy of British unions in the nineteenth century had itself been conditioned by an intellectual shift from deductive classical political economy to an inductive historicism based on detailed empirical studies of trade union activities.[50]

Empirical studies of trade unions were still produced by institutionalist economists after 1945. Their research contested many of the neo-liberal arguments, and enjoyed a measure of political influence in Britain and the United States at the height of the post-war boom. One finding of this empirical work was that there was a large variation in wage rates for similar work in the same local labour market, which suggested that a swathe of social factors inevitably played a role in setting pay rates rather than the frictionless operation of market forces. This cast doubt on the neo-liberal claim that there was a clear 'competitive' wage rate that union contracts exceeded. Many of the leading institutionalist economists in the United States had worked during the Second World War for the War Labor Board in setting wage rates and arbitrating industrial disputes. They therefore had direct experience of how difficult it was in practice to work out exactly what the 'going rate' for a particular job was and of negotiating with trade union officials and employers.[51] But the 1970s and 1980s were hardly ideal times to remind politicians about the benefits of trade unionism. The institutionalists lost their proximity to political power as the labour movement's strength waned

[48] Hutt, *Theory*, p. 120.

[49] H. G. Lewis, *Unionism and Relative Wages in the United States* (Chicago, 1963), pp. 8–9.

[50] Lawrence Goldman, *Science, Reform and Politics in Victorian Britain* (Cambridge, 2002), pp. 201–13, 226–35; Mark Curthoys, *Governments, Labour and the Law in Mid-Victorian Britain* (Oxford, 2004), pp. 52–7, 75–8, 102–6, 235–41.

[51] See e.g. J. T. Dunlop, 'Review of *Unions and Capitalism* by Charles E. Lindblom', *American Economic Review* 40 (1950), pp. 465–6; Clark Kerr, 'Labor markets: their character and consequences', *American Economic Review* 40 (1950), pp. 278–91; Richard Lester, 'A range theory of wage differentials', *Industrial and Labor Relations Review* 5 (1952), pp. 483–500; Bruce Kaufman (ed.), *How Labor Markets Work* (Lexington, Mass., and Toronto, 1988), esp. pp. 7–8, 77–80, 91–2, 118–19. For an early British study in the same vein, see H. A. Turner, 'Trade unions, differentials and the levelling of wages', *The Manchester School* 20 (1952), pp. 227–82.

and their methodological assumptions were undermined by more theoretically sophisticated economists.

However, more recent empirical work on trade unions has bolstered the institutionalists' case. This is not because the effects of unions identified by neo-liberals were necessarily absent, but because their analysis was incomplete: unions have a variety of economic effects that were excluded from the neo-liberal account. For example, a robust statistical finding across different national contexts is that unions narrow pay dispersion within workplaces and industries, and reduce income differentials between middle-class and working-class jobs, both of which empirically dominate the disequalising effect of unions stressed by neo-liberals, namely that unions raise the wages of certain groups of workers relative to others. Aside from the finding that unions narrow income inequality, however, perhaps the most notable feature of this empirical research is the sheer complexity and heterogeneity of the impact of unions on economic performance across different national contexts and economic sectors. It is hard to generalise meaningfully about the overall influence of trade unions on the economy, and economists have certainly identified efficiency-enhancing effects of trade unionism, such as reduced staff turnover.[52]

A further difficulty with the neo-liberal analysis of trade unions is its conscious abstraction from any non-economic benefits that unions might bring. Neo-liberal authors analysed trade unions by immediately bracketing off what they considered to be the 'non-economic' functions of trade unionism in order to focus on the effects of collective bargaining on wages, employment, and efficiency. In doing so, they usually noted that, while there may indeed be some important non-economic functions performed by unions, this was not to be the focus of analysis in this particular instance. This is certainly a legitimate intellectual strategy—not everything can be analysed in sufficient depth at once—but since many of these works were not in fact addressed to a purely academic audience, this strategy had problematic political consequences. Neo-liberals presented to policy-makers and a broader public audience a partial account of the functions of trade unionism, which left unscrutinised some of the most important reasons for a strong union movement.

In particular, they did not discuss the value of the 'collective voice' function of trade unions: the role played by unions in ensuring that the interests of workers have some bargaining power in industrial and political systems where the interests of employers and the wealthy are already heard and protected. Neo-liberals displayed little imaginative sympathy for the kind of lives lived by workers and

[52] Richard Freeman and James Medoff, *What Do Unions Do?* (New York, 1984); D. Card, T. Lemieux, and W. Craig Riddell, 'Unions and the wage structure', in J. T. Addison and C. Schnabel (eds.), *International Handbook of Trade Unions* (Cheltenham, 2003), pp. 246–92; D. Baker, A. Glyn, D. Howell and J. Schmitt, 'Labour market institutions and unemployment: assessment of the cross-country evidence', in David Howell (ed.), *Fighting Unemployment* (Oxford, 2005), pp. 72–118; J. Visser and D. Checchi, 'Inequality and the labor market: unions', in W. Salverda, B. Nolan and T. M. Smeeding (eds.), *Oxford Handbook of Economic Inequality* (Oxford, 2009), pp. 230–56.

their families, or for the reasons why collective action might be important to ensure that they could gain a measure of control over those lives. Instead, neo-liberal authors offered an unwavering focus on the illegitimate coercive power of trade unions, leaving undiscussed the coercive tactics used by employers to prevent union organisation; the coercion inherent in employment relations; or even the reasons why some employers were perfectly happy to collaborate with unions. Viewed in these terms, their focus on union coercion was reminiscent of a 'moral panic' rather than a balanced assessment of the evidence. And they neglected the crucial point that unions were democratic institutions that enabled employees to express a collective view about workplace conditions and benefits; to have their voice heard in management decision-making; to monitor the implementation of workplace agreements and legal regulations; and to ensure that in a democratic society politics is not dominated by wealthy individuals but also pays attention to the concerns of those citizens who lack equivalent economic power. It is the distinctive character of trade unions as vehicles of collective action that enables them to fulfil these functions; they cannot be carried out under the regime of individualised industrial relations favoured by neo-liberals. The voices of individual employees carry less weight, and are more likely to be chilled by employer intimidation, than when they are aggregated into a representative, collective voice. Yet it was precisely collective action by employees that neo-liberals found so disturbing; it was the collective pressure of the group on the individual that they sought to eliminate. 'The real exploiters in our present society', wrote Hayek, 'are not egoistic capitalists or entrepreneurs, and in fact not separate individuals, but organisations which derive their power from the moral support of collective action and the feeling of group loyalty.'[53] On this account, solidaristic sentiments between groups of workers were to be viewed with fear and suspicion, for they threatened the sovereignty of the individual.

To draw attention to the limitations of the neo-liberal critique is not necessarily to deny that the problems identified by neo-liberals existed—but it is to say, as the labour economist Richard Freeman has put it, that unions have both a 'monopoly' face and a 'collective voice' face, and that the costs and benefits of both have to be considered to give a rounded social assessment of trade unionism.[54] This point has also been made by historians of class and work. Ross McKibbin's examination of mid-twentieth century British work culture crisply summarised the need for a more balanced view, even from a purely economic perspective:

> Employers who did not recognise unions did not have to deal with stewards, and many must have thought the cost was worth it. But there was a cost: absenteeism, high labour turnover, casual strikes and walkouts . . . and the emergence of informally elected shop stewards even more truculent (though more easily dismissed) than those elected by agreement with a union. Employers often exaggerated losses due to strikes and under-estimated losses due to 'non-union' factors.[55]

[53] Hayek, *Law*, vol. 3, p. 96. [54] Freeman and Medoff, *What Do Unions Do?*
[55] Ross McKibbin, *Classes and Cultures: England 1918–51* (Oxford, 1998), p. 149.

Instead of offering a balanced assessment of trade unions, neo-liberal theorists and publicists excluded 'collective voice' as irrelevant to their analytical interests. And yet, as this chapter has shown, their partial account was used as the basis for public polemics about the need for a concerted attack on the power of the unions. It was certainly a gripping story that the erosion of union power would benefit the individual, but, as many will now be able to attest, it was more realistically a story about how to benefit certain sorts of individuals, perhaps even certain classes of individuals, at the expense of others.

17

History and the Labour Party

*Clare V. J. Griffiths**

For a party as young as ours every year is a milestone.
(Harold Wilson, writing in 1970[1])

By the end of the twentieth century, the relationship between history and the Labour Party seemed to be inherently antagonistic. The forthright launch of a 'New' Labour presented an explicit confrontation to Labour's traditions and to the ways in which historical narratives and associations shaped political identities within the party. 'Our job is to honour the past but not to live in it,' Tony Blair explained in his election statement for the party leadership.[2] The reinvention of the party during the 1990s was impatient of sentimental attachments to Labour's heritage, most particularly when these impinged on party structures or approaches to policy, with the warning from advocates of 'the project' that 'to present yesterday's solutions to today's problems is not just negligent but facile'.[3] Even in delivering a lecture to mark the fiftieth anniversary of Labour's 1945 electoral landslide—and the celebrated reforming government which that election had ushered into office—Blair declared that he wanted to see the Labour Party 'liberated from our history and not chained by it'.[4]

When modernisers presented the past as something from which one had to break away, they emphasised a myth of an 'old' Labour, drawing on very particular chapters in the party's history which were not necessarily representative of the party's traditions more broadly.[5] Historians, political scientists, and journalists, meanwhile,

* I am grateful to the participants at the workshop at St. John's College, Oxford in April 2009 for their comments on an initial version of this essay, and to David Martin and William Whyte for their very useful suggestions and help in producing the final text.

1 *Labour Organiser*, January 1970, p. 9.

2 Tony Blair, *New Britain. My Vision of a Young Country* (London, 1996), p. 3.

3 Peter Mandelson and Roger Liddle, *The Blair Revolution: Can New Labour Deliver?* (London, 1996), p. 21.

4 Tony Blair, *Let us Face the Future—the 1945 Anniversary Lecture*, Fabian pamphlet no. 571 (London, 1995), p. 12.

5 Meg Russell, *Building New Labour: The Politics of Party Organisation* (Basingstoke, 2005), pp. 250–1.

responded with a plethora of commentaries on the characteristics of 'old' Labour, emphasising traditions of revisionism within the party, and raising the question of whether New Labour was quite so 'new' after all. Blair himself took opportunities to present the 'new' Labour in the context of the party's historical development: to suggest that the Labour Party was founded on a commitment to change, and that, in this sense, his project of modernisation was in keeping with an important strand in the party's culture. Academic Labour historiography has also provided correctives to the image of 'old Labour' in ways which argue that change is itself a Labour tradition, offering the slightly paradoxical position that, in breaking with the past, New Labour represented certain continuities with the party's history. Glen O'Hara and Helen Parr suggest that, 'The constant striving for modernity, the stress on the future, and continual attempts to redefine Labour and its policies, have always been at the heart of the party's history.'[6]

Most recent discussions of the relationship between the Labour Party and its history have been conducted within such debates about New Labour: about the extent to which the party moved away from its roots during the 1990s and made deliberate efforts to distance itself from the past.[7] This essay looks at attitudes towards the party's history over a much longer period and argues that tensions surrounding ideas of 'new' and 'old' have been a feature of the party throughout its existence—that they might even be seen as a crucial part of Labour's character. Against a disputed heritage of talismanic policy commitments, leaders' betrayals, and the perennial dilemmas of reconciling values, pragmatism, interests and ideology, the party's sense of its own history has served as one means of defining and justifying Labour's existence as an enduring political formation.

Labour's past—or shared understandings and reinventions of it—became, as Jon Lawrence has described, one of the 'myths it lived by'.[8] It informed the symbolism attached to the party, shaped or bolstered members' notions of what the party was for and their own role was within it, and was implicated in debates about policy and strategy in a party whose ideological coherence was often less impressive than its organisational strength.[9]

There are a number of reasons for studying attitudes towards history within the Labour Party. First, the New Labour project implicitly construed history, and the attachment to the past, as a problem for the modern Labour Party. A second argument follows on from this: ideas about the party's history provided a particularly strong element within Labour's identity. The historicist impetus

[6] Glen O'Hara and Helen Parr, 'Conclusions: Harold Wilson's 1964–70 governments and the heritage of "New" Labour', *Contemporary British History* 20 (2006), p. 487.

[7] e.g. James E. Cronin, *New Labour's Pasts. The Labour Party and its Discontents* (Harlow, 2004); Steven Fielding, 'New Labour and the past', in Duncan Tanner, Pat Thane, and Nick Tiratsoo (eds.), *Labour's First Century* (Cambridge, 2000), pp. 367–92 and *The Labour Party: Continuity and Change in the Making of 'New' Labour* (Basingstoke, 2003); Alasdair Blair, 'New Labour's history' (review article), *Contemporary British History* 22 (2008), pp. 137–42.

[8] Jon Lawrence, 'Labour—the myths it has lived by', in Tanner et al., *Labour's First Century*, pp. 341–66.

[9] On symbolism in Labour's political culture, see Tim Bale, *Sacred Cows and Common Sense: The Symbolic Statecraft and Political Culture of the British Labour Party* (Aldershot, 1999).

within the Labour movement as a whole has been noted by many commentators, some of whom have identified its role as a point of reference in the absence of any more systematic ideology.[10] H. M. Drucker viewed Labour's 'uses of the past' as central to the party's ethos, accepting a compatibility between Labour as a party concerned with the future and Labour as a party with a strong sense of its history, associated in part with memories of political causes which were the focus of its reforming mission: the very reason for its existence.[11] Kenneth Morgan has described the Labour Party as 'captivated, even obsessed, by its history', citing its appeal to the past as a 'permanent feature' of its political style. 'More than any other party,' he wrote, 'it has praised famous men (and, just occasionally, famous women as well) and has perpetuated their imperishable memory.'[12]

The third reason for thinking about history and the Labour Party is perhaps most significant: the nature of the Labour Party's development encouraged specific responses to its own history which distinguished it from the experience of the other major political parties. Other parties, of course, have had their own genealogies, ancestral loyalties, and past troubles and triumphs on which those involved in present disputes have taken sides. What was distinctive about the Labour Party in the twentieth century was that it had a clear and recent date of foundation.[13] The party had been created as a deliberate and strategic act in ways which set it apart from its older political competitors. Despite narratives attached to the periodic rebranding and reorganisation of the Liberal and Conservative groupings, the modern forms of those parties could be traced back readily to the mid-nineteenth century, and associated with Whig and Tory labels stretching back much further. Alongside this prolonged evolution of a two-party system, Labour's appearance was sudden and novel. The implications of this new phenomenon in the electoral landscape were masked initially by Labour's relationship with the Liberal Party, but the notion of 'independence' and the goal of achieving a different kind of political representation were there from the start. At the beginning of the twentieth century, the Labour Party aspired, in its own way, to 'break the mould' of British politics. By 1918 it had already begun to realise its ambitions of becoming a political force which could compete in its own right, rather than work in electoral alliances, presenting itself as a national party, rather than as a pressure group restricted to a few areas of support.

This essay addresses a number of aspects in the relationship between the Labour Party and its past: the conflict of 'old' and 'new'; Labour's growing maturity as an institution and the impact of generational change within the party; attitudes towards the Labour movement and heritage; and the use of the

[10] See discussions in Raymond Plant, Matt Beech, and Kevin Hickson (eds.), *The Struggle for Labour's Soul. Understanding Labour Political Thought since 1945* (London, 2004).

[11] H. M. Drucker, *Doctrine and Ethos in the Labour Party* (London, 1979), pp. 24–43.

[12] Kenneth O. Morgan, *Labour People. Leaders and Lieutenants: Hardie to Kinnock* (Oxford, 1989), p. 2.

[13] Jeremy Nuttall describes the 'frequently historiographically ignored reality that the Labour Party, and indeed even socialism as an idea, were still in the 1930s and 1940s, relatively new phenomena': Jeremy Nuttall, *Psychological Socialism. The Labour Party and Qualities of Mind and Character, 1931 to the Present* (Manchester, 2006), pp. 30–2.

past in contemporary debates. These themes, running through Labour's party culture during the twentieth century, were important in shaping identities, but were often controversial. As generations grew up and came into positions of power within the party, interpretations of the past were always subject to renegotiation, leading to ambivalent attitudes towards the party's history: as something to be celebrated and a source of on-going inspiration, but also as a potential cause of inertia and a restraint on future development.

OLD AND NEW

For a long time, Old Labour itself was very conscious of being new. Seven decades after the formation of the Labour Representation Committee, Harold Wilson could still refer to 'a party as young as ours'. In the foreword to a popular history of the party produced before the 1997 general election, Tony Blair used similar language, making a distinction between Labour and the other major parties, partly on the grounds that 'we are still a young party, not yet quite a century old'.[14]

As the most recent major addition to the party political landscape in Britain, the Labour Party celebrated its anniversaries as proof of its credibility as a real political force which was here to stay.[15] Even after the landslide electoral victory of 1945 had seemed to confirm its place in the political establishment beyond any doubt, the party remained conscious of its special status, expressed by Clement Attlee in his foreword to Francis Williams's history of Labour's first half-century: *Fifty Years' March.*

> The Liberal and Conservative Parties in this country have long histories. They have evolved from their predecessors the Whigs and the Tories. Fifty years ago the Labour Party was born.... Socialists can claim fellowship with many fighters for freedom in the past, but as an organized political movement resulting in the establishment of a completely new addition to the major political parties in the State the Labour Party is unique in our history.[16]

As Attlee implied, Labour could—and often did—cite evidence from a long ancestry of radicalism to demonstrate that this modern institution had deeper foundations in the national past. Yet newness was also part of Labour's appeal.

[14] Tony Wright and Matt Carter, *The People's Party. The History of the Labour Party* (London, 1997), p. 8.

[15] There were, of course, other new entrants to the list of political parties after the formation of the Labour Party, though most of these made a minor impact and had a short life-span (for example, Common Wealth, 1942–5, and various small, single-issue parties). More significant amongst new party groupings in mainland Britain in this period were the Co-operative Party (1917), the Communist Party of Great Britain (1920), Plaid Cymru (1925), the Scottish National Party (1928), the New Party (1931—later relaunched as the British Union of Fascists, 1932), People (1973—later Ecology, 1975 and the Green Party, 1985), the Social Democratic Party (1981—most of which was absorbed within the Social and Liberal Democrats, 1988) and the British National Party (1982).

[16] Clement Attlee, foreword to Francis Williams, *Fifty Years' March. The Rise of the Labour Party* (London, 1950), p. 5.

Labour was intended to represent something different from the other two major parties: its adherents imagined that, as a product of modern social and economic developments, it was in tune with the direction of historical change, whilst its older rivals, arising out of a different age, were supposedly less well-placed to meet the needs of working people in the early twentieth century.[17] The very existence of the party offered an indictment of the failures of older political structures and their inability to rise to the challenges of a mass electorate, the economic imperatives of modern capitalism, and the labour relations which developed alongside it.

The notion of evolution—evoked by Ross McKibbin in *The Evolution of the Labour Party* (1974) as a dynamic in the early institutional development of the party—was applied by contemporaries in the early twentieth century as a broader, quasi-organic context for explaining the need for a Labour Party and its response to wider social transformations within Britain.[18] Emanuel Shinwell observed in 1944 that 'the birth of the Labour Party marked one of the great stages in the political evolution of this country'.[19] But the politician who made more use than most of the metaphor of political evolution was Ramsay MacDonald. MacDonald justified the advent and growth of the Labour Party as something fitting to its time, whilst allegiances to the Conservative and—particularly—the Liberal Party had become 'little more than labels which most people were unwilling to take off their coats; labels, which, belonging to dead days, were accepted by living electors.' In the process he also made a claim for Labour as a young person's party:

> The new movement provided not only new labels but new issues, and though, to those brought up in old political faiths and in the worship of old political heroes, it was most confusing and annoying to be told that their faiths were lifeless and their heroes antique, to the younger people entering politics for the first time and asking themselves why they should join this party or that, the propaganda ruddy with youth as themselves was commendable.[20]

For MacDonald, then, one of the great virtues of Labour was precisely that it was new and suited to modern circumstances, whilst the Liberal Party was damned as on its way to 'extinction'. Criticisms that Labour's political opponents were hangovers from a past politics remained a feature of the party's rhetoric long

[17] As an ironic twist in the reinvention of the Liberal Party grouping from the 1980s onwards, the emergent Liberal Democrats were able to harness similar rhetoric about introducing a 'new politics' to challenge the two old parties—where Labour was now securely characterised as an 'old' party. See, notably, the Lib Dem leader Nick Clegg's contributions to the televised leadership debates at the 2010 general election: Andrew Grice, Nigel Morris, and Tom Mendelsohn, 'Clegg smashes through two-party system', *Independent*, 16 April 2010.

[18] Jose Harris, 'Labour's political and social thought', in Tanner et al., *Labour's First Century*, pp. 11–12; Geoffrey Foote, *The Labour Party's Political Thought: A History* (2nd edn.: London, 1986), pp. 58–64.

[19] Steven Fielding, Peter Thompson, and Nick Tiratsoo, *England Arise! The Labour Party and Popular Politics in 1940s Britain* (Manchester, 1995), p. 87.

[20] J. Ramsay MacDonald, *Socialism: Critical and Constructive* (London, 1921), pp. 68–9. See also discussion in David Marquand, *Ramsay MacDonald* (London, 1977), pp. 89–93.

after MacDonald's departure. Labour attacks on Conservative opponents in 1945 capitalised in part on the recent history of 'guilty men' in government, but there was also a longer perspective on offer, which condemned a party political position, as well as the records of particular politicians: 'The underlying principle of honest and decent Conservatism is inertia, the hanging on in the twentieth century to opinions that might have had much to say for themselves in the nineteenth.'[21] Meanwhile, attempts to explain the decline of the Liberal Party through factors such as the role of individual personalities or party division were, Aneurin Bevan claimed, missing the point: 'they could never have led to the decline of the Liberal Party if history had still had an important role for it to play.'[22]

One consequence of the evolutionary metaphor, and the justification of Labour as a party peculiarly suited to its time, was the implication that Labour would also move with the times: that it could not be defined by timeless commitments, but by the contingencies of social and economic realities. In this sense, Labour should have remained always 'new'. Harold Wilson positioned the party as the natural representative for a modern, white-hot economy in the 1960s[23], whilst Tony Benn—though later better known as an exponent of the *longue durée* of radical tradition[24]—also emphasised the significance of Labour's mission to be at the forefront in promoting new technologies. Neil Kinnock, in the late 1980s, insisted on the importance of Labour's engagement with the aspirations of an affluent working class whose consumerism and leisure presented a notable departure from caricatures of Labour's old constituency.[25] Yet the culture of Labour's founding period continued to exert a powerful hold on many members of the party.

COMING OF AGE

However much the Labour Party claimed to relish being the newest addition to the political scene, getting older was something to celebrate. In 1921, the party conference treated the 21st anniversary of the Labour Representation Committee as a 'coming of age', and subsequent significant anniversaries have tended to be marked with pious celebration of the 'pioneers' and founding fathers, mild triumphalism at the achievements of the intervening period, taking stock of the present and making plans for future expansion. For many local Labour parties, their own 'coming of age' came later. Cottenham Labour Party, in the Cambridgeshire constituency, was one of many to be celebrating its 21st birthday

[21] 'Licinius', *Vote Labour? Why?* (London, 1945), p. 75.

[22] Aneurin Bevan, *In Place of Fear* (1952: London, 1990), p. 123.

[23] Harold Wilson, *The Relevance of British Socialism* (London, 1964).

[24] See Tony Benn, *The Levellers and the English Democratic Tradition* (Nottingham, 1976) and *Arguments for Socialism* (London, 1979).

[25] e.g. in his speech on affluence and socialism to the 1987 party conference, Neil Kinnock, *Thorns & Roses. Speeches 1983–1991* (London, 1992), pp. 123–40.

in 1939—marked with tea and a concert—and the Cambridgeshire Divisional Labour Party itself was also planning to celebrate its 'coming of age' in November 1939—though it was unlucky with its timing, and the special dinner was cancelled following the outbreak of war.[26]

Anniversaries, milestone issues of publications, formalisations of its organisation through the professionalisation of its staffing, the opening of new offices and the building of Labour clubs, provided opportunities to remember the past, marked Labour's growing maturity, and celebrated its durability as a political force. Acknowledgement of the passing years and markers of Labour's establishment as something more secure than a temporary pressure group—its own buildings, commemorative volumes, strategic schemes to undertake specific recruitment and development work—contributed to its self-assurance as a mature feature in British political life.[27] With a pride and respectability reminiscent of the stationery of commercial firms, local Labour parties headed their notepaper with the date when their organisation was 'Established'.

This growing maturity brought with it its own mid-life crisis and a consciousness of lost youth. One important context for the tendencies towards an idealisation of the party's past lay in Labour's expansion as an institution, with the professionalisation, systematization, and formalities which accompanied this. Not everyone felt entirely comfortable with the ways in which the party was changing, and by the 1930s there were expressions of nostalgia for purer, more committed forms of political action, associated with the founding generation of pioneers. '[T]he Labour Party of today is not the Party it formerly was,' Philip Snowden lamented as he wrote his memoirs (as an exile from Labour's ranks) and reminisced about missionary work for the ILP half a lifetime earlier: 'It has lost much of its idealistic quality and spiritual fervour. It has become an ordinary political party, with little to distinguish it from the quality of other parties.'[28] Such concerns were not solely the province of an older cohort with personal experience of the party in its earlier manifestations. Indeed they seem to have been taken up with notable enthusiasm by the youth sections, keen to emulate a more glorious past of commitment to the cause and a more romantic vision of socialist propaganda than was necessarily compatible with modern branch life. John Dugdale (b. 1905) moaned to the party conference in 1933 that the pre-war Labour Party had been 'a Party of adventure', whereas 'to-day Labour represents to a great extent a Party of respectability and dullness'.[29] Reference to—and reverence for—the generation of the pioneers was also adopted more strategically as part of membership crusades in the 1930s, as Labour confronted concerns about a disengagement of young people from conventional politics and attempted through pageantry and inspirational talk about the rewarding

[26] Cambridgeshire Record Office, Cambridgeshire Divisional Labour Party papers, 416/0.22; 416/0.20, Executive Committee reports for 1938–9 and 1939–40.

[27] On commemorative volumes to mark anniversaries, see Andrew Thorpe, 'Centenary histories of the Labour Party' (review article), *History* 86 (2001), pp. 523–4.

[28] Philip Snowden, *An Autobiography*, ii (London, 1934), p. 1039.

[29] *Report of the 33rd Annual Labour Party Conference* (1933), p. 147.

experience of active party life to encourage greater enrolment in its campaign to achieve a million members and establish itself as a truly mass party. As Margaret Bondfield described in relation to staging the Pageant of Labour at the Crystal Palace in October 1934, the hope was to 'inspire a revival of the spirit which animated the early trade union pioneers'.[30]

The growing size and complexity of the party as an institution and its wish to prove itself capable, modern and efficient were partly in tension with this ethos. Contrasts were drawn between the 'sacrifice' of earlier socialists and the salaried professionals who increasingly ran the modern party, insisting on recognition and suitable terms and conditions for jobs which had once been done—and in many areas of the country were still being done—in a voluntary capacity. The creation of a class of professional, paid organisers—who, by 1916, even had their own organisation (the National Association of Labour Registration and Election Agents, rechristened the National Union of Labour Organisers and Election Agents in 1920)—raised particular questions about the nature and ethos of party service. Their role became a focus for discussions about the character of the party itself and the ways in which it was changing. Party agents and organisers themselves often displayed a Janus-faced attitude towards their job. The National Union pressed for appropriate recognition of its members' professional competence, ran training schemes from 1921 to give would-be organisers a qualification in electoral law, book-keeping, and the other skills necessary for the job, and, as one would expect of a professional organisation, was antagonistic towards part-time appointments and pragmatic attempts to arrange organisational assistance at a lower rate of pay. But many of the early paid organisers had a previous record of unpaid enthusiasm in service to the Labour movement, and continued to emphasise the vital role of the rank and file in Labour's future development, insisting that older traditions of voluntarism and sacrifice should still be encouraged.

The celebration of 'servants' of the Labour movement commonly employed the same sorts of language in commemorating the work of paid employees as it did in remembering the early socialist missionaries. Herbert Drinkwater, chief spokesman for professional party agents throughout the 1920s and 1930s, argued that the spirit of sacrifice was not diminishing, despite the fears expressed by some of those nostalgic for the 'good old days' of heroic struggle. As he saw it, even paid party servants sacrificed, through working long hours and as 'casualties by way of ill-health, and even death'.[31] Obituaries of paid party agents, organisers, and professional propagandists continued to celebrate their lives as a kind of martyrdom. Some, such as the national agent Egerton Wake, who died in 1929, were seen as succumbing to an early death, worn out by their dedication to the cause. Others were commended for their physical exertions in the promotion of Labour politics: the hours they worked, the miles they travelled to attend meetings. By the time the National Union's magazine *The Labour Organiser*

[30] Modern Records Centre, University of Warwick, TUC papers, MSS292/1.91/44.
[31] *Labour Organiser*, January 1930, p. 15.

reached its 50th birthday in 1970, it was the agents of the 1920s who had become symbols of a heritage to celebrate and emulate.[32] When the *Labour Organiser* ceased publication in August 1971, its final issue was full of nostalgia for the pioneering days in which the magazine had first appeared.[33]

Such romanticisation of a past in which there had supposedly been greater commitment to and excitement about party work has been a persistent feature of Labour's political culture.[34] As he set out his vision of Labour as a 'party of advance' Roy Jenkins noted what he saw as the dangerous attractions of idealising earlier days of protest, propaganda, 'political passion', and comradeship when socialists were 'a small band, untrammelled by the responsibilities of office, and exhilarated by the feeling of being *contra mundum*': 'Doubtless . . . it was for the individual a morally exciting and emotionally satisfying movement to which to belong. Not unnaturally therefore there are many who regret the old days and the fervour that seems to have gone.'[35] In 1951, as he delivered a lecture on the future of the Labour movement, G. D. H. Cole warned his audience that he could not leave them with the satisfaction of a comforting peroration to the spirit of Keir Hardie, Robert Blatchford, or William Morris: 'For these pioneers of the modern Labour movement were products of a situation which it is impossible to recall. They were moved to strong indignation by the sight, everywhere they looked around them, of unmerited and unnecessary human suffering . . . They were men who had grown up in a social atmosphere that was at one and the same time moral and hard.'[36] Indeed Cole—himself a prolific biographer of early radicals and advocate of labour history—suggested that too much focus on valued mythologies had left some socialists isolated from the mainstream of the Labour Party, 'invoking vainly the spirits of the pioneers . . . while the leaders of the Party, with the support of most of the rank and file, got on with the "real business" of winning parliamentary power'.[37]

In Cole's view Labour had reached the end of an era and needed to acknowledge that some aspects of its heritage belonged the past rather than being of direct relevance to contemporary conditions. The lingering significance of references to an earlier politics had been encouraged to some degree by Labour's own demographics. The tendency for the first cohorts of office holders and Labour politicians to come to political work after careers in industry and trade unionism often made for a relatively elderly leadership, whose own experience and points of

[32] *Labour Organiser*, July/August 1970, p. 125.

[33] For further discussion, see Clare Griffiths, 'Savoir gérer un parti. Organisation et professionnalisation du parti travailliste britannique des années 1920 aux années 1940', *Politix. Revue des sciences sociales du politique*, 81 (2008), pp. 61–80.

[34] On this as a feature of socialism more generally, see Ralph Miliband, 'Socialism and the myth of the golden past', in Ralph Miliband and John Saville (eds.), *The Socialist Register* (London, 1964), pp. 92–103.

[35] Roy Jenkins, *Pursuit of Progress. A Critical Analysis of the Achievement and Prospect of the Labour Party* (London, 1953), p. 164.

[36] G. D. H. Cole, *British Labour Movement—Retrospect and Prospect*, Fabian Special Tract no. 8 (London, 1951), p. 18.

[37] Ibid., p. 10.

reference already stretched back to very different historical circumstances. In other words, there was both a personal investment in narratives about the circumstances which had led to the formation of the party (in which these individuals could reasonably claim to have played a part) and a close connection to the labour struggles of the nineteenth century. Family connections meant that even involvement in Chartist campaigns or early trade union struggles was not necessarily viewed as part of a distant history for some activists in the 1920s.

The impact of continuities of personnel within the party machine soon meant that, as Martin Pugh has observed with regard to the 1930s, 'though only thirty years old, Labour was already becoming an old man's party'.[38] This is not to suggest that the other major political parties were being run predominantly by young people and shaped by their new, fresh thinking, unencumbered by the legacies of the past. But, despite the emphasis on Labour as a relatively new presence in British politics, concerns were soon being expressed about the party's excessive reliance on the activities of the more aged section of the population and its apparent inability to reach out to attract youthful supporters. In the 1930s, criticisms were being laid against the less-than-enticing culture of committee structures and staid social events, at a time when extremist political movements were capitalising on the use of modern methods of propaganda and spectacle to attract membership. And as Labour gained maturity as an organisation, some argued that it was failing to keep up with the times. There were complaints in the 1950s and 1960s that party life at branch level was far too old-fashioned, operating with worn-out equipment in dingy premises which did nothing to attract new generations of members and was at odds with the proper ethos of a party concerned with visions of a better future.[39] Trade unions were likewise criticised for carrying associations with a bygone age, their activities and propaganda appearing 'increasingly anachronistic, dowdy'.[40]

Questions about the distinctive political cultures representing different generations and the implications for Labour's support have been examined by Michael Childs, who concluded that the party's electoral fortunes reflected the education and experience of different age cohorts.[41] But generations mattered within party activism as well as party support. Sometimes generational change made party unity more likely by taking the sting out of old divisions, such as the crisis of 1931, attitudes to the Popular Front, or the factionalism of the Bevanites and Gaitskellites. In the process it could also consolidate a specific vision of what the party was and what it was there to do, relying on institutional histories from the 'forward march' school, implying a united purpose which newer recruits were in no position to interrogate on the basis of their own experience. Writing in the

[38] Martin Pugh, *Speak for Britain! A New History of the Labour Party* (London, 2010), p. 218.

[39] Lawrence Black, '"Still at the penny-farthing stage in a jet-propelled era": branch life in 1950s socialism', *Labour History Review* 65 (2000), pp. 202–26.

[40] Michael Shanks, *The Stagnant Society* (1961), cited in Robert Taylor, *The Fifth Estate. Britain's Unions in the Seventies* (London, 1978), p. 4.

[41] Michael Childs, 'Labour grows up: the electoral system, political generations, and British politics 1890–1929', *Twentieth Century British History* 6 (1995), pp. 123–44.

Labour Organiser in October 1970, a party activist from South Wales reflected on a modern culture in which controversies such as the disaffiliation of the ILP (in 1932) had been forgotten, and a new generation of party workers had never even heard of the Tolpuddle Martyrs. Although trying to avoid undue nostalgia, he found himself succumbing nonetheless:

Are we becoming a Labour *Party* rather more than a Labour *Movement*? Those who went to our meeting in the 1920s went in the real spirit of revival . . . When I think back on those days I wonder have we tired on the way, or have we substantially achieved what was desired? Was it really intended, like the Liberal Party before us, that we carry the social reform another lap in human progress . . . ?[42]

HERITAGE

As the Labour Party aged, it developed—as most institutions do—a sense of its own history. Labour marked the centenary of 1906 with a project to collect 'untold stories' of rank and file members and activists. Tony Robinson, actor, television presenter of popular history programmes, and Labour Party activist, was the public face used to endorse the initiative. 'How frustrating,' he wrote, 'that those of us who continue their work today know so little about our forebears!':

If only we knew something more about their personalities, their foibles, their successes and their failures. What a source of inspiration that would be! . . . How can we learn what to do next unless we have a sense of the triumphs and failures of past generations? We sometimes talk blithely about the values of the Labour Party. But those values aren't abstract concepts. They were wrought from the experience of ordinary men and women in their restless search for a better world. Let's discover who they were, so we can honour them, learn from them, and use their experience to create a meaningful twenty-first century socialist [party].[43]

An initiative like 'Your history—your chance to play a part' was an attempt to recover a past apparently in danger of being lost from memory, reaching back to experiences that now survived only in documentary records or as traditions. For all the 'inspiration' that might be garnered from this history, its distance from the present was part of what made it safe and adaptable to modern needs. Labour had not always been so wedded to preserving its past. Concerns that being out-of-date and too beholden to the past might compromise one's efficiency, had resulted in earlier pleas to local organisers and secretaries to divest themselves of old clutter. In the 1960s and 1970s, secretaries of local organisations were encouraged to

[42] Chas. W. Bridges, 'A memorable past—but what of the future?', *Labour Organiser*, October 1970, p. 191.

[43] Text from website for the project 'Your history—your chance to play a part', http://www.1906labourcentenary.org.uk (accessed 15 February 2006). See also Dianne Hayter, 'The PLP: 1906–2006', *Parliamentary Affairs* 60 (2007), pp. 153–63. The Labour Oral History Project, begun in 1993, was also set up to record the experience of local activists: Daniel Weinbren, *Generating Socialism: Recollections of Life in the Labour Party* (Stroud, 1997).

throw out the detritus left by their predecessors in the post, fuelling concerns for some in the Movement about the need to archive and create museums of Labour's heritage.

The impetus to preserve, display, and commemorate a history of the Labour movement began most explicitly in the 1930s. In 1937 G. D. H. Cole staged one of the earliest exhibitions of Labour history in a temporary display at Collet's Bookshop on London's Charing Cross Road entitled 'The Road to '37', with objects drawn in large part from his own personal collection, aiming to demonstrate 'a story of working-class struggle through six generations to the present day'.[44] Also in the 1930s, the Co-operative movement established its museum to the Rochdale Pioneers, whilst the TUC sponsored a volume of essays accompanied by facsimiles of original documentary sources as part of its centenary commemoration of the Tolpuddle Martyrs.[45] The natural impetus in such historical projects was to define a common heritage for the Labour Movement, rather than for the Labour Party as a separate entity, and the most substantial expression of this was the collection assembled through the Trade Union, Labour and Co-operative History Society in the 1960s. This formed the basis for the National Museum of Labour History, operating initially at Limehouse Town Hall in the 1970s, and later in Manchester, where it was reincarnated as the People's History Museum in 1994.[46]

These efforts to preserve artefacts and historical accounts tended to present past radicalism and struggles as part of a unifying narrative which retained a relevance for the contemporary Labour movement. Mobilisations of Labour's heritage began as efforts to strengthen identification with the cause in the present day, encouraging respect, and even reverence for forebears in the movement, and providing inspiration, particularly through accounts of what activists had had to endure in the past. Laying claim to an extended radical tradition within British history offered respectability and a lineage for the modern Labour politics of the twentieth century.[47] It also had an educative role. G. D. H. Cole argued that history was the most important subject in workers' education, allowing men to 'feel at home in the world', to understand how changes happen, and to substitute realism for utopianism.[48] 'The greatest weakness of the workers at

[44] British Library of Political and Economic Science, London, Fabian Society papers, J14/7, f. 46, circulated letter from New Fabian Research Bureau [1937].

[45] I have written on the Tolpuddle commemorations in 'Remembering Tolpuddle: rural history and commemoration in the inter-war Labour movement', *History Workshop Journal*, 44 (1997), pp. 145–69. As Secretary to the TUC, Walter Citrine oversaw a number of other illustrated histories, including *Sixty Years of Trade Unionism* (1928) and *Seventy Years of Trade Unionism* (1938)—both of which, self-evidently, identified the history of trade unionism closely with the institutional history of the TUC (founded 1868).

[46] Chris Burgess, 'The development of Labor history in UK museums and the People's History Museum', *International Labor and Working-Class History* 76 (2009), pp. 26–35.

[47] Gerhard W. Ditz, 'Utopian symbols in the history of the British Labour Party', *British Journal of Sociology* 17 (1966), pp. 145–50.

[48] *New Standards*, 12 (October 1924), p. 357. On Cole's ideas about the power of history to equip people to shape their own lives, see Gail L. Owen, 'G. D. H. Cole's historical writings', *International Review of Social History*, 11 (1966), pp. 169–96, especially pp. 180–1.

this present time,' he argued in the 1920s, 'is not the lack of power, but the lack of the confidence to use it.' For Cole, this came down to a lack of historical perspective:

That lack of confidence comes in part, I believe, from a sense of insecurity, not only in the present, but in the past . . . [The worker] does not know how his insecurity arose; he has no sense of an historic mission to make a new society that will give him assurance and elbow-room, as rising social classes in the past have made assurance and elbow-room for themselves by the creation of new social systems.[49]

History within workers' education was often politically aligned, and worked deliberately to counteract the establishment histories taught in school and to shape the resolve of the present generation in the movement: Cole and others promoted the history of the common people and their movements as an education equipping working men and women to take a full part in political and organisational work.[50] In the late 1960s, the veteran trade unionist Will Lawther commented that, 'It's more essential for people in the Labour Movement to know their social history and to know the history of the Movement than to know anything else.'[51] There was always an ambiguity about whether Labour history should be about the social history of the working class or about organisations and institutions, but these attitudes certainly encouraged Labour history to develop as a historiography with a purpose, characterised by Eric Hobsbawm as 'at a point of junction between politics and academic study, between practical commitment and theoretical understanding, between interpreting the world and changing it'.[52]

When it came to members of the Labour Party reading about the history of the party, G. D. H. Cole's, *A History of the Labour Party from 1914* (1948) became a standard account, following on from his *British Working-Class Politics, 1832–1914* (1941). Mary Agnes Hamilton, in addition to producing a number of biographies of Labour figures (including Mary Macarthur and Ramsay MacDonald), wrote various overviews of the party history during the interwar period, claiming that an understanding of the history was necessary to explain the current form of the party's organisation.[53] But the 1960s and 1970s were a period of more formalisation and the development of a more overtly academic profile for Labour history, with the creation of institutions, organisations and projects

[49] G. D. H. Cole, 'The importance of history to the workers', *New Standards in Industry, Politics, Education—A Journal of Workers' Control*, 5 (March 1924), p. 137.

[50] For example, the influential social history which Cole co-wrote with his brother-in-law Raymond Postgate: *The Common People* (London, 1938, and later editions).

[51] J. F. Clarke, 'An interview with Sir William Lawther', *Bulletin of the Society for the Study of Labour History* 19 (1969), p. 21.

[52] From 'Labour history and ideology' (1974), cited in John McIlroy, 'Origins of the Society for the Study of Labour History', in John McIlroy, Alan Campbell, John Halstead, and David Martin (eds.), *Making History. Organizations of Labour Historians in Britain since 1960*, Labour History Review Fiftieth Anniversary Supplement (Leeds, 2010), p. 80.

[53] Mary Agnes Hamilton, *The Labour Party To-Day: What it is and How it Works* (London, [1939]), pp. 12–39, 93. Also, 'Labour Party: history and events', in H. B. Lees-Smith (ed.), *The Encyclopaedia of the Labour Movement* (London, 1928), vol. 2, pp. 164–75.

including, notably, the establishment of the Society for the Study of Labour History in 1960 and the beginnings of the *Dictionary of Labour Biography*, the first volume of which appeared in 1972.[54] One of the concerns in this period was about the condition of the sources from which historians might write new accounts of the Labour Party. Henry Pelling's *The Origins of the Labour Party 1880–1900* (1954) commented on the challenges of the unpublished source material, which was scattered and, as Pelling saw it, insufficiently well cared for.[55] The creation of archives and the pressure to make documents available to scholars contributed to the development of new historiographies. The doctoral research which informed Ross McKibbin's first book—*The Evolution of the Labour Party* (1974)—drew on the Labour Party's archives, then in the library at Transport House and relatively inaccessible to scholars up until that point.[56]

Margaret Cole, who survived her husband G. D. H. Cole by two decades, developed parts of his legacy (such as his plans for a dictionary of labour biography) in this new climate. She shared his views about the importance of history in educating political activists, which, in her case, she promoted particularly through biography, nagging Michael Foot in 1976 about the likely publication date for the second volume of his life of Aneurin Bevan, since she was 'constantly recommending it to younger workers in the Labour movement who come in knowing so little of what it has meant to hundreds of thousands'. However, as she reflected on her own contributions to this process of providing young people with edifying accounts of their political forebears, she evidently felt some reservations about the tone of some of the new histories: 'nearly 30 years ago, I wrote a book called *Makers of the Labour Movement*—and recently I reread it myself, and was delighted to find afresh how good and how *generous* it was, so different from some of the sour-mouthed stuff that too many people are putting out nowadays.'[57]

That distinction between generosity and being 'sour-mouthed' perhaps hints at the difference between a critical history and the cultivation of a sense of heritage which might reinforce the present in less problematic ways. *The Makers of the Labour Movement* (1948) drew on Margaret Cole's considerable experience in historical research and writing for a general audience in an accessible manner, offering a series of biographical portraits of radical figures, from Tom Paine and William Cobbett to George Lansbury and (less predictably) H. G. Wells. But the collection was framed by expressions of political piety. Hugh Dalton contributed a foreword claiming that the memory of these pioneers should be 'held in honour',

[54] McIlroy et al., *Making History*; Ralph Miliband, 'John Saville: a presentation', in David E. Martin and David Rubinstein (eds.), *Ideology and the Labour Movement* (London, 1979), pp. 28–30; David Howell, 'John Saville and the *Dictionary of Labour Biography*', *Labour History Review* 75 (2010), pp. 125–7.

[55] Henry Pelling, *The Origins of the Labour Party 1880–1900* (London, 1954), p. v.

[56] Foreword to 1991 impression, Ross McKibbin, *The Evolution of the Labour Party 1910–1924* (Oxford, 1991), p. vii.

[57] Margaret Cole to Michael Foot, 2 December 1976, Labour History Archive, Manchester, MF/L27/11 (emphases as in original).

and that it was fitting that Cole's book had 'made it possible for a later generation to recognise its debt to each of them'. Cole herself justified the book as an account of the political tradition that lay behind Labour's 1945 victory:

> [T]here is a long roll, extending over many centuries, of men and women who fought and died for democracy, social justice and the rights of the common people. History books make less of them, for history books are mostly written from the point of view of the other side. But they are *our* leaders and *our* pioneers, and we must make them and their lives at least as well known to the world as those of the captains and the kings. That is why this book is written.[58]

Jon Lawrence has argued that uses of the past within the Labour Party often had an instrumental value, as the 'myths [Labour] has lived by' allowed members to 'place themselves within an unfolding, seamless history of political commitment', despite substantial changes over time to the kind of party Labour was, its membership, activity, and what it stood for.[59] Lawrence was referring here to a more immediate history within the party, almost a family history, exemplified by the shaping of the life stories of party figures in biographies and memoirs. Meanwhile, alongside the relatively short history of the Labour Party's own existence as an institution, there were much longer chronologies (like that offered by Margaret Cole) in which to situate the party's experience. Fielding, Thompson, and Tiratsoo have illustrated the readiness of leading Labour figures in the 1940s to reach to examples of radical forebears in setting the work of the Attlee government in a longer national tradition.[60]

Even so, there may be a case for suggesting that the Labour *Movement* encouraged the commemoration of a much more extensive genealogy than within the party more narrowly defined. In the context of the Movement, a shared and unifying past became a source for encouraging solidarity: a social memory expressed in song, design, pageantry, literature, and as a general frame of cultural reference for 'This Great Movement of Ours'. These representations of heritage were mainly for internal consumption, strengthening working-class identities and charting an alternative national history of the people which was also to a large extent pursued within the self-identifying enterprise of labour history. They served to reinforce notions of radical chronologies, long marches, unity of purpose, continuities of struggle (even in very different historical circumstances), and a clear trajectory of progress, placing present-day concerns in the context of longer-term traditions. The majority of members of the Labour Party identified themselves whole-heartedly within 'The Movement' and were a part of this culture of celebrating a Labour heritage. But for the Labour Party there were added anxieties about the place of such narratives within its core

[58] Margaret Cole, *Makers of the Labour Movement* (London, 1948), pp. viii, ix-x (emphases as in original).

[59] Tanner et al., *Labour's First Century*, p. 342. Lawrence's essay in the volume draws mainly on auto/biographies.

[60] Steven Fielding, Peter Thompson, and Nick Tiratsoo, *England Arise! The Labour Party and Popular Politics in 1940s Britain* (Manchester, 1995), pp. 86–7.

activity of addressing and responding to the external audience of the general electorate. Moreover, the defining purposes of the political party were both less certain and more subject to change than was the case for the trade unions. What remained of greater significance for the party was the interpretation of its own immediate past—often because this could be used as a contribution to debates and power struggles within the organisation in the present.

LESSONS

For a party that purported to challenge tradition in many aspects of British life, the Labour Party's own traditions were deployed to a surprising extent within its internal debates about policy, power structures and priorities. Despite its relentless emphasis on youth and newness and modernisation, even the New Labour project made its own use of lessons from history, and Steven Fielding has described its attempt to 'construct a tradition which challenged the dominant view of the party's past'.[61] In his foreword to Austin Mitchell's study of the 1945 general election—subtitled *Reflections on the Revolution in Britain*—Blair offered the maxim: 'A party that lives in the past is doomed to die. But a party that neglects the past is doomed to fail.'[62] The important point, then, was to focus on the 'right' bits of the past.

A shared frame of reference to key episodes in the party's past certainly provided an important common vocabulary within Labour rhetoric throughout the twentieth century: about betrayals, the dangers of political pacts with other parties, the party's vulnerability to bankers' machinations and uncontrollable strikers, maverick council leaders, and the dangers of disunity in Labour ranks. Conversely, unimpeachable heroes and the great achievements of the past functioned as talismanic references to demonstrate one's loyalty to supposedly enduring principles and values. Much of Labour's historical imagination coalesced around the figures of inspirational leaders and pioneers, celebrated in memoirs that tended towards political hagiography, and evoked periodically for approval or censure of the present-day party.[63] 'If Keir Hardie were here today . . . ' was an enduring cry, harking back to the ultimate figurehead of the founding generation. But Labour had its villains, as well as heroes, offering cautionary tales to the party. None was more notorious than Ramsay MacDonald. 'Well, I mean, look at the tragedy of Snowdon (sic), Thomas and MacDonald,' observed Will Lawther in the late 1960s; 'MacDonald, his grave

[61] Fielding, 'New Labour and the past', in Tanner et al., *Labour's First Century*, p. 384.

[62] Tony Blair, in Austin Mitchell, *Election '45. Reflections on the Revolution in Britain* (London, 1995), p. 7.

[63] On memoirs and biography, see Duncan Tanner, 'Socialist pioneers and the art of political biography' (review article), *Twentieth Century British History* 4 (1993), pp. 284–91, and Jon Lawrence, 'Labour—the myths it has lived by', in Tanner et al., *Labour's First Century*, pp. 341–66.

there at Lossiemouth, there's nobody ever looks at it or anything. He's simply forgot.'[64]

The notion that MacDonald was forgotten, rather than unforgiven, sounds like wishful thinking. But the case of his infamous betrayal illustrates that attitudes within the party towards its history were not just about acknowledging the past but about taking sides. A firmly developed sense of history has been a common feature of oppositional stances in the Labour Party, both against external opponents and as a means of expressing discontent within the party. Gidon Cohen has discussed the use of myths about the ILP in debates within the Labour Party as a source of historical endorsement for Labour's ethos and approach and in re-examining its origins.[65] The use of reference to the past in arguing the moral high-ground against things with which one disagrees in the present was identified by Paul Corthorn as one of the hallmarks of Michael Foot's political career: 'a particularly pronounced example of a broader, and continuing, Labour tradition'.[66]

There were two episodes in particular which came to define the Labour Party and adopt a central role in its historical consciousness. One was the foundation itself, and the work and outlook of the pioneers responsible for bringing Labour into being. David Martin has described the political culture surrounding the first generation of Labour MPs as setting 'an unusually indelible reforming agenda', which 'provided, for good or ill, a point of reference for succeeding generations of activists'.[67] But even more powerful was the legacy of the 1945 general election and the programme enacted by the government which it brought into office. More than anything else, the reforms of Attlee's administration shaped subsequent cohorts of the party, setting the bar for what Labour might achieve in government and elevating the status of certain key policies, notably state provision of welfare and nationalisation.[68] Gareth Stedman Jones wrote in the mid-1980s about the dangers of the Labour Party focusing too much on a 'golden age' version of its past which was caught up above all with versions of the period of the Attlee governments. As Stedman Jones saw it, 'The reason why [Labour] must

[64] William Lawther, interviewed by J. F. Clarke in 1968, *Bulletin of the Society for the Study of Labour History* 19 (1969), p. 17.

[65] Gidon Cohen, 'Myth, history and the Independent Labour Party', in Matthew Worley (ed.), *The Foundations of the British Labour Party: Identities, Cultures and Perspectives, 1900–39* (Farnham, 2009), pp. 95–112.

[66] Paul Corthorn, 'Michael Foot as Labour leader. The uses of the past', in Richard Toye and Julie Gottlieb (eds.), *Making Reputations. Power, Persuasion and the Individual in Modern British Politics* (London, 2005), p. 165.

[67] David Martin, 'Labour's parliamentary pioneers of 1906', in Alan Haworth and Dianne Hayter (eds.), *Men Who Made Labour: The PLP of 1906—the Personalities and the Politics* (Abingdon, 2006), p. 20.

[68] Robert Looker, 'A golden past?: The Labour Party and the working class in 1945', in Jim Fyrth (ed.), *Labour's Promised Land? Culture and Society in Labour Britain 1945–51* (London, 1995), pp. 28–42. Note Tony Blair's caution in delivering the lecture to the Fabian Society to mark the 50th anniversary of the 1945 election, that 1945 should be remembered as 'the exception and not the rule' (*Let Us Face the Future,* p. 3).

understand its own history is to avoid attempts to perpetuate or nostalgically to recapture it.'[69]

Too much reverence for the past could reify certain policy positions and key episodes until they became articles of faith, and excessive loyalty to the party's past has often been blamed as a limitation on its future development. David Marquand, who left the Labour Party for the SDP in 1981, pointed to the constraints imposed on socialists and social democrats in Britain by operating 'through the institutions, values and collective memory of British Labourism'. A noted historian of Labour politics, Marquand observed excessive filial piety within Labour's ranks, characterising the persistence of some of the party's socialist commitments (notably in Clause Four) as essentially symbolic: 'to show that the party was true to its roots, properly respectful of past sacrifices and the memory of the pioneers'.[70] Moreover, these debts to the past amounted to more than sentiment: legacies of the peculiar origins of the party remained embodied in its structures and decision-making. In particular, the persistent influence of trade unionism was often implicated in critiques of Labour's failure to establish a more radical socialist programme and break free from 'labourism'.[71] In presenting an engaging and largely celebratory history of the achievements of the Labour movement, A. J. Davies likened the position of Labour by the 1990s to Marx's image of the weight of tradition lying 'like a nightmare on the brain of the living'.[72]

Concerns about the constraints imposed by an unhealthy focus on the past contributed to arguments that a reinvigorated Labour Party would have to rethink its attitudes towards its history. In the balance between old and new, the emphasis needed to be placed once more on the 'new'. The term 'New Labour' was considered, though not adopted, by the founders of the breakaway Social Democratic Party in 1981.[73] Many of the criticisms of Labour as a political vehicle in the later twentieth century were bound up with problems in moving away from its institutional legacies, the power of mythologies about its history and a too-literal loyalty to the past. In his speech to the 1987 party conference, Neil Kinnock quoted from Aneurin Bevan's warning that socialists must be 'on guard against the old words'. Yet it is notable that, even as his leadership focused on the need to 'modernise' the party, Kinnock's oratory drew

[69] Gareth Stedman Jones, 'Marching into history?', in James Curran (ed.), *The Future of the Left* (Cambridge, 1984), p. 4.

[70] David Marquand, *The Progressive Dilemma: From Lloyd George to Kinnock* (London, 1991), pp. 237, 22.

[71] Madeleine Davis, '"Labourism" and the New Left', in John Callaghan, Steven Fielding, and Steve Ludlam (eds.), *Interpreting the Labour Party: Approaches to Labour Politics and History* (Manchester, 2003), pp. 39–56; Eric Shaw, 'Labourism: myths and realities', in Plant et al., *The Struggle for Labour's Soul*, pp. 187–205; Willie Thompson, *The Long Death of British Labourism: interpreting a political culture* (London, 1993).

[72] A. J. Davies, *To Build a New Jerusalem: The British Labour Movement from the 1880s to the 1990s* (London, 1992), p. 284.

[73] Matthew d'Ancona, 'New Labour and a false paternity suit', *Sunday Telegraph*, 3 September 2000; Ray Dunne, 'SDP: breaking the mould', 25 January 2001, BBC News website: http://news.bbc.co.uk/1/hi/uk_politics/1136223.stm.

on references to the achievements of past Labour administrations, the historic struggles of working people and the inspiration offered by figures such as Bevan.[74]

Academic historiography of the Labour Party sometimes made its own contributions to diagnoses of what prevented Labour from fully realising its potential as a party of government.[75] Introducing a reprint of the proceedings of Labour's first party conference reports in 1967, Henry Pelling left the reader to 'judge for himself how far the strengths and weaknesses of four Labour Governments in Britain can be traced back to these early days', with the implication that this was one context in which sources from the earliest days of the party were likely to be read.[76] Nor was academic history writing always detached from modern debates going on within the Labour Party, given the tendency recognised by John Callaghan, Steven Fielding, and Steve Ludlam for historians of the Labour Party to be party members themselves and to identify a teleology for the party in keeping with their own ideological position.[77]

Appeals to history came to represent a canonisation of certain elements within Labour's past as somehow the proper embodiment of the party's traditions, from which any departure was a form of betrayal. But, for a party which was, from the outset, a federal construction populated by migrants from other political parties, the identification of unifying 'traditions' has always been selective in its treatment of Labour's heritage. Historians have pointed out that the influence of working-class patriotism and recruitment of personnel from the Conservative Party, for example, have been much less celebrated or chronicled than Labour's links to Liberalism, while the significance of nonconformity has tended to be given more prominence than connections to High-Church socialism or spiritualism.[78]

In his survey of approaches to writing about the Labour Party, Royden Harrison categorised three types of general history of the party: 'vulgar celebratory stuff [such as Francis Williams's *Fifty Years' March*], unvarnished tales [including by Pelling and, with more hesitation, G. D. H. Cole], and chronicles of a death foretold [with Ralph Miliband's *Parliamentary Socialism* (1961) as the pre-eminent example]'.[79] Such accounts informed, but also reflected a broader and persistent consciousness of the past within the party, offering a coherence, common cultural identity and purpose, but also exposing and providing much of the ammunition for the party's internal divisions. As I have argued in this essay, the functions of history within the party were connected in part to its own development as an institution: boosting the confidence and solidarity of a young

[74] Speech to 1987 Labour Party conference, in Kinnock, *Thorns & Roses*, p. 129.

[75] See e.g. Ross McKibben (sic), 'The historic Labour Party', *History Today* 33, November 1983, pp. 31–6.

[76] *The Labour Party Foundation Conference and Annual Conference Reports 1900–1905*, Hammersmith reprints of scarce documents, no.3 (London, 1967), p. 5.

[77] 'Introduction', in Callaghan, Fielding, and Ludlam, *Interpreting the Labour Party*, p. 1.

[78] Pugh, *Speak for Britain!*, p. 12, *et passim*; Raphael Samuel, 'Ancestor worship', *Island Stories: Unravelling Britain. Theatres of Memory, volume II* (London, 1998), pp. 272–5.

[79] Royden Harrison, 'Labour Party history: approaches and interpretations', *Labour History Review* 56.1 (1991), p. 8.

organisation, and bolstering its claims to be taken seriously and to make a successful transition from pressure group to enduring presence in the political landscape. History also offered reference points to define Labour on a more philosophical level, to endorse values and commitments within the party, while, in social and cultural terms, the sense of a shared past embodied and perpetuated the tribalism of being a member of the party—just as challenges to the understanding and valuing of Labour's history raised questions of loyalty and political priorities. In the broad church of Labour's affiliated bodies and individual membership, some readings of party history were as likely to focus existing tensions as to broker a contented, imagined community. Yet the ability of a shared historical narrative to act as a focus for party unity should not be underestimated. It was a tribute to the lasting power of a sense of common heritage that the modernisers at the end of the century chose to place such emphasis on liberating the membership from its attachment to 'Old Labour' and prioritising 'values' over tradition in relaunching the party as something 'new'.

REFLECTIONS

18

Communicating Interest

Emma Eadie

I remember Ross discussing, one day, some or other historical controversialist. What he didn't understand about the man was that he was supposed to be an historian but he didn't seem to have any interest in the past at all. As a teacher, I realised, communicating this interest, without resorting to exhortation, was Ross's most important achievement.

What struck me most forcibly about Ross's interest in the past was its precision. It seemed, at first, slightly out of character. He always seemed such an easy-going sort of chap; unfuddy-duddy, disappointingly so to a newcomer to Oxford. But he was a stickler for accuracy. In all things. Spelling, of course. One friend became quite distraught on receiving back his first essay and finding the word 'peasant' written with, he thought, more than usual firmness at the bottom of the page. It was simply a correction of a frequent mistake but, as such, seemed surprising and so was taken as a cruel and inexplicable insult until someone explained otherwise. Coming as I did from an altogether more casual set-up, I was slightly disconcerted at not being able just to make things up when the need arose or express them in a general sort of way which got the gist across. Ross was particularly exercised by my frequent reference to 'lords', a group of individuals who, it seemed to me, were much in evidence at mid-nineteenth century race meetings, my field of study. Not so. No such thing. I was, at first, perplexed by this but soon came to appreciate that it is that sort of precision, accuracy, respect for the past which encourages trust, not only in a reader but in a student too.

Of course, accuracy is just the beginning and reading Ross's article on late nineteenth-century working-class gambling inspired in me not so much trust as a sort of fear. I could never imagine coming up with anything as insightful, as original, as clever (and, in this respect, my imagination did not let me down). The Hon. George Lambton's *Men and Horses I have Known* didn't have quite the same impact. The surprising thing to me therefore about Ross as a teacher is how good he is. Good teachers should always be able to appreciate the trouble others might experience in understanding things; it helps when concocting explanations. Ross's explanations were always illuminating; well-informed, precise of course, but never obtrusive. I suppose many of the undergraduates he encountered were a little nervous of what might await them when dealing with Ross; that was certainly the case with those later students I sent to St John's. However, they all emerged from their tutorials looking rather pleased with themselves. Of course they had acquired a fuller understanding of the past and the means of communicating it effectively. They also had the sense that they had achieved that very much under their own steam. This is what I mean by teaching unobtrusively. Ross's students did have an interest in the past, which developed during their time at college but it was one he helped them to, not one that was imposed. And that is a very difficult thing for any teacher to do.

19

Despite His Choice of Jumpers

Rosemary Sweet

Ross was a tutor who always inspired respect, even amongst the most confident products of public school, despite his choice of jumpers, which were a perennial source of complaint amongst the student body. He was just self-evidently clever. In tutorials one was on edge, as Ross sat there, habitually scowling, poised to cut through the flannel of an ill thought through essay with his armoury of dry wit and laconic understatement. Our idleness and excesses were simply met with an attitude of world-weary resignation. But on the plus side one could always rely on him to summarise what one should have said with incisive clarity. That familiar Oxford feeling of leaving a tutorial in a bemused state of confusion, wondering what on earth the previous hour of roundabout digressions and diversions had had to do with the essay that had been set, was never something that happened with Ross. The lucidity with which he made the bewildering complexities of a reading list fall into place gave him unassailable authority amongst the undergraduate community.

But Ross was also held in deep affection as well as admiration. He did not go in for the kind of extravagantly cheerful bonhomie extended by some of the other tutors, nor did he make a habit of mixing with the students on the sports field or in the college bar. If this was a cynical ploy to ensure that his presence was doubly appreciated when he did turn up to history society dinners or other functions it certainly worked: within minutes he would be surrounded by a ring of students hanging on his every word. It was on these occasions that Ross's talents as a wickedly funny observer and raconteur would become evident. The scowl would lift as he recounted stories of his youth in Australia—including a narrow escape from a collision with Kerensky in a Sydney suburb as a boy on a bike with faulty brakes—or treated us to his astute analyses of either contemporary politics or contemporary soaps. His aperçus on the latest episode of *The Bill* were particularly valued. Ross was never effusive, indeed he always seemed rather surprised, or even alarmed, if one greeted him on the street. But he knew us far better than we realised, as I—and many others—had cause to appreciate during our undergraduate careers, when Ross's pastoral concern intervened when others had failed to notice anything wrong.

As a Junior Research Fellow I got to know Ross better and began to regret that in my enthusiasm for the early modern period as an undergraduate I had not taken the opportunity to be taught by Ross more often. What little I know of twentieth-century history owes much to Ross—but I also owe him so much more, not least in the sphere of domestic furnishings. It was Ross who offered me an invaluable tip on taking up the hems of curtains as I embarked upon furnishing a house for the first time: use a stapler.

20

A Bicycle Tour of Memories

Eve Colpus

Ross described the workshop from which sprang this collection as one of two 'unalloyed pleasures' in his life, the other was getting a bicycle for Christmas when aged ten. There was good humour in this after-dinner sketch; there was also nostalgia. Here was a glimpse of the tutor—and the boy—behind the books. Ross's reflecting back prompted me to take a bicycle tour of my memories of him. I first met Ross in 2004 when I was a finalist taking the Special Subject Political Pressures and Social Policy 1899–1914 and he was one of its elder statesmen (the other was Philip Waller). That first meeting in Ross's room at St John's was serious but animated: Ross sat on the sofa surrounded by his new tutees discussing a first edition of Seebohm Rowntree's *Poverty: A Study of Town Life*. (His commanding desk in the background to that scene told its own story.) Over the course of the term, Ross emerged as punctual (his arrival to tutorials chimed with St John's clock), sharp (to the point marking), and dryly-humoured (the Australian wit). He met my *cri de coeur* about how to tackle gobbets with a characteristically prompt and pithy reply, itself a lesson in the art of finals' gobbet writing. Ross was also a generous and warm tutor; he lent me the copy of his edition of Marie Stopes's *Married Love* that he intended as a gift for his niece.

Having the opportunity to work again in close proximity to Ross as a Research Assistant for the editors on this collection was an exciting prospect. By then a doctoral student of twentieth-century Britain, I had the beginnings of a more rounded (professional) image of the historian Ross: as understated performer of The Ford Lectures, trenchant commentator in the Modern British History and Politics seminar, and oftentimes rampaging reviewer for the *LRB*. I had few sightings of Ross in advance of the workshop held at St John's in April 2009, although one spontaneous encounter on St Giles' stands out. He stopped me in my tracks to let me know that he knew about my involvement with the festschrift. It was good to know he knew, but I had a feeling of not wanting to let the side down (and I wondered if and how he remembered me as an undergraduate?). The workshop opened my eyes both to the intellectual esteem and personal affection with which Ross was held amongst a community of scholars spanning both continents and generations. Ross was often to be seen during the two days in a familiarly thoughtful pose—head slightly bowed, cupped hand raised gently to his mouth—but he was also in a less workaday, jovial spirit. If, in a sense, the workshop was a progress through Ross's career in microcosm, it was indeed a pleasurable one.

21

A Chronicle

Mary-Kay Wilmers

Optimistic, pleased with the way things are, Ross McKibbin is the *LRB*'s ideal correspondent:

30 August 1991: Hardly anyone believes that Labour will really win the next election, or that it could cope even if it did.

28 May 1992: It seems reasonable to argue that a Labour victory was always unlikely, because 13 years of unremitting effort have gone into making it unlikely.

3 April 1997: If Labour wins the coming election it will do so for two reasons: because it is not the Conservative Party, and because it is not very different from the Conservative Party. Yet, while that may be a good way of winning this election, it is a terrible way of winning the next.

5 July 2001: The result of the election is a remarkable one: a government liked and respected by few and despised by some has preserved its already huge majority virtually intact.

3 April 2003: The comparative facility with which Blair has taken us to war highlights once again the deeply flawed relationship between the Parliamentary Labour Party and the government.

8 July 2004: The fact is that the Labour Party is led by a man who has little sympathy for its fundamental principles; a man whose conduct of Anglo-American relations has been almost inexplicably reckless and careless of the national interest and who has entangled Labour with people who despise its principles and who are in turn despised by most members of the Labour Party.

5 January 2006: Gordon Brown, though alleged by the Conservatives to personify Old Labour, differs little in substance from Cameron.

7 September 2006: The best we can hope for is that the national executive will do something to restore its authority and that the Labour Party will do likewise. That both are now merely institutional shells is central to Labour's malaise.

22 March 2007: Blair's government has been so disappointing not because it is without achievement but because its achievements are much less than they might have been and its mistakes much worse.

4 October 2007: The immense pressure on MPs to do nothing that would suggest political disagreement and the inability of the doubters to find a plausible candidate or the nerve to oppose Brown openly, demonstrate the extent to which the parliamentary party has been rendered apolitical, and Brown intends to keep it that way.

11 September 2008: Brown says little and even that is mostly a mumble—when he should be saying much loudly. But no doubt if he did that someone would say he was sending out the wrong signals.

26 March 2009: Where do we go from here? It's pretty clear that Gordon Brown doesn't know. Who would care if the Labour Party, politically and morally decrepit as it is, lost the next election?

24 September 2009: With both the government and the Labour Party in terminal condition and little time for either to do much about it, our thoughts inevitably turn to the Conservatives and what they might do after May 2010.

I very much look forward to many more cheerful pieces from Ross.

Index